CHURCHES
TO VISIT IN
SCOTLAND

ST GILES' CATHEDRAL, EDINBURGH

SCOTLAND'S CHURCHES SCHEME
gratefully acknowledges the support of
THE RUSSELL TRUST
in the production of this book

CHURCHES
TO VISIT IN
SCOTLAND

Illustrated by John R Hume

HAROLDSWICK METHODIST CHURCH, UNST, SHETLAND
(THE MOST NORTHERLY CHURCH IN BRITAIN)

PUBLISHED ON BEHALF OF
Scotland's Churches Scheme
BY THE National Museums of Scotland AND Scottish Christian Press

Published on behalf of
SCOTLAND'S CHURCHES SCHEME
by
NMS ENTERPRISES LIMITED – PUBLISHING
National Museums of Scotland, Chambers Street, Edinburgh EH1 1JF
and
SCOTTISH CHRISTIAN PRESS

ISBN 1 901663 86 8

British Library Cataloguing in Publication Data
A catalogue record for this book is available from the British Library.

Designed by Mark Blackadder.
Typeset in Columbus and Gill Sans.

DIRECTOR
Dr Brian Fraser BA PhD FIPD

Office: Dunedin, Holehouse Road, Eaglesham, Glasgow G76 0JF
Telephone: 01355 302416 *Fax:* 01355 303181
E-mail: fraser@dunedin67.freeserve.co.uk
Website: http://churchesinscotland.co.uk
Registered Charity Number: SC 022868

FRONT COVER PHOTOGRAPH
Our Lady and St Meddan Church, Troon. Photograph: Crown Copyright © Royal Commission
on the Ancient and Historical Monuments of Scotland

BACK COVER PHOTOGRAPHS
Top. Kilmaveonaig Episcopal Church, Blair Athol. Photograph: © A Stewart Brown
Bottom. Mansefield Trinity Church, Kilwinning.
Photograph: © The Property Department of National Mission, The Church of Scotland

SPINE PHOTOGRAPH
The Aberlemno Stone in Aberlemno Kirkyard, is believed to depict the great victory of the Picts over the
Northumbrians at the battle of Dunnichen (AD 685). Photograph: © Cultural Services, Angus Council

Printed in Scotland by Bell & Bain Ltd, Glasgow.

CONTENTS

Churches to Visit in Scotland

LOCAL COUNCILS

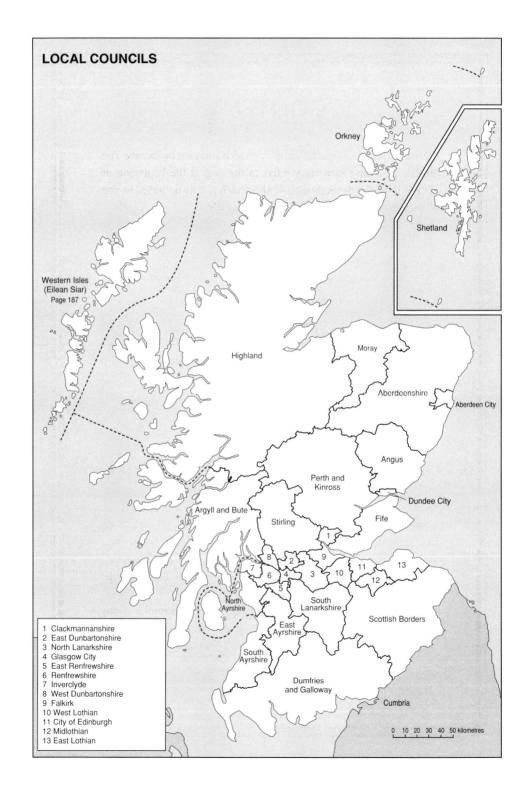

Orkney

Shetland

Western Isles
(Eilean Siar)
Page 187

Highland

Moray

Aberdeenshire

Aberdeen City

Angus

Perth and
Kinross

Dundee City

Argyll and Bute

Stirling

Fife

1

8 2 9

7 4 3 10 11 13

6 12

5

North
Ayrshire

South
Lanarkshire

East
Ayrshire

Scottish Borders

South
Ayrshire

Dumfries
and Galloway

Cumbria

1 Clackmannanshire
2 East Dunbartonshire
3 North Lanarkshire
4 Glasgow City
5 East Renfrewshire
6 Renfrewshire
7 Inverclyde
8 West Dunbartonshire
9 Falkirk
10 West Lothian
11 City of Edinburgh
12 Midlothian
13 East Lothian

0 10 20 30 40 50 kilometres

HOW TO USE THIS GUIDE

Entries are arranged alphabetically by council and then by locality. The number preceding each entry refers to the map at the beginning of each section. The denomination of the church is shown on the last line of each entry, followed by the relevant symbols:

    ♿   Access for partially abled

    ⓒ   Hearing induction loop for the deaf

    🚶   Welcomers and guides on duty

    📕   Guidebooks and souvenirs

    WC   Toilet for the disabled

    ℞   Inventory completed by Church Recorders

    👤   Features for children/link with schools

    ☕   Refreshments

    WC   Toilets on premises

    A   Category A Listing

    B   Category B Listing

    C   Category C Listing

Category A: Buildings of national or more than local importance, either architectural or historic, or fine little-altered examples of some particular period, style or type.

Category B: Buildings of regional or more than local importance, or major examples of some particular period, style or building type which may have been altered.

Category C: Buildings of local importance, or lesser examples of any period style, or building type, as originally constructed or altered; and simple traditional buildings which group well with others.

The information appearing in the gazetteer of this guidebook is supplied by the participating churches. While this is believed to be correct at the time of going to press, Scotland's Churches Scheme cannot accept any responsibility for its accuracy.

SCOTLAND'S CHURCHES SCHEME

Serving Churches of all denominations in Scotland

AIMS AND PURPOSES

I.

To promote spiritual understanding by enabling the public to appreciate all buildings designed for worship and active as living churches

2.

To advance the education of the public in history, architecture and other environmental subjects through the study of historic church buildings of all denominations in Scotland, their contents and environs

3.

To encourage co-operation among the churches themselves and between them and their local communities

4.

To publish details of churches open to visitors through a handbook *Churches to Visit in Scotland* as a guide for visitors, and to encourage support for the churches visited through donations, especially for specific appeals

5.

To receive donations for churches, in particular or in general, in order to provide when requested advice on the care and reception of visitors and the provision of historical and other information

6.

To promote the common purpose of mission through the ministry of welcome for visitors, tourists and pilgrims

FOREWORD

Post-war churches in Scotland
BREAKING THE MOULD
John R Hume

An incredible boom in church construction took place between 1840 and 1914, fuelled by denominational fission, amalgamation, rivalry, and most potently by population rise and migration. After the First World War economic depression and a stable population meant that few new churches were built in the 1920s. Most of these were 'traditional' in design, stone-faced, and only differentiated from their predecessors by lavish provision of halls. Economic depression became acute in the early 1930s, but when it began to lift in the mid 1930s a minor boom in church building took place, mainly in the new private and council house estates that spread rapidly round the larger towns and cities. These new churches (such as *King's Park, Croftfoot* and *Williamwood*) were generally modest in scale, and brick-built, often with the Romanesque arches so easy to build in brick. Most were architecturally unadventurous, but there were some notable exceptions, especially those designed by Gillespie, Kidd and Coia for the Catholic Church in Glasgow, Greenock and Ardrossan (*St Peter in Chains*), all of which were strikingly different, original, and moving in the worship spaces they provided. Though less accomplished, the Art Deco Wilson Memorial United Free church in Portobello, by James Johnston, 1933 (Fig 1) was also a daring break with tradition.

The Second World War, like the First, effectively stopped church building, but the post-war conditions were strikingly different. With a Labour government in power, and a backlog of house construction, new public housing was built on an unprecedented scale, as a priority. At first most of this new building was concentrated on the outskirts of larger towns and cities, but soon overspill

FIGURE 1

agreements boosted the population of smaller towns, and the first New Towns, East Kilbride and Glenrothes, were being laid out. Many of those rehoused in these ways came from church backgrounds, and the major denominations speedily saw the need to plant churches in these new communities, some of which were of considerable size, such as Castlemilk and Drumchapel in Glasgow, each of which had a population the size of that of Perth.

The desire to build new churches was, however, not matched by the availability of building materials, either in enough quantity or quality, or of skilled workmanship. In the aftermath of war, too, the leading denominations expected the new congregations to grow quickly. Unlike the 19th century, except in a relatively small number of cases, permanent churches were built in very large numbers to meet a largely untested demand. As shortage of materials continued, for more than twenty years large buildings were constructed as cheaply as possible. This had the effect of encouraging rapid development of innovative design, a trend encouraged by the rejection by most architects of tradition in favour of what has been termed 'international modernism', a set of design principles characterised by simple outlines, uncluttered internal spaces, absence of colour, and – flat roofs. These external pressures were accompanied, especially in the major denominations, by a desire to simplify the character of worship spaces, especially in the case of the Church of Scotland, where European trends in Protestant church design proved notably influential. There was no time for gradual evolution of design: different architectural practices were all working flat out to design on the scale the post-war building boom demanded – not just churches, but schools, housing and more housing.

The effect of these pressures was remarkable. A stream of very varied designs materialised during the 1950s, and increased into a torrent in the 1960s. At no time since the post-Disruption construction of Free churches were so many churches built so quickly. But the public at large, and the bulk of the worshipping community, were not aware of what was going on, and have remained unaware, for most of the new buildings were in housing schemes, places where the generality of people had no reason to go, and in some cases had no wish to go. Even the people for whom they were designed have rarely seen more than a handful of them in the course of their whole lives.

Because so many churches were required so quickly, rapid constructional methods were generally employed, such as steel or reinforced-concrete framing, brick skins (often made of common brick and harled), and flat or concrete-tiled roofs. The interiors were generally plastered on the hard, or left as exposed brick. Timber was expensive, and generally minimally employed, though most churches had well-made wooden pews. Largely for reasons of economy, pulpits and ambos, altars and communion tables were often brick or stone-built. Because of the techniques of construction employed, the buildings usually had large unobstructed interiors, many of them deliberately so, as they were used as halls during the week.

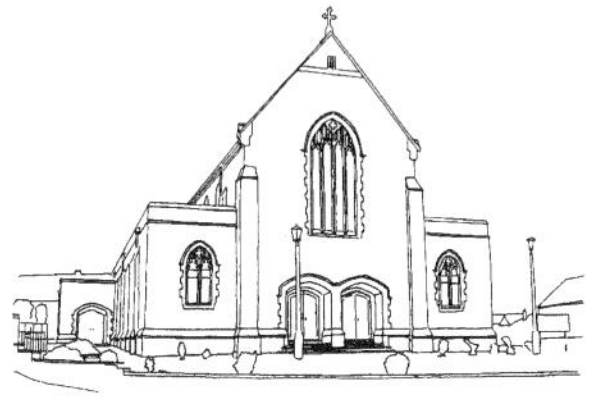

FIGURE 2

As hinted above, there was an enormous variety of architectural expression employed. The tail end of the Gothic Revival is to be seen clearly expressed in Catholic churches in Knightswood (Fig 2) and Priesthill, and more vestigially in some of the Catholic churches designed by Alexander McAnally as at St Mark's, Burnside (Fig 3), and Thomas Cordiner (*St John, Barrhead*),

FIGURE 3

though Cordiner neither in his only Church of Scotland church, St Paul's Provanmill, Glasgow (1948-51), nor in his Catholic church of the Immaculate Conception, Maryhill, Glasgow (1957, now demolished) used any vestige of the traditional. The whitewashed churches of Caithness inspired Ian G Lindsay and Partners, and Charles Gray and Partners, to build Colinton Mains, Oxgangs, Edinburgh (Fig 4) and *The Holy Name, Oakley*. Another church in the same spirit is Drylaw parish, Edinburgh (Fig 5), by William Kininmonth.

FIGURE 4

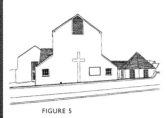

FIGURE 5

The mould was broken most effectively by the Glasgow practice of Gillespie, Kidd and Coia, whose economical designs of around 1950, though not of the quality of their 1930s churches externally, have a refreshing simplicity and modernity of approach. Their truly revolutionary period, however, began when two young designers, Andy MacMillan and Isi Metzstein, joined the practice. Thoroughly imbued with the modernist views of Le Corbusier, the practice took a fresh look at church design, and came up with *St Paul's Catholic Church, Glenrothes*, where they used rooflights to emphasise the importance of the altar and created a sanctuary of great dignity and simplicity. The firm went on to design some extraordinary buildings for the Catholic Church, like St Benedict's, Drumchapel (demolished); St Bride's, East Kilbride; St Martin's, Castlemilk, Glasgow (Fig 6), and *St Patrick's Kilsyth*. Of almost equal importance, however, was the effect St Paul's had in freeing up what was acceptable in church design. Within a year

FIGURE 6

or two, aesthetically innovative design became almost the norm for new churches, and for more than ten years challenging new designs flooded out of architects' offices. There was considerable interest in unorthodox plans – squares, polygons and circles, like Lochwood, Glasgow, by WNW Ramsay (Fig 7, now demolished), and in a sculptural approach to building exteriors, sometimes achieved at the expense of weather resistance! Among the conceptually outstanding churches of this period are the centrally-planned *St Columba's parish, Glenrothes*, by Wheeler and Sproson and St Mungo's parish, Cumbernauld, by Alan Reiach, Eric Hall and Partners, and aesthetically remarkable churches include *Craigsbank parish, Corstorphine*, by Rowand Anderson, Kininmonth and Paul; two circular Catholic churches in Prestonpans

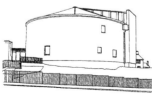

FIGURE 7

and Livingston, by Alison and Hutchison and Partners, and St Mary Magdalene Catholic church, Portobello (Fig 8). Even architectural practices that had been somewhat traditional in their approach were caught up in this visual ferment, like McAnally who broke away from his generally orthodox approach in his later churches, like St James the Great, Crookston, Glasgow (Fig 9).

By 1975, however, this wildly experimental period was over. New housing areas were not being constructed, and all the denominations were finding it difficult enough to keep churches going without commissioning new buildings. Not that new construction stopped altogether. Small, modest buildings were what was needed, and these

were provided by a number of building firms who used laminated timber beams, exposed brickwork and pyramidal roofs to make buildings of undoubted utility, but often of limited aesthetic or intellectual appeal. Some of these were new, others replacements for older buildings. In the late 1980s, however, some fine designs were produced that can stand comparison with earlier work. St Mary's Scottish Episcopal Church in Port Glasgow (Fig 10), by Frank Burnet, Bell and Partners, St Anthony's Catholic church in Kirriemuir (Fig 11), by James F Stephen Architects, and the replacement for *St Joseph's Catholic Church, Faifley* by Jacobsen and French are all fine buildings with no obvious precursors. In Ayrshire, Girdle Toll parish in Irvine, set in a former farm-

FIGURE 12

steading (Fig 12), and the new *Manse-field Trinity* in Kilwinning, are worthy of note.

If, as seems likely, we will not recapture the heady innovative 1960s approach to church design, we should be able, within more limited means, to build places of worship, suitable for all denominations, which embody the same care for the God-given creativity and visual sensitivity of human beings which has inspired church builders since the beginning of institutional Christianity. At the same time we should seek to retain and cherish the best of what the second half of the twentieth century has passed on to us. Heroic building does not come often: it can, if read aright, still powerfully inspire us with the influence of the Holy Spirit on its creators. Let us not write all these churches off as 'housing scheme' churches, mere ephemera to be thoughtlessly discarded.

John R Hume

ST JAMES THE LESS SCOTTISH EPISCOPAL CHURCH, BISHOPBRIGGS, GLASGOW

Note: the churches in *italic type* are members of the Scheme, and are included in this handbook.

SCOTLAND'S CHURCHES SCHEME

SCOTLAND'S CHURCHES SCHEME

LOCAL REPRESENTATIVES

Mrs Elizabeth Beaton, *Moray*

Mrs Margaret Beveridge, *East Lothian*

Mrs Jane Boyd, *Glasgow*

Sheriff and Mrs Vincent Canavan, *North Lanarkshire/Glasgow*

Mr and Mrs Robert Cormack, *Orkney*

Mr Michael Dunlop, *Galloway*

Miss Joan Fish, *Ayrshire*

Mr Sandy Gilchrist, *Tweedale/Clydesdale*

Mrs Lyndall Leet, *North Highland*

Mr Norman MacGilvray, *Renfrewshire*

Ms Atisha McGregor Auld, *Western Isles*

Mr Norman G Marr, *Aberdeenshire*

Mr Ian Milne, *Inverclyde*

Dr Ramsay Napier, *Shetland*

Mr Alan Naylor, *Falkirk/West Lothian*

The Rev John Paton, *Argyll & Bute*

Mrs Mary Reid, *Borders*

Miss Marion Smith, *Dunbartonshire*

Mr Louis Stott, *Stirlingshire*

The Rev J W Scott, *Dumfriesshire*

Dr Judith Spenceley, *Central Highland*

Mr Andrew Thackrey, *Edinburgh*

The Rev Malcolm Trew, *Fife*

DIRECTOR

Dr Brian M Fraser

PREFACE

From the Chairman, Robin Blair LVO WS

Welcome to the eighth edition of *Churches to Visit in Scotland*. It contains details of over 900 places of worship in Scotland who have joined Scotland's Churches Scheme. I hope that you will enjoy reading through this Guide and visiting some of the churches listed. Scotland has a remarkable ecclesiastical heritage and the enormous range of architectural and artistic styles from medieval to contemporary are reflected in this book.

People visit churches for a variety of reasons. The building may be architecturally outstanding in its setting. It may contain exceptional stained glass or a historic organ. A visitor to a busy town may feel a need for a moment of peaceful reflection. Often the church is a focal point in a community, and a visitor to, or a resident of, the town or village may wish to identify with that focal point. Whatever your reason, this Guide may help you.

We are sometimes asked, 'Why is such and such a church not in your Guide?' In this Guide we list all those churches who have chosen to apply to become members of Scotland's Churches Scheme. It is the individual churches who decide whether they wish to join.

Our members listed in this Guide come from the Church of Scotland, the Roman Catholic Church, the Scottish Episcopal Church, the Free Church, the Baptist, Methodist and United Reformed Churches, as well as the Greek Orthodox Church and the Jewish faith and a number of inter-denominational and ecumenical churches. Scotland's Churches Scheme is unique in being the only organisation in the world which provides information about the accessibility to visitors of such a range of religious buildings.

Scotland's Churches Scheme was formed just ten years ago. The story of how it all started and what has happened in the last ten years, written by Ann Davies, one of the members of the Advisory Council, appears on page 379.

I hope that you will find this book a useful companion wherever you happen to be in Scotland.

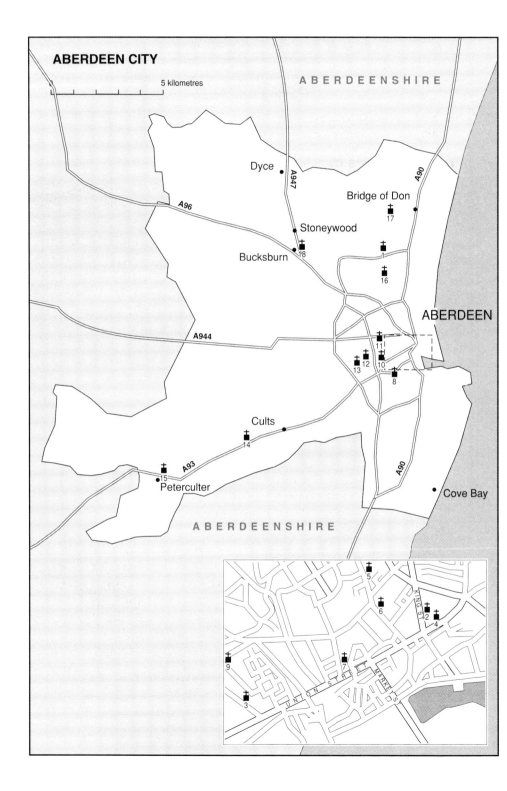

ABERDEEN

Local Representative: Mr Norman Marr, 63 Devonshire Road,
Aberdeen AB10 6XP *(telephone 01224 322937)*

I ST MACHAR'S CATHEDRAL

NJ 939 008
The Chanonry, Aberdeen
Fourteenth to 16th-century nave with
unique heraldic ceiling and fortified west
front. Interesting monuments, stained glass.
Ruined transepts. 3-manual organ by Willis
1892/97, rebuilt Rushworth & Dreaper
1928/56 and Mander 1973. Peal of eight
bells. Sunday Services: 11.00am and 6.00pm
Church website: www.ifb.net/stmachar
Open daily 9.00am-5.00pm. Recitals programme
information, telephone 01224 485988
CHURCH OF SCOTLAND [&] [symbols] A

ST MACHAR'S CATHEDRAL

2 ST ANDREW'S CATHEDRAL

NJ 945 065
King Street, Aberdeen
Built by Archibald Simpson 1817 and altered and enhanced by Sir Ninian Comper
1939-45. Gold burnished baldacchino over the high altar. National memorial to
Samuel Seabury, first Bishop of America consecrated in Aberdeen in 1784.
Interesting roof heraldry depicting American
states and Jacobite supporters of the '45
rebellion. Stained glass. Sir John Betjeman
described it as one of Aberdeen's best modern
buildings. Organ by Bruce of Edinburgh 1818,
rebuilt and enlarged by Hill, Norman & Beard.
Daily Services: Tuesday Holy Communion
8.30am; Wednesday Holy Communion 10.00am
and on Saints' Days Holy Communion at
10.00am. Sunday Services: Holy Communion
8.00am; Sung Eucharist 10.45am; Choral
Evensong 6.30pm (the Cathedral Choir is on
holiday during July and August, during which
Evening Prayers are said at 6.30pm).
Church website: www.cathedral.aberdeen.anglican.org
Open May to September, Monday to Saturday
10.00am-4.00pm
SCOTTISH EPISCOPAL [&] [symbols] [WC] A

ST ANDREW'S CATHEDRAL

3 THE CATHEDRAL OF OUR LADY OF THE ASSUMPTION

NJ 937 061
Huntly Street, Aberdeen
The principal church of the Roman Catholic Diocese
of Aberdeen, built in 1860 by Alexander Ellis. Spire
and bells added in 1877, designed by R G Wilson.
Contains religious artefacts by Charles Blakeman,
Gabriel Loire, Ann Davidson, Felix McCullough,
David Gulland and Alexander Brodie. The organ is
a rare example of the work of James Conacher,
Huddersfield, 1887. Off Union Street.
Mass Times: Saturday Vigil 7.00pm; Sunday 8.00am,
11.15am, 6.00pm
Open daily, summer 8.00am-5.00pm, winter 8.00am-
4.00pm. Also Aberdeen Doors Open Day. Clergy House
at 20 Huntly Street
ROMAN CATHOLIC 🏠 ② wc **B**

THE CATHEDRAL OF OUR
LADY OF THE ASSUMPTION

4 ST PETER'S CHURCH

NJ 942 065
Chapel Court, Justice Street (off the Castlegate)
By James Massie, 1803-4; gallery added 1815 and façade
finished 1817 by Harry Leith. Within the courtyard is the
residence occupied since 1774, including, in the 18th century,
the Vicars Apostolic of the Lowland district: Bishop James
Grant and Bishop John Geddes. Services: Saturday Vigil
6.00pm; Sunday 11.00am; weekdays as announced
Open Tuesday and Friday 9.30am-2.00pm, or by arrangement.
Celebrates 200th Anniversary in August 2004.
Doors Open Day, September each year
ROMAN CATHOLIC 🦽 wc ② **B**

ST PETER'S CHURCH

5 ST MARGARET OF SCOTLAND

NJ 942 067
Gallowgate, Aberdeen
Completed in 1869, the spacious sanctuary includes many fine examples of the
work of Sir Ninian Comper, including the chapel of St Nicholas, the first building
he designed and with the original stained glass. His style is mainly Early English
with elements of Byzantine and Renaissance. Memorial garden. Just north of
Marischal College. Sunday Services: Parish Mass 10.30am, Evensong 6.00pm
Open Tuesday mornings. Other times, telephone Canon Nimmo 01224 644969,
or A Allan 01224 872960. Gallowgate Festival Saturday in early August
SCOTTISH EPISCOPAL 🦽 ⓘ 🏠 **B**

6 GREYFRIARS JOHN KNOX CHURCH

NJ 943 044
Broad Street, Aberdeen
Striking Gothic building, designed to complement the
impressive granite front of Marischal College. Both
designed by architect A Marshall Mackenzie. Light and
airy interior. Great window from original 1532 Franciscan
church, moved here 1903. Stained glass in this and six
side windows by C E Kempe. Organ 1903 by Willis.
Chancel panelled with pew ends c.1690.
Sunday Service: 11.00am
Open 10.30am-12.30pm Thursday, Friday and Saturday,
mid-June to mid-September
CHURCH OF SCOTLAND ② Ⓘ 🏠 A

GREYFRIARS JOHN KNOX CHURCH

7 KIRK OF ST NICHOLAS

NJ 941 063
Back Wynd, Aberdeen
The 'Mither Kirk' of Aberdeen dates from the 12th century. The present building is
largely 18th and 19th century. The west end 1755 by James Gibbs, the east end by
Archibald Simpson 1837. The church contains the Chapel of the Oil Industry, and
the 15th-century St Mary's Chapel. West Kirk: 3-manual organs by Willis
1881/1927; East Kirk: organ by Compton 1933; St John's Chapel: organ by
Brewsher & Fleetwood 1825. The carillon of 48 bells is the largest in Great
Britain. Seventeenth-century embroidered wall hangings. Situated in Aberdeen city
centre. Sunday Service: 11.00am, also July and August 9.30am; daily Prayers:
Monday to Friday 1.05pm.
Open 8 May to 29 September, Monday to Friday 12.00 noon-4.00pm, Saturday 1.00-3.00pm.
Other times, on application to the Church Office 10.00am-1.00pm, telephone 01224 643494
CHURCH OF SCOTLAND 🦽 Ⓘ 🏠 ② wc A

8 FERRYHILL PARISH CHURCH

NJ 939 054
Junction of Fonthill Road and Polmuir Road, Aberdeen
Designed by Duncan McMillan for the Free Church
1874. Early Gothic style with a tall square bell tower
with octagonal spire. Side galleries added in 1896 were
reduced in 1994. From 1929-90 the building was
known as Ferryhill South Church. Contains several fine
windows by James McLundie, A L Moore and others,
including a number removed from the former Ferryhill
North Church. The sanctuary was re-ordered 1994 by
Oliver Humphries, and in 1994 the same architect was

FERRYHILL PARISH CHURCH

responsible for the creation of a fine new atrium and foyer. The memorial Chapel
incorporates the 51st (Highland) Divisional Signals War Memorial, the Piper Alpha
and Steele memorial windows, both by Jane Bayliss. Allen organ. Small historical
museum in the basement. Sunday Service: 11.00am (10.00am in July and August);
see notice boards for evening and weekday services and musical events
Church website: www.ferryhillpc.org.uk
The Church and the Foyer Coffee Shop are open 9.30am-11.30am, Monday to Friday,
9.30am-12.00 noon on Saturday. Other times, telephone 01224 584176 or 01224 589465
CHURCH OF SCOTLAND 🚹 ⊘ ⓠ wc 🏛 **B**

9 DENBURN PARISH CHURCH

NJ 936 059
Summer Street
The buildings incorporate the *Chapell of Ease* (William Smith, 1771), one of the few
surviving buildings in Aberdeen constructed of Loanhead granite. The frontage
and elegant arcaded interior date from 1878. Organ: 3-manual by Wadsworth 1893.
The great Irish preacher and character Dr James Kidd ministered here from 1802-
34. The church houses the model ship *Agnes Oswald* and an interesting 17th-century
edition of the Bible. Sunday Service: 11.00am
Open by arrangement with Mr Marr 01224 322937, or Mr Innes 01224 312426
CHURCH OF SCOTLAND 🚹 wc ⊘ ⓠ (by arrangement) 🏛 **B**

10 GILCOMSTON SOUTH CHURCH

NJ 935 059
Union Street, Aberdeen
Sandstone and granite building by William
Smith 1868. Spire added in 1875 and
rebuilt in 1995. Stained glass by David
Gauld, Douglas Strachan and Jane Bayliss.
Oak screen and choir stalls. Binns pipe
organ 1902. A hundred yards from west
end of Union Street. Sunday Services:
11.00am and 6.30pm; Tuesday (fortnightly)
12.45pm; Wednesday 7.30pm;
Saturday Prayer Meeting 7.00pm
Church website: www.fgilcomston.org
Open Aberdeen Doors Open Day.
Other times, telephone Mr John Glibborn
01224 873919
CHURCH OF SCOTLAND 🚹 ⊘ wc **C**

GILCOMSTON SOUTH CHURCH

11 ROSEMOUNT CHURCH

NJ 933 069
120 Rosemount Place, Aberdeen
Traditional church 1870 converted to multi-purpose
Celebration Centre in 1984. Ground floor accommodates
Sunday worship, weekday activities and coffee lounge.
Gallery houses 'Jonah's Journey' – children's museum.
Situated close to two municipal parks. By road or by
bus 22 from lower end of Union Street.
Sunday Service: 11.00am
Open all year (not public holidays), Monday to Saturday
10.00am-12.00 noon, Sunday 2.30-4.30pm (except July)
CHURCH OF SCOTLAND ♿ ⌾ ⍾ ☐ wc **C**

ROSEMOUNT CHURCH

12 THE CHRISTIAN COMMUNITY

NJ 919 056
8 Spademill Road, Aberdeen
Situated in the west end of Aberdeen, this small
church was built in 1991, by Camphill Architects, to
house community facilities as well as priest's office
and vestry. Simple interior in lilac wash lit by four
flanking windows; the altar is lit only by candles.
Oak candle holders, altar and pulpit. Altar painting
by David Newbatt, a local artist. Sunday Service: Act
of Consecration of Man (Communion) 10.30am
Open by arrangement with Mr William Milne,
telephone 01224 647609
CHRISTIAN COMMUNITY ♿ wc

THE CHRISTIAN COMMUNITY

13 ST MARY'S CHURCH

NJ 929 060
Carden Place, Aberdeen
The variety of granites and patterned roof tiles earned it the nickname 'The Tartan
Kirkie'. To a design by Alexander Ellis and the Rev F G Lee, dating from 1864.
The east end sustained severe damage during an air raid in April 1943.
Reconstructed 1952. Altar triptych by Westlake (c.1862) in the crypt. The church is
home to a Samuel Green chamber organ, built in 1778. Display of historical
photographs in the choir vestry (1905) adjoining church. On the left between
Skene Street and Queen's Road. Sunday Services: 8.00am and 10.15am; Tuesday
7.00pm; Wednesday 11.00am; Thursday 7.00pm
Church website: www.beehive.thisisnorthscotland.co.uk/st-marys-aberdeen
Open by arrangement, telephone the Rector 01224 584123
SCOTTISH EPISCOPAL ⌾ wc **A**

14 ST DEVENICK'S BIELDSIDE

NJ 882 025

North Deeside Road, Bieldside

Pink and grey granite church, designed by Arthur
Clyne and opened in 1903. Organ (Wadsworth)
installed in 1910: 'best specimen of its kind by
Wadsworth ever placed in Aberdeen or for a
considerable distance round about.' North transept
completed in 1959 by building of Lady Chapel, which
seats 24. West gallery and foyer added 2000. Sunday
Services: 8.30, 10.30am and 8.00pm; Thursday 10.30

Church website: www.stdevenicks.org.uk

Open by arrangement, telephone the office 01224 863574

SCOTTISH EPISCOPAL   👤 ② 🚪 ♿ wc **B**

ST DEVENICK'S BIELDSIDE

15 PETERCULTER PARISH CHURCH

NO 594 996

North Deeside Road, Peterculter, Aberdeen

Prominently sited on the main road, this church was
built in 1895 and has a recent extension built in 1995
providing a meeting place. Extensively refurbished in
2001, it now offers a multi-purpose sanctuary which
can be used by the local community.

Sunday Service: 11.00am (10.00am in July/August)

Church website: www.kirk87.fsnet.uk

Open Thursday and Saturday mornings, or by arrangement with
the church office, telephone 01224 735845 (mornings only)

CHURCH OF SCOTLAND   ② wc wc ☕

PETERCULTER PARISH CHURCH

16 THE CHAPEL OF THE CONVENT OF
ST MARGARET OF SCOTLAND

NJ 941 074

17 Spital, Aberdeen

The chapel, built in 1892, is one of the earliest works of Sir Ninian Comper, son
of the Rev John Comper, Rector of St John's Church in Aberdeen, who in 1863
had invited sisters from St Margaret's Convent, East Grinstead, to work with him.
The furnishings, fittings and windows were also designed by Sir Ninian, and
executed in his workshop. The oak panelling over the stalls was a thank offering
after the Second World War. On left hand side of road from Mounthooly
roundabout to the Old Town. Services: Vespers 5.30pm (Thursdays 5.00pm); daily
Eucharist at varying times. Please telephone 01224 632648 for exact information

Open by arrangement. Apply at front door of convent.

Chapel may be viewed through grille in west porch

SCOTTISH EPISCOPAL 🚪 **A**

ST COLUMBA'S PARISH CHURCH

17 ST COLUMBA'S PARISH CHURCH

NJ 1094

Braehead Way, Bridge of Don

St Columba's Parish Church is shared with the local Roman Catholic congregation. The most notable feature is a steel cross at rear of the church.

Sunday Services: 10am and 6.00pm

Church website: www.st-columbas.org.uk

Open by arrangement, telephone Mr Wilson 01224 703672

CHURCH OF SCOTLAND ♿ 𝄞 ② ☕ wc

18 NEWHILLS CHURCH

NJ 876 095

Bucksburn, Aberdeen

The present church was built in 1830 to a design by Archibald Simpson, near to the site of the original 17th-century church (now part of the graveyard). Painted coat of arms of the patron, Lord James Hay of Seaton, and the Earl of Fife and several modern banners add colour to the interior.

Sunday Services 10.30am and 6.00pm (not July and August)

Church website: www.newhillschurch.co.uk

Open Monday to Friday, 9.00am-1.00pm

CHURCH OF SCOTLAND ♿ ⚥ (by arrangement) ② wc **C**

NEWHILLS CHURCH

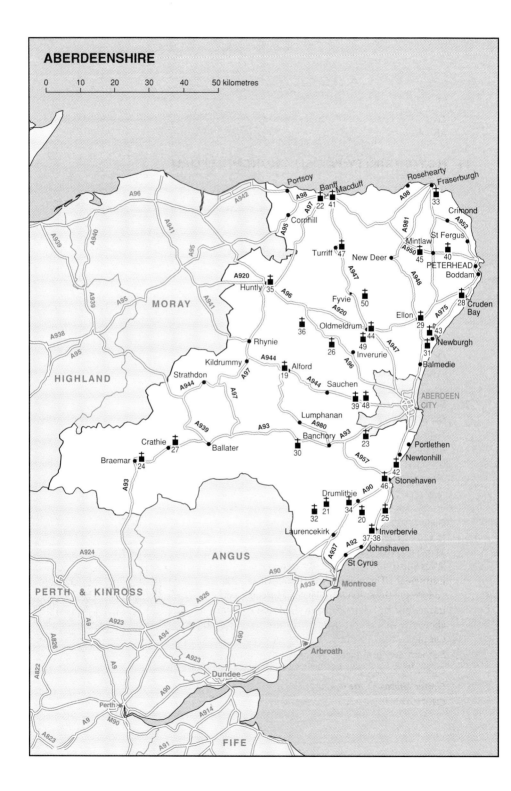

ABERDEENSHIRE

0   10   20   30   40   50 kilometres

A96
A942
A939
A940
A941
A95
A938
A95
A939
A95
A941
MORAY
HIGHLAND
A924
PERTH & KINROSS
A9
A923
A826
A822
A9
A823
A925
A935
A94
A923
A90
A914
A91
M90
FIFE
ANGUS

Portsoy
Banff
Macduff
A98
A97
22 41
Cornhill
Rosehearty
Fraserburgh
A98
33
Crimond
A952
St Fergus
A981
A95
Turriff 47
New Deer
Mintlaw
A950
45
40
PETERHEAD
Boddam
A920
Huntly 35
A96
Fyvie
50
A920
A948
A947
36
Oldmeldrum
44
Ellon
29
A975
28 Cruden Bay
Rhynie
26
49
Inverurie
43
Newburgh
31
Balmedie
Kildrummy
A944
Alford
19
A97
Strathdon
A944
Sauchen
A96
A947
ABERDEEN CITY
A944
A97
39 48
Lumphanan
A980
Crathie
27
Ballater
Banchory
A93
23
30
Portlethen
Newtonhill
Braemar
24
A957
42
46 Stonehaven
A93
Drumlithie
A90
32 21
34
20 25
Laurencekirk
Inverbervie
37-38
A937
A92
Johnshaven
St Cyrus
A90
A826
Montrose
Arbroath
Dundee
Perth

ABERDEENSHIRE

Local Representative: Mr Norman Marr, 63 Devonshire Road, Aberdeen AB10 6XP *(telephone 01224 322937)*

19 HOWE TRINITY PARISH CHURCH, ALFORD

NJ 577 151

110 Main Street

Built in 1867 as Alford Free Church and substantially reordered in 2001 by William Lippe to mark the union of Alford, Keig and Tullynessle & Forbes. Renovations include reorientation of chancel to the long wall; pews replaced with chairs; creation of glass vestibule. Set of engravings showing the parable of the Sower in modern form and stained glass window of the Burning Bush by Jane Bayliss. Sunday Service 10.00am

Church website: www.howetrinity.org.uk

Open by arrangement with the Minister, telephone 01975 562282

CHURCH OF SCOTLAND 🔾 wc ⊘

HOWE TRINITY PARISH CHURCH, ALFORD

20 ST TERNAN'S CHURCH, ARBUTHNOTT

NO 801 746

Almost certainly a St Ternan cult church long before it became a parish church by the late 12th century. The chancel dates from the early 13th century, the Arbuthnott family aisle and the bell-tower from the late 15th century and the nave is medieval or earlier but has been much altered. The church was gutted by fire in 1889 and reopened in 1890 with the nave and chancel restored as at the time of consecration in 1242; the architect for the restoration was A Marshall Mackenzie. One manual pedal organ by Wadsworth, 1890, a 'small but resourceful instrument'. The unique Arbuthnott Missal, Psalter and Prayer Book (now in Paisley Museum) were transcribed and illuminated in the Priest's Room above the Arbuthnott Aisle between 1497 and 1500. On the B967, three miles from Inverbervie. For Services, see local paper and notice board

Open all year. Refreshments in Grassic Gibbon Centre in village

CHURCH OF SCOTLAND 🔾 ⚲ A

ST TERNAN'S CHURCH, ARBUTHNOTT

21 ST PALLADIUS or AUCHENBLAE PARISH CHURCH

NO 726 784
Auchenblae, near Laurencekirk
Built by John Smith 1829 as Fordoun Parish
Church on a site known as Kirkton of Fordoun.
Religious site since 7th century. St Palladius died
and reputedly buried here. Celtic stone in
vestibule. Memorial to first Protestant martyr
George Wishart (born at Mains of Pittarrow in
old parish of Fordoun) in graveyard. Seating in
nave replaced 1990. Stained glass rose window.
Sunday Service: 11.00am, excluding first
Sunday of month
Open by arrangement, telephone
Rev Catherine Hepburn 01561 340203
CHURCH OF SCOTLAND 🦽 📖 B

ST PALLADIUS OR
AUCHENBLAE PARISH CHURCH

22 BANFF PARISH CHURCH

NJ 689 638
High Street, Banff
Built in 1789, Andrew Wilson architect and builder,
with tower added in 1849, William Robertson.
Chancel added and interior altered in 1929. Stained
glass. Small chapel created at rear of church in
1994. Pulpit, font, communion table and stained
glass in chancel all gifted in 1929. Other
furnishings from Trinity & Alvah Church, united in
1994. Beside St Mary's car park.
Sunday Services 11.00am and 6.30pm
Open mid-June to August, 2.00-4.00pm.
Also Doors Open Day, September
CHURCH OF SCOTLAND 🦽 ⓘ wc ☕ A

BANFF PARISH CHURCH

23 ST MARY'S CHAPEL, BLAIRS

NJ 883 009
The building, designed by Richard Curran of
Warrington, was opened in 1901 and follows the
neo-Gothic style, while the unusual interior design
is due to the fact that it is a former collegiate
chapel. The walls originally had painted decoration,
but in 1911 were lined with marble. At the same
time were added the reredos and baldacchino in
carved wood with its figures of the Scottish patron

ST MARY'S CHAPEL, BLAIRS

saints, Andrew and Margaret. The church also has fine stained glass windows. Four miles south of Aberdeen on B9077. Sunday Service: 9.00am. The Blairs Museum (adjacent to the chapel) is open from May to October (12.00-4.00pm)
Church website: www.blairs.net
Open Monday, Tuesday and Thursday 10.30am-2.00pm.
Saturday/Sunday by arrangement, telephone 01224 869424
ROMAN CATHOLIC 🦽 🛏 **A**

24 BRAEMAR CHURCH

NO 1591
Behind the Braemar Mews
The inspiration for the building of this former Free Church in 1870 was the Rev Hugh Cobban. Unusually, he was buried in the church, behind the pulpit. Four lancet stained glass windows with lilies, a branch with fruit and a tree with palms. Some interesting tapestry banners, described as 'living pictures'.
Sunday Service: 10.00am
Open 9.00am-9.00pm, April to October
CHURCH OF SCOTLAND ② 🛏 **C**

BRAEMAR CHURCH

25 ST PHILIP'S, CATTERLINE

NO 869 789
St Ninian was reputed to have landed at Catterline. The present building, designed by Charles Brand, dates from 1848 and was built on the site of an earlier church, retaining its historic graveyard. The style is Early English. The interior has been recently refurbished. Off A9 between Montrose and Stonehaven and near Dunottar Castle. Sunday Services: 6.45pm
Church website: www.nmearnssec.org.uk
Church open daily
SCOTTISH EPISCOPAL 🦽 **C**

ST PHILIP'S, CATTERLINE

26 CHAPEL OF GARIOCH

NK 716 242

In centre of Chapel of Garioch village

The present church, dating from 1813, was built on the site of a 12th-century church. Subsequent changes include a chancel built out from the north wall and the impressive stained glass window. Of particular interest are the baptismal basin of 1742, the mosaic plaque and the A-listed gateway in the west wall of the churchyard, dated 1626.

Sunday Service: 2003 9.30am, 2004 11.00am, 2005 9.30am

Open by arrangement with keyholder Mrs Whewell 01467 681543 or

Mrs Stannett 01467 681207

CHURCH OF SCOTLAND **B** (church) **A** (gateway)

27 CRATHIE PARISH CHURCH

NO 265 949

On A93 Ballater–Braemar

Queen Victoria laid the foundation stone in 1893, the church opened 1895. Cruciform design by A Marshall Mackenzie. The church stands on a hill overlooking the ruins of the 14th-century church and the River Dee. Memorial stones, plaques and stained glass commemorate royalty and ministers. Fine Iona marble communion table and 17th-century oak reredos.

Sunday Service: 11.30am

Open April to October, Monday to Saturday

9.30am-5.00pm; Sunday 12.45pm-5.00pm

CHURCH OF SCOTLAND  **B**

CRATHIE PARISH CHURCH

28 ST JAMES'S CHURCH, CRUDEN BAY

NK 069 356

Chapel Hill, Cruden Bay

The tall spire of St James's can be seen from miles around. Designed by William Hay in 1842. The font is from the chantry chapel, built after the battle between the Scots and the Danes in 1012. One and a half miles from Cruden Bay. Sunday Service: Family Communion 9.30am

Church website: www.saintmaryandsaintjames.net

Open daily 10.00am-dusk

SCOTTISH EPISCOPAL  **B**

ST JAMES'S CHURCH, CRUDEN BAY

29 ST MARY ON THE ROCK, ELLON

NJ 958 301
Craighall, Ellon
A superb example of the work of George Edmund
Street, built in 1871 to incorporate chancel, nave,
narthex and spire. Floor tiles by Minton. Good glass,
including windows by Clayton & Bell on the north
side of the nave, Lavers & Barreau on the south side,
all dating from the 1880s, and by Jane Bayliss 1996.
On the A90/A948, at the south end of the town.
Sunday Service: Early Eucharist 8.30am,
The Eucharist 10.30am
Church website: www.saintmaryandsaintjames.net
Open daily 10.00am-dusk. Saturday 4 September 2004 –
Flower Festival. Sunday 5 September 2004 – Marymas Festival.
SCOTTISH EPISCOPAL [♿] (?) **A**

ST MARY'S ON THE ROCK, ELLON

30 FINZEAN CHURCH (BIRSE AND FEUCHSIDE)

NO 617 924
Finzean, near Banchory
Small mission church. Includes former
congregations at Birse and Strachan. Between
Banchory and Aboyne on South Deeside Road.
Sunday Service: 11.00am
Open May to September, Monday to
Friday 10.00am-4.00pm
CHURCH OF SCOTLAND **B**

FINZEAN CHURCH

31 FOVERAN PARISH CHURCH

NJ 985 241
One mile south of Newburgh on A975
Built 1794, organ apse added 1900, interior
refurbished 1934 with pews and fittings from the
demolished Foveran United Free Church. Number of
items from medieval church (since disappeared): early
15th-century Turin Stone, 17th-century bust of Sir
John Turing, Queen Anne hour-glass attached to pulpit
and font using carved medieval column. Various
monuments including bronze plaque to painter and
etcher James McBey, born nearby. Sunday Service:
11.00am (shared with Holyrood Chapel, Newburgh)
Open by arrangement, key available from the Manse,
or from Newburgh Post Office during opening hours
CHURCH OF SCOTLAND  **B**

FOVERAN PARISH CHURCH

32 FETTERCAIRN PARISH CHURCH

No 651 735
Fettercairn near Laurencekirk
Built in 1803 and with a steeple added in 1860,
the building was completely refurbished and
extended in 1926. The interior has interesting
stained glass and locally made furnishings.
Sunday Service: 9.30am
Open by arrangement, telephone the
Minister 01561 340203
CHURCH OF SCOTLAND B

FETTERCAIRN PARISH CHURCH

33 FRASERBURGH OLD PARISH CHURCH

NJ 998 671
The Square, Fraserburgh
Present building dates from 1801, with a church on
this site since 1572. The pulpit is one of the
highest in Scotland and the superb memorial
window designed by Douglas Strachan 1906 was
gifted by Sir George Anderson, Treasurer of the
Bank of Scotland, in memory of his parents. A
front pew in the south gallery is marked as the
place where Marconi, pioneer of wireless
telegraphy, worshipped during his stay in
Fraserburgh. Untouched Forster & Andrews
2-manual organ of 1892.
Sunday Services: 11.00am and 6.00pm
Open daily June to September
CHURCH OF SCOTLAND [wc] (?) ☕ C

FRASERBURGH OLD PARISH CHURCH

34 GLENBERVIE PARISH CHURCH

No 766 807
Glenbervie, near Stonehaven
Built 1826 and preserving original
design and features. Oil lamps
electrified. Stones preserved and
sheltered. Grandparents of
Robert Burns buried in old
kirkyard. Sunday Service: 11.00am,
first Sunday of month
Open by arrangement,
telephone 01561 340203
CHURCH OF SCOTLAND B

GLENBERVIE PARISH CHURCH

35 ST MARGARET'S CHURCH, HUNTLY

NJ 528 402

Chapel Street, Huntly

Octagonal church with impressive classical front
façade built 1834. The architect was Bishop James
Kyle in collaboration with William Robertson.
Spire 80ft with fine toned bell. Altar piece and
other paintings from the Gordon family of Xeres,
Spain 1840. Restored 1990 by Doric Construction,
Aberdeen. Organ by Peter Conacher, 1871.
Sunday Service: 9.45am

Open by arrangement, telephone
Mr W McKay 01466 792409

ROMAN CATHOLIC [wc] **A**

ST MARGARET'S CHURCH, HUNTLY

36 ST DROSTAN, INSCH

NJ 630 281

Commerce Street, Insch

Alexander Ross 1894. Agreeable rustic Gothic in
red granite with sandstone dressings. Red-tiled
roof with broach-spired wooden bellcote.
Font 1892, and screen 1904. Church is on road
from Insch railway station to town centre.
B992 off A96. Service: second and fourth
Sundays, Sung Eucharist 10.00am

Open by arrangement, telephone Mrs Mitchell,
Greenhaugh, Rannes Street, Insch 01464 820276

SCOTTISH EPISCOPAL **C**

ST DROSTAN, INSCH

37 BERVIE PARISH CHURCH, INVERBERVIE

NO 830 727

43 King Street, Inverbervie

Built in 1836 with elegant clock and bell tower.
Two stained glass windows originally from United
Free Church. Lawton pipe organ 1904. To mark the
millennium, new doors were fitted to the inner
vestibule/sanctuary. Doors fitted with stained
glass overlay panels depicting significant local
landmarks/buildings, including the church. In
centre of town. Sunday Service: 11.30am

Open by arrangement, telephone Mr W Beattie, 39 King
Street 01561 361256, or 9 Farquhar Street 01561 362728

CHURCH OF SCOTLAND [wc] **B**

BERVIE PARISH CHURCH, INVERBERVIE

38 KING DAVID OF SCOTLAND EPISCOPAL CHURCH, INVERBERVIE

NO 828 733

Victoria Terrace, Inverbervie

Small, simple church with very pretty interior. Shared with the local Roman Catholic community. Sunday Service: 9.30am Holy Communion; Saturday: Roman Catholic Mass 6.30pm

Open daily 9.00am-4.30pm

SCOTTISH EPISCOPAL

39 SKENE PARISH CHURCH, KIRKTON OF SKENE

NJ 803 077

Quarter mile off A944 Aberdeen–Alford Road, 9 miles from Aberdeen city centre The church was built in 1801, architects William and Andrew Clerk, and contains stained glass by Blair & Blyth. Sunday Service: 11.15am

Open by arrangement, telephone the Minister 01224 743277 or the Beadle 01224 743534

CHURCH OF SCOTLAND ♿ ♿ⓌＣ ② B

SKENE PARISH CHURCH, KIRKTON OF SKENE

40 LONGSIDE PARISH CHURCH

NK 037 473

Inn Brae, Longside

Impressive rectangular building by John Smith, 1836. The west gable is capped by a bellcote. The adjoining old parish church, a roofless ruin, dates from 1620 and is accessed through a lychgate of 1705. Some notable monuments in the graveyard. Services: Sunday 11.30am, 2nd Sunday 6.30pm

Open by arrangement with the Minister, telephone 01779 821224

CHURCH OF SCOTLAND

♿ ② 𝙸 B (Old Parish Church) A

LONGSIDE PARISH CHURCH

41 MACDUFF PARISH CHURCH

NJ 701 643
Church Street, Macduff
Once used to guide boats to safe haven, this
white box kirk of 1805 high on the bluff above
the harbour was transformed in 1865 by
architect James Matthews of Aberdeen into a
magnificent Italianate landmark, with notable
stained glass windows and a lovely three-storey
tower with a lead-domed roof and cupola
above. Galleried interior, most of the fittings
dating from 1865. Magnificent views. Nearby
stand the town cross and an anchor, symbolic of
the message of the church.
Sunday Services: 11.00am and 6.00pm
Church website: www.macduffparishchurch.fsnet.co.uk
Open by arrangement, telephone 01261 832316
CHURCH OF SCOTLAND [&] (?) [wc] **B**

MACDUFF PARISH CHURCH

42 ST TERNAN'S, MUCHALLS

NO 891 921
Muchalls, by Stonehaven
Simple country church with attractive chancel.
The oldest church building in the Diocese of
Brechin, built 1831-70.
Sunday Service: 10.30am Holy Communion
Open by arrangement, telephone 01569 730967
SCOTTISH EPISCOPAL [wc] (?) [&]

ST TERNAN'S, MUCHALLS

43 HOLYROOD CHAPEL, NEWBURGH

NJ 999 253
Main Street, Newburgh
Built in 1838 as the original Newburgh Mathers school; converted as Chapel of
Ease for Foveran Parish Church 1882. Clock Tower added 1892, interior
refurbished 1907, including pitch pine roof in imitation of St Laurence, Forres.
Named in honour of the original medieval chapel of the Holy Rood and St
Thomas the Martyr in Inch Road, Newburgh – all that remains of this is the
Udny Family Mausoleum in the Holyrood Cemetery.
Sunday Service: 11.00am (shared with Foveran Church)
Open by arrangement, key available from the Manse,
or from Newburgh Post Office during opening hours
CHURCH OF SCOTLAND [wc] (?) **B**

HOLYROOD CHAPEL, NEWBURGH

44　ST MATTHEW & ST GEORGE, OLDMELDRUM

NJ 812 279

Ross & Joass 1863. Pleasing granite Early Decorated with striking chequered voussoirs to west window. Octagonal spire alongside the simple nave and chancel. Tendril-like freestone tracery is carved with real freedom. Stained glass by Hardman records the Life of Our Lord. Intricate Arts & Crafts monument to Beauchamp Colclough Urquhart of Meldrum. Church is at the north end of the village on A947. Sung Eucharist 11.30am

Open by arrangement, telephone the Rector 01651 872208

SCOTTISH EPISCOPAL   🕭 **B**

45　DEER PARISH CHURCH, OLD DEER

NJ 979 477

Old Deer village

Built 1789 as a simple rectangular church with Venetian windows to the east and west. The front porch with tower and spire were added in the late 1890s to a design by Sir George Reid PRSA. The pulpit table and font are by A Marshall Mackenzie, 1898. Willis pipe organ of the 1890s. Stained glass windows in memory of George Smith, local benefactor who emigrated to America and the Rev Dr Kemp, the Minister from 1899-1953 and his wife. Sunday Service 10.30am

Open by arrangement, telephone Mr Wishart 01771 623582

CHURCH OF SCOTLAND 🕭 wc ⊘ ⛲ ⛲ ☕ **B**

ST MATTHEW & ST GEORGE, OLDMELDRUM

DEER PARISH CHURCH, OLD DEER

46 ST JAMES THE GREAT, STONEHAVEN

NO 873 857

Arbuthnott Street, Stonehaven

The nave was built by Sir Robert Rowand Anderson in 1877 in Norman/Early English style. The chancel was added in 1885 and the narthex and baptistry in 1906 by Arthur Clyne. Baptistry glass by Sir Ninian Comper 1929. Elaborately sculptured reredos by Gambier-Parry of London. 2-manual organ of some merit by Wadsworth, 1881/85. Off south side of Market Square in Stonehaven.

Sunday Services: 8.30 and 10.30am; Thursday 10.30am

Church website: www.nmearnssec.org.uk

Open by arrangement with Rector

SCOTTISH EPISCOPAL   🔲 🔲 wc **A**

ST JAMES THE GREAT, STONEHAVEN

47 ST CONGAN'S, TURRIFF

NJ 722 498
Deveron Road, Turriff
Elegant church by William Ramage 1862
with a red, slender Gothic western tower.
Mural tablet of Bishop Jolly who is
depicted in the east window. Beautiful
stained glass. Oak rood screen, pulpit and
lectern are the important ornaments. A
short distance away are the ruins of the
medieval church whose elaborate belcote
of 1635 survives. Services: Sundays
11.00am (winter), 10.30am (Easter to
end-October), Wednesdays 10.00am
Open weekend: Flower/Harvest Festival 25/26
September 2004. Open by arrangement with the
Assistant Priest, telephone 01888 562530
SCOTTISH EPISCOPAL 🔣 Ⓓ 🏠 📖 wc 💺 **B**

ST CONGAN'S, TURRIFF

48 TRINITY CHURCH, WESTHILL

NJ 8307
Westhill Drive, Westhill (off A944 Aberdeen–Alford Road)
Built 1981 by Stock Brothers. Ecumenical and multi-purpose. Extension completed
in 2003. Services: Roman Catholic 9am; Church of Scotland 10am; Scottish
Episcopal 11.15am.
Open most of week, check with Minister, telephone 01224 743277
INTERDENOMINATIONAL 🔣 wc 💺

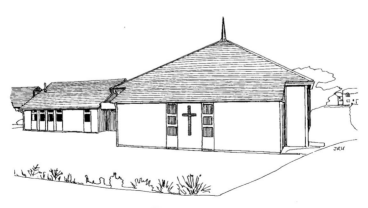

TRINITY CHURCH, WESTHILL

ALL SAINTS', WHITERASHES

49 ALL SAINTS', WHITERASHES

NJ 855 235

Gothic style nave and chancel built by James Matthews in 1858. Windows by Sir Ninian Comper of saints chosen for the Christian names of the Irvines of Drum and Straloch. On A947, three miles south of Oldmeldrum.

Service: first Sunday, Evensong 3.00pm

Open by arrangement, telephone the Rector 01651 872208

SCOTTISH EPISCOPAL ♿ (one step) **B**

50 ALL SAINTS', WOODHEAD OF FETTERLETTER

NJ 790 385

Early English aisleless nave and chancel by John Henderson 1849. The fine tower with the slated broach spire was added in 1870. Described by Pratt in Buchan as 'one of the finest examples of a Scottish village church'. Crosses and a sheaf of arrows from Fyvie Priory are incorporated in the walls. The altar and reredos are from St Margaret's, Forgue. Organ by David Hamilton of Edinburgh, recently restored by Stanley Edmonstone. One and a half miles east of Fyvie.

Sunday Service: 10.15am

Open by arrangement, telephone Mrs Cleaver, Gowanlea, Woodhead 01651 891513

SCOTTISH EPISCOPAL ♿ **B**

ALL SAINTS', WOODHEAD OF FETTERLETTER

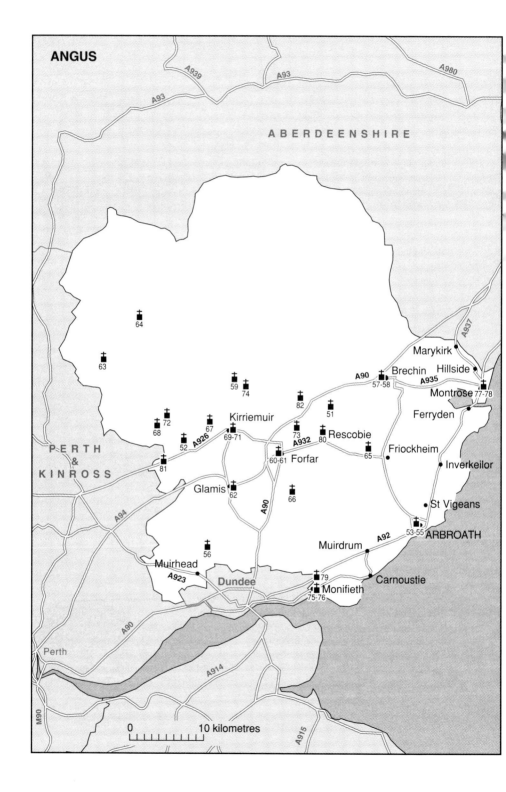

ANGUS

ABERDEENSHIRE

A939
A93
A93
A980

A937

64

63

Marykirk

Brechin   Hillside
A90
57-58   A935

59   74

Montrose 77-78

82

Ferryden

51

72

Kirriemuir

67

68

52   A926

69-71

73   Rescobie

A932   80

65   Friockheim

PERTH
&
KINROSS

81

60-61   Forfar

Inverkeilor

Glamis   62

66

St Vigeans

A94

53-55   ARBROATH

56

Muirdrum   A92

Muirhead

A923   Dundee

79

Monifieth
75-76

Carnoustie

A90

Perth

A914

M90

0   10 kilometres

A915

ANGUS

51 ABERLEMNO PARISH CHURCH

NO 523 555
5 miles east of Forfar on B9134
Small oblong church re-built 1722 on the site of pre-
Reformation church, was extended to a T-plan in 1820 and
remodelled in Gothic style in the late 19th century. The vestry
and galleries were added in 1856. Famous 8th-century standing
stone in kirkyard (covered in winter months). Pre-Reformation
stone font was brought into the church in 1992.
Sunday Services: 10.00am or 11.30am, contact the Minister
on 01241 828243 for details
Open during daylight hours
CHURCH OF SCOTLAND 🦽 wc (only available during services) 📖 **B**

ABERLEMNO PARISH
CHURCH

52 AIRLIE PARISH CHURCH

NO 313 515
Kirkton of Airlie
Stands on a site where the Gospel has been preached
for over 780 years. The present simple building was
completed in 1783. The interior was renovated in 1893
using pitch pine and an addition added to accommodate
the pipe organ and choir. Pre-Reformation relics; the
oldest gravestone is dated 1609.
Sunday Services: 9.30am most Sundays, contact the
Minister on 01575 560260 for details
Open by arrangement, telephone Mr G Bruce 01575 530243
CHURCH OF SCOTLAND 🦽 wc 🖐 **A**

AIRLIE PARISH CHURCH

53 ST JOHN'S, ARBROATH

NN 645 411
Ponderlaw Street, Arbroath
Opened for worship by the Rev John Wesley on 6 May
1772. Built in the octagonal style favoured by Wesley,
this is the only one of these churches left in Scotland.
Known as the 'Totum Kirkie'. Vestibule added 1883.
The Lifeboat Window is a memorial to the loss of the
Lifeboat *Robert L Lindsay* and six crew members in 1953.
Old manse adjacent to church. Sunday Service: 11.00am
Open by arrangement, telephone Mr Nicoll 01241 875172
METHODIST 🦽 wc 📖

ST JOHN'S, ARBROATH

54 ST THOMAS OF CANTERBURY, ARBROATH

NO 638 406
Dishlandtown Street
Church opened for worship 1848, designed by
George Mathewson of Dundee. Romanesque design
with ailsed nave and chancel. The front is a miniature
replica of St Augustine's gateway at Canterbury.
Unique 1-manual and pedal organ by Postill of York,
c.1860, recently rebuilt. Services: Saturday Vigil Mass
6.30pm, Sunday Mass 10.30am
Church website: //sites.ecosse.net/stthomas
Open daily 9.00am-6.00pm
ROMAN CATHOLIC [♿] [wc] (?) ⊑ (after Sunday Mass) **B**

ST THOMAS OF CANTERBURY,
ARBROATH

55 ST VIGEAN'S CHURCH, ARBROATH

NO 583 446
St Vigean's, Arbroath
Dedicated to St Vigean (or Fechin), Irish saint, died
664. Church rebuilt in 12th century, but not dedicated
until 1242. Some 15th-century alterations; 19th-century
restoration with lovely stained glass windows. Largely
unaltered since. Organ by Harrison, 1875.
Sunday Service: 11.30am
Key available from house opposite church main gate.
St Vigean's Museum also open
CHURCH OF SCOTLAND (?) [] ⊑ [wc] **A**

ST VIGEAN'S CHURCH, ARBROATH

56 AUCHTERHOUSE CHURCH

No 342 381
Kirkton of Auchterhouse
Built 1630 with stone from earlier churches of 1275
and 1426. Partially rebuilt 1775. Chancel and nave
with tower at west end. Burial vault at east end.
Interior completely renovated 1910. Gothic chancel
arch lends character and dignity. Three impressive
stained glass windows, medieval octagonal font, stool
of repentance and 18th-century clock. Linked with
Murroes and Tealing. Situated on south side of
Sidlaw Hills one mile east of B954 Dundee to
Meigle, six miles from Meigle.
Sunday Service: 11.30am

AUCHTERHOUSE CHURCH

Open by arrangement, telephone John Skea 01382 320257, or Heather Heggie 01382 320305
CHURCH OF SCOTLAND [♿] (?) [wc] **B**

57 BRECHIN CATHEDRAL

No 595 601

Church Lane, Brechin

Founded in the 11th century, the round tower of that date is
of Irish inspiration. Thirteenth, 14th and 15th-century
medieval architecture underwent major restoration in 1900-2
supervised by J Honeyman (Honeyman, Keppie &
Mackintosh). Special features include the 12th-century font
and a collection of Pictish sculptures. Stunning 20th-
century stained glass by Henry Holliday, Gordon Webster,
Douglas Strachan, Herbert Hendrie, William Gauld, Hugh
Easton and the firm of William Morris. The cathedral also
contains the largest group of William Wilson windows in
Scotland. Sunday Service: 11am. Short Communion in
Queen's Aisle after Service on 2nd Sunday of the month

BRECHIN CATHEDRAL

*Open most days all year 9.00am-4.00pm. With hosts in summer months (and guides by
special arrangement outwith these times). Afternoon teas in church hall, alternate Thursdays
2pm. Brechin Caledonian Railway nearby. Historical artefacts in Brechin Library. Brechin
Town Trail. Pictavia. Angus Pictish Trail*

CHURCH OF SCOTLAND 🔓 wc (100 yards) ② 📖 ⌖ ☖ **A**

58 ST NINIAN'S CHURCH, BRECHIN

NO 600 603

Bank Street

Tall simple church of 1875 in Normandy Gothic, distinctive of the architect
William Leiper. Small octagonal spire on the left of the front gable. Interior
enlivened by stained glass and murals.

Services: Sunday Mass 10.00am, Tuesday and Thursday 10.00am

Open by arrangement telephone Mrs Josephine McMahon 01356 622840

ROMAN CATHOLIC **B**

59 CORTACHY CHURCH

NO 396 597

Cortachy Church was built by the 7th Earl of Airlie, the
sole heritor, in 1828 on the site of a previous church. The
architect was David Patterson. It has a magnificent setting
overlooking the river South Esk. The gallery gives the
church a seating capacity of 300. Inside there are
memorials to the 9th and 12th Earls and against the east
gable is the Burial Aisle of the Airlie family. Sunday
Service: 10.00am, excluding 5th Sunday of month

Church website: www.gkopc.co.uk

Open by arrangement with church office, telephone 01575 572819

CHURCH OF SCOTLAND ② wc **B**

CORTACHY CHURCH

60 LOWSON MEMORIAL CHURCH, FORFAR

NO 465 509
Jameson Street, Forfar
A gem of a church designed by A Marshall
Mackenzie 1914. In the style of late Scots Gothic,
cruciform in shape with five-bay nave, aisleless
transepts and a one-bay chancel. Built of a ruddy-
hued local stone. Low central tower and squat
spire. Wooden wagon roof. Excellent stained glass,
Douglas Strachan. At east end of Forfar off
Montrose Road. Sunday Service: 11.00am
Church website: www.lowson-memorial.org.uk
Open Monday to Friday 9.30am-4.30pm all year
CHURCH OF SCOTLAND 🦽 ⊘ 🚹 WC **A**

LOWSON MEMORIAL CHURCH, FORFAR

61 ST JOHN THE EVANGELIST, FORFAR

No 458 507
71 East High Street, Forfar
Built on the site of an earlier church, the present building
was designed in Early English style by Sir R Rowand
Anderson and consecrated in 1881. The broach spire
intended for the tower was never built. Panelling and
redecoration of the roof by Sir Matthew Ochterlony, late
1940s. Altered in 1975 by Dr F R Stevenson to provide
Lady Chapel and vestries. The font has traditionally been
associated with St Margaret and Restenneth Priory. 3-
manual pipe organ by Conacher of Huddersfield. Stained glass by Charles E Kempe
and Septimus Waugh. Queen Elizabeth The Queen Mother was confirmed in the
church. Historic graveyard predates present church. Sunday Services: 8.30am and
11.00am, weekdays as announced
Open daily, summer months 9.00am-4.00pm, winter months 9.00am-2.00pm
SCOTTISH EPISCOPAL 🦽 (on request) ⊘ WC **B**

ST JOHN THE
EVANGELIST, FORFAR

62 ST FERGUS CHURCH, GLAMIS

No 386 469
Kirk Wynd, Glamis
Present church built 1792 on site of church dedicated to St Fergus 1242.
Substantially altered and beautified 1933. Classic bell tower and spire. Seventh-
century Celtic stone in manse garden and Well of St Fergus nearby. Category B
kirkyard with interesting stones. Strathmore Aisle (category A) built in 1459 by
Isabella Ogilvy on death of her husband Patrick Lyon, 1st Lord Glamis. United
with Inverarity. Sunday Service: 11.30am
Church website: www.stferguskirkglamis.co.uk
Open daily
CHURCH OF SCOTLAND 🦽 🚹 WC **A/B**

ST FERGUS CHURCH, GLAMIS

GLENISLA PARISH CHURCH

63 GLENISLA PARISH CHURCH

NO 215 604

Lovely rural setting at the head of Glenisla. Small oblong Gothic building with belfry and session house. Visitors most welcome. Sunday Services: 11.30 am 2nd Sunday, 1st and 5th Sunday rotates with Kilry and Lintrathen. 1st and 5th Sunday united service with Kilry, Lintrathen, Airlie, Ruthven and Kingoldrum

Open by arrangement, telephone 01575 560267

CHURCH OF SCOTLAND      **C**

64 GLEN PROSEN CHURCH

No 328 657

Glen Prosen, by Pitcarity, Kirriemuir

Present church built 1802, paid for by local inhabitants, ensuring continuous worship in the glen for nearly 400 years. Special features include wood carvings by Sir Robert Lorimer and war memorial porch with rare slated cross. Sunday Service: 1st and 3rd Sundays 12.00 noon; summer months Holy Communion (Scottish Episcopal) 4th Sunday 8.30am; Songs of Praise for Guide Dogs for the Blind: April to September, 1st Sunday of month 6.00pm

Open daily, access via vestry door

CHURCH OF SCOTLAND   **B**

GLEN PROSEN CHURCH

65 GUTHRIE PARISH CHURCH

NO 568 505

½ mile north of A932, 7 miles east of Forfar
Present church was built in 1826 to a
Telford design. The 15th-century
Guthrie Aisle is beside the church. Two
stained glass windows: 'The Good
Shepherd' (1920), Dickson family and
'The Sower' (1976), Guthries of
California. Sunday Services: 10.00am
or 11.30am or 6.30pm, contact the
Minister on 01241 828243 for details
Open at all times
CHURCH OF SCOTLAND [♿] [📖] **B**

GUTHRIE PARISH CHURCH

66 INVERARITY CHURCH

No 460 440

Inverarity
Church built 1754 with recent impressive
renovation. Kirk Bell by Peter van dem
Heim dated 1614, cast in Holland. Gable
porches added 1854. Modern
church/community hall next to church.
Situated at eastern boundary of village on
triangle of ground at division of B9127.
Sunday Service: 10.00am
Church website: www.stferguskirkglamis.co.uk
Open by arrangement, telephone
Mr A L Ingram 01307 840223
CHURCH OF SCOTLAND [♿] [wc] **B**

INVERARITY CHURCH

67 KINGOLDRUM PARISH CHURCH

NO 334 550

There has been a church in Kingoldrum since
earliest times, a carved stone coffin lid found in
the churchyard dates to 12th or 13th century.
The present church is a small oblong Gothic
church with a pinnacled belfry and projecting
porches of 1840. Pews and panelling were the
gift of Betty Sherriff, in memory of her
husband, and the pulpit fall of her parents.
Sunday Service: 11.00am
Open by arrangement, telephone 01575 574727
CHURCH OF SCOTLAND [♿] **C**

KINGOLDRUM PARISH CHURCH

68 KILRY PARISH CHURCH

NO 246 538
Stands in a valley on the edge of the hills at the
entrance to Glenisla. Visitors most welcome.
Sunday Services: 11.30 am 3rd Sunday, 2nd and
4th Sunday rotates with Glenisla and Lintrathen.
1st and 5th Sunday united service with Glenisla,
Lintrathen, Airlie, Ruthven and Kingoldrum
Open by arrangement, telephone 01575 560267
CHURCH OF SCOTLAND [♿] [wc] (❓) ☕ **c**

KILRY PARISH CHURCH

69 KIRRIEMUIR OLD PARISH CHURCH

No 386 539
Bank Street, Kirriemuir
Ninth-century stones were found when the church was
rebuilt on this earlier Christian site in 1788 to a design
by James Playfair, father of William Henry Playfair.
The steeple was completed in 1790. Stained glass
includes the triple window of The Last Supper, a Violet
Jacobs window, and windows by William Wilson.
Interesting kirkyard, the earliest stone dating from 1613.
In centre of the town, behind Bank Street's shops.
Sunday Services: 9.00am and 11.15am
*Open Monday to Friday, 10.00am-12.00 noon and
1.30-3.30pm (call at office if door locked)*
CHURCH OF SCOTLAND [♿] (❓) ♟ **B**

KIRRIEMUIR OLD PARISH CHURCH

70 ST ANDREW'S CHURCH, KIRRIEMUIR

No 386 535
Glamis Road, Kirriemuir
Late Gothic style church (originally the South
United Free Church) with a 60-ft tower by
Patrick Thoms 1903. It replaced an earlier
church (the South Free Church) built in 1843 for
those who left the South Church (across the
road) at the 'Disruption'. In the grounds are the
headstones of the Rev Daniel Cormick, first
minister of the South Free Church and of the
Rev A Duff, minister of the South Church.
Linked with Oathlaw and Tannadice.
Sunday Service: 11.15am
Open daily 9.00am-5.00pm
CHURCH OF SCOTLAND [♿] (❓)

ST ANDREW'S CHURCH, KIRRIEMUIR

71 ST MARY'S CHURCH, KIRRIEMUIR

NO 383 544
West Hillbank, Kirriemuir
Gothic revival church by Sir Ninian Comper 1903
built to replace classical church of 1797 destroyed by
fire. Stained glass by Comper and William Wilson. 2-
manual tracker organ, Hamilton of Edinburgh 1906.
Sanctus bell 1741. Conspicuous red sandstone bell-
tower. Signposted to north side of the town. Sunday
Services: 1st, 2nd and 3rd Sundays 10.00am Sung
Eucharist; 4th Sunday 10.00am; Matins 11.30am Said
Eucharist; 5th Sunday 10.00am Family Service:
11.30am Said Eucharist; Wednesday 10.00am
Key at Rectory, 128 Glengate, or 91 Glengate, Kirriemuir
SCOTTISH EPISCOPAL **A**

ST MARY'S CHURCH, KIRRIEMUIR

72 LINTRATHEN PARISH CHURCH

NO 286 546
Beautiful wooded setting near the banks of
Lintrathen Loch. Small oblong Gothic church
of 1802, remodelled and extended to T-plan in
1875. Visitors most welcome. Sunday Service:
11.30am 4th Sunday; 2nd and 3rd Sunday
rotates with Glenisla and Kilry; 1st and 3rd
Sunday united service with Glenisla, Airlie,
Ruthven and Kingoldrum
Open by arrangement, telephone 017575 560267
CHURCH OF SCOTLAND 🔲 Ⓒ 🔲 **B**

LINTRATHEN PARISH CHURCH

73 ST MARGARET'S CHURCH, LUNANHEAD

No 476 522
Carsebarracks, Lunanhead
Built in the planned village of Carsebarracks on the site of an earlier chapel in
1907 by the builder/architect William L McLean of Forfar as a gift of Mrs Susan
Helen Gray of Bankhead House in memory
of her husband. Stained glass window of
the Crucifixion (1913), by A D Fleming of
London. Mural (1909) by Miss W M Watson
of Edinburgh. On the B9134, one mile east
of Forfar. Service: 1st and 3rd Sundays,
excluding July and August 2.00pm
Open by arrangement, telephone
Mr Orrock 01307 468156
SCOTTISH EPISCOPAL

ST MARGARET'S CHURCH, LUNANHEAD

74 MEMUS CHURCH

NO 427 590
Memus Church was built as the Free Church
of Tannadice in 1843 in an outlying part of
the parish. It is a plain rectangular building
free of external ornamentation apart from the
bellcote. The internal furnishings are of very
fine pitch pine. The church had only two
ministers in 103 years. Sunday Service:
10.30am, 1st and 3rd Sundays
Church website: www.gkopc.co.uk
Open by arrangement with church office,
telephone 01575 572819
CHURCH OF SCOTLAND **B**

MEMUS CHURCH

75 HOLY TRINITY CHURCH, MONIFIETH

NO 499 327
High Street, Monifieth
Black and white half-timbered style
building by Mills & Shepherd 1909.
Originally intended as church hall,
adapted to church. Pleasant sheltered
garden. Buses from Dundee to
Monifieth, Carnoustie and
Arbroath stop outside.
Sunday Services: 8.00am, 10.30am
Open daily
SCOTTISH EPISCOPAL [&] [wc] **B**

HOLY TRINITY CHURCH, MONIFIETH

76 ST BRIDE'S, MONIFIETH

NO 499 325
6-8 Brook Street, Monifieth
The original church was established in 1880 in a converted cottage, which became
the hall when the new church was built in 1983. A light airy building, it was
designed by Brock's Bros of Leeds. Stained
glass by Gail Donovan. Services: Monday to
Friday in St Bride's 10am; Saturday 9.30am;
Wednesday in St Mary's Home 6.30pm;
Saturday Vigil Mass 6.00pm;
Sunday 10.30am and 6.15pm
Church website:
www.catholic-forum.com/churches/stbrides
Open daily 8.30am-7.30pm
ROMAN CATHOLIC [&] [⊘] [▯] [wc]

ST BRIDE'S, MONIFIETH

77   MONTROSE OLD CHURCH

NO 715 778

High Street, Montrose

Built 1793 by John Gibson with a 'lovely flying-buttressed spire (J Gillespie
Graham 1832) which is Montrose's town-mark' (Colin McWilliam, *Scottish
Townscape*). By rail Intercity London to Aberdeen. Sunday Service: 11.00am,
also last Sunday 6.30pm

Open June to August, Monday to Friday 2.00pm-4.30pm

CHURCH OF SCOTLAND ♿ ⓨ 🕯 📖 **A**

78   ST MARGARET'S, MONTROSE

NO 716 581

23 Market Street

Opened 1886. Font by David Lamb. Painting of St Margaret for 900th anniversary
in 1993. Services: Sunday Mass 11.30am, Monday, Friday, Saturday 10.00am,
Eucharist Tuesday and Thursday 10.00am

Open 7.30am-6.00pm Entry restricted to back of church

ROMAN CATHOLIC ♿ 🚻 **B**

79   MURROES AND TEALING CHURCH

No 461 351

Murroes, near Broughty Ferry

T-plan church by William Smith 1848 on a site occupied by a church for 750 years.
Church records from 1202. Interesting gravestones and coping on churchyard wall
carved with texts in English, Latin and Greek. Interior is simple and relatively
original. Pews with doors, four impressive stained glass windows in south wall and
small pipe organ in gallery recently restored. Former coach house and stables
restored to provide hall, chapel, kitchen and toilet facilities. Linked with
Auchterhouse. Sunday Service: 9.30am and 10.45am alternate Sundays

Open by arrangement, telephone Gordon Laird 01382 350242

CHURCH OF SCOTLAND ♿ ⓨ

MURROES AND TEALING CHURCH

80 RESCOBIE PARISH CHURCH

NO 509 521

3 miles east of Forfar on B9113
Built 1820 to a Telford design
incorporating a 17th-century mural
monument in the south wall. Very fine
oak ceiling. Single-manual pipe organ
by Millar of Dundee. Sunday Services:
10.00am or 11.30am, contact the Minister
on 01241 828243 for details
Open by arrangement, telephone
the Minister 01241 828243
CHURCH OF SCOTLAND & B

RESCOBIE PARISH CHURCH

81 RUTHVEN PARISH CHURCH

NO 286 489

Ruthven Parish was first noted in 1180, the present red sandstone church of 1859
is the fourth on this site overlooking the River Isla. Two ancient stone crosses in
the west wall, a ship's bell marked 'The Enterprise WW 1735', and the Royal
Warrant appointing John G McPherson Minister in 1874 are of interest, as is the
adjoining graveyard with headstones dating from the early 17th century. Annual
Music Festival mid-June weekend. Services: Monthly evening service, twice-yearly
Communion and twice-yearly joint service with Isla Parishes
Open by arrangement, telephone 01828 632558
CHURCH OF SCOTLAND ⌙ ⌂ C

82 TANNADICE CHURCH

NO 475 581

Present church by John Carver built 1866 on site
of previous buildings. Place of Christian
worship since 7th century. Monastery recorded
in 1187 and Kirk of Tanatheys consecrated by
the Bishop of St Andrew's 1242. Union with
Oathlaw 1982. St Columba and St Francis
windows at west end of church 1976 in memory
of 2nd Lord Forres of Glenogil. Former
Oathlaw war memorial windows on north wall,
by James Ballantine 1923 and Neil Hamilton
1949. Linked with St Andrew's, Kirriemuir four
miles north of Forfar on B957, A90 from
Dundee. Sunday Service: 9.45am
Key available at Post Office 9.30-11.30am. Or by
arrangement, telephone Mrs Davidson 01307 850345
CHURCH OF SCOTLAND ⌓ wc C

TANNADICE CHURCH

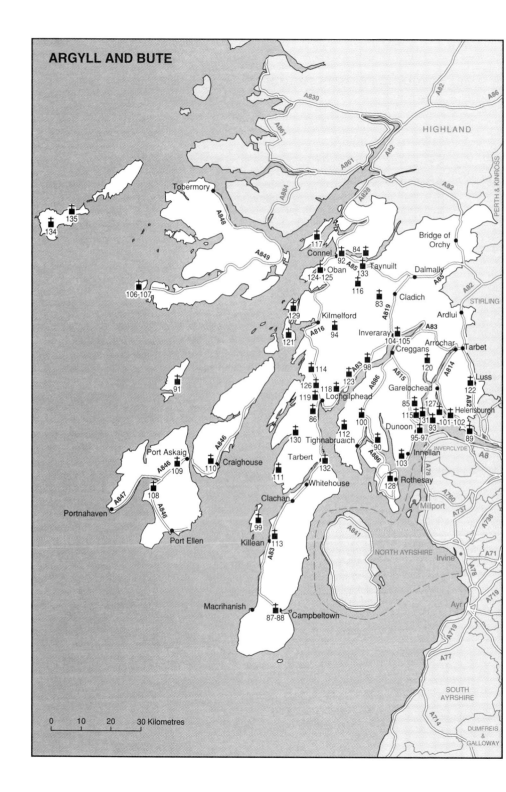

ARGYLL AND BUTE

HIGHLAND

PERTH & KINROSS

Tobermory

135
134

Bridge of
Orchy

Connel
117
84
92 Taynuilt
Oban 133
124-125 116

Dalmally

STIRLING

106-107

129
Kilmelford

Cladich
83

Ardlui

121

94
Inveraray
104-105
Creggans

Arrochar
Tarbet

91

114
123
98
120

Luss
122

126
118
119 Lochgilphead
100
Garelochhead
85
127
115 131
101-102
Helensburgh

86

112
130 Tighnabruaich
Dunoon 93
95-97
89

Port Askaig
109

110 Craighouse

Tarbert
132

Whitehouse

90
Innellan
103

128 Rothesay

108
Portnahaven

Clachan

Millport

99
Port Ellen
Killean 113

NORTH AYRSHIRE
Irvine

INVERCLYDE

Macrihanish
87-88 Campbeltown

Ayr

SOUTH
AYRSHIRE

DUMFRIES
&
GALLOWAY

0   10   20   30 Kilometres

ARGYLL & BUTE

Local Representative: The Rev John Paton, Muasdale, by Tarbert
(telephone 01583 421249*)*

83 ST JAMES' CHURCH, ARDBRECKNISH

NN 072 212
Built 1891, stone interior with fine series of
monuments and excellent windows. Bells
rehung 1991. Grass churchyard overlooking
Loch Awe. Sunday Service: in summer
11.00am, 3.00pm Eucharist on 3rd Sunday of
the month (winter). Linked with St John's
Cathedral, Oban
Church website: www.scotland.anglican.org/argyll
Open daylight hours in summer
SCOTTISH EPISCOPAL

ST JAMES' CHURCH, ARDBRECKNISH

84 CHURCH OF THE HOLY SPIRIT, ARDCHATTAN

NM 971 349
Built 1886. Fine First World War memorial incorporating the three banners of
Scotland, England and Ireland. Ardchattan crucifix on south wall. Stone pedestal
font and ancient stone stoup. One mile west of Bonawe Quarry, beside Loch Etive.
Sunday Service: 2nd Sunday, 12.15pm. Linked with St John's Cathedral, Oban
Website: www.scotland.anglican.org/argyll
Open by arrangement, contact Mrs Colquhoun, The Ferry House, Ardchattan
SCOTTISH EPISCOPAL

85 ARDENTINNY

NS 188 876
Shore Road, Ardentinny
Simple oblong kirk of 1838-39 with three
tall windows each side. Gabled front with
gabled porch and arched bellcote at apex.
Pulpit with sounding board decorated
with finials. The church contains the
memorials to the men of *HMS Armadillo,*
the wartime Royal Navy Commando Unit
who trained in Ardentinny.
Sunday Service: 2.30pm
Open daily
CHURCH OF SCOTLAND 🏠 wc B

ARDENTINNY

86 ARDRISHAIG PARISH CHURCH

NR 854 852

Tarbert Road, Ardrishaig

Gothic tower-fronted nave church of 1860 with low
semi-octagonal transpets and vestibule added 1904. The
octagonal castellated stage of the tower and the sharp
spire were added in 1868. Edwardian Art Nouveau
patterned stained glass in all windows.

Sunday Service: 11.00am

Open by arrangement with the Minister, telephone 01546 603269

CHURCH OF SCOTLAND wc

ARDRISHAIG PARISH CHURCH

87 HIGHLAND PARISH CHURCH, CAMPBELTOWN

NR 720 201

New Quay Street, Campbeltown

'To be causewayed with whinstone and paved with
hewn flags. The lock on the front door to be of
20/- value and the rest to have snecks and wooden
bolts': the instruction of the architect George
Dempster of Greenock, for a new church, built for
the Highland, Gaelic-speaking, congregation of the
area, and completed in 1807. Harled rubble with red
sandstone dressings, an oblong with rectangular stair
towers at each end of the front. Three galleries. The planned belfry was not large
enough for the heritors, so a steeple was built; twice since it has been rebuilt, the
casualty of lightning strikes. Allen Renaissance organ 2000. The organ screen
bears a memorial to the fallen of the Second World War.

HIGHLAND PARISH
CHURCH, CAMPBELTOWN

Sunday Services: 11.15am and 6.30pm, except July and August

Open daily

CHURCH OF SCOTLAND **B**

88 LORNE AND LOWLAND CHURCH, CAMPBELTOWN

NR 718 206

Longrow, Campbeltown

Built in 1872 to the design of John Burnet, historically
called The Longrow Church. Classical, influenced by
Italian Renaissance style. Its bell-tower is a well known
landmark. Two stairways lead from the entrance foyer
to a horse-shoe gallery. Fine plaster ceiling. Pulpit 1895.

Sunday Services: 11.15am

Church website: www.lorneandlowland.com

Open July to August, Monday to Friday 11.00am-4.00pm.

Other times, telephone Mr Robert Young 01586 552601

CHURCH OF SCOTLAND wc **C**

LORNE AND LOWLAND
CHURCH, CAMPBELTOWN

89 CARDROSS PARISH CHURCH

NS 345 775
Station Road, Cardross
Church founded 1225 on west bank of River
Leven and rebuilt in village 1640. Present building
1872. Stained glass windows, Sadie McLellan 1972,
embroidered panels, Hannah Frew Paterson 1981,
woven silk hangings, Sarah Sumsion 1990, and
engraved glass windows, John Lawrie 1992. Peal of
six bells augmented to eight for the Millennium.
A82 from Glasgow; half-hourly train service from
Glasgow Queen Street. Sunday Services: 9.30am
and 11.00am; June, July, August 10.00am only
Open Monday, Wednesday, Thursday and Friday
mornings, or by arrangement, telephone
Mrs S McLatchie 01389 841509
CHURCH OF SCOTLAND [♿] ⊘ [wc] **B**

CARDROSS PARISH CHURCH

90 COLINTRAIVE CHURCH

NS 045 735
Erected 1840 by Mrs Campbell of Southhall as a chapel-of-ease, part of
Inverchaolain parish. Became a Free Church in 1843, United Free in 1900 and
returned to the Church of Scotland in 1929. United with Kilmodan Church.
Spectacular views over Kyles of Bute.
Sunday Service: 10.00am or 11.30am, alternating monthly with Kilmodan
Open daily
CHURCH OF SCOTLAND [📖]

91 COLONSAY PARISH CHURCH

NR 890 941
By Scalasaig ferry terminal
Built by Michael Carmichael, 1802, on a site of a medieval chapel and close to a
Bronze Age burial site. Neighbouring former Parochial School is mentioned in
John Buchan's *Island of
Sheep*. The church originally
had galleries at both ends,
accessed by extramural stair-
cases. Attractive wooden
ceiling.
Sunday Service: 11.30am
Normally open at all times.
*For assistance, telephone Kevin
Byrne 01951 200320*
CHURCH OF SCOTLAND **B**

COLONSAY PARISH CHURCH

92 ST ORAN'S CHURCH, CONNEL

NM 914 343
Gothic Revival cruciform church of 1888
with lancet and pointed traceried windows,
gabled porch and a central tower with
corbelled parapet. Good interior with open
timbered ceiling. Fine collection of 20th-
century glass by various artists. Beautiful
views up Loch Etive from garden. On A85.
Sunday Service: 10.30am
Open during daylight hours
CHURCH OF SCOTLAND ♿ ? 📖 ⚲ **B**

ST ORAN'S CHURCH, CONNEL

93 CRAIGROWNIE CHURCH, COVE

NS 224 810
Church Road, Cove, near Helensburgh
Daughter Church of Rosneath, opened 1853.
Architect David Cousin, enlarged by
Honeyman & Keppie 1889. Organ by James J
Binns of Leeds. Various examples of stained
glass including J Benson, S Adam, Mayer &
Co Frescoes by the sisters Doris and Anna
Zinkeisen of the four Evangelists. Nearby
Church Hall in a former church designed by
Hugh Barclay, 1858, with windows by F Hase-
Hayden, A Webster, A McW Webster and
others. Sunday Service: 11.30am, in 2003 and
10.00am in 2004

CRAIGROWNIE CHURCH, COVE

Open by arrangement with the Minister, telephone 01436 842274
CHURCH OF SCOTLAND ♿ wc ? ⚲ ☕ (by arrangement) **B**

94 DALAVICH CHURCH

NM 968 124
15 miles from Taynuilt
The building dates from about
1770. Linked with Muckairn and
Kilchrenan. A small bell-tower
built on the gable to celebrate the
Millennium. Sunday Services:
10.00am, 2nd and 4th Sundays
of the month
Open by arrangement, MacIntosh,
1 Dalavich, by Taynuilt
CHURCH OF SCOTLAND ?

DALAVICH CHURCH

95 DUNOON BAPTIST CHURCH CENTRE

NS 171 770
9 Alexandra Parade, Dunoon
Formerly the American servicemen's YMCA. The centre welcomes all visitors to the
beautiful Cowal Peninsula. Browse in the well-stocked Christian book and gift
shop. Sample excellent coffee and home baking with a splendid view of the Clyde
estuary. Next to Tourist Information Centre and five minutes from the pier.
Sunday Services: 11.00am and 6.30pm
Open Monday to Saturday 10.00am-4.00pm
BAPTIST ② 🛈 📷 🖵 wc **A**

96 DUNOON THE HIGH KIRK

NS 173 769
Church Square, Dunoon
The present building probably stands on the site of a much earlier church which
until 1688 was the Cathedral Church of both the Roman Catholic and
Episcopalian Bishops of Argyll. Towards the end of the 18th century the building
became dilapidated and was demolished, the stone being used to build Gillespie
Graham's Late Decorated Gothic Revival church of 1816. The belfry tower was
added in 1839 and the church was lengthened and widened by Andrew Balfour in
1909. Chancel window 1939 by Douglas Hamilton. Gravestones of the 13th and
17th century in the kirkyard. Sunday Service: October to May 11.00am, June to
September 10.30am; mid-week service Wednesday 10.30am
Church website: www.highkirkdunoon.co.uk
First Thursday to Saturday in August, Flower Festival. June to September inclusive: exhibition
(history and memorabilia), Monday to Saturday 10.30am-4.00pm. Other times open by
arrangement, telephone Mr James Brogan, Church Officer 01369 702241
CHURCH OF SCOTLAND 🚹 ② 🛈 📷 🖵 wc **B**

97 ST JOHN'S CHURCH, DUNOON

NS 172 769
Argyll Street, Dunoon
A magnificent nave and aisles kirk by R A Bryden 1877, built to supersede the
original Free Church of 1843. Normandy Gothic spired tower. Galleried 'concert
hall' interior. Raised choir behind central pulpit.
3-manual pipe organ by Brook & Co 1895. Interesting
stained glass including windows by Stephen Adam and
Gordon Webster, also Lauder Memorial. Sunday Services:
10.15am and 6.30pm (last Sunday of the month)
Church website: www.stjohnsdunoon.org.uk
Open June, July, August and September: Monday to Friday
10.00am-12.00 noon. September Sunday concerts at 3.00pm
(last 3 Sundays in September), includes organ recitals,
visiting choirs, etc 01369 830639
CHURCH OF SCOTLAND 🚹 ② 🛈 📷 🖵 wc **A**

ST JOHN'S CHURCH, DUNOON

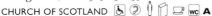

98 CUMLODDEN PARISH CHURCH, FURNACE

NS 014 994

Built in 1841 by local mason, David
Crow, to a design by James Nairn of
Balloch. Interior redesigned 1894.
Contains an early Christian cross-shaft
showing a bearded figure, 8th or 9th
century, removed from Killevin Burial
Ground. Stained glass, 1924, by
William Meikle & Sons, Glasgow.
Sunday Service: 10.30am, 4th Sunday
11.00am
Open by arrangement with the Minister,
telephone 01499 500288
CHURCH OF SCOTLAND [wc] **C**

CUMLODDEN PARISH CHURCH, FURNACE

99 GIGHA AND CARA PARISH CHURCH, ISLE OF GIGHA

NR 643 481

Built 1923. Windows by Gordon Webster. First minister Dr Kenneth MacLeod,
author of 'The Road to the Isles'. Gigha Gardens and nine-hole golf course ten
minutes walk from church. Ferry from Tayinloan/Kintyre 20 minutes.
Sunday Service: 12.00 noon
Open daily
CHURCH OF SCOTLAND [&] [wc] [book] [cup] (at village shop)

100 KILMODAN CHURCH, GLENDARUEL

NR 995 842

Clachan of Glendaruel

A Georgian T-plan church of 1783 on site of an earlier church of 1610.
Completely restored in 1983. Segmental-arched windows; lofts in the three arms.
Two long narrow communion tables. Memorial to Rev John MacLaurin and his two
famous sons (Colin, author of
MacLaurin's *Mathematical*
Theorem). Bus and post bus
from Dunoon. On A886.
United with Colintraive.
Sunday Services: 10.00am or
11.30am, alternating monthly
with Colintraive
Open daily
CHURCH OF SCOTLAND
[&] [wc] (nearby)

KILMODAN CHURCH, GLENDARUEL

101 ST MICHAEL AND ALL ANGELS, HELENSBURGH

NS 292 825

William Street, Helensburgh

Built by Robert Rowand Anderson in 1868 in French Gothic style. Tower with peal of eight bells added in 1930. Richly decorated interior with oak chancel screen elaborately carved Austrian oak north porch screen. West porch screen (1996) of light oak and engraved glass by James Anderson. Alabaster and mosaic reredos against encaustic tiling. Organ originally by August Gern, foreman to Cavaille-Coll. Fine sculpted west portal nave and chancel capitals. Good stained glass; light by Clayton & Bell, Shrigley & Hunt, Adam & Small, and Barraud & Westlake, with five windows by C E Kempe including fine rose window in west façade. 800m west of Central railway station, off Clyde Street. Services: Sunday 8.00am, 10.15am and 6.30pm; Tuesdays 10.30am; Wednesdays 7.30pm

ST MICHAEL AND ALL ANGELS, HELENSBURGH

Open daily 9.00am-5.00pm

SCOTTISH EPISCOPAL ⓐ 🛈 wc **A**

102 THE WEST KIRK OF HELENSBURGH

NS 295 825

Colquhoun Square, Helensburgh

Victorian Gothic building of 1853, J, W H & J M Hay, restored after disastrous fire in 1924 by Robert Wemyss, with a porch by William Leiper. Impressive panelled interior, with fine woodwork and half-timbered ceiling. Organ by Hill, 1894, rebuilt Hill, Norman & Beard. Exceptionally fine stained glass including memorial windows to Andrew Bonar Law, one time Prime Minister, and to John Logie Baird, inventor of television and son of the Manse in Helensburgh. Hill House (Charles Rennie Mackintosh) is one mile away. Sunday Service: 10.00am May to August, 11.00am September to April

Open daily all year 9.00am-5.00pm; and with guides June to August, Monday, Wednesday and Friday 2.00-4.00pm. Exhibition summer months

CHURCH OF SCOTLAND ⓐ 🛈 ⧘ ⧘ wc **B**

THE WEST KIRK OF HELENSBURGH

103 INNELLAN PARISH CHURCH

NS 152 707

7 Matheson Lane, Innellan

Built of local whin rubble in 1852 and expanded
in 1867 and again in 1887. Fine stone pulpit from
1887 re-ordering. The central stained glass
window is a version of Holman Hunt's 'The
Light of the World' which glows whatever the
lighting conditions. The church is best known for
its association with George Matheson who
ministered for 18 years from 1869 during which
time he wrote 'O Love that wilt not let me go'.

INNELLAN PARISH CHURCH

Sunday Service: 11.30am

Open by arrangement with the Clerk to the Congregational Board, telephone 01369 830554

CHURCH OF SCOTLAND 🔾 ⓓ

104 ALL SAINTS CHURCH AND BELL-TOWER, INVERARAY

NN 095 085

The Avenue, Inveraray

Gothic-style church built 1885 in local red granite, designed by Wardrop and
Anderson of Edinburgh. Many of the interior furnishings given by Niell Dairmid,
10th Duke of Argyll. Belltower, in Gothic revivial by Hoare & Wheeler, built 1923-
31 as a memorial to Campbell dead of First World War and previous wars. Peal of
ten bells by John Taylor of Loughborough, 1926. Exhibition in entrance to ringing
chamber. Sunday Service: 2nd Sunday 3.00pm

Church website: www.scotland.anglican.org/inveraray.htm

Open daily, early April to end September

SCOTTISH EPISCOPAL 🔾 **B** (Church) **A** (bell-tower)

105 GLENARAY & INVERARAY PARISH CHURCH, INVERARAY

NN 096 084

Church Square, Inveraray

Designed by Robert Mylne in 1792 to
house two congregations, English and
Gaelic. A solid wall separated the two.
Gaelic portion converted to church
hall 1957. Chamber organ by David
Hamilton of Edinburgh, 1840s.

Sunday Service: 11.15am

Open July and August on request at
Church exhibition and sale in Church Hall
at rear of Church

CHURCH OF SCOTLAND **A**   GLENARAY & INVERARAY PARISH CHURCH, INVERARAY

106 IONA ABBEY

NM 287 245
Isle of Iona
On the original site of St Columba's monastery c.563. St Columba's Shrine dates from the 9th century, most of the present buildings from around 1200. The massive restoration of the Abbey Church was undertaken by the Iona Cathedral Trust, who own the buildings, and was completed in 1910. The Iona Community now occupy the monastic buildings which they restored under the leadership of the Rev Dr George MacLeod. Historic Scotland now have the resposibility to care for the Abbey and associated monuments. Beautiful Augustinian nunnery, 12th-century ruin, Reilig Odhrain (Royal burial ground), 'Street of the Dead', imposing standing crosses and one of the largest collections of early Christian carved stones in Europe. Ferry from Oban to Mull, by bus/car to Fionnphort, pedestrian ferry to Iona. Services: Sunday 10.30am and Monday to Saturday 2.00pm, March to October; also Monday to Saturday 9.00am all year
Open at all times (Historic Scotland)
INTER-DENOMINATIONAL 🕯 📖 ☕ wc A

107 IONA PARISH CHURCH

NM 285 243
Isle of Iona
A Thomas Telford church of 1828. Pews, pulpit and communion table realigned in 1939. Former manse of same date now a heritage centre with picnic area adjacent. Ferry from Oban to Mull. Bus/car to Fionnphort for ferry to Iona.
Sunday Service: 12.00 noon. Short Service: Tuesday 1.00pm and each weekday in high summer
Open daily
CHURCH OF SCOTLAND **B**

IONA PARISH CHURCH

108 KILARROW PARISH CHURCH, BOWMORE, ISLE OF ISLAY

KILARROW PARISH CHURCH

NR 312 596
This 18th-century church, known as 'The Round Church', was built by Daniel Campbell of Shawfield and Islay in 1767 at a cost of £1000. A year after the building commenced, the village of Bowmore came into being as a 'planned village' to rehouse those of the village of Kilarrow who were not directly involved in the work of Islay Estate, mainly agricultural workers and weavers. The two-storey circular body of the church has a main central pillar 19 inches in diameter, possibly of hemlock oak, harled and plastered. Above the coved ceiling is a radial king-post roof truss into which eight major beams are jointed. The gallery was added in 1830, increasing its capacity to 500. Extensive renovation has been carried out in recent years. At the top of Main Street. Linked with Kilmeny. Sunday Service: 11.00am
Open daily all year, 9.00am-6.00pm
CHURCH OF SCOTLAND ♿ ⚲ (during summer months) ② ⛪ **A**

109 KILMENY PARISH CHURCH, BALLYGRANT, ISLE OF ISLAY

NR 353 636
Kilmeny Parish Church is situated in sheltered wooded grounds which are at the moment being developed. The present church was remodelled in 1828 to plans by Thomas Telford and stands about 400m NE of its medieval predecessor. There is evidence of a number of early Celtic Church foundations within the parish boundary, and nearby is the famous Finlaggan site, administrative centre of the Lords of the Isles. The church has been the recipient of some fine gifts, the most recent being an organ donated by the Caol Ila Distillery Company during their 125th anniversary in 1996. The interior has recently been upgraded with confortable seating both on pews and padded chairs. Linked with Kilarrow. Situated above the main Port Askaig/ Bowmore road. Sunday Service: 12.30pm, 10.00am July and August
Open July to August, Thursday 10.30am-12.30pm and 2.00-4.00pm
CHURCH OF SCOTLAND ⚲ 🚻 ⛪ ☕ **B**

110 JURA PARISH CHURCH

NR 527 677
Craighouse, Isle of Jura
The harled church was built in 1776. Pennant in his *Voyage to the Hebrides* (1776) says 'land in Jura, at a little village, and see to the right on the shore the church, and the minister's manse'. Alterations 1842 and 1922. Superb photographic exhibition of 'Old Jura' in gallery behind the church. Sunday Service: 11.30am
Open at all times
CHURCH OF SCOTLAND ♿ ② ⛪ 🚻

JURA PARISH CHURCH

KILBERRY PARISH CHURCH

111 KILBERRY PARISH CHURCH

NR 741 620

The church was built in 1821. A plain oblong building, galleries on three sides, later alterations provided an internal stair and removed the original external access. At Lergnahension, twelve miles from Tarbert on the B8024.

Sunday Services: fortnightly, summer 10am, winter 2.00pm

Open all year during daylight hours

CHURCH OF SCOTLAND  **B**

112 KILFINAN PARISH CHURCH

NR 934 789

A place of worship since 1235. Gothic 1759, including the earlier Lamont Vault of 1633. Stones of interest. B8000 from Tighnabruaich or Strachur.

Sunday Service: 12.00 noon

Open all year

CHURCH OF SCOTLAND **B**

113 KILLEAN & KILCHENZIE KIRK, A'CHLEIT, KINTYRE

NR 681 418

A83, 1 mile north of Muasdale

The church, 1787-91 by Thomas Cairns, is set on a rocky promontory out to sea. White harled with round arched windows. Belfry added 1879 by Robert Weir. The pulpit, in the long west wall, is a First World War memorial with Celtic style carving and faces a large laird's loft. Beside the pulpit is a marble monument of 1818 to Col Norman Macalister. Sunday Service: 11.15am *Flower Festival mid-July 2002.*

Open daily

CHURCH OF SCOTLAND

♿ ② wc (on request) **A**

KILLEAN & KILCHENZIE KIRK, A'CHLEIT, KINTYRE

114 KILMARTIN PARISH CHURCH

NR 836 993

Kilmartin, by Lochgilphead

On the site of earlier churches, the
present building opened in 1835. The
architect was James Gordon Davis. Three
interesting memorial panels from the
18th and 19th centuries to members of
the family of Campbell of Duntroon.
The church has two outstanding crosses,
with explanatory panels provided by
Historic Scotland. The kirkyard contains
the mausoleum of Bishop Neil
Campbell and medieval tomb slabs.
Extensive views over Bronze Age burial
cairns. Services: see local paper and
notice board

Open April to October, 9.30am-6.00pm

CHURCH OF SCOTLAND ♿ ⓘ **B**

KILMARTIN PARISH CHURCH

115 KILMUN PARISH CHURCH, ST MUNN'S

NS 166 821

Kilmun, by Dunoon

On the site of a Celtic monastery, overlooking Holy Loch. Tower of 15th-century
collegiate church. Present building dates from 1841, by Thomas Burns with interior
remodelled by P MacGregor Chalmers in 1899. Important stained glass by Stephen
Adam and Alfred Webster. Water-powered organ by Norman & Beard, 1909.
Ancient graveyard with fine 18th-century carved stones. Mausoleum of Dukes of
Argyll, Douglas vault. Grave of Elizabeth Blackwell, first lady doctor. On A880,
six miles from Dunoon. Sunday Service: 12.00 noon

*Open May to end September, Tuesday to Thursday 1.30-4.30pm (last tour 4.00pm). Other
days and times, throughout the year by appointment. Groups welcome. Telephone Valerie Gilles
01369 840342. Benmore Botanic Gardens (RBGE), two miles, open April to October*

CHURCH OF SCOTLAND ⓘ ⛪ 🏠 ☕ wc **B**

KILMUN PARISH CHURCH, ST MUNN'S

116 KILCHRENAN PARISH CHURCH

NN 037 229

The building was built in 1770 on the site of an earlier church dating back to the 12th century. Some stones from that church have been incorporated into the present building. There are interesting tombstones in the graveyard including that of Cailean Mor in 1294. Linked with Muckairn and Dalavich.

Sunday Services: 10.00am on the 1st, 3rd and 5th Sundays of the month

Open during daylight hours

CHURCH OF SCOTLAND Ⓐ

KILCHRENAN PARISH CHURCH

117 ST MOLUAG, ISLE OF LISMORE, KENTALLEN

NN 007 573

'The Cathedral of Argyll' was built in late 14th to early 15th century and attributed locally to 'The Roman' or 'An Roimhanach'. Six stained glass windows, two modern by Mitton. Eight medieval carved slab-stones, said to be of the 'Loch Awe' school and recumbent carved stone within the building. Traditional Baptismal font is carved in a natural rock surface. Exhibition on 800 years of Christianity on Lismore

Open at all times

CHURCH OF SCOTLAND wc Ⓘ (by arrangement) 🗋

ST MOLUAG,
ISLE OF LISMORE, KENTALLEN

118 LOCHGAIR PARISH CHURCH

NR 922 905

Originally Mission Church of Glassary Parish. Built 1867 to a simple oblong design. Half-octagon box pulpit centred between blind lancets. Services: 1st and 3rd Sundays 3.00pm; 2nd Sunday of the month Gaelic Service 3.00pm; 5th Sunday 6.30pm

Open during daylight hours

CHURCH OF SCOTLAND wc C

LOCHGAIR PARISH CHURCH

119 CHRIST CHURCH, LOCHGILPHEAD

NR 860 884

Bishopton Road, Lochgilphead

Church and adjoining rectory designed by John
Henderson, 1850-51. Nave-and-chancel church
with an arch-braced nave roof. Organ chamber
built 1887-88 to house the organ by William
Hill & Son 1876. Sunday Services: 9.00am
(except 1st Sunday) and 11.00am

Church website:

www.scotland.anglican.org/lochgilphead.htm

Open during daylight hours

SCOTTISH EPISCOPAL ♿ (ramps available) ⏿ **B**

CHRIST CHURCH, LOCHGILPHEAD

120 LOCHGOILHEAD & KILMORICH PARISH CHURCH

NN 198 015

Lochgoilhead

Dedicated to the Three Holy Brethren, the church is first mentioned in papal
letters of 1379. It was rebuilt in the 18th century incorporating the medieval walls.
Many features of interest. A83 Arrochar–Inveraray, top of Rest and Be Thankful,
B828 and B839 into village. Sunday Service: 10.30am

Open by arrangement, telephone Mr W Workman 013013 280.

Church Fair in August. Coffee mornings depending on local weather conditions

CHURCH OF SCOTLAND **B**

121 KILCHATTAN KIRK, TOBERONOCHY, ISLE OF LUING

NM 743 104

Toberonochy, Isle of Luing

Kilchattan Kirk was built in 1936 and houses a beautifully carved, floor-standing,
wooden lectern and two wooden offering plates donated by Latvian ship owners to
mark the rescue efforts of the islanders when one of their ships foundered in a
storm on the island of Belnahua in 1938. Just beyond the school on the road to
Toberonochy. Sunday Service: 11.30am, except last Sunday in month 3.15pm

Open all year

CHURCH OF SCOTLAND ⏿ wc

122 LUSS PARISH CHURCH

NS 361 929

This picturesque church, the third built on this site on the banks of Loch Lomond,
with its beautiful stained glass windows and uniquely timbered roof, features
frequently in 'Take the High Road'. The ancient graveyard has 15 listed ancient
monuments. Luss Village, off A82. Sunday Service: 11.45am

Open daily from 10am

CHURCH OF SCOTLAND **B**

LUSS PARISH CHURCH   LOCHFYNESIDE PARISH CHURCH, MINARD

123 LOCHFYNESIDE PARISH CHURCH, MINARD
NR 978 962
Good example of a corrugated-iron church by Speirs & Co of Glasgow,
'Designers and Erectors of Iron and Wood Buildings'. Stained glass window by
Sax Shaw, 1984. Pulpit of ancient ash from Crarae estate, designed by Ilay M
Campbell. Service: 12.00 noon except 4th Sunday
Open by arrangement with the Minister, telephone 01499 500288
CHURCH OF SCOTLAND

124 CATHEDRAL CHURCH OF ST JOHN THE DIVINE, OBAN
NM 859 304
George Street, Oban
The cathedral is a small part of the projected building, consisting of chancel,
crossing, nave of one bay and one transept by James Chalmers, 1908, attached at
right angles to existing church by Charles Wilson and David Thomson, giving an
extraordinary building internally. Tall reredos on a Scottish theme with painting of
Ascension set in the West
Highlands by Norman
Macdougall. Vast hovering
bronze eagle. Choir stalls in form
of Celtic graveyard. Much Iona
marble and terrazzo. Sunday
Services: 8.00am, 10.15am,
Wednesdays 11.00am
Church website:
www.scotland.anglican.org/argyll
Open daily
SCOTTISH EPISCOPAL

CATHEDRAL CHURCH OF
ST JOHN THE DIVINE, OBAN

 C

125 ST COLUMBA'S CATHEDRAL, OBAN

NM 855 307
Corran Esplanade, Oban
Built between 1932 and 1958, St Columba's
Cathedral is the principal Church of the Roman
Catholic Diocese of Argyll and the Isles. Designed
by Giles Gilbert Scott in the neo-Gothic style, of
highly distinctive, lofty, pink granite. The tower
soars above the Esplanade. High timber reredos
with intricate Gothic fretwork, designed by Scott
and carved by Donald Gilbert. Services: Saturday,
Vigil Mass 7.00 pm; Sunday, Mass 10.30am
Church website: www.dioceseofargyllandtheisles.org
Open dawn to dusk
ROMAN CATHOLIC ⓢ **A**

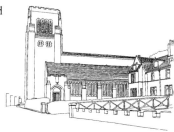

ST COLUMBA'S, OBAN

126 ST COLUMBA'S, POLTALLOCH

NR 816 965
Poltalloch Estate, by Kilmartin
In the gentle parkland of ruined Poltalloch House (William Burn 1849), St
Columba's was conceived as a private chapel but built as a church with
congregation and incumbent. Built 1852 to a design by William Cundy of London
in Early English style with leafy carvings and pointed arches. Complete set of
stained glass by William Wailes. Organ by Gray & Davison, 1855. Two
Whitechapel Foundry bells. Three misericord seats. Sunday Services: 1st Sunday
9.00am, 3rd Sunday 3.30pm
Church website: www.scotland.anglican.org/kilmartin.htm
Open daily
SCOTTISH EPISCOPAL **B**

127 ST MODAN'S PARISH CHURCH, ROSNEATH

NS 2583
A814 to Garelochhead, then B833 to Rosneath
There has been a church at Rosneath since the time of St Modan c.AD 600-50, the
present building, 1853, is by architect David Cousin. The bell from the earlier
church, and now on display in the present building, was made by Ian Burgerhuis
in 1610 and was rung as a summons to arms during the 1715 Jacobite rebellion. 2-
manual organ by Hill, 1875. Queen Victoria's Bible was gifted by Princess Louise.
Reredos of ten commandments by W A Muirhead and The Last Supper by
Meredith Williams, carved by Thomas Wood. Mural of St Modan by Mary
Ainsworth, 1995. Stained glass by Clayton & Bell, Douglas Strachan, Stephen
Adam & Co, Gordon Webster, Crear McCartney.
Sunday Service: 11.00am in 2003 and 11.30am in 2004
Open by arrangement, telephone the Minister 01436 842274
CHURCH OF SCOTLAND wc ⓘ 🛈 ⌷ (by arrangement) **A**

ST MODAN'S PARISH CHURCH, ROSNEATH

TRINITY PARISH CHURCH, ROTHESAY

128 TRINITY PARISH CHURCH, ROTHESAY

NS 089 645
Castle Street, Rothesay
Opened as the Free Church in 1845. Designed by Archibald Simpson in severe Gothic with a square tower surmounted with a slender spire. The interior, in contrast, is softened by the warmth of the hammer-beam roof and colourful stained glass windows, a triple lancet First World War memorial by Oscar Paterson and, adjacent to the pulpit, the Second World War memorial by Gordon Webster. Only Church of Scotland church in the centre of Rothesay.
Sunday Services: 11.00am and 6.30pm, 1st Sunday of the month
Open by arrangement with Mrs O'Neille, telephone 01700 502900
CHURCH OF SCOTLAND   👤 ⓘ wc **B**

129 KILBRANDON KIRK, BALVICAR, ISLE OF SEIL

NM 758 155
Kilbrandon Kirk was built in 1866 and contains a beautiful set of five stained glass windows – the work of Douglas Strachan. The windows were commissioned by Miss Mackinnon of Ardmaddy Castle in 1937 in memory of her friend the Marchioness of Breadalbane. On the B8003, one mile south of the Balvicar turn-off.
Sunday Service: 10.00am, except last Sunday 11.00am

Open all year
CHURCH OF SCOTLAND
👤 (two steps) ⓘ wc **C**

KILBRANDON KIRK, BALVICAR, ISLE OF SEIL

130 SOUTH KNAPDALE PARISH CHURCH

NR 781 775
Achahoish, by Lochgilphead
Parish of South Knapdale was formed in
1734 and churches were built at Achahoish
and Inverneill (now a ruin). Achahoish was
completed 1775, rectangular in plan with a
square castellated tower added in the 19th
century. Ancient font basin from St
Columba's Cave.
Sunday Services: May to September
9.45am, October to March 12.30pm
Open by arrangement with Mr Brown, Inn
Cottage, Achahoish, telephone 01880 770269
CHURCH OF SCOTLAND 🦽 👐 wc **C**

SOUTH KNAPDALE PARISH CHURCH

131 STRONE (ST COLUMBA'S)

NS 193 806
Shore Road, Strone
The square, battlemented tower and spire survive of the original 1858 church and
are used as a navigation aid for shipping. The rest of the building 1907-8 by Peter
MacGregor Chalmers using material from the old church. Stained glass by Stephen
Adam and Gordon Webster. United with Ardentinny in 1932.
Sunday Service: 10.30am
Open daily
CHURCH OF SCOTLAND 🦽 ⓓ 👐 wc 🍵 (after Service) **B**

132 TARBERT PARISH CHURCH

NR 863 686
Campbeltown Road, Tarbert
Built in 1886 on the site of an earlier
mission church dating from 1775 and
granted *quoad sacra* status in 1864. Architects
J McKissack and W G Rowan of Glasgow.
The building features an imposing square
tower rising over 100ft, surmounted by a
crown and lantern. Stained glass windows
and unusual roof decoration. Eighteenth-
century graveyard within walking distance.
Sunday Service: 11.30am
Open April to September, 10.00am-5.30pm
CHURCH OF SCOTLAND ⓓ 👐 **B**

TARBERT PARISH CHURCH

133 MUCKAIRN PARISH CHURCH, TAYNUILT

NN 005 310

Built in 1829 the church stands adjacent
to the ruins (1228) of Killespickerill,
once the seat of the Bishop of Argyll.
Two stones of antiquity are built into
the walls of the present Church.
Tombstones from the 14th century can
be seen in the graveyard. Linked with
Kilchrenan and Dalavich.
Sunday Service: 11.30am
Open during daylight hours
CHURCH OF SCOTLAND ◎ 🚪 wc

MUCKAIRN PARISH CHURCH, TAYNUILT

134 HEYLIPOL CHURCH, TIREE

NM 964 432

Barrapol, Tiree

The distinctiveness of Heylipol church or Eaglais na Mointeach – the Church of
the Moss – is enhanced by its location at a crossroads in a stretch of open country.
Built 1902 by architect William MacKenzie of Oban, in cruciform Gothic with a
bell-tower over the porch.
Sunday Services: 11.30pm and 6.00pm (alternating with Kirkapol Church)
Open at all times. Information on a Tiree pilgrimage route linking ancient and modern
ecclesiastical sites can be obtained from the Tiree Heritage Society, c/o Miss Fiona
MacKinnon, Lodge Farm, Kirkapol, Tiree PA77 6TW
CHURCH OF SCOTLAND wc

135 KIRKAPOL CHURCH, TIREE

NM 041 468

Kirkapol, Gott Bay, Tiree

The current church of Kirkapol (Norse for
'Church Town') is a continuing witness to the
Christian faith that stretches back to Columban
times. Built in 1842 by architect-contractor Peter
MacNab as a simple square box with galleries
on three sides focused on a central pulpit. Some
of the granite came from the same quarry as
that for the Skerryvore lighthouse. Inside, the
focus is the box pulpit of 1893 at the centre of
the north wall. Sunday Services: 11.30pm and
6.00pm (alternating with Heylipol Church)
Open at all times
CHURCH OF SCOTLAND wc **B**

KIRKAPOL CHURCH, TIREE

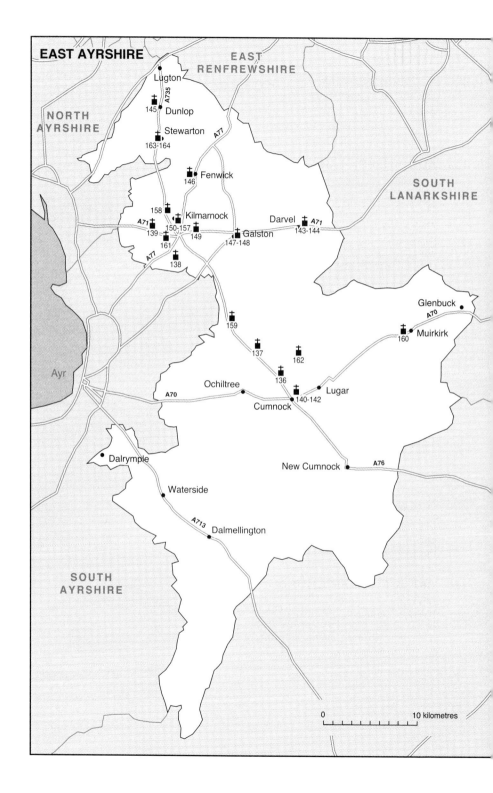

EAST AYRSHIRE

EAST
RENFREWSHIRE

NORTH
AYRSHIRE

SOUTH
LANARKSHIRE

Lugton

Dunlop
145
A735

Stewarton
163-164

A77

Fenwick
146

Kilmarnock
158
A71
139 150-157
161 149
138

Darvel A71
143-144

Galston
147-148

Glenbuck
A70

Muirkirk
160

159

137

162

136

Ochiltree
A70

Lugar
140-142

Cumnock

Dalrymple

New Cumnock A76

Waterside

A713 Dalmellington

SOUTH
AYRSHIRE

Ayr

0   10 kilometres

EAST AYRSHIRE

Local Representative: Miss Joan Fish, 31 Oaklands Avenue, Irvine
(*telephone* 01294 272654)

136 AUCHINLECK PARISH CHURCH

NS 552 216
Church Hill
There has been a church on this site since the 12th century. The present building, designed by James Ingram, was begun in 1833 and was funded by the Boswell family. The bell tower, designed by Robert Ingram, was added 1897. The interior was completely rebuilt after a fire in 1938. Organ by Hill, Norman & Beard. James Chrystal, a Moderator of the Church of Scotland, served as Minister for over 60 years. In the churchyard is the Boswell Aisle of 1754. Sunday Service: 11.15am
Open by arrangement, telephone 01290 422946
CHURCH OF SCOTLAND 🚫 wc ⌀ **c**

137 CATRINE PARISH CHURCH

NS 528 260
Chapel Brae, Catrine
Charming church, built as a chapel-of-ease in 1792, financed by Sir Claud Alexander of Ballochmyle. It was established as a parish church when Catrine was made a *quoad sacra* parish in 1871. Major renovations in 1874, 1960, 1992 and 2003. Stained glass. Harrison & Harrison pipe organ 1883. Overlooking Catrine in the river Ayr valley. B713, off A76 Dumfries–Kilmarnock, between Mauchline and Auchinleck. Sunday Service: 10.00am
Open by arrangement, telephone Mr McIlvean 01290 551521
CHURCH OF SCOTLAND 🚫 ⌀ wc **A**

CATRINE PARISH CHURCH

138 CRAIGIE PARISH CHURCH

NS 427 323
Pleasant traditional country kirk built 1776. Remains of previous church c.1580, but the site was occupied by a church from medieval times. Three miles from Prestwick Airport off A77 (two miles along Tarbolton Road). Sunday Service: 12.00 noon first and third Sundays

Open by arrangement, telephone
Mrs J Morris 01563 860283
CHURCH OF SCOTLAND 🚫

CRAIGIE PARISH CHURCH

139 CROSSHOUSE PARISH CHURCH

NS 395 384

25 Kilmarnock Road

Designed by Bruce and Sturrock, the church
was built 1882 in red sandstone with a 60ft
steeple over the front door. Stained glass
windows on all sides with a rose window on
the rear elevation. Traditional layout to seat
500. Manual pipe organ with pedal board in
the chancel has a beautiful sound. The church
is the focal point of the parish.

Sunday Service 11.00am

Open weekends and by arrangement with

Session Clerk, telephone 01563 535975

CHURCH OF SCOTLAND ♿ wc ② ⌻ ⌷

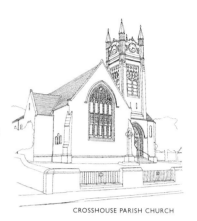

CROSSHOUSE PARISH CHURCH

140 OLD CUMNOCK OLD CHURCH

NS 508 202

The Square, Cumnock

Commanding a prominent position in the
square of this old market town, the church was
built in 1866 through the patronage of the
Marquess of Bute and the Bute family seats
remain in the Memorial Chapel. Organ 1966.
Mosaic of Jesus walking on the water by James
Harrigan. Bell in vestibule was cast in 1697 by
Quinus de Vesscher of Rotterdam, and was
used in the two churches which preceded the
present building. Services: Sunday 11.30am; on
days of opening 12.30pm; plus Friday 12.30pm

Church website: www.e-ayrshire.co.uk/local/oldcumnock

OLD CUMNOCK OLD CHURCH

Open July and August Tuesday and Fridays 12.00 noon-4.00pm, Thursdays 11.00am-2.00pm

CHURCH OF SCOTLAND ♿ wc ② ☕ (at Words of Wisdom opposite church, closed on

Wednesday) **B**

141 ST JOHN THE EVANGELIST, CUMNOCK

NS 572 196

92 Glaisnock Road, Cumnock

Rare Scottish example of the work of William Burges, 1882, for the Marquess of
Bute, and the first ecclesiastical building in Scotland to be lit by electricity. Lush
feast of painted surfaces, rich furniture, glorious stained glass and an altarpiece by
J F Bentley and N J Westlake. Services: Saturday 6.00pm, Sunday 11.45am

Open by arrangement with Parish Priest, telephone 01290 421031

ROMAN CATHOLIC ② wc **B**

142 CUMNOCK CONGREGATIONAL CHURCH

NS 566 203

4 Auchinleck Road, Cumnock

The Church began with twelve members in 1838. The present building is situated beside the River Lugar at the entrance to Woodroad Park. This friendly, compact sandstone church was dedicated in 1883. The first ever Labour Member of Parliament, Keir Hardie, served on the Diaconate. Impressive 2-manual organ with eleven ranks of pipes. Sunday Services: 11.00am and 6.30pm

Open by arrangement with Mr Mitchell, telephone 01290 421982

CONGREGATIONAL [wc] (♪) **C**

143 DARVEL PARISH CHURCH

NS 563 375

Hastings Square

The church is prominently set in the centre of the village square, adjacent to the memorial to Sir Alexander Fleming, the discoverer of penicillin. Designed by Robert S Ingram and built 1887-88 in Early English style with a tower and spire 130ft high. The Sanctuary has a nave, transept, aisles and a back gallery with woodwork of pitch pine. The pulpit of carved oak is particularly handsome and incorporates a Forster and Andrew pipe organ and backed by a triple lancet stained glass window. In the east wall is the Morton of Gowanbank memorial stained glass window of 1958. Sunday Service 11.00am

Open by arrangement telephone 01560 322924

CHURCH OF SCOTLAND [♿] [wc] (♪) **B**

DARVEL PARISH CHURCH

144 OUR LADY OF THE VALLEY, DARVEL

NS 5637

4 West Donington Street, Darvel

Church built by seceders in 1874 and closed in 1927. Various users of the building, *eg* Girl Guides, until early 1950s when it again lay empty. Purchased in mid-1960s by Darvel Parish Church and used as a church hall before being sold to the Catholic community and opened by Bishop Maurice Taylor on 25 November 1984. Sunday Service: 10am

Church website: www.saintsophias.fsnet.co.uk

Open by arrangement, contact Mr A Dougherty

telephone 01560 320346

ROMAN CATHOLIC [wc]

OUR LADY OF THE VALLEY, DARVEL

145 DUNLOP PARISH CHURCH

NS 405 494
Main Street, Dunlop
A Christian site since the 13th century, the present
church dates from 1835, though the sculptured
stonework of the Dunlop Aisle, 1641, was
preserved. Magnificent collection of stained glass by
Gordon Webster. Beside the church is Clandeboyes
Hall, 1641, built as a school. Built onto the back of
Clandeboyes is the early 17th-century monumental
tomb of Hans Hamilton, first Protestant minister of
Dunlop. Sunday Service: 11.00am
Open Sunday 2.00-4.00pm, June-September
CHURCH OF SCOTLAND [wc] [ ] [ ] [ ] **B** (church) **A** (tomb and hall)

DUNLOP PARISH CHURCH

146 FENWICK PARISH CHURCH

NS 465 435
Kirkton Road, Fenwick
Built 1643, in the shape of a Greek cross,
with four arms of equal length. Features
of note include outside stairs to Rowallan
loft with the coat of arms of the Mures
of Rowallan above the door, crowstepped
gables and 'the jougs' on the south wall.
Several Covenanting artefacts, including
the battleflag of the Fenwick
Covenanters. Walled graveyard contains
several notable graves and monuments.
Sunday Service: 11.00am September to
May, 10.00am June to August
Open for half an hour after morning worship
or by arrangement with the Minster,
telephone 01560 600217
CHURCH OF SCOTLAND [♿] [ ] [ ] [wc] (in Hall) [wc] **A**

FENWICK PARISH CHURCH

147 GALSTON PARISH CHURCH

NS 500 367
Cross Street, Galston
Present church, designed by John Brash of Glasgow, erected
1809 on site of Christian worship since 1252. Third church
since Reformation. Spire 120ft. Chancel added 1912 and
3-manual pipe organ by J J Binns 1913. Stained glass
windows the work of Oscar Paterson, a contemporary of
Charles Rennie Macintosh. Full restoration of church

GALSTON PARISH CHURCH

building completed in 1999. Floodlit since 2000. Ministers include Dr George Smith, great-grandfather of Robert Louis Stevenson and mentioned by Robert Burns in 'The Holy Fair' (grave on north side of church). Also Rev Robert Stirling, inventor of the Stirling Engine. Gravestone of Andrew Richmond, killed by Graham of Claverhouse, on south porch door along with a memorial to five Covenanters. Sunday Service: 11.00am

Church website: www. galstonparish.org.uk

Open by arrangement, telephone Mrs May McHoull 01563 820890

CHURCH OF SCOTLAND ♿ ➁ ♀ ▭ **B**

148 ST SOPHIA, GALSTON

NS 504 365

Bentinck Street, Galston

Constructed 1885-86, architect Sir R Rowand Anderson, the church is a distinctive building freely based on Hagia Sophia in Istanbul. At the behest of Lord Bute, who commissioned the church, Anderson, and possibly Weir Schultz, brought to Galston this dark brick echo of the Byzantine Empire. Services: Saturday 6.00pm, Sunday 11.30am; daily Mass as announced

Church website: www.saintsophias.fsnet.co.uk

Open by arrangement, telephone Mr T Heggan 01563 821587

ROMAN CATHOLIC ♿ (disabled access available on request) [wc]

149 ST PAUL'S ROMAN CATHOLIC, HURLFORD

NS 458 370

Galston Road, Hurlford

The church is a yellow brick building dating from the 1850s. Gothic arches feature in the light and bright interior. Services: Saturday 6.30pm, Sunday 10.30am

Open by arrangement, telephone 01563 525963

ROMAN CATHOLIC ➁ [wc] ♀ **A**

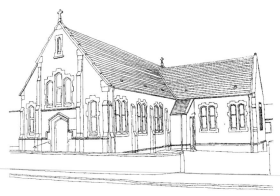

ST PAUL'S ROMAN CATHOLIC, HURLFORD

150 OLD HIGH KIRK, KILMARNOCK

NS 430 382
Soulis Street, Kilmarnock
Kilmarnock's oldest church building built
1732 of local stone by the Hunter
Brothers to a design adapted from St
Martin's-in-the-Fields, London. Austere
exterior contrasts with pleasing interior
enhanced by unique set of 23 stained
glass windows by W & J J Keir, glaziers
to Glasgow Cathedral. Graveyard with
tombs including John Wilson, publisher of
Robert Burns' first book of poems.
Sunday Service: 11.00am
Church website: www.old-high-kirk.org.uk
Open July and August 2.00-4.00pm or by
arrangement, telephone Mr G Thomson
01563 526064. Doors Open Day –
September of each year
CHURCH OF SCOTLAND ⓘ 🏛 wc A

OLD HIGH KIRK, KILMARNOCK

151 LAIGH WEST HIGH KIRK, KILMARNOCK

NS 428 379
John Dickie Street, Kilmarnock
Body of the church by Robert
Johnstone 1802. Enlarged 1831 with
later 19th-century session room.
Major refurbishment 1996 by
W I Munro Architects, winning 1997
Civic Trust Award for part of town
centre regeneration. Interesting
monuments and stained glass.
Covenanters' graves in adjacent
kirkyard. Close to bus and rail
stations. Sunday Services: 11.00am,
also 9.30am June to August
Open Monday, Wednesday and Friday
12.00 noon-2.00pm. Tuesday, Thursday
and Friday mornings. Other times,
telephone 01563 528051
CHURCH OF SCOTLAND
♿ ⓘ 🏛 wc A

LAIGH WEST HIGH KIRK, KILMARNOCK

HOLY TRINITY CHURCH, KILMARNOCK

152 HOLY TRINITY CHURCH, KILMARNOCK

NS 426 377

Portland Road, Kilmarnock

The nave to a design by James Wallace 1857, with chancel and sanctuary by Sir George Gilbert Scott 1876. Wall and ceiling murals in the chancel; stained glass. At the junction of Portland Road with Dundonald Road, 200 yards from King Street. Sunday Services: 9.15am Holy Communion, 11.00am Sung Eucharist, 6.00pm Evensong; Matins 11.00am, first Sunday if not a festival

Church website: www.copinger.org.uk/htk/

Open daily (except when Rector is on holiday)

SCOTTISH EPISCOPAL   **B**

153 HENDERSON PARISH CHURCH, KILMARNOCK

NS 431 380

London Road, Kilmarnock

Brilliantly individual Arts & Crafts treatment of Gothic motifs by Thomas Smellie, Kilmarnock, completed in 1907. Very tall tower above church built on rising ground, with halls below. Carillon of bells 1950. Fine Norman & Beard 3-manual organ restored in 1987. Stained glass windows by Gordon Webster 1907, and, in side chapel, by Wendy Robertson 1987. On Burns Heritage Trail, leading to Dean Castle Country Park (open all year). Church in town centre, adjacent to Grand Hall, Palace Theatre and bus station.

Sunday Services: 9.45am and 11.00am

Open by arrangement, telephone Mr J Neil 01563 528212

CHURCH OF SCOTLAND   **B**

HENDERSON PARISH CHURCH, KILMARNOCK

154 OUR LADY OF MOUNT CARMEL, KILMARNOCK

NS 428 401

Kirkton Road, Onthank, Kilmarnock
Opened in 1963, Our Lady of
Mount Carmel serves the areas of
Onthank, Altonhill and Wardneuk
in Kilmarnock as well as the
villages of Kilmaurs and Fenwick.
A large church, possibly its most
distinctive features are its stained
glass windows and the figure of
Christ Crucified. Services: Saturday
6.30pm; Sunday 10.00am
*Open by arrangement with the Parish
Priest, telephone 01563 523822*
ROMAN CATHOLIC ⍰ wc

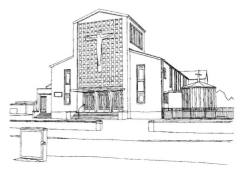

OUR LADY OF MOUNT CARMEL, KILMARNOCK

155 ST MARNOCK'S PARISH CHURCH, KILMARNOCK

NS 427 377

St Marnock's Street, Kilmarnock
Perpendicular Gothic, rectangular plan 6-bay
church with centrally placed tower on north gable
end, by John Ingram 1836. Fine carillon of bells.
3-manual pipe organ 1872, painted organ screen.
Extensive restoration programme completed in
1997. In centre of town with easy access from bus
and railway station. Sunday Service: 11.00am (and
9.30am June to mid-August)
*Open first Sunday in September each year 12.00 noon-
4.00pm. Or by arrangement, telephone the Session
Clerk 01563 520210. E-mail: jwrca@globalnet.co.uk*
CHURCH OF SCOTLAND ⍰ 🍴 📖 ☕ (free) wc **B**

ST MARNOCK'S PARISH CHURCH, KILMARNOCK

156 ST MATTHEW'S, KILMARNOCK

NS 442 388

Grassyards Road, Kilmarnock
Modern building built in 1977 to have a dual purpose of both hall and church
combined. Services: Saturday 6.30pm; Sunday 9.30am and 11.00am; Monday,
Tuesday, Friday and Saturday 10.00am; Wednesday 8.15am
Open for services
ROMAN CATHOLIC ♿ wc

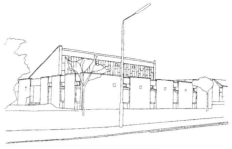

ST MATTHEW'S, KILMARNOCK

157 WINTON PLACE E U CONGREGATIONAL CHURCH, KILMARNOCK

NS 426 377

Dundonald Road

Founder church of the Evangelical Union, started in 1843 by the Rev James Morrison. The present grey sandstone building, designed by James Ingram, was built in 1860. Three stained glass windows behind the pulpit by Keir of Irvine, 1890, restored 1995. 3-manual pipe organ by James Conacher.

Sunday Service: 11.00am

Open by arrangement, telephone Dr Barclay 01292 313139

CONGREGATIONAL [wc] **B**

158 ST MAUR'S GLENCAIRN PARISH CHURCH, KILMAURS

NS 415 408

The church at Kilmaurs was in the possession of Kelso Abbey as early as 1170. In 1413 the present foundation was endowed by Sir William Cunninghame as a collegiate church. Rebuilt by Robert S Ingram 1888 in a cruciform shape. Stained glass, 20th-century, including a window by Roland Mitton of Livingston, and three rose windows. The clock tower holds the original bell inscribed 'Michael Burgerhuys Me Fecit 1618'. Glencairn Aisle adjacent to the church with sculptured mural 1600 commissioned by James 7th Earl of Glencairn, in memory of the Earl and Countess of Glencairn, and worked by David Scougal, mason and burgess. On A735.

Sunday Service: 11.00am

Open by arrangement, telephone

Rev John Urquhart 01563 538289

CHURCH OF SCOTLAND [♿] [?] **B**

ST MAUR'S GLENCAIRN
PARISH CHURCH, KILMAURS

159 MAUCHLINE PARISH CHURCH

NS 498 272

Loudoun Street, Mauchline

Present church by William Alexander 1829 stands
on site of St Michael's Church founded in 13th
century. Single bell cast in 1742. Willis pipe organ
1888 rebuilt in 1980. Associations with Covenanters
and Robert Burns, many contemporaries of whom
are buried here. At junction of B743 with A76.
Sunday Service: 11.00am

Open June to August, Tuesday and Wednesday
2.00-4.00pm. Also Ayrshire Doors Open Day
(date to be announced)

CHURCH OF SCOTLAND   wc **B**

MAUCHLINE PARISH CHURCH

160 ST THOMAS THE APOSTLE, MUIRKIRK

NS 699 278

Wellwood Street, Muirkirk

The material for this church, built in 1906, was transported from Belgium.
Sunday Service: 10.00am

Open by arrangement with Parish Priest, telephone 01290 421031

ROMAN CATHOLIC

161 RICCARTON PARISH CHURCH

NS 428 364

Old Street, Riccarton, Kilmarnock

Classical square-plan church of 1825 by John Richmond with the chancel added in
1910. Beautiful War Memorial window of 1919 in memory of those of the
congregation and parish who gave their lives in the Great War. A former Minister,
the Rev Alexander Moodie, mentioned by Burns in 'The Twa Herds' and 'The
Holy Fair' is buried in the churchyard. Sunday Service: 11.00am

Open by arrangement with John Henderson, telephone 01563 537982

CHURCH OF SCOTLAND wc **B**

162 SORN PARISH CHURCH

NS 550 268

Main Street, Sorn

A rather splendid edifice, quietly assured, built in 1656 and much reconstructed in
1826. Outside stairs to three galleries. Jougs on the west wall. East wall memorial
to George Wood, last Covenanter to die 1688. Sunday Service: 10.00am

Open by arrangement, telephone Miss McKerrow 01290 551256

CHURCH OF SCOTLAND wc **B**

SORN PARISH CHURCH

163 OUR LADY AND ST JOHN'S, STEWARTON

NS 417 457

69 Lainshaw Street, Stewarton

Our Lady and St John's was built in 1974 and functions as church and hall. Modern stations of the Cross by a local arts teacher. Services: Tuesday, Wednesday, Friday 11.00am; Monday, Thursday 10.00am; Saturday Vigil 5.00pm; Sunday 11.45am

Open by arrangement with the Sisters, telephone 01560 483322

ROMAN CATHOLIC

164 ST COLUMBA'S PARISH CHURCH, STEWARTON

NS 419 457

1 Kirk Glebe, Stewarton

Built in 1696, renovated in 1775, and widened in 1825 with later additions. Bell-tower. Lainshaw Loft used for smaller services. New and restored windows installed for tercentenary in 1996. Beside the mini-roundabout at the south end of Stewarton.

Sunday Service: 11.00am

Open by arrangement, telephone the Minister 01560 482453

CHURCH OF SCOTLAND

ST COLUMBA'S PARISH CHURCH, STEWARTON

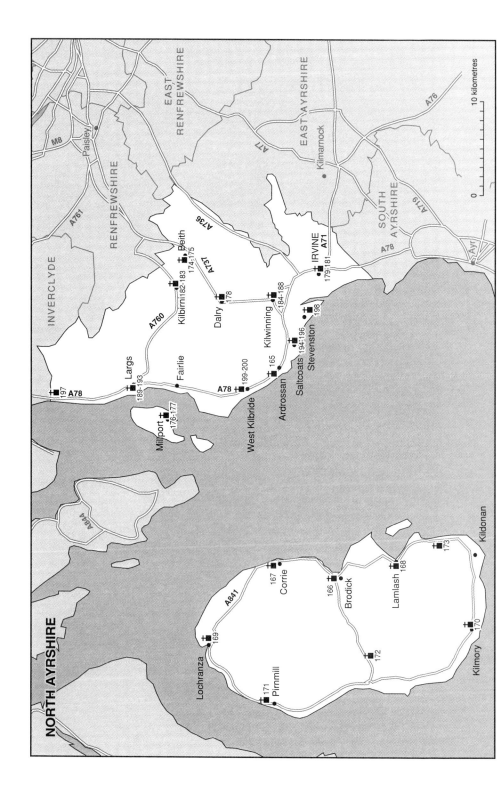

NORTH AYRSHIRE

EAST
RENFREWSHIRE

EAST AYRSHIRE

Kilmarnock

Paisley

M8

RENFREWSHIRE

A761

A77

A76

SOUTH
AYRSHIRE

A71

A78

Ayr

A76

A719

10 kilometres

0

INVERCLYDE

A760

A736

Beith
174-175

A737

Kilbirnie 182-183

Dalry
178

Kilwinning
184-188

IRVINE
179-181

A71

Largs
189-193

Fairlie

A78

Ardrossan

Saltcoats 194-196

Stevenston
198

197
A78

Millport
176-177

West Kilbride
199-200

165

A844

A841

Lochranza
169

Corrie
167

Brodick
166

Lamlash
168

Kildonan
173

Pirnmill
171

172

Kilmory
170

NORTH AYRSHIRE

Local Representative: Miss Joan Fish, 31 Oaklands Avenue, Irvine
(*telephone* 01294 272654)

165 ST PETER IN CHAINS, ARDROSSAN

NS 233 421
1 South Crescent, Ardrossan
Designed by Jack Coia and opened in 1938, St Peter in
Chains is probably the most academic of this period. The
church, in reddish facing brick, has a high west gable as at St
Columba, Hopehill Road, Glasgow and a tower to the right
reminiscent of Stockholm Town Hall. Striking brick main
doorway with stone keystone; the door feature continues to
the gable roof and ends in a small well-detailed cross.
Services: Monday to Saturday Mass 9.30am, 7.00pm; Saturday
Vigil Mass 6.30pm; Sunday 10.00am, 12.00 noon and 6.30pm
Open daily 9.00am-7.30pm
ROMAN CATHOLIC 🔊 **A**

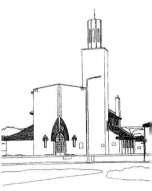

ST PETER IN CHAINS,
ARDROSSAN

166 BRODICK CHURCH, ISLE OF ARRAN

NS 012 359
Knowe Road, Brodick (1 mile north of pier, turn left at sports park)
The present church was built in 1910 from local red sandstone. The pulpit, built by
local craftsmen, is an exact replica of John Knox's pulpit. Two stained glass
windows are in memory of church member Bethia Torrance who died in 1958.
Originally the church hall was Bennecarrigan Free Church on the west side of the
island. Since it was no longer in use it was transported in March 1950 alongside
Brodick Church as a hall. Sunday Service: 10.45am
Open by arrangement, telephone Mr Hannah 01770 302248
CHURCH OF SCOTLAND ♿ wc 🔊 **B**

167 CORRIE CHURCH, ISLE OF ARRAN

NS 024 437
6 miles north of Brodick
Designed by J J Burnet 1887 as 'one of a family of long, low friendly churches'.
Constructed in red sandstone in an early Gothic style with a simple stone belfry
and wooden porch. An unusual baptismal font is set into the arch and church wall
and rush-bottomed chairs take the place of pews. Lit by circular candelabra. Two
tapestries by Mrs Sandeman and two recently installed stained glass windows by
Richard Leclerc. Sunday Service: 12.00 noon
Open by arrangement, telephone the Session Clerk, E Stevenson 01770 810268,
Mr McConnachie 01770 810246 or Mrs Pringle 01770 810210
CHURCH OF SCOTLAND wc **B**

CORRIE CHURCH, ISLE OF ARRAN

168   LAMLASH PARISH CHURCH, ISLE OF ARRAN

NS 026 309

Shore Road, Lamlash, Isle of Arran

A massive campanile tower over 90ft high sits above
this Gothic-style, red sandstone building by H & D
Barclay 1886. The church was built by 12th Duke of
Hamilton to replace an earlier building of 1773.
Boarded, barrel-vaulted ceiling and carved, wooden
tripartite Gothic sedilia. The tower hosts a peal of nine
bells played every Sunday before service, the largest
peal still existing, cast for a Scottish church in a
Scottish foundry. Seven stained glass windows by
Anning Bell, Meiklejohn, Gordon Webster and
Christian Shaw; all other windows are hand painted,
German cathedral glass. Pipe organ, William Hill,
Norman and Beard 1934. In the front grounds are an
ancient cross and baptismal font from the old monastery
on Holy Isle in Lamlash Bay. Major restoration
programme begun 1997.

LAMLASH PARISH CHURCH,
ISLE OF ARRAN

Sunday Service: from start to end of BST, 10.00am, otherwise 11.45am

Church website: www.isle-of-arran.co.uk

*Open by arrangement. See Church notice board for information, or contact
Captain J L Davidson, Rock Cottage, Cordon, Lamlash, telephone 01770 600787*

CHURCH OF SCOTLAND

♿ ⊘ 🏠 wc 🚹 A

169   ST BRIDE'S, LOCHRANZA

NR 937 503

At T-junction in centre of Lochranza

The present church was rebuilt in 1712 on the site of the previous church of 1654. A
beautiful, simple and attractive church featuring a circular stained glass window in

the east gable depicting the Ship of the Gospel sailing through the troubled Sea of
Life. This window and the unusual lych gate were given by Miss Edith Kerr in
memory of the Rev John Colville, minister here 1922-31. Sunday Service: 10.30am

Key available from Lochranza Field Centre 01770 830637 or May Fenton 01770 830222

CHURCH OF SCOTLAND ♿ wc ☕ **A**

170 KILMORY PARISH CHURCH, ISLE OF ARRAN

NR 700 449

Present church built 1880 over previous building 1765. Small, delightful church
with plain windows surrounded by red-coloured stained glass, providing a warm
ambience. Situated in village of Kilmory, turn right after Creamery on road from
Whiting Bay. Sunday Service: 10.00am

Open by arrangement, telephone Mrs Mairi Duff 01770 870305

CHURCH OF SCOTLAND **B**

171 PIRNMILL CHURCH, ARRAN

NR 873 443

On main street, at the north end of the village

Known locally as 'the tin kirk', the building previously belonged to the Free Church
of Scotland. A small and friendly congregation which warmly invites visitors to join
them for worship. Access is by a footpath through a field – it looks worse than it is!
Sunday Service: 12.00 noon

Open for services

CHURCH OF SCOTLAND **B**

172 ST MOLIOS, SHISKINE

NR 910 295

On B880 1 mile north of junction with A841

Known locally as 'The Red Kirk' because the local Machrie sandstone of its
construction is of a warm, red hue, this church
was built in 1889 to a design by John J Burnet.
The tower contains a single bell. Set into the
west wall of the tower is a carved stone
graveslab, possibly of a 13th-century abbot
taken from Clauchen graveyard. The north
gable has a double window in Norman style
with Celtic motifs. A small wooden carving of
St Molios, who lived as a hermit
on Holy Island, is set into a bench end on the
south side of the sanctuary. Sunday Service:
11.45am in summer, 10.00am in winter

*Church website: http://homepage.ntlworld.com
/morritek/lamlashchurch/index.htm*

Open during daylight hours

ST MOLIOS, SHISKINE

CHURCH OF SCOTLAND ♿ wc ② ☕ **B**

173 ST MARGARET OF SCOTLAND, ARRAN

NS 047 273

On main road just inside northern boundary of Whiting Bay

Built c.1960 for the Free Church; acquired (after a period as a holiday home) with
a legacy from Elsie Wood, widow of Canon Charles Wood; dedicated 1995.
Friendly ambience. Stained glass window by Eilidh Keith of Glasgow. Eagle
lectern from St Andrew's-on-the-Green, Glasgow, and a Slavonic (possibly Serbian)
icon. Sunday Service: 11.00am Holy Communion (1970 Liturgy on 2nd Sunday);
Evensong 4th Sunday 6.00pm March to September, 3.00pm October to February

Church website: www.scotland-anglican.org/argyll

Open by arrangement with the Minister, telephone 01770 700225

SCOTTISH EPISCOPAL 🦽 wc ☕ (after Sunday service) 📖 **B**

174 BEITH HIGH CHURCH

NS 350 539

Kirk Road, Beith

Built in 1807 and extended in 1885. Gothic
T-plan kirk dominated by the tall five-stage
tower. Stained glass by Gordon Webster.
Harrison & Harrison pipe organ 1885. From
Beith bypass along Barrmill Road to Kirk
Road. Sunday Service: 10.30am.
Joint service with Beith Trinity during the
month of August

Open by arrangement, telephone 01505 502686

CHURCH OF SCOTLAND 🦽 ⊘ 📖 📖 ⓘ wc **B**

BEITH HIGH CHURCH

175 BEITH TRINITY CHURCH

NS 351 544

Wilson Street, Beith

Built 1883, architect Robert Baldie. The
chief external feature is a graceful octagonal
tower. Interior destroyed by fire 1917, rebuilt
1926. Gothic style, with rectangular nave,
Gothic arched chancel and one transept on
the east side. Stained glass by John C Hall
& Co. Organ 1937 by Hill, Norman &
Beard. Sunday Service: 11.00am
Joint service with Beith High during the
month of July

Opening by arrangement,
telephone 01505 502131

CHURCH OF SCOTLAND wc ⊘

BEITH TRINITY CHURCH

176 THE CATHEDRAL OF THE ISLES, CUMBRAE

NS 165 561

College Street, Millport, Isle of Cumbrae

Cathedral, college and cloister by William Butterfield 1851. A Tractarian church built by 6th Earl of Glasgow. Peal of bells, organ, stained glass by William Wailes and Hardman. Visitors welcome to picnic in the grounds. Ferry from Largs and bus to Millport. Sunday Service: 11.00am Sung Eucharist; other times see notice board in porch

Church website: www.scotland.anglican.org/argyll

Open daily

SCOTTISH EPISCOPAL ☐ wc **A**

177 CUMBRAE PARISH CHURCH

NS 160 550

Bute Terrace, Millport

The church, with battlemented tower, pinnacles and clock, was erected in 1837. There are two very interesting grotesques, from the old Kirkton Church, in the chancel, also a lintel with inscribed Hebrew lettering. Flower Festival 8-10 August 2004 and 10-12 August 2005, Floral Service 11 August 2004 and 13 August 2005. Flower Festival 2005.

Services: Sunday 11.00am, Thursday 9.30am

Open by arrangement with Mr McCubbin,

telephone 01475 530393

CHURCH OF SCOTLAND wc ☺ **B**

CUMBRAE PARISH CHURCH

178 ST MARGARET'S PARISH CHURCH, DALRY

NS 291 496

The Cross, Dalry

David Thomson was the architect of this landmark Victorian Gothic building (1871-73) on an earlier site. Inventive 159ft broach spire 'worthy of the many tasks thrust upon it'; the whole building is a 'powerful, carefully handled composition'. The restored interior (with good acoustics) of the early 1950s presents 'a space of deep solemnity enhanced' by Beith-made pulpit, table, lectern and stained glass by Guthrie & Wells, Charles Payne, C L Davidson, plus the only decent amount of Munich glass and only Francis Hemony bell (1661) in a UK church. 3-manual Blackett & Howden organ (1899) moved here in 1953. Communion silver of 1618. Bronze sundial and some interesting stones in Kirkyard. Kirk bears the name of the original medieval dedication: St Margaret of Antioch (see modern Rona Moody window) the only such in Scotland. In the vicinity – Blair House may be viewed from outside; Cleeves Cove (interesting limestone cave system). Sunday Services: 10.30am all year round

Open by arrangement, telephone 01294 833135. Also Ayrshire Doors Open Day

CHURCH OF SCOTLAND ☐ wc **B**

ST MARGARET'S PARISH CHURCH, DALRY

179 IRVINE OLD PARISH CHURCH

NS 322 387

Kirkgate

The church, 1774 by David Muir, is the third to occupy the site. A large classical building with round-headed windows lighting the gallery. The clock in the 6-stage octagonal steeple was presented by Irvine Volunteers in 1803. The stained glass windows are a fine example of Keir brothers work. The graveyard contains fine classical monuments. Sunday Service: 11.00am

Open by arrangement with the Minister, telephone 01294 279265

CHURCH OF SCOTLAND   🚹 wc ✋ **A**

180 ST ANDREW'S PARISH CHURCH (FERGUSON MEMORIAL), IRVINE

NS 3239

Caldon Road x Oaklands Avenue, Irvine

St Andrew's was gifted in 1957 to commemorate the centenary of the death of John Ferguson, founder of the Ferguson bequest. Architect Rennie & Bramble of Saltcoats. Stained glass windows by Mary Wood 1957, Ann Marie Docherty 1998 and Stained Glass Designer Partnership of Milngavie 2000. The congregation shares the church with the local Scottish Episcopalian congregation who built on a chapel/meeting room, containing tapestry by Vampboulles, and coffee lounge in 1981. Architect R L Dunlop of Troon. Sunday Services: Scottish Episcopal 9.30am; Church of Scotland 11.15am

Open Tuesdays 9.45-11.00am

October to May

CHURCH OF SCOTLAND   🚹 ✋ wc ☕

ST ANDREW'S PARISH CHURCH
(FERGUSON MEMORIAL), IRVINE

181 FULLARTON PARISH CHURCH, IRVINE

NS 316 389

Church Street, Marress Roundabout

Built 1838 and designed by Ingram of Kilmarnock. School of 1640 now forms part of the halls. Vestry of 1907. Two stained glass windows of 1958 by G Maille & Son of London depicting 'the Good Shepherd' and 'Christ blessing little children' in memory of the Rev John Paterson, much loved Minister from 1903-37. Memorial to James Montgomery, Christian poet and hymn writer. Digital organ by the Bradford Computing Organ Co., 1994. Sunday Service: 11.00am and 6.30pm

Church website: www.fullartonchurch.co.uk

Nearby Fullarton Centre Café open Monday, Tuesday, Thursday and Friday 10.00am-12.00 noon and 2.00-4.00pm. Closed July and August. Church open by arrangement with the Minister 01294 279909 or the Session Clerk 01299 216942

CHURCH OF SCOTLAND   🦽 wc ⍥ ☕ **B**

182 THE AULD KIRK OF KILBIRNIE

NS 315 536

Dalry Road, Kilbirnie

A pre-Reformation church on the site of 6th-century cell dedicated to St Brendan of Clonfert. The nave dates from 1470 and the bell-tower from 1490. Glengarnock aisle added 1597. Crawfurd aisle added in 1642 with unique Renaissance-style carving. Pulpit c.1620. At junction of B780 and B777. Bus to Kilbirnie, rail to Glengarnock.

THE AULD KIRK OF KILBIRNIE

Sunday Services: 9.30am and 11.00am

Church website:

www//members.tripod.co.uk/auldkirk/

Open July to August, weekdays 2.00-4.00pm except Mondays; Ayrshire Doors Open Day, September. Other times, telephone Mr J Lauchland 01505 683459

CHURCH OF SCOTLAND 🦽 ⍥ 🏠 wc **A**

183 ST COLUMBA'S, KILBIRNIE

NS 314 546

Glasgow Street

The old church was built in 1843 and reconstructed and enlarged 1903. The design of a sloping floor and balcony is unusual. The balcony front is French Fibre plasterwork. Table runner by Malcolm Lochhead. Three-light window by Stephen Adam in the hall which is the former Kilbirnie West Church.

Sunday Service: 11.15am

Church website: www.broster.org

Open by arrangement, telephone the Minister 01505 683342

CHURCH OF SCOTLAND 🦽 wc ⍥

184 THE ABBEY CHURCH, KILWINNING

NS 303 433
Main Street, Kilwinning
Built in 1774 by John Garland and John
Wright. The church is on the site of the
ruined abbey, founded in 1188, and
replaced the first reformation church built
in 1590. The organ built by Foster &
Anderson of Hull was first played in 1897
and is highly regarded. The church has
strong links with the Earls of Eglinton.
Sunday Services: 9.15am and 11.00am
September to May; 10.00am June, July
and August
Or by arrangement, telephone Mr J Muir,
30 Underwood, Kilwinning 01294 552929
CHURCH OF SCOTLAND

THE ABBEY CHURCH, KILWINNING

185 ERSKINE CHURCH, KILWINNING

NS 303 434
Main Street, Kilwinning
Simple UP-style building, 1838, down a
lane from Main Street. Pedimented open
bellcote flanked by ancones. Gable finials.
Pleasant restored interior with gallery.
Sunday Service: 11.30am
Open by arrangement, telephone
Mr Welsh 01294 554376
CHURCH OF SCOTLAND WC c

ERSKINE CHURCH, KILWINNING

186 FERGUSHILL CHURCH, KILWINNING

NS 337 430
Benslie Village, Kilwinning
Church extension for the mining
community from Kilwinning Parish
Church in 1879 to a plan prepared
by William Railton of Kilmarnock.
Attractive church with bell-tower.
Fine views to Arran.
Sunday Service: 10.00am
Open by arrangement, telephone
Mrs Borland 01294 850257
CHURCH OF SCOTLAND WC

FERGUSHILL CHURCH, KILWINNING

187 ST WININ'S, KILWINNING

NS 300 432

St Winning's Lane, Kilwinning

Modern functional building with basic decoration. Seats 400 and is well-used by the 700 or 800 congregation who attend weekend masses.

Services: Saturday 6.30pm, Sunday 10.00am and 12.00 noon

Church website: www.st-winins.com

Open by arrangement with Parish House, telephone 01294 552276

ROMAN CATHOLIC [♿] (side entrance) [②] [wc] (in Hall) [wc]

188 MANSEFIELD TRINITY CHURCH, KILWINNING

NS 301 433

West Doura Way, Stevenston Road

The first church opened by the Church of Scotland in the new millennium. Designed by architects James F Stephens, the building is multi-purpose and reflects current thinking, being open, accessible, full of light and atmosphere.

Sunday Service: 11.00am October to June, 10.30am July to Septmber

Open 10.00am-2.00pm Tuesday and Thursday otherwise by arrangement telephone 01294 550746

CHURCH OF SCOTLAND [♿] [wc] [②] [☕]

MANSEFIELD TRINITY CHURCH, KILWINNING

189 CLARK MEMORIAL CHURCH, LARGS

NS 202 593

Bath Street, Largs

Gifted by John Clark of the Anchor Thread Mills, Paisley, and designed by William Kerr of T G Abercrombie, Paisley 1892. Red sandstone from Locharbriggs and Corsehill in Early English Gothic style. Superb stained glass, all manufactured in Glasgow at height of Arts & Crafts movement. Hammer-beam roof. Organ by 'Father' Willis, 1892. Views of the Clyde and Cumbraes.

Sunday Service: 10.00am, Thursday 10.30am

Open daily 10.00am-4.00pm (except Tuesdays).

Viking Festival one week each September

CHURCH OF SCOTLAND [🕯] [📖] [②] [wc] **A**

CLARK MEMORIAL CHURCH, LARGS

190 ST COLUMBA'S PARISH CHURCH, LARGS

NS 203 596

Gallowgate, Largs

The old parish church was replaced by
the present building in 1892. It is a
handsome structure, architects Henry
Steele and Andrew Balfour, of red stone
with a three-stage tower with spire and
clock. Interesting carved octagonal oak
pulpit and notable windows. 'Father'
Willis organ, 1892, generally regarded
as one of the finest church instruments
in Scotland. Memorial to General Sir
Thomas MacDougall Brisbane,
astronomer, soldier and Governor
of New South Wales.

ST COLUMBA'S PARISH CHURCH, LARGS

Sunday Service: 11.00am

Church website: www.btinternet.com /~jfultonmurdoch/columba.htm

Open 10.00am-12.00 noon, Monday to Friday

CHURCH OF SCOTLAND

 (by arrangement) ⑦ ☐ ☕ (Saturdays June to September) wc **B**

191 ST MARY'S STAR OF THE SEA, LARGS

NS 201 603

28 Greenock Road, Largs

A bright modern building opened
in 1962. The architect was Mr A
R Conlon of Reginald Fairlie &
Sons. Features include a tapestry
at the High Altar depicting Jesus
and two disciples at Emmaus,
eight stained glass panels above
the main door, and a statue
outside the main door of Our
Lady, Star of the Sea, by eminent
Scottish sculptor, Hew Lorimer.

Services: Saturday Vigil 6.30pm,
Sunday 9.00am and 11.30am

Open 8.30am-8.00pm in summer,
8.30am-3.30pm in winter

ROMAN CATHOLIC ⑦ wc wc

ST MARY'S STAR OF THE SEA, LARGS

192 ST COLUMBA'S, LARGS

NS 201 603

Aubery Crescent

Built in 1876 on land gifted by the Brisbane family and the construction funded
by the Earl of Glasgow. Charming and delicate exercise in the Early English style
by Ross and McBeth of Inverness. Victorian stained glass, including a rose window
depicting a dove, symbol of the Holy Spirit and St Columba. Memorials to the
Brisbane and Boyle (Earls of Glasgow) families and to the scientist Lord Kelvin.
Embroidered kneelers made for the centenary. Services: Sunday 8.00am, 11.00am,
6.30pm and Wednesday 10.00am

Church website: www.geocities.com/largschurch

Open 9.00am-5.00pm daily except Friday

SCOTTISH EPISCOPAL   🚹 wc ② ｉ ☕ 📖 **B**

193 ST JOHN'S, LARGS

NS 201 593

Bath Street

Built as a Free Church in 1843 and named St
John's in 1900 after union with the Free and
United Presbyterian Churches. Designed by A J
Graham, the building is in the Romanesque style
with the tall tower at the north-west corner and
vestry to the south-west linked by an arcaded
narthex. Sunday Services: 11.00am and 6.30pm

Open by arrangement, telephone the Session Clerk,
Mr McGregor, 01475 686729

CHURCH OF SCOTLAND   🚹 ② **B**

ST JOHN'S, LARGS

194 ST BRENDAN'S, SALTCOATS

NS 247 430

63 Corrie Crescent

St Brendan's has a magnificent contemporary stained glass window depicting the
life of St Brendan and a unique crucifix, designed locally and fabricated in steel.
Services: Saturday 6.30pm, Sunday 11.00am

Open by arrangement, telephone 01294 463483

ROMAN CATHOLIC   🚹 ② wc

ST BRENDAN'S, SALTCOATS

195 ST CUTHBERT'S PARISH CHURCH, SALTCOATS

NS 244 418

Caledonia Road, Saltcoats

Designed by Peter MacGregor Chalmers and
dedicated in 1908, the fourth building of the
congregation of Ardrossan Parish. The
chancel displays a marble reredos of the Last
Supper. Sixteen stained glass windows on the
Life of Christ by William Wilson 1947; two
windows by Gordon Webster 1976. Model
of a French frigate of 1804, by a sailor
William Dunlop, hangs in the church. He
made it as a thanksgiving for his surviving
the Napoleonic wars when a cannonball
narrowly missed his hammock!

Sunday Service: 11.15am

Open by arrangement, telephone

Mrs Hanlon 01294 466636

CHURCH OF SCOTLAND ♿ ⟲ wc **B**

ST CUTHBERT'S PARISH
CHURCH, SALTCOATS

196 NEW TRINITY PARISH CHURCH, SALTCOATS

NS 246 414

Chapelwell Street

Congregation formed by the union of Erskine and Landsborough Trinity Churches
in 1993. The former Erskine Church buildings of 1866 are used. The building,
designed by William Stewart, has a spire and pinnacles above a polychrome
Venetian Gothic façade. Additional halls built 1970. Organ, Forster & Andrews,
1899. Four stained glass windows depicting 'Music', 'The Good Shepherd',
'Dorcas' and 'The Sower of the Seed'. Services: Sunday 11.15am, Thursday 10.30am

Open by arrangement, telephone 01294 602410

CHURCH OF SCOTLAND ♿ wc ⟲ **C**

197 SKELMORLIE & WEMYSS BAY

NS 192 681

Shore Road, Skelmorlie

Gothic church with nave and chancel and a square tower, built 1895 and designed
by John Honeyman to replace a 'chapel-of-ease' of 1856. Free-standing wrought-
iron lamp by Charles Rennie Mackintosh, 1895, at the entrance. Stained glass by
Douglas Strachan ('Stilling the Storm'), Stephen Adam, Edward Burne Jones and
Charles E Kempe. Organ by Binns, 1910. Services: Sunday 11.00am

Church website: www.newtrinity.co.uk

Open Saturdays July and August 2.00-4.00pm, otherwise by arrangement with

Minister telephone 01475 520703

CHURCH OF SCOTLAND wc ⟲ 🕯 **B** (Lamp **A**)

198 ST JOHN, STEVENSTON

NS 272 425

Hayocks Road, Stevenston

Built 1963 to designs by Mr Houston Jr.
Features laminated trusses supporting the
roof and beautiful stained glass by M
Gabriel Loire of Chartres representing
biblical scenes and St John the Evangelist.
Brass baptismal font depicting a half tree
trunk sheltering a fawn: 'As the deer longs

ST JOHN, STEVENSTON

for streams of water, so my soul yearns for you, my God.' Services: Saturday Vigil
6.30pm, Sunday 10.30am, weekdays 10am (subject to change)

Church website: www.stjohnsrc.force9.co.uk

Open by arrangement with Parish Priest,

telephone 01294 463225

ROMAN CATHOLIC [&] [?] [wc]

199 OVERTON CHURCH, WEST KILBRIDE

NS 203 481

Ritchie Street, West Kilbride

Just over 100 years old, designed by Mr Le Blanc
(of Glasgow Baths fame). Very good stained glass
with two recent modern additions. Two manual
Binns Organ – tubular pneumatic. Unusual hipped
wooden ceiling to nave. Sunday Service: 11.00am
all year, 6.30pm during autumn and winter.

Open Thursday 10.00am–12.00 noon

CHURCH OF SCOTLAND

[&] [wc] [?] [ ] (by arrangement) [cup] (Thursday mornings)

OVERTON CHURCH, WEST KILBRIDE

200 ST BRIDE'S, WEST KILBRIDE

NS 206 484

9 Hunterston Road

The church was built and opened in
1908. The Marian shrine in the grounds
was erected in 1958 for the Golden
Jubilee. Services: Saturday Vigil 6.30pm,
Sunday 10.30am, weekdays (including
Saturdays) 9.30am

Open daily 9.00am-6.00pm

ROMAN CATHOLIC [?] [wc]

ST BRIDE'S, WEST KILBRIDE

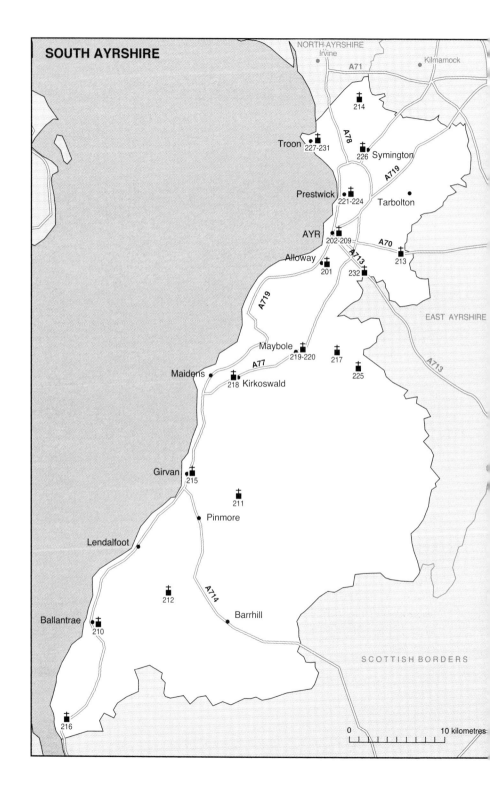

SOUTH AYRSHIRE

NORTH AYRSHIRE
Irvine
Kilmarnock
A71
214
A78
Troon
227-231
A719
226 Symington
Prestwick
221-224
Tarbolton
AYR
202-209
A70
A713
213
Alloway
201
232
EAST AYRSHIRE
A713
Maybole
219-220
217
A77
225
Maidens
218 Kirkoswald
Girvan
215
211
Pinmore
Lendalfoot
212
A714
Barrhill
Ballantrae
210
SCOTTISH BORDERS
216

0   10 kilometres

SOUTH AYRSHIRE

Local Representative: Miss Joan Fish, 31 Oaklands Avenue, Irvine
(*telephone* 01294 272654)

201 ALLOWAY PARISH CHURCH

NS 332 181

ALLOWAY PARISH CHURCH

Built in 1858, architect Campbell Douglas. South
transept added in 1877, chancel built and nave
extended in 1890. Excellent stained glass including
Stephen Adam, Clayton & Bell, Gordon Webster, W
& J J Keir. Douglas McLundie's memorial window
to D F McIntyre, pilot on first flight over Mount
Everest in 1933. Two windows by Susan Bradbury
were installed in 1996, one depicting the four
seasons, the other in memory of Robert Burns.
Three further Bradbury windows were added in
2001, enhancing the porch and sanctuary area throughout with stained glass.
B7024 south of Burns' cottage. Sunday Services 9.45am and 11.15am
Open June to September, Monday to Friday 10.00am-4.00pm. Conducted tours,
contact local tourist office
CHURCH OF SCOTLAND ♿ ⚲ 📖 **B**

202 THE AULD KIRK OF AYR (ST JOHN THE BAPTIST)

NS 339 219

Off High Street, Ayr
The approach to the Auld Kirk is through Kirkport and the 1656 Lychgate into the
kirkyard. The Commonwealth Government paid for the 1654 T-plan kirk after
Cromwell's troops had occupied the old Church of St John on the sands.
Respectful alterations by David Bryce of 1836. High-quality interior with three
lofts on Corinthian columns and a splendid double-decker pulpit. One of the few
remaining 'Obit' boards records money donated to the poor. This church is not a
museum, but living and active. Sunday Service: 11.00am
Church website: www.auldkirk.org
In 2004 The Auld Kirk celebrates its 350th
anniversary and many events are planned every
month. January 1, floodlighting of the Church.
Easter Sunday, the release of 350 Balloons. May
22, Ballyclare Male Choir from Northern Ireland.
June 20, Thanksgiving Service. November 3,
Alexander Brothers. December 2,3 and 4, Flower
Festival. Open Saturday mornings by arrangement,
telephone the church office 01292 262938
CHURCH OF SCOTLAND ♿ ⚲ 📖 🚾 **A**

THE AULD KIRK OF AYR
(ST JOHN THE BAPTIST)

203 ST QUIVOX, AUCHINCRUIVE, AYR

NS 375 241

Christian presence on the site dates back to the
13th century. The medieval building was
restored 1595 and extended 1767 to create a T-
plan church. Interior fittings date largely from
the late 18th century, including a good pulpit. In
the kirkyard, mausoleum of the Campbells of
Craigie, by W H Playfair 1822.

Sunday Service: 11.30am

Open by arrangement, contact Mrs A C Taylor,

telephone 01292 269746

CHURCH OF SCOTLAND 🦽 wc **A**

ST QUIVOX, AUCHINCRUIVE, AYR

204 HOLY TRINITY CHURCH, AYR

NS 336 218

Fullarton Street, Ayr

Dedicated in 1888. Scotland's major example of the work
of J L Pearson, designer of Truro Cathedral. Pulpit of Caen
stone and very fine stained glass windows by, among others,
Clayton & Bell. Next to Ayr bus station, walking distance
from railway station. Sunday Services: 8.00am, 10.30am
and 6.30pm; Wednesday Eucharist 11.00am

Church website:

//website.lineone.net/~holytrinitychurch/southayrshire/indexx.html

Open mornings in summer. Concert series

SCOTTISH EPISCOPAL

🦽 ⏰ 🍴 📷 ☕ (for visiting groups by arrangement) wc **A**

HOLY TRINITY CHURCH, AYR

205 ST ANDREW'S, AYR

NS 338 222

39 Park Circus, Ayr

St Andrew's, identified by its tall red sandstone spire, was opened in November
1893. The worshipping congregation came from the Wallacetown Free Church
disruption. The design, by John B Wilson, is Perpendicular Gothic. The beautiful
stained glass includes work by John Blyth, Marcus McLundie and G Maile Studios,
Canterbury. The church hall (1897) is by William McClelland, major extensions to
provide additional accomodation were carried out in 1963 and 1983. The church
is on the south side of the town between the railway and the sea front.

Sunday Service: 11.00am

Church website: wwwstandrewsayr.cwc.net

Open last Wednesday of the month, May to September 2.00-4.00pm

CHURCH OF SCOTLAND 🦽 ⏰ wc 🍴 ☕ **B**

206 ST COLUMBA, AYR

NS 337 201
Midton Road / Carrick Park
Originally known as Trinity Church, Ayr.
St Columba was dedicated in 1902. Built of red
sandstone to designs by John B Wilson of Glasgow.
Fine pipe organ 1904 by J J Binns, restored by
Harrison & Harrison 1985. Stained glass by Sidney
Holmes, C C Baillie, Susan Bradbury and Rowland
Mitton. Resurrection window unveiled by HRH the
Princess Royal, 2002. Cultured octagonal pencil
tower with carillon of bells. Sunday Services: 9.30
and 11.15am, 1st Sunday of month 6.30pm
Church website: www.ayrstcolumba.co.uk
Open 9.00am-12.00 noon, Monday, Tuesday, Thursday, Friday
CHURCH OF SCOTLAND [&] [?] [wc] **B**

ST COLUMBA, AYR

207 ST JAMES'S PARISH CHURCH, AYR

NS 342 232
Prestwick Road / Falkland Park Road, Ayr
St James's Church was built as a chapel-of-ease in 1885 to
designs by John Murdoch. Murdoch, an engineer before he
became an architect, was the most ambitious of the
architects of Ayr in the late 19th century and received many
important commissions. There is a rose window above the
pulpit. Sunday Service: 11.00am
Open by arrangement with the Minister, telephone 01292 262420
CHURCH OF SCOTLAND [wc] **B**

ST JAMES'S
PARISH CHURCH, AYR

208 ST LEONARD'S, AYR

NS 338 204
St Leonard's Road / Monument Road, Ayr
Built in 1886, several hundred yards from the site of the
ancient chapel of St Leonard, the patron saint of
prisoners. The architect was John Murdoch and the style
belongs to the geometric period of decorated Gothic.
The building comprises a nave with aisles, transepts and
chancel (added in 1911). 2-manual pipe organ by
Harrison & Harrison, rebuilt 1992. Many beautiful
stained glass windows. Sunday Service: 10.00am
Open by arrangement, telephone Mr William Bruce
01292 263694
CHURCH OF SCOTLAND [&] [?] [wc] **B**

ST LEONARD'S, AYR

209 ST PAUL'S ROMAN CATHOLIC, AYR

NS 348 200

Peggieshill Road, Ayr

The dedication stone was laid in 1966 and the
church was opened 1967. Wall hanging by
members of the parish of St Paul's meeting on
the road to Damascus. Altar, lectern and
baptismal font in Creetown granite. Services:
Saturday Vigil 6.30pm, Sunday 10.00am and
12.00 noon, daily usually at 10.00am

Open by arrangement with Parish Priest,

telephone 01292 260197

ROMAN CATHOLIC

ST PAUL'S ROMAN CATHOLIC, AYR

210 BALLANTRAE PARISH CHURCH

NX 084 825

Main Street, Ballantrae

Built in 1819. Memorial to Lord Ballantrae.
Regency pulpit. Nephew of Robert Burns was
minister 1826-30. Kennedy tomb beside church.
Ruins of Ardstinchar Castle. A77. Railway station
at Girvan, 13 miles. Buses from Glasgow. United
with Glenapp. Sunday Service: 11.00am

Church website: www.ballantraeparishchurch.org.uk

Open daily, May to September 10.00am-sunset

CHURCH OF SCOTLAND (in village) **B**

BALLANTRAE PARISH CHURCH

211 BARR PARISH CHURCH

NX 275 941

Main Street, Barr, by Girvan

Dating from 1878, built to a design by
A Stevenson. Early Gothic gabled chapel.
Slate roof, skew gables, rubble walls,
freestone dressings. Picturesque south-
east bellcote. Fine wooden ceiling.
Restored 1978 P J Lorimer, London.
B734 from Girvan, occasional buses
from Girvan. Sunday Service: 12.00 noon

Open all year, 9.00am-7.00pm.

Teas in July and August: Monday, Friday

and Saturday 2.30-5.00pm

CHURCH OF SCOTLAND   **C**

BARR PARISH CHURCH

212 COLMONELL CHURCH

NX 145 858

Built 1849 and renovated when the organ was installed. Organ screen and chancel by Robert Lorimer. Exceptional stained glass, including windows by Louis Davis and Douglas Strachan. Martyr's stone in graveyard from the time of the Covenanters, and Kennedy vault dating from 1620. Local lore gives a Christian presence here from AD c.600 when St Colman of Ella built his cell.

Sunday Service: 10.30am

Open daily

CHURCH OF SCOTLAND **B**

213 ST CLARE'S, DRONGAN

NS 441 185

Watson Terrace, Drongan
(1 mile south of A70, 7 miles east of Ayr)
Unassuming church building opened in 1967. Sunday Service: 9.45am

Open only for Sunday Service

ROMAN CATHOLIC wc

ST CLARE'S, DRONGAN

214 DUNDONALD PARISH CHURCH

NS 366 343

Main Street, Dundonald
Tranquil setting for this traditional stone church of 1804, built on the site of an earlier building. The clock tower was added 1841, and the chancel 1906. Some fine stained glass, particularly Henry Dearle's unique 'Last Supper'. Pipe organ, Norman & Beard 1906. Interesting grave stones in the tidy graveyard. Sunday Service: 11.00am

Church open by arrangement, telephone
Rev Robert Mayes 01563 850703

CHURCH OF SCOTLAND ♿ ⊘ wc **B**

DUNDONALD PARISH CHURCH

215 SACRED HEARTS OF JESUS AND MARY, GIRVAN

NS 183 979

Harbour Lane, Girvan
A plain Gothic structure of 1860 with a huge prow-like porch added in 1959 by Stevenson & Ferguson. Stained glass windows of 1860.
Services: 7.00pm Saturday, 9.00am and 11.00am Sunday

Open during daylight hours

ROMAN CATHOLIC

SACRED HEARTS OF
JESUS AND MARY, GIRVAN

216 GLENAPP CHURCH

NX 075 746

This church has a memorial window to Elsie
Mackay, third daughter of Earl of Inchcape. She
was killed in 1928 attempting to fly the Atlantic.
Modern stained glass window above door, 'The
Stilling of the Tempest', in memory of first Earl.
Graveyard contains tombs of the three Earls of
Inchcape. Seven miles south of Ballantrae on A77,
ten miles north of Stranraer. United with
Ballantrae. Sunday Service: occasional

Church website: www.ballantraeparishchurch.org.uk

Open summer and autumn

CHURCH OF SCOTLAND

GLENAPP CHURCH

217 KIRKMICHAEL PARISH CHURCH

NY 005 884

80 Patna Road, Kirkmichael, near Maybole

Believed to stand on the site of a 13th-century church under the care of the monks
of Whithorn, the present church was built 1787 by Hugh Cairncross, and the
belfry rebuilt 1887. Stone pulpit of 1919 depicting St Michael, St George, St
Andrew and St Patrick incorporates the war memorial. Two large stained glass
windows on either side of the pulpit, one by Christopher Whitworth Whall. The
oldest building is the lychgate, the bell inside is dated 1702 and is still rung when
a bride leaves the church after her wedding. Interesting stones in surrounding
graveyard, including Covenanter's memorial, open every day. Two miles east of
Maybole. Sunday Service: 10.30am

Open by arrangement, telephone the Minister 01655 750286

CHURCH OF SCOTLAND 🦽 ⛪ (in village) wc **B**

218 KIRKOSWALD PARISH CHURCH

NS 240 074

Robert Adam 1777, contemporary with Culzean Castle.
It is suggested that while working with Lord Cassillis,
his client at Culzean, Robert Adam came across the
church during construction and recommended some
changes, giving the building fine Palladian details. The
church was visited by Robert Burns and more recently
by President Eisenhower. Following a fire, the church
was fully restored in 1997 and the opportunity was
taken to research original Adam colour scheme. Burns'
characters, Tam o' Shanter, Souter Johnnie and
Kirkton Jean, are buried in the old graveyard, where
also can be seen the baptismal font used to baptise

KIRKOSWALD
PARISH CHURCH

Robert the Bruce. The church is situated just off the A77, in Kirkoswald 5 miles south of Maybole, and 7 miles north of Girvan. Sunday Service: 11.00am

Open by arrangement, telephone 01655 760210 or 01655 760238

CHURCH OF SCOTLAND   ♿ ⑦ 🏺 📖 **A**

219   ST OSWALD'S, MAYBOLE

NS 299 101

Cargill Road / Garden Path

Built 1883 on land gifted to the church and seating about 90 people. Organ by Alfred Kirkland, 1892. Hall and toilets added 1970s. Convenient for Maybole Railway Station. Services: Sunday 11.30am, Wednesdays 10.00am

Open by arrangement with keyholders, Mr & Mrs Pope, telephone 01655 882452

SCOTTISH EPISCOPAL   ♿ 🚾

220   OUR LADY & ST CUTHBERT, MAYBOLE

NS 299 094

Dailly Road, Maybole

Gothic church with presbytery to west and hall to east, linked to form a T-plan complex. Built of yellow sandstone with white ashlar dressings with an octagonal spire on the north-west corner and a gabled porch at the north-east corner. Opened in 1878, the church has unusual bosses depicting the saints looking out into the church. Services: Saturday 6.30pm, Sunday 10.00am – please telephone 01655 882145 to confirm

Church website: www.maybole.org / community / churches

Open by arrangement, telephone 01655 882145

ROMAN CATHOLIC   🚾 ⑦ 💻 (after Sunday service) **B**

OUR LADY &
ST CUTHBERT, MAYBOLE

221   MONKTON & PRESTWICK NORTH

NS 350 263

10 Monkton Road, Prestwick

The church was built as a Free Church in 1874, architect James Salmon & Son, and the bell-tower was added 1890, architect John Keppie. The congregation, united with the Church of Scotland in 1900, now uses a computerised communication system for hymn singing and visual aids. The pulpit, from St Cuthbert's, Monkton, is mobile. The original St Cuthbert's Communion Table has been fixed as a panel between two stained glass windows. Sunday Service: 11.00am

Open by arrangement, telephone the
Rev A Christie 01292 477499

CHURCH OF SCOTLAND   ♿ ⑦ 🚾

MONKTON & PRESTWICK NORTH

222 KINGCASE PARISH CHURCH, PRESTWICK

NS 348 244

Waterloo Road, Prestwick (behind Safeway store)

The church was built in 1912, extended 1956, in attractive red sandstone with three small but beautiful stained glass windows. Fairly small building in excellent state of repair. Sunday Services: 9.45am and 11.15am, 7.00pm. Large-print hymn books available

Church website: www.kingcase.freeserve.co.uk

Open by arrangement with Church Office, telephone 01292 470755

CHURCH OF SCOTLAND [wc] (?) [?]

KINGCASE PARISH
CHURCH, PRESTWICK

223 PRESTWICK SOUTH PARISH CHURCH

NS 352 260

Main Street, Prestwick

First church commission 1879 for James A Morris, a contemporary of Charles Rennie Mackintosh. Adept, light handling of Gothic forms, enlivened by Glasgow-style carving. Carefully chosen interior fittings include glass by Oscar Paterson. Sunday Service: 11.00am

Church website: www.south-church.org.uk

Open by arrangement with the Minister, telephone 01292 478788

CHURCH OF SCOTLAND [&] (?) [ ] [wc]

224 ST QUIVOX, PRESTWICK

NS 352 257

St Quivox Road, Prestwick

The building was completed in 1933 and is built of Accrington brick in Romanesque style. The church was extended in 1969 and incorporates the old building to form a rectangular-shaped church. Inside are a sanctuary mosaic panel and the Stations of the Cross. Jubilee 2000 window. Sunday Services: 10.00am, 11.30am and 6.00pm

Open daily 10.00am-5.00pm

ROMAN CATHOLIC (?)

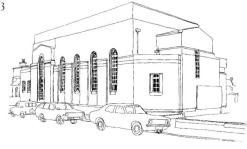

ST QUIVOX, PRESTWICK

225 STRAITON PARISH CHURCH (ST CUTHBERT'S)

NS 380 049

The main part of the church dates from 1758. The piscina of the original church is still visible on the east wall. Chantry chapel of late 15th century containing various memorial plaques to members of the Hunter Blair family. In 1901 the church was renovated by John Kinross and the bell-tower was added to the design of John Murdoch. The interior is noted for its beautiful carvings, especially on the ceiling and pulpit. Striking 'Millennium Banner' mounted on a pedestal made from a former pew. Tapestry cushions, 1993, depict themes from the life and work of the community. The stone font is the gift of the Fergusson family. Splendid stained glass. Covenanter's memorial in graveyard, open every day. Of special interest is the artwork undertaken by the ladies of the local Sewing Guild to commemorate 1997 as 'The Year of Faith'; 1998 as 'The Year of Hope'; and 1999 as 'The Year of Love'. Straiton is four miles east of Kirkmichael.
Sunday Service: 12.00 noon

Open by arrangement with the Minister, telephone 01655 750286
CHURCH OF SCOTLAND ♿ wc (nearby) **A**

STRAITON PARISH
CHURCH (ST CUTHBERT'S)

226 SYMINGTON CHURCH

NS 999 352

Known as Ayrshire's Norman church, the rectangular building with three-feet thick walls was founded c.1160 by Symon de Loccard whose own story in itself makes a visit worthwhile. Restored 1919 by P MacGregor Chalmers. Norman arched windows, piscina and ancient oak-beamed ceiling. The stained glass, much of it by Douglas Strachan, is glorious in creation and colour. Though small in size, its stones breathe the atmosphere of prayer and praise of all the saints over 800 years. Two miles from Prestwick Airport on A77. Sunday Service: 10.30am

Church website: www.symingtonchurch.com
Open by arrangement, telephone
Mrs Margaret Kerr 01563 830289,
or Jim Knox 01563 830043
CHURCH OF SCOTLAND ♿ 🍴 📖 👤 **A**

SYMINGTON CHURCH

227 TROON OLD CHURCH

NS 321 309
Ayr Street, Troon
Neo-Gothic building in red sandstone by Hippolyte
Blanc and dedicated in 1895. The stained glass of
the Ascension window is by the Morris Studio; other
windows by Gordon Webster. Alabaster reredos
depicting Moses, St Paul and the Last Supper has a
finely carved canopy and stands above a mosaic
pavement of the Paschal Lamb. Richly carved pulpit,
communion table and font. Various memorials.
Sunday Service: 10.30am; Wednesday 11.15am
Church website: www.troonold.org.uk
Open Tuesday to Sunday 10.00am–12.00 noon
CHURCH OF SCOTLAND ʷᶜ Ⓓ 👤 (by arrangement), 📖 🍵 (Saturday and Sunday) **B**

TROON OLD CHURCH

228 OUR LADY AND ST MEDDAN CHURCH, TROON

NS 327 311
4 Cessnock Road, Troon
Built to a design by Reginald Fairlie 1910, this church is a
mixture of architectural styles and also copies the rear view
of Holy Rude Church in Stirling. The church has undergone
major restoration funded by Historic Scotland. Two minutes
from railway station, Glasgow–Ayr, half-hourly train service.
Sunday Mass 9.00am and 11.15am; Saturday Vigil Mass
6.00pm
Open daily until 4.00pm, and Ayrshire Doors Open Day, September
ROMAN CATHOLIC Ⓓ ʷᶜ **A**

OUR LADY AND
ST MEDDAN CHURCH, TROON

229 PORTLAND PARISH CHURCH, TROON

NS 323 309
South Beach / St Meddan's Street, Troon
Opened in 1914 as a United Free Church by H E Clifford & Lunan. Perpendicular
Gothic in white sandstone with fine tracery in the great north window which is
repeated in the nave windows. Interior has exposed
stone with blonde Austrian oak pews and fittings. The
stained glass chancel window was donated in 1920 as
a war memorial by Mr A F Steven. Harrison &
Harrison 2-manual organ, rebuilt 1970. Halls extension
added 1964. Two minutes' walk from railway station.
Sunday Service: 10.30am
Open July and August, Sunday and Thursday 2.00–4.30pm,
and Ayrshire Doors Open Day, September
CHURCH OF SCOTLAND Ⓓ 👤 📖 🍵 ʷᶜ **B**

PORTLAND PARISH
CHURCH, TROON

230 ST MEDDAN'S, TROON

NS 323 309

Corner of Church Street and St Meddan's Street, Troon
Built 1888-89 for the United Presbyterian Church,
architect J B Wilson, St Meddan's has many
noteworthy features. The tall and stately spire houses
a clock which was originally part of the University
of Glasgow's Old College in High Street, Glasgow.
Many beautiful stained glass windows; the largest,
opposite the pulpit, depicts the healing of Jairus's
daughter. Sunday Services: 9.30am and 11.15am
Church website: www.troonstmeddanschurch.org
Open Monday, Tuesday and Thursday 9.00am-2.00pm
CHURCH OF SCOTLAND ♿ wc ② B

ST MEDDAN'S, TROON

231 ST NINIAN'S, TROON

NS 327 304

Bentinck Drive
Designed in Arts & Crafts Gothic by James A Morris, nave dedicated 1913, chancel
built and dedicated 1921. Twenty years of planning culminated when the church
was consecrated in 1931. The church contains many examples of fine woodwork by
Yorkshire carver Robert Thomson of Kilburn, whose signature is the carved mouse
(look closely at the main door). Organ by J J Binns, rebuilt 1987. Services: Sunday:
8.00 am Holy Communion, 10.30 am; Sung Eucharist; 1st/3rd Sunday 5.00pm
Evening Prayers; Wednesday 10.00am Holy Communion
Open daily 9.00am-4.00pm
SCOTTISH EPISCOPAL ♿ wc ② B

232 ST FRANCIS XAVIER, WATERSIDE

NS 445 080

On A713, 10 miles south-east of Ayr
Brick-built church with red
sandstone dressings. The church
was opened 1895 to cater for the
workers of Waterside ironworks.
At its peak, the ironworks was one
of the largest in Ayrshire and is
now being developed as an
interpretative centre for the
industrial heritage of Ayrshire.
Saturday: Vigil Mass 6.00pm
Open only for Services
ROMAN CATHOLIC ♿ wc

ST FRANCIS XAVIER, WATERSIDE

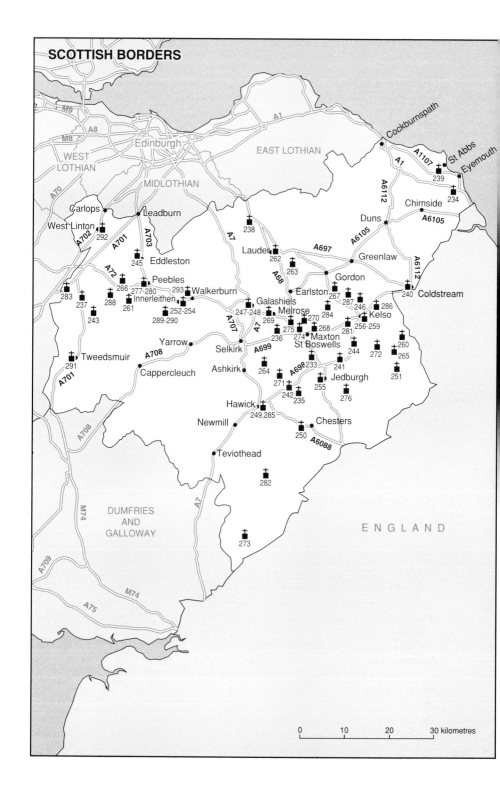

SCOTTISH BORDERS

BORDERS

Local Representatives: Mrs Mary Reid, 2 Crookhaugh, by Biggar
(*telephone* 01899 880258) and Mr Sandy Gilchrist, 11 Mercat Loan,
Biggar (*telephone* 01899 221350) – Tweedale

233 ANCRUM KIRK

NT 627 246

The present church, built of red sandstone, was opened
in 1890 to replace an 18th-century building, the remains
of which may be seen in the kirkyard, approximately
one mile west of the present church. Four stained glass
memorial windows. Sunday Service: 10.00am
*Open by arrangement with keyholder Mr Rogerson, telephone
01835 830321*
CHURCH OF SCOTLAND 📖 wc

ANCRUM KIRK

234 AYTON PARISH CHURCH

NT 927 609
South side of village, opposite road to Chirnside
First-pointed Gothic style building with 36-metre spire designed by James
Maitland Wardrop 1864-66. High quality stained glass by Ballantine & Sons. Fine
organ by Forster & Andrews of Hull 1894, restored by James Lightoller of
Berwick 1997. Occasional organ recitals. In the burial ground are the ivy-clad ruins
of the 12th-century St Dionysius's church. Service on 1st and 3rd Sunday: 2004
9.30am; 2005 11.00am
Open by arrangement with the Minister, telephone 01890 781333
CHURCH OF SCOTLAND wc 👤 (by arrangement) **A**

235 BEDRULE CHURCH

NT 599 179
Bedrule, by Jedburgh
Beautifully rebuilt in 1914 by T Greenshields Leadbetter,
the church has a plaque commemorating Bishop Turnbull,
founder of Glasgow University in 1451. Stained glass,
including Guild centenary window 1992 and windows by
Douglas Strachan 1922. Memorial with interesting link to
war-time 'Enigma' decoding project. Fine views over Rule
Valley to Ruberslaw. Linked with Denholm and Minto. Time
of fortnightly Sunday Service, which alternates with Minto,
changes every four months: 11.30am February to May;
10.00am June to September; 11.30am October to January
Open during daylight hours.
CHURCH OF SCOTLAND 📖 (free) **B**

BEDRULE CHURCH

236 BOWDEN KIRK

NT 554 301

Sitting by St Cuthbert's Way, the pilgrim route from
Melrose to Lindisfarne, the church has a wealth of
architectural history. It was founded in 1128, part of
the north wall is possibly 15th century, east end from
1644, cross aisle from 1661, west gable and doorway
at west end of north wall 17th century. Repaired in
1794 and with major alterations in 1909 by P
MacGregor Chalmers. Carved wooden 17th-century
laird's loft for Riddell-Carre family. Burial vaults of
Riddell-Carre of Cavers-Carre and Dukes of

BOWDEN KIRK

Roxburghe. Memorials, including one to Lady Grizell Baillie, first Deaconess of
the Church of Scotland. Many notable tombstones in graveyard.

Sunday Service: 11.00am

Open during daylight hours

CHURCH OF SCOTLAND   (from Post Office) wc ☕ ℞ **A**

237 BROUGHTON, GLENHOLM AND
KILBUCHO PARISH CHURCH

NT 111 368

Broughton, Biggar

Built in 1804 and extended by Robert Bryden of
Broughton and Glasgow 1886 to whom there is a
memorial stained glass window in the north wall. Roof
lights above the communion table are based on
originals in Copenhagen Museum. Linked with
Tweedsmuir, Skirling and Stobo with Drumelzier.

Sunday Service: 10.00am

Open by arrangement, telephone

Mr Ian Brown 01899 830365

CHURCH OF SCOTLAND ② wc

BROUGHTON, GLENHOLM AND
KILBUCHO PARISH CHURCH

238 CHANNELKIRK PARISH CHURCH

NT 481 545

2 miles west of Oxton

Commanding a fine view down the valley, this is a
historic site dating back to St Cuthbert, the Mother
Kirk of Lauderdale, established by Dryburgh Abbey.
Present building erected 1817 by James Gillespie
Graham in Perpendicular Gothic. Original pulpit and
fittings. Bell of 1702 still rung each Sunday.

Sunday Service: 10.00am

Open at all times

CHURCH OF SCOTLAND ♿ 📖 **A**

CHANNELKIRK PARISH CHURCH

239 THE PRIORY CHURCH, COLDINGHAM

NT 904 659

Coldingham, Berwickshire

Influential centre of Christian witness in Scottish
Borders since 7th century. Present church formed
from the choir and sanctuary area which comprised
the eastern arm of the early 13th-century cruciform-
plan Priory Church of St Mary. Splendid free-
standing arch of original church to the east of the
main building. South and west walls rebuilt 1662
and extensive renovation in 1850s. Interior
renovation 1950 providing present chancel and its
furnishings. Nine modern stained glass windows.
Detailed scale model of the Priory on exhibition.
Sunday Service: 12.00 noon

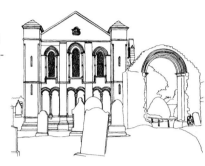

THE PRIORY CHURCH, COLDINGHAM

Church website: www.stebba-coldinghampriory.org.uk

Open Wednesdays, May to September 2.00-4.00pm, and by arrangement,

telephone Mr G Johnston 018907 71880

CHURCH OF SCOTLAND 👤 📖 **A**

240 COLDSTREAM PARISH CHURCH

NT 844 400

High Street, Coldstream

The square church tower with its four stages, clocks and octagonal stone roofed
bell-tower and weathervane is a distinctive feature of the outline of Coldstream. It
and the west entrance are part of the original church built in 1718. The rest of the
church was rebuilt in 1905 to a design by J M
Dick Peddie. A classical nave and aisles church
with barrel-vaulted roof supported by eight
Tuscan columns. A fine stone pulpit sits in front
of the semi-circular arch which leads into the
chancel. The church contains many reminders of
its close association, along with the town, with
the Coldstream Guards. The King's and
Regimental Colours hang in the chancel. Plaque
to the Rev Adam Thomson who formed the
Coldstream Free Bible Press in 1845, thus
breaking the monopoly held by Oxford and
Cambridge Universities and the King's printers
in Scotland. Sunday Service: 11.15am

Open June to August, Thursday 2.00-4.30pm. Other
times by arrangement, telephone Dr B J Sproule
01890 882271

CHURCH OF SCOTLAND 🎧 📖 🚻 ☕ **B**

COLDSTREAM PARISH CHURCH

241 CRAILING KIRK

NT 682 250

Built c.1775 on an ancient site of worship; the
bell is dated 1702. Aisle added in the early
19th century and further alterations and
additions 1892. Restoration by P Macgregor
Chalmers 1907. On A698 Jedburgh–Kelso.
Services: 2nd and 4th Sunday 10.30am, 1st
Sunday of winter months 6.30pm.
See local press for more details
Open by arrangement, telephone Mrs Rose,
The Braeheids, Crailing 01835 850268
CHURCH OF SCOTLAND ♿ ⓒ **B**

CRAILING CHURCH

242 DENHOLM CHURCH

NT 569 186

Denholm, by Hawick

Dates from 1845. Interior much altered 1957. 150th
anniversary wall hangings. Situated in a beautiful
conservation village. Best small village in 'Beautiful
Scotland in Bloom' 1999 and 2000. A698
Jedburgh–Hawick. Time of weekly Sunday Service
changes every four months: see notice boards for details
Key from the Manse in Leyden's Road, or Robert L Brown,
Marybank, Douglas Drive, Denholm 01450 870218
CHURCH OF SCOTLAND ♿ ⓒ 📖 (free) |wc| **C**

DENHOLM CHURCH

243 DRUMELZIER KIRK

NT 135 343

Drumelzier, by Broughton

A simple rectangular building of pre-Reformation origins. The original date is
uncertain, but it owes its present appearance largely to major alterations carried out
in 1872. Bellcote, 17th-century, on the west
gable. Burial vault 1617 for the Tweedies of
Drumelzier. United with Stobo and linked
with Broughton, Tweedsmuir, Skirling. One
hundred yards off B712 in Drumelzier village.
Sunday Service: 1st and 3rd of the month
6.30pm (not January, February, July and
August)
For information on access, telephone the
Rev Rachel Dobie 01899 830331, or
Mr and Mrs Julian Birchall 01899 830319
CHURCH OF SCOTLAND **B**

DRUMELZIER KIRK

244 ECKFORD KIRK

NT 706 270
Eckford, by Kelso
Built 1771 on an ancient site of worship,
incorporating fragments of the 1668 building
and the north aisle of 1724. Very sweet interior
with rich turn-of-the-century furnishings in the
sanctuary. Jougs 1718, mort bell and 19th-
century watch-tower. Many fine 17th-century
gravestones. On A698 Jedburgh–Kelso.
Service: first Sunday of summer months at
6.30pm, see local press for details
Open by arrangement, telephone
Mrs Jean Dyet 01573 850308
CHURCH OF SCOTLAND **B**

ECKFORD KIRK

245 EDDLESTON PARISH CHURCH

NT 244 472
Bellfield Road
The site has been in continuous occupation since the 12th century, the present
building being erected in 1829 and incorprates a number of carved stones of the
17th and 18th centuries. The church was rebuilt after a fire in 1897 and the vestry
and chancel added. The restoration was paid for by the then Lord Elibank, and Mr
Somerville of Portmore. The church bell, one of the oldest in the country, was cast
in 1507. The 2-manual pedal organ of 1907 from St Blane's in Dunblane was
rebuilt here in 1980. Sunday Service: 11.45am except last Sunday 6.00pm
Open by arrangement with Mrs Margaret Love, 11 Old Manse Road, 01721 730263
CHURCH OF SCOTLAND ♿ wc ⌖ 📖 **B**

246 EDNAM PARISH CHURCH

NT 737 372
Ednam, by Kelso
Church built 1800 and recast 1902.
Situated in the village of Ednam where
hymnwriter Henry Francis Lyte was
born. In union with Kelso North.
Sunday Service: 10.00am
Open daily 10.00am-4.00pm,
July and August
CHURCH OF SCOTLAND ♿ ⌖ 📖 wc

EDNAM PARISH CHURCH

247 GALASHIELS OLD PARISH CHURCH & ST PAUL'S

NT 490 362

Scott Crescent, Galashiels

Built in 1881 to plans in the Gothic Revival style by
George Henderson, the main feature is the 190ft
spire. Front porch added 1922. Good glass, including
some by Douglas Strachan. Stone carvings by John
Rhind and wood carving by Francis Lynn. Willis
organ. Sunday Services: 11.00am and 6.30pm

Open by arrangement, telephone

Mrs N Noble 01896 752724

CHURCH OF SCOTLAND [♿] (via hall) ⊘ [wc] **B**

GALASHIELS OLD PARISH
CHURCH & ST PAUL'S

248 ST PETER'S CHURCH, GALASHIELS

NT 496 356

Abbotsford Road, Galashiels

Gothic Revival style Hay & Henderson 1853.
Reredos Sir Robert Lorimer 1914. Stained glass,
memorial brasses. Setting of church with lawns,
graveyard, hall and rectory encapsulated the
Tractarian ideal. Quarter mile south of town centre
on A7. Fine 2-manual tracker organ by Brindley
and Foster 1881. Sunday Services: Holy
Communion 8.30am, Sung Eucharist 10.30am

Open by arrangement. Key from the Rectory, Parsonage Road,
Galashiels, telephone 01896 753118, or contact Mr R Brown,
54 Croft Street, Galashiels, telephone 01896 754657

SCOTTISH EPISCOPAL [♿] [🏠] [wc] **C**

ST PETER'S CHURCH,
GALASHIELS

249 ST CUTHBERT'S CHURCH, HAWICK

NT 501 141

Slitrig Crescent, Hawick

A Sir George Gilbert Scott building of 1858. Reredos
J Oldrid Scott 1905. Chancel screen Robert Lorimer.
Some fine stained glass including contemporary
windows of 1995 and 2002. Sunday Services: Holy
Communion 9.30am, Family Eucharist 10.30am;
Wednesday 10.30am Holy Eucharist

Open Monday 8.30-10.15am, Tuesday 10.30-11.00am,
Wednesday 10.15-11.45am, Thursday 9.00-10.30am
and Saturday 1.30-4.30pm

SCOTTISH EPISCOPAL [♿] ⊘ [👤] [🏠] [wc] **B**

ST CUTHBERT'S CHURCH, HAWICK

250 HOBKIRK PARISH CHURCH

NT 587 109

Hobkirk, Bonchester Bridge, by Hawick

A Christian site for over 900 years. The
present church was built in 1862. Stones from
the earlier churches are incorporated in the
font. The bell is inscribed 'I was made for
Hobkirk in 1745'. One mile west of
Bonchester Bridge on the A6088 Hawick–
Newcastle (off A68). United with Southdean.
Sunday Service: 11.00am

Open daily all year

CHURCH OF SCOTLAND

HOBKIRK PARISH CHURCH

251 HOWNAM PARISH CHURCH

NT 778 193

Hownam, Morebattle, Kelso

In an idyllic situation on the haugh by the Kale Water.
The original building appears to have been cruciform,
but was remodelled in 1752 as a rectangle, and
substantially modernised in 1844. The interior was
refurbished in 1986. From the original church there
remains a round-headed doorway in the south wall,
dating from the turn of the 15th and 16th centuries.
Linked with Linton, Morebattle and Yetholm. Sunday
Service: 2nd and 4th of every month 12.30pm

Open all year during daylight hours

CHURCH OF SCOTLAND B

HOWNAM PARISH CHURCH

252 INNERLEITHEN CHURCH

NT 332 369

Leithen Road

Built between 1864 and 1867, the church is the work of
Frederick Thomas Pilkington. Its most striking features
are the beautiful east elevation, the minaret windows
and the elaborate carving. The chancel was added by
J McIntyre Henry in 1889. Stained glass windows by
Ballantine and son, 2-manual pipe-organ by Brook
& Co, 1892. On a plinth in front of the church stands
part of the shaft of a 9th-century decorated cross,
discovered in the foundations of the earlier church.
Sunday Service: 11.30am

Open by arrangement with Mr Lunn, telephone 01896 830598

CHURCH OF SCOTLAND wc B

INNERLEITHEN CHURCH

253   ST JAMES CHURCH, INNERLEITHEN

NT 329 366

High Street, Innerleithen

Built in 1881 to a design by John Biggar, a church with
some interesting works of art including a large icon of
Our Lady of Czestochowa, Poland. This is by K Kryska
1944, the captain of Polish Forces based in Peeblesshire.
Other monuments include ones dating from 1861 and a
copy of the bust of John Ogilvie. The sanctuary has
been brought back into use, and a narthex has been
built inside the church to provide toilet and kitchen
facilities. A rood screen division within the church
provides a gathering and social space towards the rear of
the nave. Sunday Service: 11.30am; Holy Days 7.00pm

Open summer 10.00am-4.00pm, and by arrangement,

telephone Mrs Helen Garrett 01896 830025,

or Mrs Anne Tait 01896 831184

ROMAN CATHOLIC 📖 **B**

ST JAMES CHURCH, INNERLEITHEN

254   ST ANDREW, INNERLEITHEN

NT 333 371

Church Street

A small yet beautiful church, dedicated in 1904. The altar screen attractively
separates the nave and sanctuary. A mural behind the altar depicts the 'Visitation of
the Shepherds', painted in the style of Phoebe Traquair by William Blacklock of
Edinburgh. Two stained glass windows either side of the sanctuary, in memory of
Capt R M B Welsh, depict St George and the Dragon. A window in the nave, in
memory of Mrs F Ballantyne, illustrates the hymn 'All things bright and beautiful',
with local scenery, flora, animals and birds.

Sunday Service: 9.30am except 1st Sunday 11.00am

Open Thursdays by arrangement, telephone Julia Sharpe 01896 830637

or Frank Neville 01896 830084

SCOTTISH EPISCOPAL ♿ wc

255   ST MARY'S, THE IMMACULATE CONCEPTION, JEDBURGH

NT 653 210

2 Old Bongate

A good example of architect Reginald Fairlie's simple Catholic churches with
attached priest's house. Built in 1937, on the site of a previous building,
with an aisleless nave and a semi-octagonal apse; traditional and with good use
of materials. Services: Saturday Vigil Mass 5.30pm, Sunday 11.30am;
details of other services on notice board

Open by arrangement, telephone 01835 862426

ROMAN CATHOLIC wc 💻 (Sunday) **B**

256 KELSO NORTH PARISH CHURCH

NT 727 341
Roxburgh Street, Kelso
Erected 1866 for the congregation of Kelso North
Free Church, architect Frederick T Pilkington. The
front of the church is very ornate, being designed
in the Gothic style, with the tower and spire rising
to some 180ft. Extensively renovated in 1934 and
1984-89. Although the exterior is quite massive, in
contrast the interior is fairly neat and compact.
Sunday Services: 11.30am; Evening Worship 6.30pm
1st Sunday October to June
*Open July and August, Monday to Friday 10.00am-
4.00pm. Also Saturdays all year for coffee mornings*
CHURCH OF SCOTLAND   ♿ ② 👤 📖 ☕ wc **A**

KELSO NORTH PARISH CHURCH

257 KELSO OLD PARISH CHURCH

NT 729 339
The Butts, Kelso
Octagonal plan church, James Nisbet, dating from
1773, and altered by William Elliot in 1823. Built
to continue worship begun in Kelso Abbey in 1128.
Recently extensively restored. Banners of Blues &
Royals, presented to the church by the Duke of
Roxburghe 1927. Off Market Square, by Knowes
car park and adjacent to Kelso Abbey.
Sunday Service: 11.30am
*Open Easter to September, Monday to Friday
10.00am-4.00pm*
CHURCH OF SCOTLAND   ♿ ② 👤 📖 wc **A**

KELSO OLD PARISH CHURCH

258 KELSO QUAKER MEETING HOUSE

NT 729 339
Abbey Row
A former coach house adjoining the Old Priory, the Meeting House is a traditional
two-story building of stone and slate, probably dating from before 1800.
Collection of eight lino-cut prints of Border views by Earlston artist Tom
Davidson. Ministry is welcome in any language, but it is most often in English!
Sunday Meeting for Worship: 10.30am
Open after Sunday Meeting for Worship 11.30am-12.30pm
QUAKER ♿ wc ② ☕ (after Meeting for Worship) **B**

259 ST ANDREW'S CHURCH, KELSO

NT 728 337

Belmont Place, Kelso

Situated close to the banks of the River Tweed, built 1868 by Sir Robert Rowand Anderson. Altar, reredos, font and Robertson memorial sculpted in marble and Caen stone. Decorative wooden chancel roof and decorated pulpit. Stained glass. Small garden to rear (including Garden Room for meetings and Junior Church). Opposite Kelso Abbey on B6089. Sunday Services: 8.30am and 10.30am; Wednesday Eucharist 10.30am; Thursday Eucharist 7.00pm

Open daily 8.30am-5.00pm

SCOTTISH EPISCOPAL (?) [wc] [R] **B**

ST ANDREW'S CHURCH, KELSO

260 THE KIRK OF YETHOLM, KIRK YETHOLM

NT 826 281

The church for the delightful twin villages and parish of Yetholm stands on a site in use since David I's apportionment of parishes. Built by Robert Brown 1837 to replace a small dank thatched affair, it is a rectangular plan Gothic church of local whinstone with cream sandstone dressings, and a tower to the south. A remodelling in 1935, and the creation of an upper room out of the gallery in the 1970s, gives the interior a lightness belied by the sombre imposing exterior. Stained glass by Ballantine & Son, Edinburgh. The medieval bell is still in use. As the nearest burial ground to Flodden, the graveyard is believed to have interred officers fallen in that battle (1513). Gravestones 17th-century. Linked with Linton, Morebattle and Hownam. Sunday Service: 10.00am

Open daily during daylight hours

CHURCH OF SCOTLAND [♿] **B**

THE KIRK OF
YETHOLM,
KIRK YETHOLM

261 MANOR KIRK

NT 220 380

Kirkton Manor, by Peebles

First referred to in 1186 as 'the chapel of Maineure'. Tradition speaks of an earlier chapel of the 4th century dedicated to St Gordian, a martyred Roman soldier. The present building was completed in 1874. The bell, rung before every service, is inscribed '*In honore Santi Gordiani MCCCCLXXVIII*' and is one of the oldest bells in use in Scotland. Pewter baptismal basin, inscribed '*Manner Kirk 1703*'. The pipe organ, originally built by Peter Conacher in 1889, came from Pencaitland Church an was re-built in Manor Kirk in October 2002. Services: 2nd, 3rd and 4th Sundays of each month 11.00am, 5th Sunday 6.30pm

Open daily

CHURCH OF SCOTLAND [♿] (ramp) []

262 LAUDER OLD CHURCH

NT 531 475
Market Place
Built, 1673, by Sir William Bruce, in the shape of a Greek cross with four equal arms and a central octagonal bell tower. Various alterations were made through the 18th and 19th centuries. The porches were added later. Walled graveyard with watchtower of 1830. Pulpit of 1820. Sunday Service: 11.30am
Open most days 9.00am-5.00pm
CHURCH OF SCOTLAND 🦽 wc 🔊 📖 **A**

LAUDER OLD CHURCH

263 LEGERWOOD PARISH CHURCH

NT 594 434
Legerwood, Berwickshire
The church dates from 1127. Repaired in 1717 and 1804. Its chancel has a fine Norman arch. Sunday Service: 11.45am, 1st Sunday of each month
Open daily
CHURCH OF SCOTLAND 🦽 **B**

LEGERWOOD PARISH CHURCH

264 LILLIESLEAF KIRK

NT 539 253
East of Lilliesleaf village
The church of 1771 was extended in 1883 and transformed by the addition of west part of nave and belltower in 1910. Good stained glass by William Wilson, 1966. Medieval font and a child's ancient stone coffin.
Sunday Service: 11.30am
Open during daylight hours
CHURCH OF SCOTLAND
🦽 📖 wc

LILLIESLEAF KIRK

265 LINTON KIRK & HOSELAW CHAPEL

NT 773 262 and NT 802 318

Near Morebattle, Kelso

On a sandy knoll, a 12th-century
church much altered in 1616, 1774,
1813 and finally restored to an
approximation of its Romanesque
appearance in 1912 by P MacGregor
Chalmers. It retains its Norman feel
and today the visitor enters under a
unique stone tympanum to discover an
attractive nave and substantial chancel,
the arch richly carved (1912). A
Norman font and chancel stalls are of
particular interest. Linton Kirk is most
noted for the stone above the porch

LINTON KIRK & HOSELAW CHAPEL

said to depict a knight on horseback lancing two creatures – the stone is Norman
and unique in Scotland, and legend suggests that this is the first known Somerville
killing a worm. The Leishman father and son ministries completed most of the
present improvements; the son Thomas also had a small chapel built in the district
of Hoselaw (seven miles away) to serve the cottagers; architect P MacGregor
Chalmers. Linked with Morebattle, Hownam and Yetholm.

Sunday Service: 1st, 3rd and 5th of every month; and 5th Sunday at Hoselaw
Chapel (except December and January) 12.15pm

Open daily during daylight hours

CHURCH OF SCOTLAND   ⃝R **B**

266 LYNE KIRK

NT 192 405

On A72 from Peebles

Located on the site of a 12th-century church,
the present church was built between 1640
and 1645 by John Hay of Yester (later 1st Earl
of Tweeddale). The porch was added in the
19th century. The church retains its 17th-
century interior and of particular interest are
the Dutch pulpit and canopied pews dated
1644. Pre-Reformation font. The earliest stone
in the graveyard is dated 1707; the Adam and
Eve stone dated 1712 is uncommon. Roman
fort of Lyne immediately to the west.

Service: 11.00am, 1st Sunday of each month

Open daily

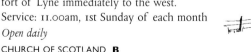

CHURCH OF SCOTLAND **B**   LYNE KIRK

267 MAKERSTOUN CHURCH

NT 669 331

⅓ mile north of Makerstoun village, 4 miles north-west of Kelso

Built 1808, the bell tower on the south wall, recently repaired, has 1808 inscribed on it. The church is light, with plain windows and original pine pews, pulpit and precentor's desk. Gallery and Sunday School upstairs. The setting of the church and churchyard is beautiful and peaceful.

Sunday Service: 10.00am, 2nd and 4th Sunday

Open at all times

CHURCH OF SCOTLAND **B**

268 MAXTON PARISH CHURCH

NT 610 303

On the north-west edge of Maxton village

On St Cuthbert's Way and dedicated to St Cuthbert. Reputed to have been a place of worship on this site for almost 1000 years. Originally oblong, thatched until 1790. North aisle added 1866, vestry 1962. Wyvern organ. Stained glass by J H Corham gifted 1914, Hebrew and Latin inscriptions, Maxton War Memorial within church. Burgerhuys bell 1609. Burial vault of Kers of Littledean.

Sunday Service: 11.30am, 2nd and 4th Sunday

Church website: www.maxton.bordernet.co.uk/chutch.html

Open by arrangement, telephone 01835 823745

CHURCH OF SCOTLAND  **B**

MAXTON PARISH CHURCH

269 HOLY TRINITY, MELROSE

NT 540 342

High Cross Avenue, Melrose

Built in the Early English style by Benjamin Ferrey 1846-50. Decorated chancel and transepts by Hay & Henderson 1900. The chancel floor is mosaic. Open timber roof carried on mask corbels. Stained glass windows in transept 1900, by Kempe, other commemorative glass by Mayer & Co and W Wilson 1963. Quarter mile from Melrose centre, on road to Darnick. Services: Sunday 8.30 and 11.00am; Wednesday 10.30am; Evensong 1st Sunday of month 6.30pm

Open by arrangement, telephone the Rector 01896 822626. Occasional concerts

SCOTTISH EPISCOPAL  **B**

HOLY TRINITY, MELROSE

270 MERTOUN KIRK

NT 615 318

The original church of 1241, not on this site, was
dedicated to St Ninian. The present church was
built 1652, renovated 1820 and enlarged 1898
with the addition of the north aisle and vestry.
On the outside of the south wall, the remains
of a set of jougs can be seen. Bird-cage belfry,
bell dated 1707, sundial on south-east corner.
Rose window in west gable.
Sunday Service: 11.30am, 1st, 3rd and 5th Sunday
Open by arrangement: key available from
Mertoun Estate Office
CHURCH OF SCOTLAND [♿] (✋) **B**

MERTOUN KIRK

271 MINTO CHURCH

NT 557 201

Minto, by Hawick

Designed by William Playfair, the church dates from 1830, the interior recast in 1934.
Fine external war memorial. Panoramic views of Teviotdale and Minto Hill. Linked
with Bedrule and Denholm. Time of fortnightly Sunday Service: alternates with
Bedrule, changes every four months: February to May 11.30am, June to September
10am, October to January 11.30am, and so on

Key from Mrs Marjorie Walton, Kirk View, Minto, Hawick 01450 870351

CHURCH OF SCOTLAND (✋) **C**

272 MOREBATTLE PARISH CHURCH

NT 772 250

Morebattle, Kelso

The church of 'Mereboda' is recorded as belonging to the Diocese of Glasgow
from about 1116. The building was burnt down in 1544 and rebuilt; the present
structure dates substantially from 1757, extensions having been made in 1899 and

1903. It is oblong in plan, with chancel,
porch and vestry which seem to be
additions. The bellcote at the west end is
currently being rebuilt. Look for the plan in
the porch which shows the archaeological
work carried out in the early 1900s, and
inscriptions painted on fabric on the west
wall. Linked with Hownam, Yetholm and
Linton. Sunday Service: 11.15am
Open all year during daylight hours
CHURCH OF SCOTLAND [♿] (✋) **B**

MOREBATTLE PARISH CHURCH

273 NEWCASTLETON CHURCH

NY 482 877
Montague Street
A bright and welcoming building dating from 1888 but with a more modern feel. Memorial to George Armstrong, founder of the World's first children's hospital. Millennium stained glass window by Alex Haynes of Brampton.
Sunday Services: 10.00am and 6.00pm
Open Wednesdays 10.00am-11.30am (coffee stop), or by arrangement with Mrs M Henry,
01387 375353 or Mrs A Forster 01387 375767
CHURCH OF SCOTLAND 👤 wc ✎ ☕ 📖

274 ST BOSWELLS PARISH CHURCH

NT 594 310
South side of St Boswells main street near village hall
Built 1844 as Free Church, originally square with earth floor. Wooden floor and seating added later in 19th century. Became United Free Church in 1900 and St Modans Church of Scotland in 1929 and St Boswells Parish Church in 1952 when old church at Benrig was abandoned. Substantially renovated 1957-59 and chancel added. Pipe organ. Stained glass in chancel by Liz Rowley 1988; other glass by Ballantine. Sunday Service: 10.00am
Open April to September 9.00am-9.00pm,
October to March 9.00am-5.00pm
CHURCH OF SCOTLAND 👤 wc (service times only) ✎

ST BOSWELLS PARISH CHURCH

275 NEWTOWN CHURCH

NT 315 693
St Boswells Road, Newtown St Boswells
Church opened in 1868. Contains memorials to past ministers.
On bus routes between Jedburgh to Edinburgh and Galashiels.
Sunday Service: 9.45am
Open by arrangement, telephone the
Minister 01835 822106
CHURCH OF SCOTLAND wc

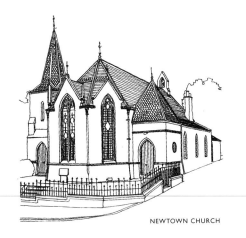

NEWTOWN CHURCH

276 OXNAM KIRK

NT 701 190

Oxnam, by Jedburgh

On the site of a medieval church
dating from before 1153. The present
church was built in 1738 and enlarged
to form a T-plan in 1874. A
characteristic Scottish 18th-century
church with plain glass and whitewashed walls. Many fine 17th- and
18th-century gravestones. Continuo
pipe organ by Lammermuir Pipe
Organs 1990. Signposted from A68 at
Jedburgh. Services: 1st and 3rd
Sundays, Christmas and Easter 10.30am

OXNAM KIRK

Open by arrangement, telephone Patrick Wood, Ladfield 01835 840358.
Pennymuir Fair, ancient Border hill sheep fair, 1st Saturday in September

CHURCH OF SCOTLAND   **B**

277 LECKIE MEMORIAL CHURCH

NT 253 404

Eastgate, Peebles

Handsome Gothic style church with a fine
terraced situation, built 1875-77, to designs
by Peddie & Kinnear, in memory of Thomas
Leckie, the first pastor of the Associate
Burgher Congregation from 1794-1821.
Gifted in trust, by the surviving members of
his family. Following union in 1976 with St
Andrews Church, now home of the St
Andrews Leckie congregation. The pews have
been removed and replaced with removable
seating so the building is now multi-
functional. Sunday Services: 10.30am
and 6.00pm

Church website: www.standrewsleckie.co.uk
Open by arrangement, contact church office,
Monday to Friday 9.30am-12.30pm,
telephone 01721 723121

CHURCH OF SCOTLAND   wc

LECKIE MEMORIAL CHURCH

278 PEEBLES OLD PARISH CHURCH

NT 246 406

High Street, Peebles

1887 by William Young of London in Gothic
style containing features from earlier church.
Fine crown spire dominates the High Street. An
inviting flight of steps leads up to the entrance.
The chancel was reconstructed by J D Cairns
1937. Entrance screen of 1965, woodwork by
Messrs Scott Morton, metalwork by Charles
Henshaw & Son, glass by Helen Turner. Pulpit
1913 by P MacGregor Chalmers. Part of pre-
Reformation font incorporated in table in
crossing, by Mitchall Design 1998. Pipe organ
by August Gern 1887, extensively rebuilt.
Stained glass by Cottier of London and
McCartney of Wiston. Sunday Service: 10.00am;
Holy Communion 10am on last Sunday of
month, January, April and October

Open 10.00am-4.00pm, mid-April to mid-October

CHURCH OF SCOTLAND 📖 wc **B**

PEEBLES OLD PARISH CHURCH

279 ST JOSEPH'S CHURCH, PEEBLES

NT 248 407

Rosetta Road, Peebles

The present building was opened in 1858.
The couthy interior was reordered in 1971.
The church includes various stained glass
windows and statues. The most significant
is the recently restored 14 Stations of the
Cross by the Alinari Brothers of Florence.
Services: Saturday Vigil 6.00pm,
Sunday 9.30am

Open daily 9.00am-6.00pm

ROMAN CATHOLIC 📖 **B**

ST JOSEPH'S CHURCH, PEEBLES

280 ST PETER'S EPISCOPAL, PEEBLES

NT 253 405

Eastgate, Peebles

Built 1836-37 in finely hewn ashlar
with an open timber roof. The floor
is paved with mosaic tiles as is the
reredos, beautifully executed with
devices in gold and colour. Choir seats
and altar of oak. Piscina on the south
side with stone shelf and foliated
basin. Fine stained glass. The organ,
1909 by Harrison, is one of the
smallest 3-manual instruments ever
built and has been praised for its
compactness and excellence of tone.
Sunday Services: Holy Communion
8.30am, Eucharist 10.30am; Thursday:
Holy Communion 10.00am
Open 9.00am-5.00pm, or daylight hours
SCOTTISH EPISCOPAL

ST PETER'S EPISCOPAL, PEEBLES

281 ROXBURGH PARISH CHURCH

NT 700 307

Built in 1752, repaired in 1828, with additions of 1865. Fine painted heraldic panels.
Stained glass 1947 by W Wilson. The exterior has a pair of cubical sundials. In the
graveyard the (roofless) burial-vault of the Kers of Chatto. Fine modern continuo pipe
organ, Lammermuir Pipe Organs 1990. Signposted two and a half miles west of
Kelso on A699. Services: 2nd and 4th Sundays 11.30am
Open by arrangement, telephone Mrs Palmer, North Cliff Cottages,
Roxburgh 01573 450263
CHURCH OF SCOTLAND ② **B**

ROXBURGH PARISH CHURCH

282 SAUGHTREE KIRK

NY 562 968

9 miles north of Newcastleton on B6357

A simple country kirk dating from 1872 enjoying views to the English Border. Fine patterned coloured glass window. Interesting embroidered pulpit fall depicting the Trinity. Sunday Services: 9.30am on 2nd Sundays and occasional evening services

Open by arrangement with Mr A Douglas, telephone 01387 376224

CHURCH OF SCOTLAND

283 SKIRLING PARISH CHURCH

NT 075 390

By Biggar

The earliest reference to a church in Skirling is in 1275. It was probably situated near to the present war memorial. It is not known when a church was built on the present site. However, records show that the church was virtually rebuilt in 1720. Further significant alterations were made in 1891. The bellcote is of particular interest, as is the sundial on the tower. The floral design of the stained glass east window forms a backdrop to the communion table and matching chairs presented by the artist, Sir D Y Cameron, in 1948. Round churchyard enclosed by a ha-ha and entered through fine wrought-iron gates. Two miles east of Biggar on A72, approached from opposite village green by a steep metalled access road. Sunday Service: 11.30am

Open by arrangement, telephone
A S Goodere 01899 860251

CHURCH OF SCOTLAND

SKIRLING PARISH CHURCH

284 SMAILHOLM CHURCH

NT 649 364

Smailholm village

Built 1630s on 12th-century foundations, altered 1820s and the interior re-ordered during the 20th century. The east window, depicting St Cuthbert & St Giles, was erected in memory of Sir Walter Scott, whose family farmed at Sandyknowes by Smailholm Tower. Birdcage belfry with external bell-rope and outside stairs to the laird's loft. Sunday Service: 10.00am, 1st and 3rd Sunday

Open at all times

CHURCH OF SCOTLAND **B**

285 SOUTHDEAN PARISH CHURCH

NT 631 092
Southdean, by Hawick
Built in 1876 to a design by George Grant of
Glasgow on a site near to the ruins of two previous
churches of 12th and 17th centuries. Font, 12th-
century. Super-altar set into the communion table,
one of only two known in Scotland. Good stained
glass. Memorial to James Thomson (1700-48),
author of 'Rule Britannia' and 'The Seasons', whose
father was parish minister. Prior to the Battle of
Otterburn 1388, the Earl of Douglas and his army
met at the 12th-century church, whence the
survivors returned to bury their dead. United with
Hobkirk. Special Services only and used by
children in winter
Open by arrangement, telephone 01450 860692
CHURCH OF SCOTLAND

SOUTHDEAN PARISH CHURCH

286 SPROUSTON KIRK

NT 757 353
There has been a church in Sprouston since the
17th century. The present building was built in
1781, though the belcote bears the date 1703 and
a 12th-century piscina is built into the chancel.
The Minister in 1911 won first and third prize
out of 36,000 entries in the *Daily Mail* National
Sweet Pea Competition, enabling the new
chancel to be built with the £1500 prize money.
Douglas Strachan window of 'The Fall of
Lucifer'. Pulpit falls of sweet peas embroidered
by Mrs Doreen West. Sunday Service: 10.00am
Key available from Mr Tom Walker, telephone 01573 228172
CHURCH OF SCOTLAND  **B**

SPROUSTON KIRK

287 STICHILL, HUME & NEWTHORN PARISH CHURCH

NT 711 383
West end of Stichill village, 3 miles north of Kelso
This is the second (or third) church on the site, built around 1780s. It has an
outside stairway to the laird's loft, and a burial aisle to the Pringle family on the
east gable. The interior is light, with stained glass only in the chancel. Adjoining
the church is a stable, altered in 2003 to a small church hall, kitchen and toilet.
Sunday Service: 11.00am
Open at all times
CHURCH OF SCOTLAND **B**

288 STOBO KIRK

NT 183 377
Stobo, by Peebles
One of the oldest churches in the
Borders, and of historical importance.
Much of the present building dates
from 12th century. It stands on the site
of a 6th-century church reputedly
founded by St Kentigern (St Mungo).
The 12th-century building comprised
nave, sanctuary and tower, the latter
rebuilt from first floor level, probably
16th century. Major restoration in 1863,
John Lessels. North aisle chapel
restored in 1929, James Grieve. A new
stone floor laid and a meeting room
formed at first floor level of the tower in 1991. Linked with Broughton,
Tweedsmuir and Skirling and united with Drumelzier. Stands 100 yards from B712,
off A72, four miles west of Peebles or off A701, one and a half miles south of
Broughton. Sunday Service: 11.30am

STOBO KIRK

For information on access, telephone Mrs Loudon Hamilton 01721 740393,
or Rev Rachel Dobie 01899 830331
CHURCH OF SCOTLAND B

289 TRAQUAIR KIRK

NT 320 335
There has been a church at Traquair
since the early 12th century. The present
simple, elegant country church is dated
1778 and has a traditional plan with a
central pulpit. Comprehensive restoration
completed 2001. A monument on the
outside wall commemorates Alexander
Brodie (d.1811), 'Iron Master ... a native
of Traquaire [*sic*], First Inventor of the
Register Stoves and Fore Hearths for
Ships'. Many notable gravestones, the
earliest from the late 17th century.
Sunday Services: 10.00am on 2nd
and 4th Sundays; as announced for
5th Sunday
Open by arrangement with Mr Donald,
 telephone 01896 830781
CHURCH OF SCOTLAND B

TRAQUAIR KIRK

290 TRAQUAIR HOUSE CHAPEL

NT 331 355

Traquair House, near Innerleithen

The chapel, formerly the billiard room above the brewhouse, replaced the 'secret chapel' in the main house used in penal times. Related memorabilia on view in house, which also contains a priest's hole and secret stairway. Chapel has carved oak panels said to have come from the chapel of Mary of Guise in Leith, and to be of Flemish origin. Service: Mass 7.00pm, last Wednesday April to October

Easter Egg Extravaganza (April). Traquair Fair first weekend in August. Christmas opening last weekend in November. Open April 12.00 noon-5.00pm, June, July and August 10.30am-5.00pm, October 11.00-4.00pm. Access to Chapel is included in admission to grounds

ROMAN CATHOLIC 🚻 wc 🍴 ☕ **A**

291 TWEEDSMUIR KIRK

NT 101 245

Tweedsmuir, by Broughton

The present building was erected in 1874 by John Lessels, to replace a much earlier church of 1643. Bell of 1773 still in use. Major restoration in 2002. Two high circular windows in the north and south transepts and some interesting stained glass. Oak for the panelling in the porch is from a tree planted at Abbotsford by Sir Walter Scott. First and Second World War memorials. The churchyard dates back to the first church and contains table-stone graves of the 18th century and several other stones of interest, including a Covenanter's grave and one, near the gate, to the many men who died in the construction of the Talla reservoir. Linked with Broughton, Skirling and Stobo with Drumelzier. Village six miles south west of Broughton on A701.

Sunday Service: 10.00am

Open daily all year

CHURCH OF SCOTLAND 📖 **B**

TWEEDSMUIR KIRK

292 ST MUNGO'S CHURCH, WEST LINTON

NT 148 519

Chapel Brae, West Linton

A 'Gladstone Church' built in 1851 when it served as both church and school. Unusually, the church runs from north to south instead of east to west. Fine stained glass by C E Kempe. Services: every Sunday 11.00am; 2nd Sunday Choral Evensong 5.30pm

Open by arrangement, telephone the Rector 01968 672862

SCOTTISH EPISCOPAL

ST MUNGO'S CHURCH, WEST LINTON

293 WALKERBURN CHURCH

NT 364 373

Walkerburn came into being as a tweed manufacturing village following the establishment of the first mill by Henry Ballantyne in 1855. After first using the school for worship, the present building was consecrated in 1875 and enlarged 1896. Pipe organ by Ingram. Gallery and space below remodelled in 1979 to create halls separate from the nave. Stained glass windows celebrate the Ballantyne family. Sunday Services: 10.00am on 1st and 3rd Sundays, as announced on 5th Sunday

Open by arrangement with the Minister, telephone 01896 870535

CHURCH OF SCOTLAND

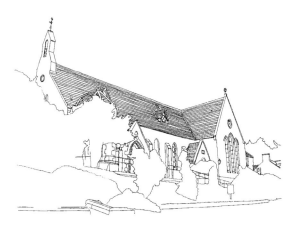

WALKERBURN CHURCH

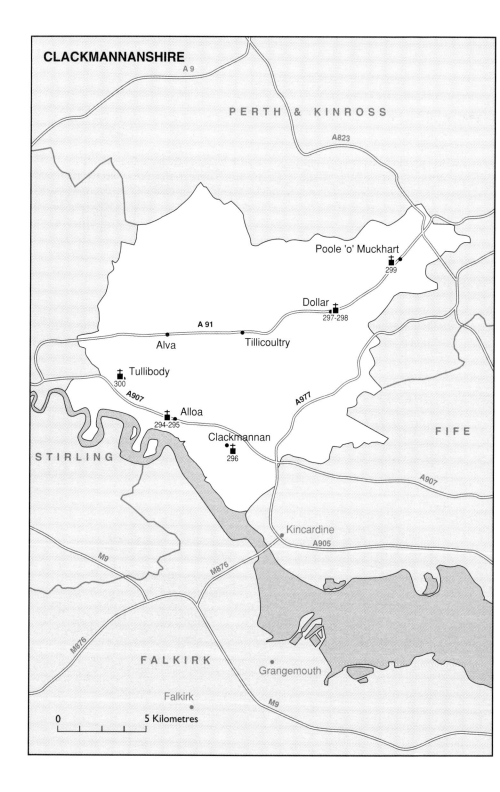

CLACKMANNANSHIRE

294 ALLOA PARISH CHURCH (ST MUNGO'S)

NS 886 929

Bedford Place, Alloa

Delicate and picturesque Gothic Revival church by James Gillespie Graham 1819. Usual symmetry in plan, but greater felicity than normal in lacy Perpendicular. The 207ft spire with flying buttresses is visible from most parts of the town. Interior is by Leslie Grahame MacDougall in Lorimer-derived Gothic.

Sunday Service: 11.15am

Open by arrangement, telephone 01259 721553. Close to Alloa Tower

CHURCH OF SCOTLAND   🦽 📖 🔊 wc **B**

295 ST JOHN'S CHURCH, ALLOA

NS 886 923

Broad Street, Alloa

Sir Robert Rowand Anderson designed St John's which was opened in 1869 and enlarged in 1873. Described by Thomas Bradshaw then as the 'most elegant place of worship in the County'. Early Geometric Gothic with a notable broach spire. The rich interior includes glass by Kempe, and a reredos with a mosaic of the Last Supper by the Italian Salviatti. The chancel was refurbished in 1913, its roof bearing 106 carved bosses. These, together with the woodwork of the choirstalls 1902, organ screen and war memorial, are all by Lorimer. The tower contains a ring of eight bells, six hung in 1871 and a further two in 1925. Sunday Service: Family Eucharist 11.00am

Open usually Wednesday and Friday 10.00am-12.30pm.

Other times, telephone 01259 212836

SCOTTISH EPISCOPAL   🦽 🔊 wc **B**

ST JOHN'S CHURCH, ALLOA

296 CLACKMANNAN PARISH CHURCH

NS 910 918

High Street, Clackmannan

There has been a church at
Clackmannan since St Serf visited from
Culross in the 8th century. The present
church was built in 1815 by James
Gillespie Graham to replace a 13th-
century church. Perpendicular Gothic
with buttressed tower at the west end.
Stained glass by Herbert Hendrie,
Gordon Webster, Sadie Pritchard and
Douglas Hamilton. Modern Makin
Toccata digital computerised organ.
Graveyard has stones dating from the
17th century with several Bruce family
memorials. Views over Carse of Forth.

CLACKMANNAN PARISH CHURCH

Sunday Services: 11.00am, 10.30am July and August

Open weekdays 2.00-4.00pm, third Monday in June to second Friday in September.

Other times, telephone 01259 214238 or 01259 211255

CHURCH OF SCOTLAND ♿ ② ⛪ 📖 wc **B**

297 DOLLAR PARISH CHURCH

NS 964 980

East end of Dollar, north side of A91,
Bridge Street

Built 1842/3 to replace 18th-century church
(ruin to north), designed by architect Tite of
London. Chancel added 1926, porch added
1963. Triple stained glass window in
memory of Rev Angus Gunn 1910. Three
stained glass windows by Adam Robson and
Jennifer Campbell, Union window 1979 by
Douglas Hogg. Millennium glass screens
designed by Angus Maclean 2003.
Rushworth and Dreaper organ 1926.
Reredos tapestry based on Ardchattan
Cross designed by Adam Robson 1963.

Sunday Service: 11.15am

Open by arrangement, telephone
Rev John Purves, 01259 743432

CHURCH OF SCOTLAND ♿ wc ② 📖 **B**

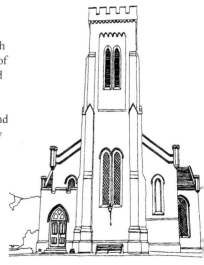

CLACKMANNAN PARISH CHURCH

298 ST JAMES THE GREAT, DOLLAR

NS 958 980

Harviestoun Road, Dollar

A small country church with a prayerful atmosphere, set in a well-kept garden. Consecrated in 1882, the building was designed by Thomas Frame & Son, Alloa. The font is a memorial to Archbishop Archibald Campbell Tait of Canterbury (1868-83). Sunday Services: 8.30am and 10.30am, Thursday 9.45am

Open daily all year

SCOTTISH EPISCOPAL ⑦ &. C

ST JAMES THE GREAT, DOLLAR

299 MUCKHART PARISH CHURCH

NO 001 010

North side of A91 at west end of Pool of Muckhart

Church 18th century. Stained Glass windows removed to Fossoway Church, Crook of Devon. Various plaques. Large gravestone on east wall of the church for the Christie family, Cowden. Nearby stone to Matsui, Japanese gardener to Miss Ella Christie. Sunday Service: 9.45am

Open at all times

CHURCH OF SCOTLAND wc B

MUCKHART PARISH CHURCH

300 ST SERF'S PARISH CHURCH, TULLIBODY

NS 860 954

Menstrie Road

Charmingly simple Norman-style church of 1904 by Peter McGregor Chalmers, with a nave and side aisles separated by five pillared arches, apse and transepts and an open dressed-timber roof. Stained glass by Stephen Adam, Norman M McDougall. Nearby ruins of the former church. Centenary events in 2004 including Flower Festival 14-16 May (telephone 01259 213236 for information). Sunday Services: 11.00am and 6.30pm

Open Tuesdays 9.30am-2.00pm

CHURCH OF SCOTLAND &. wc ⑦ ⅰ B

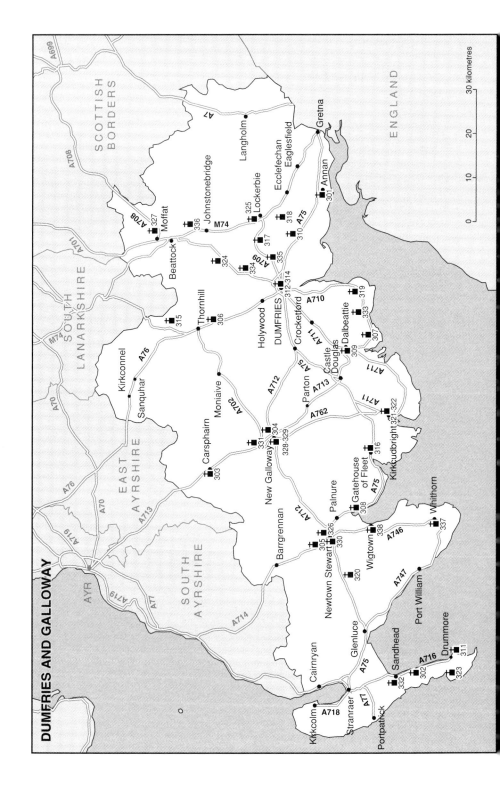

DUMFRIES AND GALLOWAY

DUMFRIES & GALLOWAY

Local Representatives: The Rev J W Scott, The Manse of Durisdeer, Thornhill (*telephone* 01848 500231); Mr Michael Dunlop, Baltersan, Newton Stewart (*telephone* 01671 402543)

301 ST COLUMBA'S CHURCH, ANNAN

NY 199 665
Scott's Street, Annan
Built as a Congregational Church in 1794 on the site of a Secession Meeting House and re-opened as a Catholic Church in 1839. Extended at both ends in 1904 by Charles Walker of Newcastle as the gift of the parish priest the Rev Lord Archibald Douglas. Stations of the Cross by Brendan Ellis 1984. Painted panels in sanctuary, Joe Burns 1997. The parish priest also serves St Francis' Church, Drove Road, Langholm (1960) and St Ninian's Church, Victory Avenue, Gretna (1925, 1918). Services: Saturday Vigil Mass 6.00pm, Sunday Mass 11.00am
Open daily 9.00am-6.00pm. When closed, key from adjacent presbytery or at 32 Scott's Street
ROMAN CATHOLIC ⚲ 📖 wc **B**

ST COLUMBA'S CHURCH, ANNAN

302 ARDWELL

NX 100 457
One kilometre west of Ardwell village
Surrounded by trees and shrubs and fronted with grass and flowerbeds, Gothic cruciform church by P MacGregor Chalmers 1901. Tower with octagonal spire and corner pinnacles. Notable inside are the inscriptions in the masonry. Pulpit, reredos, screen and communion table in oak, elaborately carved. Stained glass window of 'The Calming of the Storm'. Sunday Service: every two weeks (normally) 10.00am
Church website: www.ardwell-church.org.uk
Open by arrangement, telephone Mrs H McCreadie, Merkland Stoneykirk
CHURCH OF SCOTLAND ♿ wc **B**

ARDWELL

303 CARSPHAIRN PARISH CHURCH

NX 563 932
Carsphairn, Castle Douglas
Built in 1815 to replace church of 1636 destroyed by
fire. Central communion table. Memorials including
John Semple, Covenanting minister, and John
Loudon MacAdam, roads pioneer. Covenanter's grave.
A713 Ayr–Castle Douglas. Linked with Balmaclellan,
Kells and Dalry. Sunday Service: 10.30am
Open by arrangement, telephone Mrs Campbell 01644
460208. Carsphairn Pastoral & Horticultural Show,
first Saturday in June
CHURCH OF SCOTLAND Ⓟ wc **B**

CARSPHAIRN PARISH CHURCH

304 BALMACLELLAN CHURCH, CASTLE DOUGLAS

NX 651 791
A harled, T-plan kirk, the body was built in 1753,
with the north aisle added in 1833 by William
McCandlish. The stained glass west window is
dated 1928 and is by Gordon Webster. The
graveyard has an early 18th-century table-stone
commemorating the Covenanting martyr Robert
Grierson. Statue and plaque in churchyard
commemorate Sir Walter Scott's 'Old Mortality',
who came from Balmaclellan. Sunday Service: first
Sunday of every month at 12.00 noon
Open by arrangement, telephone the
Minister 01644 430380
CHURCH OF SCOTLAND

BALMACLELLAN CHURCH,
CASTLE DOUGLAS

305 ALL SAINTS CHURCH, CHALLOCH

NX 385 675
Challoch, by Newton Stewart
Built as private chapel of Edward James Stopford-Blair of Penninghame House
and consecrated 1872. Designed by W G Habershon & Pite of London and an
excellent example of a small Victorian church. Ten stained glass windows, 17
memorial plaques, pine altar and wrought iron and brass rood screen. Fine Harston
2-tracker organ 1881, restored 1993, and the only example of Harston's work still in
use. Located two miles north of Newton Stewart on road to Girvan, A714.
Sunday Services: 9.00am Holy Eucharist, 10.30am Sung Eucharist, first in month
10.30am Choral Matins; daily 8.00am Morning Prayer, 5.30pm Evening Prayer.
Feast days 7.00pm Holy Eucharist
Open daily, or telephone 01671 402101
SCOTTISH EPISCOPAL Ⓟ wc **A**

306 CLOSEBURN PARISH CHURCH

NX 904 923
Closeburn, by Thornhill
Built by James Barbour 1878 alongside former
(1741) church. In Gothic style with a three-stage
tower. Spacious interior with an elaborate
hammerbeam roof supported on foliaged
corbels. Pipe organ by Henry Willis & Sons
1887. Window in the north transept by the St
Enoch Glass Studios 1948. Font originally from
Dalgarnock. In the graveyard is the smart
mausoleum built by Thomas Kirkpatrick of
Closeburn in 1742. Sunday Service: 10.30am
Open by arrangement, keys from either
Mrs Lorimer, Lakehead Farm Cottages or
Mr Menzies, Closeburn Village
CHURCH OF SCOTLAND 👤 📖 wc **B**

CLOSEBURN PARISH CHURCH

307 COLVEND PARISH CHURCH

NX 862 541
Rockcliffe, by Dalbeattie
A chaste Early Christian church by P MacGregor Chalmers 1911, of granite with
red sandstone dressings and set on a rise overlooking the Solway Firth. Its bell-
tower is topped by a steep pyramid roof. A pretty interior with nave, aisle and
transept and a timbered roof. Plain plastered walls are a foil for the sandstone
columns which support round-headed arches springing from cushion capitals to
form arcades into the aisle and transept. In the chancel, the deep colour of the
stained glass window, the Ascension by Stephen Adam & Co 1918, forms a lovely
backdrop to the High
Presbyterian arrangement of
furnishings. Other windows
by Adam & Co and by
Margaret Chilton and Marjorie
Kemp 1926. A710 from
Dalbeattie, turn right onto
unclassified road signposted
Rockcliffe (quarter mile on the
right). Linked with Southwick
and Kirkbean.
Sunday Service: 11.30am
Open daily 10.00am-6.00pm
CHURCH OF SCOTLAND
🔈 📖 wc

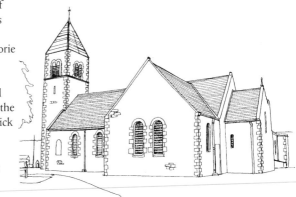

COLVEND PARISH CHURCH

308 KIRKMABRECK PARISH CHURCH, CREETOWN

NX 493 565
Large and tall with a tower above the
front gable, built in 1834 by John
Henderson. Panelling 1645 with Muir
family coat of arms. In spring,
churchyard and graveyard are carpeted
with crocuses. On A75, six miles from
Newton Stewart, signposted in village.
Sunday Service: 11.30am
Open by arrangement, telephone Mr J Cutland,
5 Chain Road, Creetown 01671 820228
CHURCH OF SCOTLAND [&] (?) [wc]

KIRKMABRECK PARISH
CHURCH, CREETOWN

309 ST PETER'S CHURCH, DALBEATTIE

NX 831 613
Craignair Street, Dalbeattie
Hall church 1814 of pinky granite
with red sandstone dressings. Grey
granite tower added c.1850.
Sunday Mass 9.00am and 11.00am
Open daily 9.00am-5.00pm
ROMAN CATHOLIC [&] **B**

ST PETER'S CHURCH, DALBEATTIE

310 DALTON KIRK

NY 114 740
Dalton, by Lockerbie
Close by the roofless shell of the 1704 parish
church stands J M Dick Peddie's 1895 sturdy
Romanesque church. Unusually colourful
kingpost-truss roof over the nave and scissors
roof in the chancel. Three-light stained glass
window of the Ascension by A Ballantine and
Gardiner 1896. The graveyard contains a late
Georgian burial enclosure and the suave classical
monument to the Carruthers of Whitecroft.
B725, signposted off A75 Annan–Dumfries.
Sunday Services: 9.45am, 11.15am by rotation
with Hightae and St Mungo
Open by arrangement, telephone the Manse,
Hightae, Lockerbie 01387 811499
CHURCH OF SCOTLAND () [] [wc] **B**

DALTON KIRK

311 ST MEDAN'S, DRUMMORE

NX 135 367
Stair Street, Drummore
Built 1903 in red Dumfries sandstone with
an attractive roof of red and yellow pine.
Hymnus IV electronic organ. Morrison
memorial window behind choir 1951. John
McGuffog memorial window above pulpit,
designed and made by Arthur C Speirs DA
of Greenock 1996. Sunday Services:
11.30am, except last Sunday of month from
May to September, when service is in
Kirkmaiden Old Church
Open by arrangement, telephone Mrs Beck,
01776 840210
CHURCH OF SCOTLAND [♿] [wc] **B**

ST MEDAN'S, DRUMMORE

312 CRICHTON MEMORIAL CHURCH,
THE CRICHTON, DUMFRIES

NY 983 742
The Crichton, Bankend Road, The Crichton, Dumfries
Designed by architect Sydney Mitchell, Crichton Memorial Church was completed
in 1897. The cathedral-style church is richly detailed and has a square tower 123ft
high. The exterior is of red sandstone from Locharbriggs, Dumfries, whilst the
elegant interior features pink sandstone from nearby Thornhill. Ornate oak roof.
Stone carving by William Vickers of Glasgow. The boldly designed floor is of
Irish and Sicilian marble. Impressive stained glass by Oscar Paterson of Glasgow
1896 features throughout. Pulpit and choir stalls date from 1897. The magnificent
organ by Lewis, 1902, has richly carved screens. Brass angel lectern 1910. Inter-
denominational. Regular services take place. Popular venue for weddings, concerts
and other special events
Church website: www.crichton.co.uk
Open by arrangement, telephone Crichton Development Company 01387 247544
NON-DENOMINATIONAL [♿] [wc] **A**

CRICHTON MEMORIAL CHURCH, THE CRICHTON, DUMFRIES

313 GREYFRIARS CHURCH, DUMFRIES

NX 971 763
Church Crescent, Dumfries
A richly ornamented Gothic edifice by John Starforth 1868
with plenty of crisply carved detail, all in red sandstone
snecked rubble. The steeple dominates both the building
and the townscape. The interior is a huge, almost square
space, richly decorated. Clustered shafts with leafy capitals
support collar-braced and kingpost-truss roofs over the
nave and transepts. Stained glass by James Ballantine &
Son, Powell Bros, Camm Bros and L C Levetts. Pipe organ
1921 by Ingram. Sunday Services: 11.00am and 9.30am
during summer; Evening Services: fortnightly
Details of opening times on notice board
CHURCH OF SCOTLAND ☻ 🍴 📖 wc **A**

GREYFRIARS CHURCH, DUMFRIES

314 ST GEORGE'S, DUMFRIES

NX 971 764
George Street, Dumfries
Built as a Free Church in 1844 by William
McGowan, and remodelled in 1893 by
James Halliday who added the Italianate
front of red sandstone. Almost square
interior with north and south aisles marked
off by superimposed Corinthian columns.
Compartmented and coved main ceiling.
Sunday Service: 11.00am, additionally July
and August 9.30am (Family Service)
Church website: www.saint-georges.org.uk
Open by arrangement, telephone Dr Balfour 01387 253696
CHURCH OF SCOTLAND ♿ wc **B**

ST GEORGE'S, DUMFRIES

315 DURISDEER PARISH CHURCH

NS 894 038
Unspoilt, peaceful, Georgian country parish church, rebuilt 1716, topped by a
belfry tower. X-plan, one arm of the cross is taller and more sophisticated, built for
the Duke of Queensberry and remaining from the earlier church. Inside is the most
amazing monument over the Queensberry burial vault, a baroque baldacchino
carved in 1695 by John van Nost to the design of James Smith who was also
architect of the later church. 'There are few buildings in which baroque
magnificence and presbyterian decency are so happily combined' (George Hay,
Architecture of Scottish Post-Reformation Churches). Martyr's Grave 1685. One mile east
of A702 (signposted). Sunday Service: 11.45am
Open during daylight hours. Drumlanrig Castle nearby
CHURCH OF SCOTLAND ♿ 🏛 ☕ (afternoon teas, Sundays, July, August, September) wc **A**

DURISDEER PARISH CHURCH   ST MARY'S CHURCH, GATEHOUSE OF FLEET

316 ST MARY'S CHURCH, GATEHOUSE OF FLEET

NX 597 562

Dromore Road

Episcopalians in the area worshipped in the private chapel of Cally house until the
present building of 1840 was purchased from the United Presbyterian Church and
dedicated to St Mary in 1909. It is probably unique among Scottish Episcopal
Churches in having a stained glass window commemorating John Knox! Sunday
Service: Holy Communion 9.45am; Wednesday: Holy Communion 9.30am

Open by arrangement, telephone P Taylor 01557 330146

SCOTTISH EPISCOPAL   ♿ ② **B**

317 HIGHTAE KIRK

NY 090 793

Built as a Relief meeting house in 1796
and remodelled for the Reformed
Presbyterians in 1865, when the windows
were enlarged and the gableted west
bellcote and small porch were added. On
the B7020, two and a half miles south of
Lochmaben. Sunday Services: 9.45am,
11.15am by rotation with Dalton and St
Mungo

Open by arrangement, telephone the Manse,
Hightae, Lockerbie 01387 811499

CHURCH OF SCOTLAND

♿ ⚲ wc (adjoining manse)

HIGHTAE KIRK

318 ST MUNGO PARISH CHURCH, KETTLEHOLM

NY 143 771

Built under the patronage of the Rt Hon Robert Jardine
MP of Castlemilk. Late Scots Gothic by David Bryce
1877 with a pinnacled-buttressed porch decorated with
grotesque carved heads. Inside, a magnificently elaborate
open roof. Organ 1905 by Abbot & Smith. Stained glass
by James Ballantine & Son 1876. First World War
memorial by F M Taubman. On the B723, three miles
south of Lockerbie. Sunday Services: 9.45am, 11.15am
by rotation with Dalton and Hightae

ST MUNGO PARISH
CHURCH, KETTLEHOLM

Open by arrangement, telephone the Manse, Hightae, Lockerbie 01387 811499

CHURCH OF SCOTLAND   🚻   ⚲   wc   **B**

319 KIRKBEAN PARISH CHURCH

NX 980 592

Harled T-plan kirk said to have been designed by William
Craik, sometime Laird of Arbigland. The tower on the west wall
is of two lower stages, 1776, with a Diocletian window in its
second stage, and two upper stages added in 1836 are by Walter
Newall, the first with a clock and the top with a big octagonal
belfry cupola of polished ashlar under a lantern. Venetian
window in the east gable of the tail of the church. Inside, plain
furnishings of 1883. A memorial font, presented by the United
States Navy in memory of John Paul Jones, a gardener's son
from Arbigland, who founded it; designed and sculpted by
George Henry Paulin 1946. In the village, turn left at the road
junction to Carsethorn. Adjacent to the school on left. Linked
with Colvend and Southwick. Sunday Service: 10.00am

KIRKBEAN
PARISH CHURCH

Open by arrangement, telephone Mr George Fazakerley 01387 880662

CHURCH OF SCOTLAND   **B**   wc

320 KIRKCOWAN PARISH CHURCH

NX 327 610

Main Street, Kirkcowan

At the west end of the village, built in 1834 to replace a former church, of which
only an ivy-clad east gable remains in its kirkyard (east end of village). The present
church is a harled T-plan building with external stairs at the east and west gables
leading to two galleries. A tower at the north side. Inside, three galleries in all,
supported by marbled cast-iron columns. Tall pulpit of 1834 and a late 19th-
century chamber organ by J & A Mirrlees, brought here in 1966. Linked with
Wigtown. Sunday Service: 10.00am

Open by arrangement, telephone Mr J Adair 01671 830214

CHURCH OF SCOTLAND   &   ⊘   wc   **A**

321 KIRKCUDBRIGHT PARISH CHURCH

NX 683 509

St Mary Street

The present neo-Gothic building dates from 1838 and was designed by William Burn. Cruciform in shape, the nave and gallery together comprise the 'Country End', with the south transept referred to as the 'Town End' and the north transept as the 'Trades End'. A substantial pulpit, also designed by Burn, incorporates a sounding board and a precentor's box. Stained glass window of 1913 in south transept by William Meikle in memory of the Rev A C Campbell. Sunday Services: September to May 11.00am, plus 9.30am on 4th and 5th Sundays, Christian Healing 6.30pm on 2nd Sunday; June to August 9.30am and 11.00am, Christian Healing 6.30pm on 2nd Sunday

KIRKCUDBRIGHT PARISH CHURCH

Open June to August 9.00am-5.00pm. At other times open by arrangement, telephone Neil Cavers 01557 331217

CHURCH OF SCOTLAND ♿ wc 👂 ⛪ **B**

322 GREYFRIARS (ST FRANCIS OF ASSISI), KIRKCUDBRIGHT

NX 682 511

Mote Brae, Kirkcudbright

The sanctuary of Greyfriars Church is the last remaining fragment of a Franciscan friary. Dating from either the 13th or 15th centuries, it has undergone many changes in both design and use over the years. The MacClellan Monument, erected in 1597, is one of the most interesting features of the church. On the left of the High Altar is an ancient piscina. There are also three fine modern stained glass windows including work by Gordon Webster.

The cross and candlesticks are the work of Mabel Brunton, a distinguished member of the artists' colony which flourished in the town in the 1920s. Other interesting furnishings are the 17-century dower chest and the medieval holy water stoup. Sunday Services: Holy Communion 11.30am all year, and 8.15am end May to August; Friday: Holy Communion 10.00am

Open Easter week, July to August, and by arrangement, telephone the Rector 01557 330146

SCOTTISH EPISCOPAL **A**

GREYFRIARS (ST FRANCIS OF ASSISI), KIRKCUDBRIGHT

323 KIRKMAIDEN OLD KIRK

NX 139 324
Kirkmaiden, Drummore
Built 1638 to replace St Catherine's at Mull of Galloway
in the most southerly parish in Scotland. T-shaped
church with vaults of the McDouall family of Logan
underneath balcony. 'Treacle' Bible on display. Bell from
Clanyard Castle, a gift from the Earl of Dalhousie 1532.
Sunday Service: 11.30am last Sunday May to September
Open daily Easter to October, or by arrangement with
Mrs Symonds, telephone 01776 840601
CHURCH OF SCOTLAND [♿] [wc] ⌂

KIRKMAIDEN OLD KIRK

324 KIRKMICHAEL KIRK

NY 005 884
Parkgate, off A701
Built in 1815 in the location of churches thought to date
from 9th and 10th centuries. Constructed of rough
dressed whinstone with sandstone facings in the classic
T-plan of the period with large round-headed windows
and a birdcage bellcote. Three stained glass memorial
windows ('Our Lord stilling the storm', 'Our Lord the
Good Shepherd' and 'Our Lady with Faith and Hope'),
three memorial plaques and a laird's loft. Good collection
of 18th-century stones in the graveyard.
Sunday Services: 9.45am or 11.15am
Open by arrangement, telephone Mrs Copeland 01687 860235
or Mr Findlay 01387 860642
CHURCH OF SCOTLAND [♿] [wc] ⟨⟩ **B**

KIRKMICHAEL KIRK

325 HOLY TRINITY, LOCKERBIE

NY 136 815
Arthurs Place, Lockerbie
Built as Trinity Church 1874 for the United Presbyterian
Church, became Church of Scotland 1929 and acquired in 1973
by the Catholic Church and renamed Holy Trinity. Designed by
Ford Mackenzie, built in Corncockle sandstone in Gothic style
with a large rose window and steeple. The organ, Ingram of
Edinburgh, is a prominent feature. Plaque in vestibule
commemorates 1000 years of Christianity in the Ukraine. Copy
of Lockerbie Book of Remembrance and Memorial Plaque.
Services: Sunday Mass 11.15am; other days as announced
Church website: www.lockerbie-and-moffat-rc-churches.freeola.com
Open daily 9.00am-5.00pm
ROMAN CATHOLIC **B**

HOLY TRINITY,
LOCKERBIE

326 MONIGAFF PARISH CHURCH, MINNIGAFF

NX 410 666

Minnigaff, Newton Stewart

Church completed in 1836 to a design by William Burn.
Stained glass by William Wailes of Newcastle 1868 and
Ballantine, Edinburgh 1910. Font from Earl of Galloway's
private chapel. Organ built in 1873, Bryceson Brothers,
London. Ruins of pre-Reformation church on medieval
foundations. East gable 12th or early 13th-century. Motte and
ditch. Eighth-century stone slab of Irish missionary
influence. Grave stones including B-listed Heron monument.
Yew tree 900 years old. Sunday Service: 10.00am, first
Sunday of month Holy Communion 9.25am

Open July and August, Monday and Friday 2.00-4.30pm.

Or by arrangement, telephone Mrs Shankland 01671 402164.

Historical display June to September

CHURCH OF SCOTLAND (?) ⬚ ⬚ wc ⬚ ⬚ (free) **B**

MONIGAFF PARISH
CHURCH, MINNIGAFF

327 ST ANDREW'S, MOFFAT

NT 075 051

Churchgate, Moffat

Impressive church in Early English style by John Starforth 1884, with a central
tower flanked by bowed stair towers. Richly carved entrance leads to a wide
interior with galleries on slender iron columns. Profusion of stained glass including
rose window above the pulpit by Starforth. Other windows by James Ballantine &
Son, Ballantine & Gardiner, and William Meikle & Sons. Pipe organ by Eustace
Ingram 1894. Sunday Service: 11.15am

Open June to September 10.30am-12.30pm and 2.00-4.00pm

CHURCH OF SCOTLAND ♿ (rear door) (?) wc **B**

328 KELLS PARISH CHURCH, NEW GALLOWAY

NX 632 784

Kirk Road, New Galloway

Built in 1822 to a design by William McCandlish. A
granite T-plan church with three-stage square tower at
the centre of south wall. Interior mainly reconstructed in
1911 following original layout. Galleries on three sides
with pulpit on long south wall. Notable churchyard with
three 'Adam and Eve' stones of 1706-7, and a delightful
upright for Captain Gordon's gamekeeper, John Murray.
Linked with Carsphairn, Balmaclellan and Dalry.
Sunday Service: 10.30am, not first Sunday

Open by arrangement, telephone 01644 430380

CHURCH OF SCOTLAND (?) **B**

KELLS PARISH CHURCH,
NEW GALLOWAY

329   ST MARGARET'S NEW GALLOWAY

NX 636 778

On edge of New Galloway on Ken Bridge road
Built 1904, chancel added 1908. The walls of the
church are harled and the roofs are red tiled. The
wooden panelling and furnishings are a mixture of
Oregon pine and oak and the windows are variously
by Kempe, Clayton & Bell, and James Powell & Sons.
Services: 10.30am every Sunday and Wednesday
Key at Rectory next door, telephone Rev John Repath
01644 420235
SCOTTISH EPISCOPAL ♿ 📖

ST MARGARET'S
NEW GALLOWAY

330   PENNINGHAME ST JOHN'S CHURCH, NEWTON STEWART

NX 410 654

Church Street, Newton Stewart
Church completed in 1840 to a design by William Burn. Groome's *Gazetteer*
describes it as 'a handsome Gothic edifice'. Major restoration work on tower and
steeple carried out in 2000. Organ by J F Harston of Newark in 1878, believed to be
the largest and most intact of all organs built by him. Renovated by Hill, Norman
and Beard 1962. Spire 151ft. All glass replaced 1996. Interesting display of
Communion silver including two chalices dated 1711. Church Street is parallel to
town's main street. Sunday Service: 10.30am
Open Tuesday 12.30-2.00pm for lunchtime prayer meeting, or by arrangement,
telephone Mr M C Dunlop 01671 402543
CHURCH OF SCOTLAND ② wc **A**

331   DALRY PARISH CHURCH, ST JOHN'S TOWN OF DALRY

NX 618 813

Main Street, St John's Town of Dalry
Completed in 1831 to a design by William McCandlish
to replace a ruinous building of 1771, it is probably the
third church to occupy the site. Early records are scarce,
but a church, a dilapidated one at that, existed in 1427.
Traditional T-shaped interior, plainly furnished. Pulpit
with carved wooden canopy. Galleries on three sides.
Stands near the Water of Ken with wide views of the
Rhinns of Kells. Avenue of lime trees. Interesting old
kirkyard with Covenanters' stone and Gordon Aisle,
burial place of the Gordons of Lochinvar. Robert Burns
fashioned his poem 'Tam o' Shanter' on a local tale. On
A713 Castle Douglas–Ayr. Linked with Balmaclellan and
Kells and Carsphairn. Sunday Service: 12.00 noon
Open by arrangement, telephone Mr D M Bell 01644 430273
CHURCH OF SCOTLAND wc ② **B**

DALRY PARISH CHURCH,
ST JOHN'S TOWN OF DALRY

332 SANDHEAD

NX 097 500

Main Street, Sandhead

Substantial timber construction with steeply pitched tiled roof and cedar-board clad walls by architects Goudie & Hill 1962. The unusual structure uses laminated timber portal frames with obscured glass between the frames in both side walls. Flat-roofed porch with masonry bell-tower. Internally, much varnished wood. Inverted-pyramid shaped pulpit. Sunday Services: 10.00am

Open by arrangement, contact Mrs C McKay, 25 Main Street or Mr Cowan, Dorlin, Main Street

CHURCH OF SCOTLAND

SANDHEAD

♿ wc ☕ (Wednesdays and Sundays, 2.00-4.00pm in summer)

333 SOUTHWICK PARISH CHURCH

NX 906 569

Caulkerbush, by Dumfries

Standing by woodland just outside the policies of Southwick House, a stone church of local grey granite with dressings of red sandstone. By Peddie & Kinnear 1891, a mixture of Early Christian and Norman. Its crossing tower was derived from the 14th-century tower of St Monans Parish Church. A wagon roof over the nave, the chancel arch enriched with chevron decoration. On either side of the chancel arch, a neo-Norman font by Cox & Buckley 1898 and a neo-Jacobean pulpit. Wrought iron Arts & Crafts light fittings, once for oil lamps. Late 19th-century stained glass. Organ replaced in May 1999 with Ahlborn SL100. A710 from Dumfries, turn right immediately over Southwick Bridge onto B793 Dalbeattie. Linked with Colvend and Kirkbean. Sunday Service: 10.00am

Open by arrangement, telephone Geo Fazakerley 01387 880662

CHURCH OF SCOTLAND

SOUTHWICK PARISH CHURCH

 wc

334 TINWALD CHURCH

NY 003 816

Off A701, 3 miles north of Dumfries

A plain rectangle with bell-finialled birdcage
bellcote built in 1769 on the foundations of an
earlier medieval church. Four stained glass
windows by Gordon Webster. Interior, with fine
hammerbeam roof, has the matching pews
arranged to form a central aisle. Chancel area
furnished in oak with octagonal pulpit, pedestal
font, communion table and Minister's and Elders'
chairs. Session Room added 2000. Covenanters'
Monument in graveyard. Striking views over
Nithsdale. Sunday Services: 9.45am or 11.15am
*Open by arrangement, telephone Mrs Carroll 01387
710551 or Mrs F Little 01387 711196*
CHURCH OF SCOTLAND ♿ wc 🅰 **B**

TINWALD CHURCH

335 TORTHORWALD CHURCH

NY 035 783

Off A709, 4 miles east of Dumfries

A church was founded in Torthorwald in the mid-13th century by Trinitarian or
Red Friars from Fail Monastery near Tarbolton, Ayrshire. A white T-plan kirk built
in 1872 to replace an earlier church on an adjacent site, stones dated 1450 and 1644
are set into the walls of the vestry. Pipe organ, 1904. The entrance gates are a
memorial to Dr John G Paton, a pioneer missionary to the islands of the South
Pacific. Sunday Services: 9.45am or 11.25am
Open by arrangement, telephone Mr Cowan 01387 750245 or Mrs Mitchell 01387 750673
CHURCH OF SCOTLAND wc 🅰 ⌷ **B**

336 WAMPHRAY PARISH CHURCH

NY 131 965

Neat rectangle by William
McGowan 1834, with a slender
tower and bellcote. Notable 18th-
century headstones in the graveyard
and a monument to the Rt Rev A H
Charteris, Founder of The Woman's
Guild and Moderator of the General
Assembly in 1892.
Sunday Service: 12.30pm
*Open by arrangement, telephone
Mrs Braid 01576 470275*
CHURCH OF SCOTLAND

WAMPHRAY PARISH CHURCH

337 ST NINIAN'S PRIORY CHURCH, WHITHORN

NX 444 403
Bruce Street, Whithorn
Built 1822 with later 19th-century tower.
Simple rectangular hall church. Carved oak
pulpit. Stained glass east windows gifted by
the daughter of Gemmell Hutcheson RSA in
memory of her father. Located on the site of
Whithorn 'dig' in the former precincts of
Whithorn Priory. First Scottish Christian
community founded here by St Ninian, pre-
dates Iona. From A75 turn south at Newton
Stewart on A714 then A746.
Sunday Services: 10.30am and 7.00pm
Open Easter to end of October, 10.00am-5.00pm
CHURCH OF SCOTLAND   ♿ ⊘ 📖 **A**

ST NINIAN'S PRIORY
CHURCH, WHITHORN

338 WIGTOWN PARISH CHURCH

NX 436 555
Bank Street, Wigtown
The parish church on an ancient ecclesiastical site, largely rebuilt in 1730, was by
the middle of the next century thought to be 'an old mean-looking edifice'. A new
church, by the London architect Henry Roberts, was built nearby in 1851, still
using the Georgian T-plan with a French pavilion roof on the tower. Built of
granite, it encloses a broad nave and east transept. P MacGregor Chalmers added a
communion table and font, an organ chamber, and rearranged the seating in 1914.
In the transept are three carved stones, one a Celtic cross shaft decorated on both
faces with interlaced rings, similar to those of the same period at Whithorn.
Stained glass in the east transept window by James Ballantine & Son 1867. Linked
with Kirkcowan. Sunday Services: 11.30am and 6.30pm (in church hall)
Open Easter to September, Monday to Friday 2.00-4.00pm
CHURCH OF SCOTLAND   ♿ ⊘ 📖 ⛪ WC ⚲ **B**

WIGTOWN PARISH CHURCH

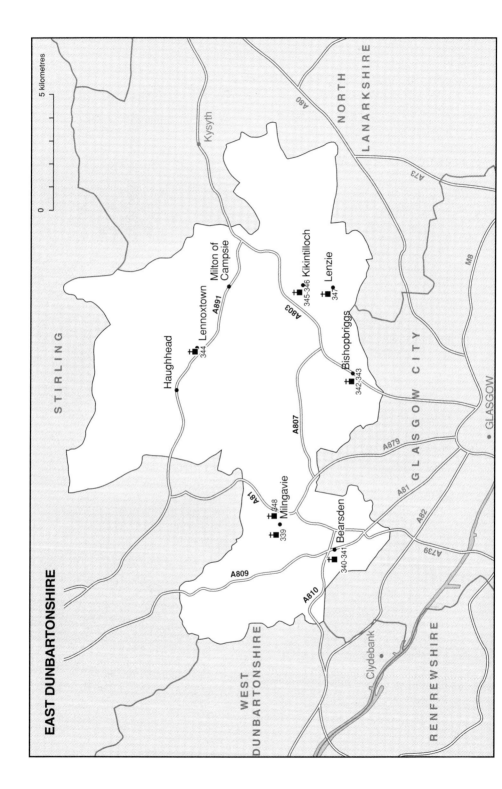

EAST DUNBARTONSHIRE

5 kilometres

0

STIRLING

NORTH LANARKSHIRE

Kysyth

A80

A73

M8

Haughhead

Lennoxtown
344

Milton of Campsie

A891

Kikintilloch
345-346

Lenzie
347

A803

Bishopbriggs
342-343

A807

Mingavie
348
339

A81

Bearsden
340-341

A809

A810

A879

A81

A82

A739

GLASGOW CITY

GLASGOW

WEST DUNBARTONSHIRE

RENFREWSHIRE

Clydebank

EAST DUNBARTONSHIRE

Local Representative: Miss Marion Smith, 30 Roman Court, Roman Road, Bearsden
(*telephone* 0141 942 1236)

339 BALDERNOCK PARISH CHURCH

NS 577 751
Near Milngavie
The religious history of the site goes back
to the 13th century. The present church was
built in 1795 on the site of an earlier church.
The bell-tower contains a curious panel
which may have come from the nearby
Roman wall. The octagonal gatehouse and
stone stile feature in Moffat's play 'Bunty
Pulls the Strings'. Interesting gravestones,
including Archibald Bulloch from whom
President Theodore Roosevelt and Eleanor
Roosevelt descended. The church stands at
the end of a lovely one-mile walk from
Milngavie. Sunday Service: 11.00am
Open Sunday 2.00-4.00pm, May to September
CHURCH OF SCOTLAND 🚹 ② 👤 📖 wc **B**

BALDERNOCK PARISH CHURCH

340 BLESSED JOHN DUNS SCOTUS CHAPEL, BEARSDEN

NS 535 720
2 Chesters Road, Bearsden, Glasgow
The Chapel of Scotus College was
designed by J F Stephen and dedicated
in 1997. The main internal features are
its barrel-vaulted ceiling and glass walls.
The 14 stained glass panels representing
the Stations of the Cross are by Shona
McInnes and are full of rich symbolism.
A number of other items were specially
commissioned for the chapel, including
processional cross, presidential chair,
candlesticks and a Christ-figure. A
pamphlet is available giving excellent
details
Open during term time 7.00am-9.00pm.
Also telephone 0141 942 8384
ROMAN CATHOLIC 🚹 wc

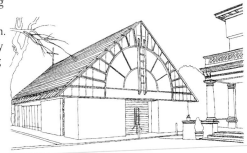

BLESSED JOHN DUNS SCOTUS CHAPEL,
BEARSDEN

NEW KILPATRICK PARISH CHURCH, BEARSDEN

341 NEW KILPATRICK PARISH CHURCH, BEARSDEN

NS 543 723

Manse Road, Bearsden

Building began in 1807 on the site of an earlier church 1649, and within the
original settlement established by Paisley Abbey in 1232. Very fine collection of
stained glass including windows by Stephen Adam, Alfred and Gordon Webster,
Norman M Macdougall, C E Stewart, James Ballantine and Eilidh Keith. By rail to
Bearsden, by bus 59 and 17 to Bearsden Cross. Services: Sunday 10.30am and
6.30pm, Wednesday 12.00 noon

Church website: www.nkchurch.org.uk

*Open by arrangement, telephone M L Smith 0141 942 1236. Close to Roman Bath House east
of Bearsden Cross*

CHURCH OF SCOTLAND ⟨&⟩ ⟨?⟩ ⟨⟩ ⟨⟩ wc **B**

342 ST JAMES THE LESS, BISHOPBRIGGS

NS 612 712

Hilton Road, Bishopbriggs

Built 1980 when the congregation moved from Springburn, this church by
Glasgow architects Weddell and Thomson preserves the most striking features of
the 1881 Springburn building and contains many items from other Glasgow
churches: stained glass by Edward Burne-Jones and Stephen Adam and part of the
old High Altar of Iona Abbey. Pipe organ by J W Walker & Sons 1964.
Sunday Services: 9.00am Eucharist, 10.30am Sung Eucharist; Thursday 10.30am
Morning Prayer and Eucharist

Church website: www.stjamesbishopbriggs.org.uk

*Open Sundays and Thursdays 10.00am-12.00 noon, or by arrangement with the Rector,
telephone 0141 772 4514*

SCOTTISH EPISCOPAL ⟨&⟩ wc ⟨?⟩ ⟨⟩

343 CADDER PARISH CHURCH

NS 616 723

Cadder Road, Bishopbriggs

A simple country church in a delightful and peaceful setting, built 1825 to designs by David Hamilton. The chancel was added in 1908 and the gallery altered 1914. Finely carved screen at the front of the gallery of Austrian oak. Very fine stained glass windows by Steven Adam, Gordon Webster, Sadie McLellan and Crear McCartney. Pipe organ by Norman & Beard. Watch-house and cast-iron mort safe in the graveyard. Sunday Service: 11.15am (plus 9.30am in summer)

Church website: www.greyfriars@webartz.com

Open by arrangement with the Minister, telephone 0141 772 1363

CHURCH OF SCOTLAND ② wc **A**

344 CAMPSIE PARISH CHURCH, LENNOXTOWN

NS 629 777

Main Street, Lennoxtown

Modern church with interesting wood carving and stained glass. Craft centre and old church with fascinating graveyard at Campsie Glen, two miles. Bus 175 Campsie Glen via Kirkintilloch. Sunday Service: 11.00am

Open by arrangement, telephone Mrs M Tindall 01360 310 911

CHURCH OF SCOTLAND ♿ ② ☕ 📖 wc **A**

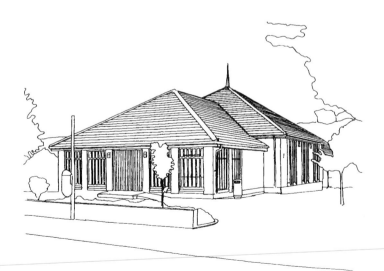

CAMPSIE PARISH CHURCH, LENNOXTOWN

ST DAVID'S MEMORIAL PARK CHURCH, KIRKINTILLOCH

345 ST DAVID'S MEMORIAL PARK CHURCH, KIRKINTILLOCH

NS 654 737

Alexandra Street, Kirkintilloch

The present church by P MacGregor Chalmers 1926, adjacent to site of the original
building (1843), was dedicated as a gift of Mrs Paton Thomson in memory of her
parents. 2-manual pipe organ, a significant Anneessens 1899 rebuilt and enlarged.
Off A803. Sunday Services: 11.00am and (most Sundays) 6.30pm

Open every Wednesday 11.00am-2.00pm for meditation and prayer

CHURCH OF SCOTLAND [&] [◎] [Å] [wc]

346 ST FLANNAN'S, KIRKINTILLOCH

NS 663 743

91 Hillhead Road

Parish founded 1948, the present building, close to the Antonine Wall, was
designed by William Gilmour and opened in 1970. The form of the building
represents praying hands. Services: Saturday 7.00pm, Sunday 10.00am, 12.00 noon,
6.30pm, Monday 7.00pm

Open for services

ROMAN CATHOLIC [&] [wc] [◎] [Å]

ST FLANNAN'S, KIRKINTILLOCH

347 ST CYPRIAN'S CHURCH, LENZIE

NS 653 727

Beech Road, Lenzie

Built in 1873 by Alexander Ross of Inverness in Gothic style with a three-stage tower at the east end and a gabled porch at the west end. The use of contrasting materials gives a colourful interior. Painting of the Last Supper on the reredos. Memorial choir screen made in local iron foundry. Half-mile north from Lenzie Cross. Sunday Services: 8.30am, 11.00am and 6.30pm (not July and August)

Open by arrangement, telephone the Rector 0141 776 4149

SCOTTISH EPISCOPALIAN ⓐ wc **B**

348 CAIRNS CHURCH, MILNGAVIE

NS 556 748

Buchanan Street, Milngavie

The longest serving congregation in Milngavie, services were first held on Barloch Moor before the first building was erected in 1799. The present church was built to the design of J B Wilson in a late decorated Gothic style, and was opened in 1903. The red tiled spire rises above the surrounding roofs. New halls and rooms by Page & Park, 2000, provide a new dimension to the presentation of the church – intimate, welcoming and friendly – a partnership with history. Interior features a range of banners. A light lunch is available every Tuesday (except during holiday periods). Sunday Services: 10.45am and 7.00pm (summer 10.00am only)

Access by arrangement with church office, telephone 0141 956 4868

Monday to Friday 09.30am-2.30pm

CHURCH OF SCOTLAND ♿ ⓐ wc ☕ **B**

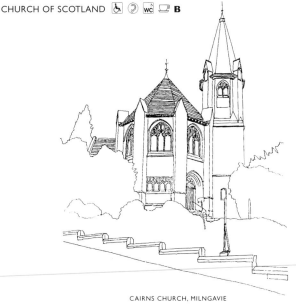

CAIRNS CHURCH, MILNGAVIE

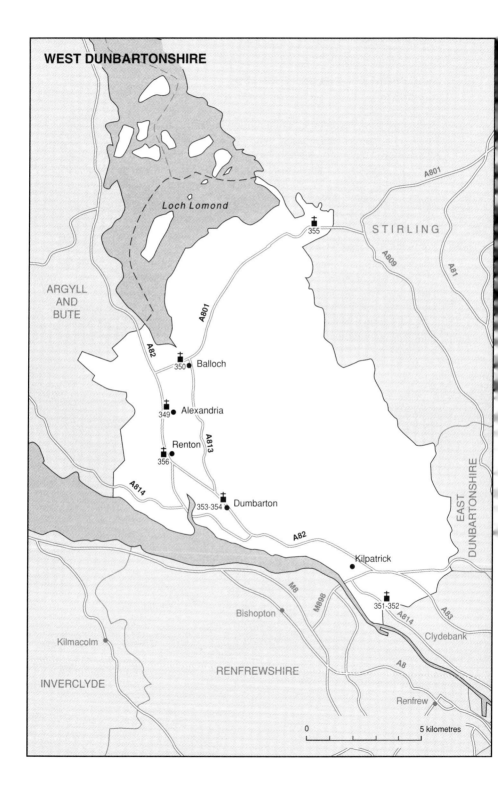

WEST DUNBARTONSHIRE

Loch Lomond

STIRLING

ARGYLL
AND
BUTE

A801

A809

A81

A82

350 ● Balloch

349 ● Alexandria

A813

356 ● Renton

A814

353-354 ● Dumbarton

A82

Kilpatrick ●

EAST
DUNBARTONSHIRE

M8

M898

Bishopton ●

351-352

A814

A83

Clydebank

Kilmacolm ●

A8

INVERCLYDE

RENFREWSHIRE

Renfrew ●

355

0   5 kilometres

WEST DUNBARTONSHIRE

Local Representative: Miss Marion Smith, 30 Roman Court, Roman Road, Bearsden (*telephone* 0141 942 1236)

349 ST MUNGO'S CHURCH, ALEXANDRIA

NS 389 796

Main Street, Alexandria

Dedicated 1894, J M Crawford, architect, in pointed Gothic style. Early 20th-century addition of side aisle. Simple interior with plain altar furniture. Open timber roof with curved brace supported on stone corbels. Three-light stained glass window in memory of Agnes J Burham of New York featuring Christ in Majesty, St Michael the Archangel, St Agnes and St Agatha. Sunday Services: Eucharist 9am, Sung Eucharist 11.00am; Wednesday: Eucharist 10.00am

Church website: //dspace.dial.pipex.com/town/plaza/aaj50/

Open by arrangement, telephone the Priest-in-charge, St Mungo's Rectory 01389 752633

SCOTTISH EPISCOPAL wc **B**

350 ALEXANDRIA PARISH CHURCH, BALLOCH

NS 389 798

Lomond Road, Balloch

Building refurbished and upgraded 1995-96. Digital organ by Allen. A number of items produced by the congregational Sewing Group include the Heritage Tapestry 30 by 27 inches, finely embroidered pulpit falls and communion table cords, four hand-sewn banners (two on local themes) crafted in 1998 and 1999 for the millennium. Several noteworthy items of stained glass. Contemporary Noah's Ark mural in main hall. In the grounds, a war memorial commemorating members of the congregation killed in action 1914-18 and 1939-45. Off A82. Five to ten minutes' walk from Balloch railway station. Sunday Service: 11.00am also during summer (mid-June to last in August at 9.30am); and Jazz Praise services at 7.00pm usually on last Sunday of February and following alternate months

Church website: www.alexandriaparishchurch.co.uk 10th Anniversary events during 2004.

Open by arrangement lunches/afternoon teas for groups by arrangement, telephone Mrs M Thomson 01389 756553

CHURCH OF SCOTLAND

ALEXANDRIA PARISH CHURCH, BALLOCH

351 KILBOWIE ST ANDREW'S PARISH CHURCH, CLYDEBANK

NS 497 702
Kilbowie Road, Clydebank
For the congregation founded as St John's on the Hill
1897, the present church was built in 1904 on land
gifted by William Black of Auchentoshen. In simple
Perpendicular style, a low cruciform church of red
sandstone. Battlemented belfry added 1933. Recent
refurbishment. Memorial side chapel with tapestry and
stained glass window by Eilidh Keith 1997, dedicated
to the victims of the Clydebank Blitz. The bell 1933 is
one of few remaining in this former industrial
community of Scotland. M8 Junction 19, A82 to A8014
turn off. Five minutes' walk from railway station.

KILBOWIE ST ANDREW'S PARISH
CHURCH, CLYDEBANK

Sunday Service: 11.00am, except July and August
Open 13 March each year 10.00am-4.00pm (Blitz Memorial
Day), Commemorative Service 12.00 noon. Other times by arrangement,
and Doors Open Day, telephone Rev R Grahame 0141 951 2455
CHURCH OF SCOTLAND ♿ ⊙ 🚹 📖 wc ☕

352 ST JOSEPH'S CHURCH, CLYDEBANK

NS 510 733
Faifley Road, Clydebank
Replacing a Coia church which was burned down,
the building is one of the newest in the country,
being opened in 1997. The award-winning design
by Jacobsen & French utilises tall windows to
provide light while natural wood is featured extensively.

ST JOSEPH'S CHURCH,
CLYDEBANK

Sunday Services: 9.00 and 11.30am; Saturday Vigil 6.00pm; daily Mass 9.30am
Open Wednesday 9.00-11.00am, Saturday 5.00-7.00pm, Sunday 9.00am-12.30pm
ROMAN CATHOLIC ♿ ⊙

353 RIVERSIDE PARISH CHURCH, DUMBARTON

NS 398 752
High Street, Dumbarton
Built in 1811 to a design by John Brash on the site of earlier 13/14th-century and
17th-century churches. The steeple and pedimented gable command the westward
curve of the High Street. Urns perch on the belfry and adorn the gatepiers. The
interior was refurbished 1886. Stained glass includes the Queen Margaret window
by the Abbey Studio of Glasgow and Ascension window by C E Stewart.
Spectacular new millennium window by John Clark 2002. Crusader stone of
11th/12th century now housed in gallery. Sunday Service: 11.15am
Church website: www.dumbartonriverside.org.uk
Open weekdays 9.30am-12.30pm
CHURCH OF SCOTLAND ♿ ⊙ 📖 wc **A**

354 ST AUGUSTINE'S CHURCH, DUMBARTON

NS 397 752
High Street, Dumbarton
Built in 1873, the architect Sir Robert Rowand
Anderson designed the building in the Gothic Revival
Style. Stained glass at baptismal font by Stephen
Adam with others to a design by Carl Alnquist. The
organ was designed and built for the church by
Smith and Brock. Total restoration of building 2003.
Sunday Services: 9.00am and 11.00am
Church website: www.staugustinesdumbarton.co.uk
Open Saturday mornings, and by arrangement, telephone church office 01389 734514
SCOTTISH EPISCOPAL   ♿ **A**

ST AUGUSTINE'S CHURCH,
DUMBARTON

355 THE CHURCH OF KILMARONOCK

NS 452 875
By Drymen
The present church building dates from 1813 and
has a stout classical dignity. Parish long-
established when documented records began; the
screen at the entrance to the nave lists
incumbents since 1325. Memorial wall plaques.
Ancient stones in graveyard. North side of
A811, three miles west of Drymen.
Sunday Service: 11.00am, May to September
*Open by arrangement. Occasional events by
the Friends of Kilmaronock*
CHURCH OF SCOTLAND ♿ 🚻 📖 **B**

THE CHURCH OF KILMARONOCK

356 RENTON TRINITY PARISH CHURCH

NS 390 780
Building originally constructed as Renton Old
Parish Church 1892, architects H & D Bradlay.
United with Renton Union Church and Renton
Millburn Church 1969. Has since been refurbished
and upgraded. Five stained glass windows by Oscar
Paterson, Glasgow 1912-22. Sunday Services:
11.00am and at 6.30pm 2nd Sunday of March,
June, September, December
*Open Thursdays 10.30am-1.30pm or by arrangement,
telephone Rev Cameron Langlands 01389 752017*
CHURCH OF SCOTLAND ♿ ☕ 📖 🕯 ☕ **A**

RENTON TRINITY PARISH CHURCH

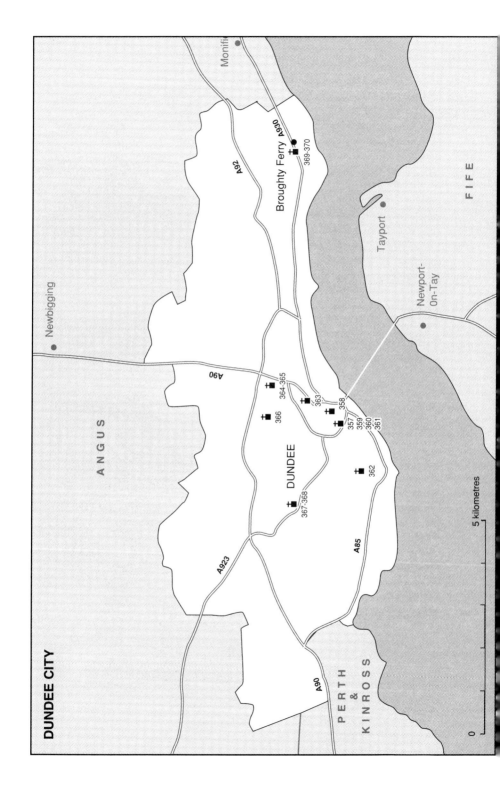

DUNDEE CITY

ANGUS

DUNDEE

PERTH
&
KINROSS

FIFE

Newbigging

Monifi...

Broughty Ferry

Tayport

Newport-
On-Tay

A90

A92

A930

A923

A85

369-370

364-365

363

366

358

357

359

360

361

362

367-368

0   5 kilometres

DUNDEE

357 DUNDEE PARISH CHURCH (ST MARY'S)

NO 401 301

Nethergate, Dundee

Founded in 1190 by Earl of Huntingdon. Rebuilt 1844 by William Burn. Beautiful 19th and 20th-century stained glass windows. War memorial 1914-18. Impressive organ installed 1865. Reading desk with interesting history. North of Discovery Point and railway station. Sunday Service: 11.00am; Holy Communion last Sunday of month

Open May to September, Tuesday, Thursday, Friday 10.00am-12.00 noon

CHURCH OF SCOTLAND  **B**

358 ST PAUL'S CATHEDRAL

NO 404 303

Castlehill, 1 High Street, Dundee

Designed by Sir George Gilbert Scott, the cathedral stands on the site of Dundee's ancient castle. Gothic in style, but Gothic with a difference. Tall, graceful columns give an impression of lightness and airiness. Organ by Hill, 1865, rebuilt, Hill, Norman & Beard 1976. East end of High Street at junction with Commercial Street. Walking distance from rail and bus stations.
Sunday Services: 8.00am, 9.40am, 11.00am and 6.30pm

Open Monday to Saturday 11.00am-5.00pm

SCOTTISH EPISCOPAL **A**

359 ST ANDREW'S CATHEDRAL

NO 400 299

150 Nethergate, Dundee

Designed by George Mathewson in 1835, impressive arcaded interior. Outstanding 19th and 20th-century stained glass by Mayer of Munich. Sunday Mass: 11.30am and 7pm; weekday Mass: 10.00am

Open Monday to Saturday 9.00am-3.00pm

ROMAN CATHOLIC

ST ANDREW'S CATHEDRAL

360 THE STEEPLE CHURCH

NO 402 301

Nethergate, Dundee

Church building dates from 1788, Samuel Bell. Entry through 15th-century St Mary's Tower. A landmark, known as 'Old Steeple'. City centre.
Sunday Services: 11.00am and 7.00pm

Open July to August, Tuesday and Saturday 12.00 noon-3.00pm. Also Doors Open Day and other summer activities. Mary Slessor Exhibition, July to August (details in church)

CHURCH OF SCOTLAND **B**

361   MEADOWSIDE ST PAUL'S CHURCH

NO 401 300

114-116 Nethergate, Dundee

Built in 1852, replacing the Mariners' Church, to a design by Charles Wilson. It 'boasts a fine spire terminating the elevation of Nethergate before it is disrupted by the ring road'. Hammerbeam roof. Organ by Walcker & Co 1902, overhauled by Rushworth & Dreaper 1971. Stained glass, some by Jones & Willis, and by Alexander Russell. Sets of tapestried pulpit falls, tapestry kneelers. Doorway mosaics by Elizabeth McFall. A hall complex, M J Rodgers 1988, the location of regular meetings of Presbytery of Dundee, as well as providing storage for the Presbytery Resources Centre. A feature of the garden is an artistic stone wall by David Wilson. Sunday Service: 11.00am

Open Wednesday 12.00 noon-1.30pm for prayer and meditation

Key from Cornerstone on weekdays

CHURCH OF SCOTLAND [♿] [?] [📖] [☕] (Cornerstone Coffee House adjoining) [wc] **B**

362   ST PETER'S FREE CHURCH

NO 390 298

St Peter Street, Dundee

Built by Hean Brothers, 1836. Remarkably douce for a revivalist kirk; yet this was the seat of the Rev Robert McCheyne (1813-43), a major player in the Evangelical revival, who made these sober rafters ring. An elegant, classical church with a gallery carried on cast-iron columns. Original pulpit. The plain simplicity of the building is ennobled by the tower and stone spire against its east gable. The church has served different denominations since its opening: Free, United Free, and

ST PETER'S FREE CHURCH

Church of Scotland. It became a Free Church again in 1987. From city centre, west for one mile along High Street, Nethergate and Perth Road. Turn right into St Peter Street. Sunday Services: 11.00am and 6.30pm; Wednesday: Prayer Meeting 7.30pm

Open by arrangement, telephone Rev D Robertson 01382 861401

FREE CHURCH OF SCOTLAND [♿] [📖] [wc] **B**

363   ST ANDREW'S PARISH CHURCH

NO 404 307

King Street, Dundee

Trades kirk with interesting history, dating from 1774, Samuel Bell with plans by James Craig, Edinburgh. Beautiful stained glass. Includes Glasite Kirk 1777, now part of church hall complex. Handsome spire with peal of fine musical bells. Lovely gardens. Teas on Saturdays. Next to Wellgate Shopping Centre. Sunday Service: 11.00am all year; also 9.30am June, July and August

Church website: www.standrewschurch.co.uk

Open Tuesday, Thursday, Saturday 10.00am-12.00 noon all year. Also Doors Open Day

CHURCH OF SCOTLAND [♿] [?] [🍴] [📖] [?] [☕] (Saturdays) [wc] **A**

GLASITE KIRK, NOW PART OF THE CHURCH HALLS
OF THE ST ANDREW'S PARISH CHURCH

ST ANDREW'S PARISH CHURCH

364 ST JOHN THE BAPTIST CHURCH

NO 411 314

116 Albert Street, Dundee

The present building was consecrated in 1886. Designed with a French-style roof by the Rev Edward Sugden 1885. The sanctuary and chancel are panelled in late Gothic style, the details suggested by the woodwork in King's College Chapel, Aberdeen. Open wood roof and pillars give this interior a Scandinavian feel. Reredos by William Hole. The font cover is a splendid carved wooden spire.

Services: Sunday 10.15am; Thursday 10.00am

Open Thursday 9.00-11.00am. Other times by arrangement,

telephone Rev James Forbes 01382 461640

SCOTTISH EPISCOPAL   🦽 📖 wc **B**

365 STOBSWELL PARISH CHURCH

NO 411 315

Albert Street, Dundee

On a prominent site, by Charles Edward and Thomas S Robertson 1874. The buildings have recently undergone extensive refurbishment. L-shaped church. Fine stained glass windows by William Wilson. From city centre buses 15, 17, 32, 33, 35 and 36. Sunday Service: 11.00am (July and August 10.30am)

Dundee Doors Open Day, September

CHURCH OF SCOTLAND

🦽 ♿ wc (for disabled) **B**

STOBSWELL PARISH CHURCH

366 ST SALVADOR'S CHURCH

NO 403 313

Church Street, Dundee

Glorious painted interior with stencilled wall decoration and open roof, built in 1868 in early Arts & Crafts Gothic by G F Bodley. Organ by Wadsworth & Maskell, 1882, recently restored. Carnegie Street end of Church Street, off Hilltown. Buses 20 and 22. Daily Services: Tuesday 9.30am, Wednesday 10.00am, Thursday 12.30pm, Friday/Saturday 8.00am. Evensong daily 5.30pm except Sunday 5.00pm. Sunday Services: 9.00am, 11.00am, 5.00pm

Open most mornings. Also Doors Open Day, September

SCOTTISH EPISCOPAL ⊘ ⬤ ⬚ ⬚ **B**

367 ST MARGARET'S, LOCHEE

NO 382 312

17/19 Ancrum Road, Dundee

The roof of this church, 1888, designed by the Rev E Sugden, has attracted the attention of the Architecture Department of Duncan of Jordanstone College. The font, in the form of an angel holding a large shell, is thought to be a copy of a font by Danish artist Bertel Thorvaldsen in Copenhagen Cathedral. Services: Sunday: Holy Communion 8.00am, Sung Eucharist 11.00am; Thursday: Holy Communion 10.00am

Open by arrangement, telephone the Rector, Fr James Milne 01382 667227

SCOTTISH EPISCOPAL ⬤ ⬚ ⬚ ⬚ (after Sunday Sung Eucharist)

ST MARGARET'S, LOCHEE

IMMACULATE CONCEPTION (ST MARY'S), LOCHEE

368 IMMACULATE CONCEPTION (ST MARY'S), LOCHEE

NO 380 314

41 High Street, Lochee

Remarkable Gothic revival church of 1866 by Joseph A Hansom ennobled by a polygonal chancel which soars up into the spire and gives a contrast between the dark nave and well-lit chancel. Notable stonework and superb detail and craftsmanship. Flamboyant altarpiece by A B Wall of Cheltenham, 1897. Stained glass by Mayer of Munich. Floodlit well 12 metres deep. Services: Saturday 6.00pm Vigil, Sunday 10.00am and 11.30am, Monday-Saturday 10.00am

Open by arrangement, telephone Mr McLean 01382 611662

ROMAN CATHOLIC 🦽 wc ② 📖 **A**

369 ST MARY'S CHURCH, BROUGHTY FERRY

NO 461 310

Queen Street, Broughty Ferry

Designed by Sir George Gilbert Scott 1858 and added to 1870. Sir Robert Lorimer extended the chancel 1911. The pulpit, screen, choir stalls and reredos are all by Lorimer. Garden of Remembrance. On the main road from Carnoustie and Monifieth to Dundee. Frequent bus service. Sunday Services: 8.30am, 11.00am, 6.30pm; weekdays: Matins 7.00am, Evensong 6.00pm

Open daily all year

SCOTTISH EPISCOPAL 🦽 ② **A**

370 OUR LADY OF GOOD COUNSEL, BROUGHTY FERRY

NO 458 309

Westfield Road, Broughty Ferry

Designed by T M Cappon in a Gothic style, the centenary of church falls in 2004. The tower at the west end has a statue of the Madonna and Child. Services: Sunday Mass 9.00am and 11.00am, Monday, Wednesday, Friday 9.00am, Tuesday, Thursday, Saturday 10.00am

Open by arrangement with the Parish Priest, telephone 01382 778750

ROMAN CATHOLIC 🦽 wc ⚱ ☕ **C**

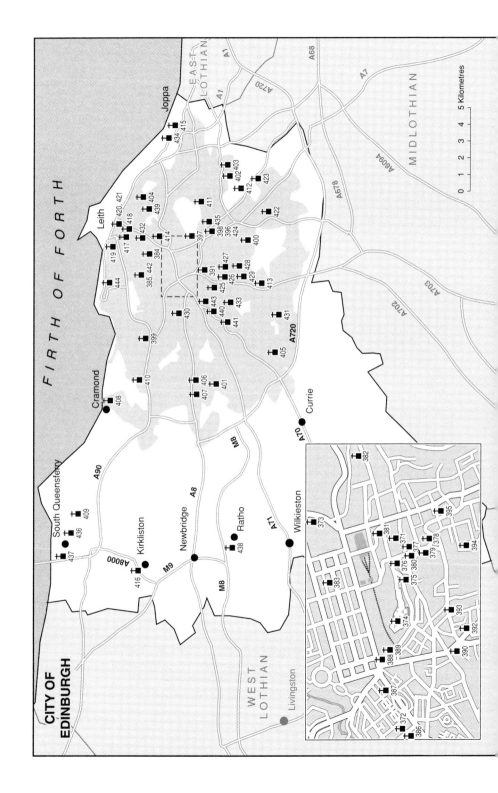

EDINBURGH

Local Representative: Andrew Thackrey, 3 Strathearn Place, Edinburgh
(*telephone* 0131 447 3232)

371 ST GILES' CATHEDRAL

NT 257 736
High Street, Edinburgh
The Cathedral was founded in the 1100s and mostly rebuilt during the 15th and 16th centuries. It was the church of John Knox during the Reformation and played an important part in the history of that time. The church contains fine examples of late medieval architecture and a wide range of traditional and modern stained glass and memorials. The magnificent Rieger organ was installed in 1992. The Thistle Chapel, designed by Robert Lorimer for the Order of the Thistle, was added in 1911.
Sunday Services: 8.00am, 10.00am, 11.30am, 6.00pm and 8.00pm
Church website: www.stgiles.net
Open May to September, Monday to Friday 9.00am-7.00pm, Saturday 9.00am-5.00pm,
Sunday 1.00-5.00pm. October to April, Monday to Saturday 9.00am-5.00pm, Sunday 1.00-
5.00pm. Dates for the diary: 'St Giles at six' recital series: Sundays at 6.00pm all year.
Lunchtime concert series: Monday to Saturday 12.15pm. Lunchtime organ music: Thursday
1.10pm May to June, September to October. Celebrity organ recitals: Wednesday 8.00pm July
to August. February 2004 the Cathedral will host 'The Quaker Tapestry' travelling exhibition.
For further details telephone 0131 225 9442
CHURCH OF SCOTLAND ⊘ ⌇ ⌂ ⊑ wc A

372 ST MARY'S EPISCOPAL CATHEDRAL

NT 242 735
Palmerston Place, Edinburgh
Built in 1879 to the award-winning design of Sir George Gilbert Scott, this neo-Gothic building reflects the spirit of that age: it is massive, its three spires lend distinction to the Edinburgh skyline and it rejoices in a wealth of ornate and symbolic detail, the evidence of a flourishing craftsmanship. Of particular note are the pelican lectern, Lorimer's rood and the J Oldrid Scott's reredos of the high altar, featuring the Scottish saints Columba and Margaret. Organ by 'Father' Willis 1879, rebuilt by Harrison & Harrison of Durham. In the grounds stand the 17-century Old Coates House (now the Theological Institute of the Scottish Episcopal Church) and the Song School, famous for its recently restored murals, painted by Phoebe Anna Traquair 1888-92 on the theme of *'Benedicite omnia opera'*. The Cathedral maintains an internationally renowned choir, which sings on Sundays and for Evensong on weekdays. During holiday periods the Cathedral welcomes visiting choirs.
Services: for full details contact the Cathedral answering machine on 0131 225 6293
Church website: www.cathedral.net
Open daily 7.30am-6.00pm (5.00pm Saturday). The Song School may be visited by
appointment
SCOTTISH EPISCOPAL ⊘ ⌇ ⌂ ⌇ wc A

373   ST MARY'S R C CATHEDRAL

NT 259 743
Broughton Street, Edinburgh
St Mary's Cathedral occupies the site of the much
smaller chapel of St Mary's, 1814. The church was
created a pro-Cathedral on the restoration of the
Scottish Hierarchy in 1878 and when 'Edinburgh'
was added to the ancient title of the see of St
Andrews, that had been vacant for 307 years. In
1886, at the request of Bishop Smith, the church
was raised in status to that of Metropolitan
Cathedral of the new Archdiocese of St Andrews
& Edinburgh, with all the rights and privileges
thereof. On the Gothic central section, at the front
of St Mary's, are remains of the 1814 chapel.
Organ by Ernest Lawton, 1932. Other areas have

ST MARY'S R C CATHEDRAL

been subject to ongoing lateral enlargement and vertical modifications.
Sunday Masses: 9.30am, 11.30am and 7.30pm; Holy days of Obligation: 6.00pm
previous evening, 9.30pm, 12.45pm and 7.30pm; daily Mass: Monday to Friday
12.45pm; Saturday: Vigil Mass 6.00pm
Church website: www.stmaryscathedral.co.uk
Open daily 8.00am-6.00pm (later on Saturday/Sunday)
ROMAN CATHOLIC ♿ ⊘ **A**

374   ST MARGARET'S CHAPEL

NT 253 735
Edinburgh Castle, Edinburgh
The oldest surviving structure in the castle built by King David I (1124-53). Interior
divided into two by a fine arch decorated with chevron ornament. Semi-circular
east chancel. Copy of the Gospel Book owned by St Margaret to whom the chapel
was dedicated by her son, David I. Stained glass windows depicting St Andrew, St
Ninian, St Columba and St Margaret by Douglas Strachan c.1930. Magnificent
views from castle ramparts. Other attractions within the castle (Historic Scotland)
include 'Honours of the Kingdom' exhibition, now with the Stone of Destiny
Open summer 9.30am-6.00pm, winter 9.30am-5.00pm (last ticket sold 45 minutes before closing)
NON-DENOMINATIONAL ♿ ⓘ ⬜ ☕ wc **A**

375   ST COLUMBA'S BY THE CASTLE

NT 254 735
Johnston Terrace, Edinburgh
By John Henderson, 1847, a single-nave building of six bays under a pitch-slated
roof with a battlemented tower. Four-bay aisleless nave and one-bay chancel; the
sixth bay forms the entrance and vestibule to the west end. Triple arcading at the
west wall, originally supporting a gallery, now subsumed into a suite of rooms

served by a new staircase. Stone altar, font and pulpit. Gifted oak panelling on lower east wall c.1914. The blocked east window has been filled with a mural of 'Christ Enthroned' by John Busby 1962. Pipe organ, James Conacher & Sons 1880, rebuilt in 1965 by N P Mander and relocated in 1998 by Lightoller. Church hall, originally a school, below the church. Redevelopment and refurbishment, Simpson & Brown 1998. Sunday Service: Eucharist 10.00am, and other times as announced

Open by arrangement, telephone the Rector 0131 228 6470

SCOTTISH EPISCOPAL   🦽 ② 📖 👤 **B**

376 QUAKER MEETING HOUSE

NT 256 736

7 Victoria Terrace, Edinburgh

Built originally as a chapel for the United Original Secession Church (Paterson & Shiells, 1865) as part of the City's Victoria Street redevelopment. Following the return of the 'Auld Seceders' to the Kirk, it became 'Kirk House', headquarters of the Edinburgh Battalion of the Boys' Brigade (conversion by Basil Spence & Partners, 1960). Converted as Quaker Meeting House by Religious Society of Friends in 1987 (Architects Walmesley & Savage). Festival venue with vegetarian café during the Edinburgh Festival Fringe in August.

Services: Sunday 11.00am; Wednesday 12.30pm

Church website: www.quaker-scotland.gn.apc.org/edinburgh

Open by arrangement, telephone the Wardens 0131 225 4825

QUAKER 🦽 wc ② 👤 **B**

377 AUGUSTINE UNITED CHURCH

NT 257 734

41 George IV Bridge, Edinburgh

Built 1857-61 by J J M & W H Hay with Romanesque, Renaissance and Classical elements for the congregation of the second Scottish Congregational Church in Edinburgh. The projecting centre of the gable front is carried up as the 'bride's-cake' tower which is topped by a spire of three diminishing octagonal stages. Composite hammerbeam and kingpost roof. The Bradford computer organ 1994 uses the pipes and case of the former Ingram organ 1929. Major alterations to interior, to plans by Stewart Tod and Partners 1995. Two stained glass windows by Robert Burns, formerly in the gallery, now at ground-floor level. Now, with the meger of several congregations, a member of the United Reformed Church. Sunday Service: 11.00am; Holy Communion first and third Sundays

Church website: www.augustine.org.uk

Open by arrangement, telephone 0131 220 1677

or e-mail auc@augustine.org.uk

UNITED REFORMED ② 👤 wc **B**

AUGUSTINE UNITED CHURCH

378 EDINBURGH SEVENTH-DAY ADVENTIST CHURCH

NT 258 732
3 Bristo Place, Edinburgh
A red sandstone building, by Sydney Mitchell &
Wilson 1900, this church is unusual in having its
sanctuary on the first floor. The rather handsome
staircase is flanked by a tiled wall. The sanctuary
interior is well lit by four large windows looking onto
the street. Pulpit and furnishings in pine; two
galleries, one of which houses a pipe organ by Gray
& Davison 1900. Services: Saturday 10.00am (Bible
Study) and 11.15am (Worship Service)
*Open by arrangement, telephone Pastor Dr Claude Lombart
01883 729432, mobile 07939 263660. Secretary:
Ms Audrey Ogilvie 01383 822343, mobile 07909 573557
Edinburgh Fringe Festival Venue, August*
SEVENTH-DAY ADVENTIST

EDINBURGH SEVENTH-DAY
ADVENTIST CHURCH

379 GREYFRIARS TOLBOOTH & HIGHLAND KIRK

NT 256 734
Greyfriars Place, Edinburgh
The first post-Reformation church built in Edinburgh 1620, altered 1722, 1858,
1938 and 1990. The National Covenant signed here in 1638. Fine 19th-century
coloured glass by Ballantine, and Peter Collins organ 1990. Historic kirkyard,
former Franciscan Friary garden, has fine examples of 17th-century monuments,
the Martyrs' Monument, Covenanters' Prison and memorial to Greyfriars Bobby.
South end of George IV Bridge. City buses 2, 12, 23, 24, 27, 28, 29, 40, 42, 45, 47.
Sunday Services: 11.00am and 12.30pm (Gaelic), first Sunday of month Holy
Communion 9.15am; Thursdays all year Lunchtime Service with organ
music 1.10-1.30pm
*Open April to October, Monday to Friday
10.30am-4.30pm, Saturday 10.30am-
2.30pm, November to March, Thursday
1.30-3.30pm. Churchyard open all year
Monday to Friday 8.00am-6.00pm,
Saturday and Sunday 10.00am-4.00pm.
Special events: year round programme of
concerts and lectures (programme available).
Tours for groups, telephone Visitors Officer
0131 226 5429*
CHURCH OF SCOTLAND
(by arrangement) **A**

GREYFRIARS TOLBOOTH
& HIGHLAND KIRK

380 MAGDALEN CHAPEL

NT 256 734

41 Cowgate, Edinburgh

The chapel was built in 1541 by Michael McQuhane and his wife Janet Rhynd. Its main features are the medieval stained glass roundels. The panelling records gifts from members of the Incorporation of Hammermen who were patrons of the chapel until 1862. The chapel is now owned by the Scottish Reformation Society and serves as its headquarters

Open Monday to Friday 9.30am-4.00pm.

Other times by arrangement. Parties welcome, telephone

Rev A S Horne 0131 220 1450

INTER-DENOMINATIONAL  **A**

MAGDALEN CHAPEL

381 OLD ST PAUL'S

NT 260 737

Jeffrey Street, Edinburgh

The hidden gem of the Old Town. Dating from 1884, Hay & Henderson. Entrances in Carrubber's Close and Jeffrey Street give little clue to the splendour within. Historic Episcopal church with Jacobite past has magnificent furnishings. A living church with daily worship and a prayerful atmosphere. Off Royal Mile. Sunday Services: Holy Eucharist 8.00am, 10.30am and 5.00pm; Evensong 6.30pm; daily Worship 12.20pm

Open daily, 9.00am-6.00pm

SCOTTISH EPISCOPAL **B**

OLD ST PAUL'S

382 CANONGATE KIRK

NT 265 738

Canongate, Royal Mile, Edinburgh

This interesting and recently restored 17th-century church was opened in 1691, its plan by James Smith being unique among 17th-century Scottish churches. Restored in 1991, Stewart Tod Partnership. The churchyard contains the remains of many famous Scots, including economist Adam Smith. 'Open Kirk' information sheets in several languages. New Frobenius organ Opus 1000, first in Scotland. On the Royal Mile, opposite Huntly House Museum. Sunday Services: Family Service 10.00am, Parish Worship 11.15am

Open mid-June to mid-September, Monday to Saturday, 10.30am-4.30pm. Churchyard open all year

CHURCH OF SCOTLAND  **A**

CANONGATE KIRK

383 ST ANDREW'S AND ST GEORGE'S PARISH CHURCH

NT 255 741

George Street, Edinburgh

This beautiful elliptical church with its delicate spire and Adam-style plaster ceiling
has been described as the architectural gem of the New Town. Built in 1784,
designed by Major Andrew Frazer. Two fine 20th-century stained glass windows, one
by Douglas Strachan (1875-1950), the other by Alfred Webster (1884-1915). Organ by
Wells-Kennedy, 1984. Light lunches in undercroft. At the east end of George Street
and one block north of Princes Street. Sunday Services: 9.00am (Communion),
9.45am, 11.00am; weekday Prayers: 1.00pm (Communion Service: Tuesday)

Church website: www.standrewsandstgeorges.org.uk

Open all year, Monday to Friday 10.00am-3.00pm. Undercroft open 12.00-2.00pm,
telephone 0131 225 3847/fax 0131 225 5921. Special Edinburgh Festival programme of
events. Week-long Christian Aid book sale in May

CHURCH OF SCOTLAND ⑦ 📖 ☕ ⓘ 📶 A

384 BROUGHTON ST MARY'S PARISH CHURCH

NT 256 748

12 Bellevue Crescent, Edinburgh

A burgh church, built to serve Edinburgh's spreading New
Town. Designed in 1824 by Thomas Brown as centrepiece of
Bellevue Crescent. Neo-classical style, graceful interior with
fluted Corinthian columns supporting gallery. Unaltered organ
by Lewis, 1882, recently restored. Original pulpit. Nathaniel
Bryson's stained glass 'Annunciation' is of particular note.
Robert Stevenson, lighthouse builder and grandfather of

BROUGHTON ST MARY'S
PARISH CHURCH

Robert Louis Stevenson, elder 1828-43. Ten to fifteen minutes walk from east end of
Princes Street. City buses 8, 17 to Bellevue Crescent. Sunday Service: 10.30am

Church website: www.broughtonstmarys.org.uk

Open May to September, Wednesday 10.00am-12.00 noon, and Monday to Saturday during
the first week of the Edinburgh Festival in August 10.00am-4.00pm

CHURCH OF SCOTLAND ⑦ ⓘ 📖 ☕ 📶 A

385 ST STEPHEN'S CENTRE

NT 250 746

St Vincent Street, Edinburgh

Built 1828 as St Stephen's Church, this is the ecclesiastical masterpiece of W H
Playfair. Severe Greek detail but Baroque in spirit, with a large tower dominating
the vista from Queen Street downhill through the northern New Town. Interior
recast in 1956 when a floor was inserted at the level of the former gallery whose
cast-iron Egyptian columns were retained. Outstanding original example of an
organ by 'Father' Willis. Built 1880. No Services

Open Monday to Friday 9.00am-9.00pm, telephone Development Officer,

David Nicholson 0131 556 2661

CHURCH OF SCOTLAND 📖 ☕

386 PALMERSTON PLACE CHURCH

NT 241 734
Palmerston Place, Edinburgh
Inspiration for Peddie & Kinnear's design of 1875
came from the 17th-century St Sulpice in Paris. A
notable feature is the central ceiling motif of a dove
within a sunburst. Wells Kennedy organ, 1991,
incorporates the oak case of the earlier 1902 organ.
Meeting place for the Presbytery of Edinburgh and
the Synod of the Scottish Episcopal Church. Sunday
Services: 11.00am, 6.30pm (except July and August)
Church website: www.palmerstonplacechurch.com
Open by arrangement, telephone 0131 220 1690
CHURCH OF SCOTLAND [wc] 🦻 **B**

PALMERSTON
PLACE CHURCH

387 ST GEORGE'S WEST CHURCH

NT 245 736
Shandwick Place, Edinburgh
Designed by David Bryce 1869 with campanile by
Sir R Rowand Anderson 1881. Special features are the rose
window and the pulpit. Woodwork excellent, mainly original.
The organ by Thomas Lewis 1897. The first organist was
Alfred Hollins, famous blind organist and composer (1897-
1942). City Centre West End. Sunday Services: 11.00am and
7.00pm; Prayers: Monday to Friday 1.00pm
*Busy Church Centre and café open Monday to Friday 10.00am-
3.30pm; Saturday 10.30am-12.30pm, all year*
CHURCH OF SCOTLAND [♿] 📖 🦻 ☕ [wc] **B**

ST GEORGE'S
WEST CHURCH

388 ST JOHN THE EVANGELIST

NT 247 736
Princes Street, Edinburgh
St John's Edinburgh, is one of architect William Burn's finest
early 19th-century buildings and is known for having perhaps
the finest collection of stained glass in the country. Organ
originally by 'Father' Willis, 1901. In addition to daily worship in
the church, it also houses a vibrant community including One
World Shop, Cornerstone Bookshop, Peace and Justice Centre
and Cornerstone Café. Sunday Services: Holy Communion
8.00am, Sung Eucharist 9.45am, Choral Matins 11.15am, Choral
Evensong 6.00pm, Eucharist with music from Taizé 8.00pm;
weekday Service: 1pm; Communion Service: Wednesday 11.00am
Church website: www.stjohns-edinburgh.org.uk
Open 8.00am-4.15pm each weekday, 9.00am-12.00noon on Saturday
SCOTTISH EPISCOPAL [♿] 🦻 🚻 📖 ☕ (Cornerstone Café) [wc] **A**

ST JOHN THE
EVANGELIST

THE PARISH CHURCH ,OF ST CUTHBERT

389   THE PARISH CHURCH OF ST CUTHBERT

NT 248 736

Lothian Road, Edinburgh

The present church, the seventh on the site, is over 100 years old, 1894 by Hippolyte
Blanc, retaining the 1790 spire. Altered in 1990, Stewart Tod. Tradition has it that St
Cuthbert had a cell church here. If so, Christian worship has taken place here for
1300 years. Furnishings include scroll-topped and Renaissance-style stalls, marble
communion table, murals and stained glass window by Tiffany. Fine organ originally
by Hope-Jones 1899, rebuilt 1928, 1957 and 1997. Display of life of St Cuthbert in
vestibule. Interesting graveyard, with many famous names, is an oasis in the centre of
the city. Gift shop and refreshments. Buses to Princes Street and Lothian Road.
Sunday Services: 9.30am, 11.00am and 6.30pm (Service of Healing)

Church website: www.st-cuthberts.net

Open 28 April to 5 September, Monday to Saturday 10.00am-4.00pm,

CHURCH OF SCOTLAND 🦽 📖 ② 🧍 🧍 wc ☕ **A**

390   EDINBURGH METHODIST MISSION

NT 248 730

Central Hall, 2 West Tollcross, Edinburgh

1901 by Dunn & Findlay, Edinburgh. Several alterations have been made to suit the
changing needs of the congregation. Main hall has a curved and ribbed ceiling on
arches rising from Ionic columns. Leaded windows of clear 'cathedral' glass
embellished in the style of Glasgow Art Nouveau. Lower landings are decorated
with mosaic tiles. A well-known venue for concerts, conferences and meetings. Half-
mile south of Princes Street west end, via Lothian Road. LRT buses 10, 11, 15-18,
23, 24, 27, 45, 47. Sunday Services: 11.00am

Open Monday to Friday 9.00am-10.00pm. Venue for the National Association of Youth
Orchestras during Edinburgh Festival, daily performances

METHODIST 🦽 (lift access via Dunbar Street) ② wc **B**

391 BARCLAY CHURCH

NT 249 726
Bruntsfield Place, Tollcross, Edinburgh
1864 in powerful Ruskinian Gothic, this is
Frederick T Pilkington's greatest
achievement. Spire 230ft is well-known
landmark. Spectacular theatrical space
within with double gallery. Painted ceiling.
Organ originally by Hope-Jones,
reconstructed by Lewis. Removal of centre
and other pews in sanctuary with other
minor alterations and the installation of
spiral staircases to the first gallery 1999,
by Gray, Marshall Associates of Edinburgh.
One hundred metres south of King's
Theatre.
Sunday Services: 11.00am and 6.30pm
*Open by arrangement, telephone church office 0131
229 6810 (afternoons)*
CHURCH OF SCOTLAND ♿ ⊘ 👤 📖 ☕ WC **A**

BARCLAY CHURCH

392 ST MICHAEL'S AND ALL SAINTS' CHURCH

NT 251 729
Brougham Street, Edinburgh
A shrine of the Anglo-Catholic movement in Scotland. The church was mostly built
in 1867 but the west end not completed until 1876 and the Lady Chapel added in
1897, all to designs by R Rowand Anderson. Austere Gothic externally but the
interior is a magnificently spacious setting for a sumptuous display of furnishings,
including an elaborate Spanish pulpit of c.1600, carved and painted altarpieces by
William Burges 1867, and Hamilton More-Nisbet 1901, and a huge high altar
reredos, again carved and painted, by C E Kempe 1889. Extensive collection of
stained glass with windows by Wailes, Clayton & Bell, Kempe, and Sir Ninian
Comper. Organ originally by Forster & Andrews, installed in 1992.
Sunday Services: Low Mass 8.00am, High Mass 11.00am, Choral Evensong and
Benediction 6.30pm; Tuesday: Low Mass 8.00am; Wednesday: Low Mass 12.30pm;
Thursday: Low Mass 6.00pm; Friday: Low Mass 10.30am; Saturday: Low Mass
12.30pm
*Open all year Wednesday 12.00 noon-2.30pm, Friday 10.00am-2.00pm,
Saturdays during Edinburgh Festival, and by arrangement, telephone the Rector
0131 229 6368*
SCOTTISH EPISCOPAL ♿ 📖 WC ☕ (Saturdays during Edinburgh Festival) **A**

393 SACRED HEART CHURCH

NT 252 730
28 Lauriston Place, Edinburgh
Stone-fronted building designed by Father Richard
Vaughan SJ 1860, altered by Archibald Macpherson 1884.
Holyrood Madonna of carved wood, probably late 16th
century. Stations of the Cross by Peter Rauth 1874. Organ
originally constructed by Hamilton of Edinburgh, 1874,
rebuilt, 1907, by Scovell (who also designed the pulpit).
A gift of fine oak panelling from St Margaret's Convent
(now Gillis Centre) has enabled the Choir Loft to be
greatly enhanced. Restoration and conservation completed
in December 2002. Buses to Tollcross. Masses: Saturday
Vigil 6.30pm; Sunday 7.45am, 11.45am, and 8.00pm
Church website: www.rc.net/standed/sacredheart
Open every day
ROMAN CATHOLIC 🚹 ⏺ 📖 🚾 ⛪ **B**

SACRED HEART CHURCH

394 ST ANDREW'S ORTHODOX CHAPEL

NT 257 728
23a George Square, Edinburgh
Built in 1779 as a one-storey and basement villa across
the centre lane on the west side of George Square. Large
Venetian window faces onto George Square. Orthodox
furnishings and icons. Services: daily 6.30pm, Sunday
and Feasts 9.00am Matins, and Liturgy 10.30am
Church website: www.edinburgh.orthodox.org.uk
Open by arrangement, telephone Archimandrite
John Maitland-Moir 0131 667 0372
ORTHODOX 🚾 📖 ☕ **A**

ST ANDREW'S ORTHODOX CHAPEL

395 NICOLSON SQUARE METHODIST CHURCH

NT 261 732
Nicolson Square, Edinburgh
By Thomas Brown 1815 set diagonally across the corner of the square behind a
forecourt. Classical two-storey front based on Adam's design for the west block of
the university. Inside, fluted cast-iron columns support the U-plan gallery.
Substantial modernisation 1972. Organ by Forster & Andrews of Hull dating from
1864. Interesting modern chapel in basement created in 1989 by Nira Ponniah.
Small public garden at rear. Sunday Services: 11.00am and 6.30pm
Church website: www.nicsquare.freeserve.co.uk
Open Monday to Friday 9.30am-3.30pm. Fringe performances during Edinburgh Festival,
and concerts at other times
METHODIST 🚹 ⏺ 📖 ☕ (café in basement) 🚾 **A**

396 BUCCLEUCH & GREYFRIARS FREE CHURCH

NT 261 728

West Crosscauseway (off Nicolson Street)
Built 1857 by Hays of Liverpool in Gothic style
for the Free Buccleuch congregation established
at the 1843 Disruption. The congregation has
sought to remain true to the original Free Church
vision of reformed theology and evangelical
outreach. One of the largest hammerbeam roofs
in the country and an impressive spire. Services:
Sunday 11.00am and 6.30pm; Wednesday 7.30pm
Open by arrangement with the Minister,
telephone 0131 664 6306
FREE CHURCH OF SCOTLAND 🦽 ⟢ wc **A**

BUCCLEUCH & GREYFRIARS
FREE CHURCH

397 KIRK O' FIELD PARISH CHURCH

NT 264 732

140 Pleasance, Edinburgh
Built as Charteris Memorial Church in 1912. Late Scots Gothic by James B Dunn.
Lorimerian vine enrichment on the vestibule ceiling. Wagon-roofed nave with west
gallery. Memorial to the Rev A H Charteris 1908. Mission Hall 1891 dedicated to
St Ninian. City buses 2, 21. Sunday Service: 11.00am
Open the first Saturday in September, 10.00am-1.00pm
CHURCH OF SCOTLAND ⟢ ⫯ ▯ ☕ wc

398 ST COLUMBA'S CHURCH, NEWINGTON

NT 265 721

9 Upper Gray Street, Edinburgh
A free treatment of the classic Renaissance style by
R M Cameron 1888. West façade has a large semi-
circular window and pedimented gable finished
with a plain Latin cross. Oblong interior with
open timber roof and semi-circular end forming a
chancel and apse. The chancel arch is a later
addition. Notable features include a collection of
statues in the window niches. Extensive natural
lighting from roof lights and west window. 2-
manual pipe organ by Matthew Copley, 1997.
Masses: Monday-Friday 9.30am; Saturday 11.00am;
Sunday 11.00am and 6.30pm
Open after Masses, or by arrangement with the
Parish Priest, telephone 0131 667 1605
ROMAN CATHOLIC

wc wc (toilet adapted in church hall) ⟢ **B**

ST COLUMBA'S CHURCH, NEWINGTON

399 BLACKHALL UNITED FREE CHURCH

NT 216 750
1 House o' Hill Road, Edinburgh
Modern church completed in 1968.
A90 at the junction between
Telford Road and Queensferry
Road. LRT buses 32, 52 and 41a,
SMT 43.
Sunday Service: 11.00am
UNITED FREE CHURCH OF SCOTLAND
wc

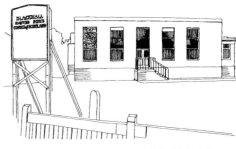

BLACKHALL UNITED FREE CHURCH

400 REID MEMORIAL CHURCH

NT 261 710
West Savile Terrace, Edinburgh
Church, hall and church officer's house by Leslie G Thomson 1933 form an
architectural oasis. A lofty, cruciform church with meticulous neo-Perpendicular
detail. Stained glass windows by James Ballantine, pipe organ Rushworth &
Dreaper, painting on reredos of 'Last Supper' by William R Lawson. Cloister court
to rear with carved panel of 'Christ at the well of Samaria' by Alexander Carrick.
On local bus routes 24, 38, 38a and 41.
Sunday Services: 10.30am and first Sunday of month 6.30pm
Open 12.30-3.00pm on Fridays during Edinburgh Festival, also open by arrangement,
telephone Henry Philip 0131 662 1494. Organ recitals at 1.10pm
CHURCH OF SCOTLAND ♿ ⊘ 🗋 ⛲ wc **A**

REID MEMORIAL CHURCH

CARRICK KNOWE PARISH CHURCH

401 CARRICK KNOWE PARISH CHURCH

NT 203 721

Saughton Road North, Edinburgh

Built in 1953, and described as of Norman design with a strong Scottish character. The last post-war church to be built of stone – the external walls of Blaxter dressed stone, and Darney rubble, both from Northumberland Quarries. Furnishings in Scottish Border oak, commissioned by the Church of Scotland as part of their exhibit for the Empire Exhibition in Glasgow of 1938 – beautiful examples of ecclesiastical craftsmanship. Baptismal bowl gifted by Her Majesty Queen Elizabeth The Queen Mother. Tapestry, Dovecot Studios, Edinburgh. Organ installed by Ronald Smith 1973. Opposite Union Park. Buses 1 and 6.

Sunday Service: 11.00am

Open every morning except Wednesday 9.30am-12.00 noon

CHURCH OF SCOTLAND   🦽 ⚲ 📖 ⓓ ☕ **A**

402 ST TERESA OF LISIEUX

NT 295 716

120 Niddrie Mains Road

Octagonal church with pebble-dashed walls, green copper roof topped by a cross. Designed by architect Charles W Gray, it was opened in 1962. Stone statue of St Teresa above the main entrance. Pipe organ. Redecorated 2002. In the weekday chapel is a copy of the San Damiano crucifix, a reminder that the church has been staffed since its opening by Franciscan Friars. Services: Monday-Friday 6.55am, 9.30am; Saturday 10.00am, Vigil 6.00pm; Sunday 10.30am

Open for services and by arrangement, telephone 0131 661 2185

ROMAN CATHOLIC   🦽 wc

403   THE ROBIN CHAPEL

NT 295 715

Thistle Foundation, Niddrie Mains Road
Memorial to Robin Tudsbery, killed in the
last days of the Second World War, built by
Architect John F Matthew 1950, at the
centre of a housing complex for physically
disabled people and their families. Peaceful
and secluded interior enhanced by stone
capitals carved by Maxwell Adam, wood
carvings by Thomas Good, wrought-iron
work by James Finnegan and stained glass
by Sadie McLellan.
Sunday Service: 4.30pm
Open by arrangement with the Chaplain,
telephone 0131 661 3366
NON-DENOMINATIONAL [&] (?) [wc] **A**

THE ROBIN CHAPEL

404   ST CHRISTOPHER'S

NT 292 748

Craigentinny Road, Edinburgh
Built by James McLachlan in 1934-38, the foundation stone was laid by John
Buchan, author of *The Thirty Nine Steps*. The exterior is of variegated red brick
with round arched windows and tiled roof. The interior is a darker plum-coloured
brick with a low wagon roof and segmental arches. The organ, Ingram 1900, came
from St Catherine's Argyll and was installed here in 1969. There are two stained
glass windows by Sax Shaw and one by George Reid. Sunday Service: 10.30am;
Communion on last Sunday in January, March, June and October.
Short Communion after Family Services on the first Sunday of the month
Open Saturday 10.00am-12.00 noon Tuesdays and Saturdays, and by arrangement,
telephone Mr R Mutch 0131 669 6735
CHURCH OF SCOTLAND (?) [wc]

ST CHRISTOPHER'S

405   COLINTON PARISH CHURCH (ST CUTHBERT'S)

NT 216 692

Dell Road, Edinburgh, at foot of Colinton village, beside Water of Leith.

The church of 1650 was rebuilt in 1771 and enlarged by David Bryce in 1837. Sydney Mitchell transformed the building in a neo-Byzantine style between 1907 and 1908. The angel-decorated, barrel-vaulted nave is supported on sandstone columns. Mitchell adorned the semi-circular apse with murals and fine woodwork including the pulpit, communion table and rood-screen. Both the latter and the marble font are beautifully inscribed. To the south of the church, Page and Park have built new rooms which, through their contemporary design, embrace the wonderful woodland setting. The Offertory House of 1807 heralds this most interesting of buildings with its ancient graveyard set within a bend of the Water of Leith. Sunday Services: 9.30 and 11.15am

COLINTON PARISH CHURCH
(ST CUTHBERT'S)

Church website: www.colintonparish.org

Open Monday to Friday 9.00am-4.00pm. Swing Café – open for morning coffee and light lunches, Monday to Friday 10.00am-2.00pm. Contact the church office, telephone 0131 441 2232

CHURCH OF SCOTLAND ♿ ⊘ ☕ ⚞wc⚟ **B**

406   CORSTORPHINE OLD PARISH CHURCH

NT 201 728

Kirk Loan, Corstorphine, Edinburgh

Interesting 15th-century church with tower, pre-Reformation relics, Scottish heraldic panels and fine medieval tombs, including those of the founders Sir Adam Forrester, Lord Provost of Edinburgh (died 1405) and Sir John Forrester, Lord Chamberlain of Scotland in the reign of James I. Fine Victorian stained glass. Interesting gravestones in churchyard. Sunday Services: 10.00am and 11.30am

Open Wednesdays 10.30am-12.00 noon, except December and January. Coincides with opening of Dower House (Corstorphine Trust) during summer

CHURCH OF SCOTLAND ♿ (partial) ⚱ ⛪ 📖 ⊘ **A**

CORSTORPHINE OLD
PARISH CHURCH

407 CORSTORPHINE UNITED FREE CHURCH

NT 199 727

Glebe Terrace, Corstorphine (off St John's Road, opposite Harp Hotel)
Intimate, secluded, friendly little church. Various ante-rooms and large hall, with
new modern kitchen. Good grassed area for barbecues. Sunday Service: 10.30am
Open by appointment, telephone Pastor George Banks 0131 552 3666
UNITED FREE CHURCH OF SCOTLAND

408 CRAMOND KIRK

NT 190 768

Cramond Glebe Road, Edinburgh
A cruciform kirk of 1656 with 15th-century tower. Interior altered 1701, 1811, large
reconstruction 1911 by Donald McArthy and James Mather. Pitch pine
hammerbeam roof, oak furnishings, white marble font. Burgerhuys bell 1619. Jock
Howieson mosaic. Plan of kirkyard available. Roman settlement remains. Off
Whitehouse Road. City buses 40 and 41/41A.
Sunday Services: 9.30 and 11.00am, July and August 10.00am
Church website: www.cramondkirk.org.uk
Open daily during Edinburgh Festival 2.00-5.00pm. Cramond Village exhibition
at the Maltings
CHURCH OF SCOTLAND   **B**

409 DALMENY PARISH CHURCH (ST CUTHBERT'S)

NT 144 775

Main Street, Dalmeny, near South Queensferry
The most complete example of
Romanesque architecture in
Scotland. Dates from c.1130.
Superb medieval south doorway,
arch stones elaborately carved
with animals, figures and
grotesque heads. Historic
graveyard. Pipe organ by
Lammermuir 1984. Off A90,
follow signs for Dalmeny and
South Queensferry.
Sunday Service: 11.30am
Open April to September, Sunday
2.00-4.30pm. Other times, key from
the Post Office, or 5 Main Street.
Parties please telephone Mr W Ross
in advance 0131 331 1479
CHURCH OF SCOTLAND
A

DALMENY PARISH CHURCH
(ST CUTHBERT'S)

410 DAVIDSON'S MAINS PARISH CHURCH

NT 207 752

1 Quality Street, off Queensferry Road

Originally Cramond Free Church. A small T-plan kirk with flat Gothic windows by David Cousin 1843. The timber bellcote with a prickly slated hat was added to the centre gable in 1866. Interior enlarged to the north in 1970. Major refurbishment to the chancel area in 1999. To the east the little school and house by Robert R

DAVIDSON'S MAINS PARISH CHURCH

Raeburn 1846 were extended with a hall by Auldjo Jamieson & Arnott 1933 maintaining the domestic scale by means of a dormered roof. Fully refurbished in 1995. Essentially a village church. Sunday Services: 10.30am and 6.30pm

Church website: www.davidsonsmainsparishchurch.org.uk

Open Tuesday to Thursday 10.00am-2.00pm

CHURCH OF SCOTLAND

411 DUDDINGSTON KIRK

NT 284 726

Old Church Lane, Duddingston Village, Edinburgh

Attractive 12th-century church, situated beside Duddingston Loch bird sanctuary, south of Arthur's Seat. Dr Neil's garden lies adjacent in the church glebe land. During the ministry of the Rev John Thomson 1804-40 (himself a noted landscape painter), the English painter Turner and the Scottish writer Sir Walter Scott both visited the manse. City bus 42/46 to Duddingston Road. Sunday Services: 10.00am and 11.30am

Open June to September, Saturday 11.00am-5.00pm, Sunday 2.00-5.00pm

CHURCH OF SCOTLAND   A

DUDDINGSTON KIRK

412 ST BARNABAS EPISCOPAL CHURCH

NT 290 693

4 Moredun Park View, Edinburgh

Small modern church in housing scheme 1950. Altered in 1969. St Barnabas tapestry. Moredun Scheme is between A7 and A772 on south side of city. Sunday Service: Eucharist 10.30am; Tuesday: Prayer Group 6.30pm

Open Wednesday mornings

SCOTTISH EPISCOPAL   A

GREENBANK PARISH CHURCH

413 GREENBANK PARISH CHURCH

NT 243 702

Braidburn Terrace / Comiston Road

Founded in 1900 as the last United Presbyterian congregation in Edinburgh.
Original building now used as halls. The present Gothic-style church (A Lorne
Campbell 1927) is an early example of reinforced concrete construction, with stone
cladding. Furnishings to Campbell's designs by Scott Morton & Co. Current
scheme of decoration by Sir William Kininmonth. Organ by A E Ingram 1927,
rebuilt R L Smith 1972. Stained glass by James Ballantine, Alexander Strachan (2),
William Wilson (3). Pulpit falls by Archibald Brennan, Penelope Beaton and
Malcolm Lochhead. New suite of halls by Lee Boyd Partnership 2001.
Sunday Services: 10.30am all year plus 9.30am September to May and 1st Sunday,
June to August 9.30am

Church website: www.greenbankchurch.org

Open by arrangement, telephone the Minister 0131 447 4032

CHURCH OF SCOTLAND ⬦ wc ⏺ ☕ (after service)

414 GREENSIDE PARISH CHURCH

NT 263 745

Royal Terrace, Edinburgh

T-plan design by Gillespie Graham 1839 with
tower added in 1851, set amidst Playfair's great
terraces. Connections with Robert Louis Stevenson
who knew it as 'the church on the hill'. Pipe
organ, rebuilt here by Ingram 1933. Off London
Road. Sunday Services: 11.00am and 6.30pm
(no evening service July and August)

Open by arrangement, telephone the

Session Clerk 0131 669 5324

CHURCH OF SCOTLAND ⏺ wc **B**

GREENSIDE PARISH CHURCH

415 ST PHILIP'S, JOPPA

NT 313 736

Abercorn Terrace, Joppa, Edinburgh

A really striking edifice in the Early Decorated style by J Honeyman 1877. Ravaged by fire 1998 and fully restored. Broach spire 170ft over a lofty belfry. Aisled nave with entry in the south gable. Inside, a remarkably complete interior. Clustered piers with leafy capitals support the nave arcade, foliated corbels on the clerestorey support the wood-lined tunnel-roof. Fine stained glass windows to aisles.

Sunday Service: 11.00am

Open by arrangement, telephone Mr Lockhart 0131 669 3641

CHURCH OF SCOTLAND   ♿ ② wc **B**

416 KIRKLISTON PARISH CHURCH

NT 125 744

The Square, Kirkliston

Mainly 12th-century church. Two Norman archways, the largest of which was blocked up in the 19th century. Two beautiful modern stained glass windows. Organ by Ingram of Edinburgh 1925. In the 19th century a small watchtower was built in the graveyard where the earliest identifiable stone is dated 1529.

Sunday Service: 11.00am

Open by arrangement, telephone Mrs Keating 0131 333 3298, or Mrs Brechin 0131 333 3252

CHURCH OF SCOTLAND   ♿ ② 🍴 📖 wc **A**

KIRKLISTON PARISH CHURCH

417 EBENEZER UNITED FREE CHURCH, LEITH

NT 266 764

31 Bangor Road, Leith

The Ebenezer congregation was founded in 1891. The original church building in Great Junction Street was demolished in 1979 to make way for new housing. The present building, by Sir Frank Mears & Partners, was opened in 1984. Bangor Road runs south from Great Junction Street in Leith.

Sunday Services: 11.00am and 6.30pm

Open first Saturday of each month, 10.00am-12.00 noon

UNITED FREE CHURCH OF SCOTLAND   ♿ wc

EBENEZER UNITED FREE CHURCH, LEITH

418 LEITH METHODIST CHURCH

NT 268 761
1 Junction Place, Leith
Built 1932 by Maclennan & Cunningham as 600-seater Central Hall in artificial
stone and harl on site of former Secession Church. In Methodist use from 1868.
Horizontally subdivided in 1987 with flexible worship area upstairs and
community centre downstairs. Off Great Junction Street, behind McKenzie-Millar.
Sunday Service: 11.00am
Open weekdays, except Wednesday 10.00am-2.00pm, Saturday 10.00am-12.00 noon
METHODIST   **A**

419 NORTH LEITH PARISH CHURCH

NT 263 765
Madeira Street, Leith
Georgian building designed by William
Burn 1816. Renovated by Ian G Lindsay &
Partners 1950, and Stewart Tod & Partners
1993. Impressive two-storey 'country house'
front. Light interior with galleries supported
by Ionic columns. Stained glass James
Ballantine. 3-manual pipe organ, built by
Wadsworth of Manchester 1880. Small
graveyard and garden. Off Ferry Road, close
to Leith Library. Sunday Services: 11.00am
all year, 6.30pm (excluding July and August)
Church website: www.northleith.freeserve.co.uk
Open by arrangement, telephone the
church office 0131 553 7378
CHURCH OF SCOTLAND   **A**

NORTH LEITH PARISH CHURCH

420 SOUTH LEITH PARISH CHURCH

NT 271 761
Kirkgate or Constitution Street, Leith
A church was erected in 1483 as a chapel attached to the collegiate Church of
Restalrig. The present building dates from 1847, built to a design by Thomas
Hamilton. Tower and porch incorporate coats of arms of four successive Scottish
monarchs. Fine hammerbeam roof. Italian marble pulpit. Stained glass and emblems
of the Trade Guilds. Organ by Brindley & Foster 1887. Set in ancient graveyard
with interesting monuments. At the foot of Leith Walk.
Sunday Services: 11.00am, also 6.30pm October to May, and 9.30am June to July
Church website: www.slpc.co.uk
Open Thursdays 12.30-1.30pm. Other times by arrangement, telephone 0131 554 2578
CHURCH OF SCOTLAND   **A**

SOUTH LEITH PARISH CHURCH

421   ST MARY, STAR OF THE SEA, LEITH

NT 272 762

106 Constitution Street, Edinburgh

E W Pugin and Joseph A Hansom's church of 1854 had no chancel, no north aisle and was orientated to the west. The north aisle was added in 1900 and the chancel in 1912 when the church was turned round and the present west entrance made. Inside, the church has simple pointed arcades and a high braced collar roof. Organ originally by Brindley & Foster 1897. Access from Constitution Street or New Kirkgate. Services: Monday to Friday 10am; Saturday 10am and Vigil Mass 6.00pm; Sunday 10.00am and 11.30am

Open Monday to Friday 9.00-11.00am, Saturday 9.00-11.30am,

Sunday 9.00am-12.30pm

ROMAN CATHOLIC ♿ ⟳ wc **B**

ST MARY, STAR OF THE SEA, LEITH

422 LIBERTON KIRK

NT 275 700

Kirkgate, Liberton, Edinburgh

Sitting in a commanding position overlooking the city, a church was founded here in 1143 by David I, although there is evidence of an earlier church dating from AD 800. The present building was erected in 1815 to replace former church sites. Designed by James Gillespie Graham, it is a rectangular semi-Gothic building with corbelled parapet tower and thin pinnacles. A memorial stained glass window depicting Cornelius, by Ballantine 1905. Three striking contemporary pulpit falls and four outstanding wall hangings by D Morrison. The kirkyard contains many stones of special interest, including a table-top tomb to a local farmer, its ends carved in relief with agricultural scenes.

Sunday Services: 9.30am and 11.00am (10.30am, July and August)

Church website: www.libertonkirk.freeserve.co.uk

Open Monday to Friday 9am-5pm by arrangement, telephone Mrs W Munro 0131 664 3795

CHURCH OF SCOTLAND ♿ ⓘ 🚪 wc **A**

423 LIBERTON NORTHFIELD PARISH CHURCH

NT 280 699

280 Gilmerton Road, Edinburgh

Built 1869 as a Free Church to designs by J W Smith. North-east tower and broach spire added by Peddie & Kinnear 1873. Interior with raked floor and an ornate arch-braced timber roof springing from short ashlar colonnettes with a variety of leafy capitals. Transepts entered by triple arches expressed on the exterior by triple gables. Virtually unaltered organ by E F Walcker 1903. Sunday Services: 11.00am and 6.30pm

Open by arrangement, telephone Rev John McPake

0131 658 1754. Flower Festival weekend, late September

CHURCH OF SCOTLAND wc **B**

LIBERTON NORTHFIELD
PARISH CHURCH

424 MAYFIELD SALISBURY CHURCH

NT 266 717

West Mayfield

Originally built as Mayfield Free Kirk 1897, this is a fine example of the French Gothic style of Hippolyte Blanc. Spire 48ft added 1894. Magnificent collection of stained glass by Ballantine & Gardiner, Charles L Davidson, Henry Dearl of Morris & Co, Guthrie & Wells and William Meikle. Church House, orginally the manse, now houses the Mayfield Radio Unit which broadcasts to hospitals in the Edinburgh area. Sunday Services: 10.30am and 6.30pm September to June; 9.30am, 10.30am and 8.00pm July to August

Open weekdays 9.00am-4.00pm, except Wednesdays, Saturday 9.00am-12.00 noon (coffee)

CHURCH OF SCOTLAND ♿ ⓘ wc **B**

425 CHRIST CHURCH, MORNINGSIDE

NT 245 719

Holy Corner, Bruntsfield, Edinburgh

French Gothic by Hippolyte Blanc, a member of the congregation, 1876. Gables and flying buttresses face onto the road; the main entrance is beneath the tower. Original murals in chancel and nave roof. Extensive stained glass by Ballantine. Sunday Services: Holy Communion 8.00am, Sung Eucharist 10.00am, Evensong (winter) 6.30pm, Compline (summer) 9.00pm; Monday to Friday: Morning Prayer and Eucharist 8.00am; Thursday: Holy Communion 11.00am

Church website: www.christchurchedinburgh.org.uk

Open 11.00am-3.00pm Wednesday and Friday

SCOTTISH EPISCOPAL wc ☺ ⓘ **B**

426 ERIC LIDDELL CENTRE

NT 246 719

15 Morningside Road, Holy Corner

Former North Morningside Church of Scotland in neo-Norman by David Robertson 1879-81. Dramatic intervention by Nicholas Groves-Raines 1992 and 1999 for conversion to Eric Liddell Centre which provides community services and accommodation for organisations of Christian witness. Galleries provide viewing of impressive collection of stained glass, including windows by William Wilson and John Duncan. Chinese Evangelical Church Services in Mandarin and Cantonese 1.00pm every Sunday

ERIC LIDDELL CENTRE

Church website: www.eric-liddell.org

Open daily 10.00am-5.00pm, or in evenings by

arrangement with reception, telephone 0131 447 4520

CHINESE EVANGELICAL CHURCH ♿ ☺ ⓘ (on request) 🏠 wc ☕ (The 1924 café and cards) **B**

427 ST BENNET'S

NT 248 717

42 Greenhill Gardens, Church Hill, Edinburgh

The chapel attached to the home of the Archbishops of St Andrews and Edinburgh. A charming Byzantine church built by R Weir Schultz 1907, under the will of the 3rd Marquess of Bute, to take the outstanding Italianate classical interior designed by William Frame in 1889 for the chapel at House of Falkland. Porch by Reginald Fairlie 1934. There are examples of stained glass windows by Gabriel Loire of Chartres dating from the 1970s; other windows were installed in 1999 commemorating the 1600th anniversary of St Ninian and the 1400th anniversary of St Columba, as well as a millennium window. The chapel contains memorabilia of the Archbishops since the restoration of the hierarchy. Buses 11, 15, 16, 17 and 23 to Church Hill. Service times as announced

Open weekdays 9.00am-5.00pm

ROMAN CATHOLIC ♿ wc **A**

ST BENNET'S

428 ST PETER'S CHURCH

NT 248 715

77 Falcon Avenue

Regarded as Robert Lorimer's most innovative design, St Peter's was built in two
stages: 1906-27 and the nave completed 1928-29. A tall square Italianate campanile
watches over a welcoming courtyard. Sculpture on the apse of 'The Crucifixion' by
Joseph Hayes. The towering nave in white-washed brick is lit by six tall windows.
Stained glass by Morris and Gertrude A Meredith Williams, Nina Millar Davidson,
and Pierre Fourmaintraux. Lead font with fish motif by G P Bankart. Masses:
Sunday 9.00am, 11.00am and 5.30pm; Saturday 12.00 noon; weekdays 9.00am
Open 20 minutes before services and during confessions on Saturdays 11.15-11.45am
and 6.30-7.00pm

ROMAN CATHOLIC 🦽 ⌂ **A**

429 MORNINGSIDE PARISH CHURCH

NT 246 707

Cluny Gardens, Morningside, Edinburgh

Built as St Matthew's 1890 by Hippolyte Blanc, inspired by late 13th-century
Gothic. Fourteen stained glass windows on side aisles of nave, including the new
St Cuthbert window to mark the 2003 union, and the St Andrew Window in
North Transept. East window: 'Four Apostles', Sir Edward Burne-Jones 1900; west
window: four scenes from the ministry of Jesus, Percy Bacon & Co 1905. Last
'Father' Willis organ in Scotland, installed 1901. Morningside Parish Church is a
union of five former churches – the former St Matthew's and then Cluny Parish
Church, now the new Morningside Parish Church; Morningside Parish Church
(Newbattle Terrace); Morningside High Church, now the Churchill Theatre; South

Morningside Church now the Cluny Centre; Braid Church, now the Braid Centre. Sunday Services: autumn, winter, spring 11.00am and 6.30pm; summer 9.30am and 11.00am

Church website: www.morningsideparishchurch.net

A regular venue for concerts, open also during Edinburgh Festival with organ recitals at 1.00pm as advertised. The church, the Cluny Centre and the Braid Centre can be opened for viewing by arrangement, telephone church office 0131 447 6745

CHURCH OF SCOTLAND ♿ ⓐ 🚹 📖

430 CHURCH OF THE GOOD SHEPHERD

NT 228 734

Murrayfield Avenue, Edinburgh

Designed by Sir Robert Lorimer and dedicated in 1899, the building contains some fine examples of stained glass, including a modern window depicting 'The Good Shepherd'. There is a fine Brindley and Foster organ which was rebuilt by Willis in 1967. Sunday Services: Holy Communion 8.30am, Sung Communion 10.00am; Wednesday Holy Communion 11.00am

Open Edinburgh and Scottish Churches Doors Open Days, or by arrangement, telephone James Young 0131 337 7615

SCOTTISH EPISCOPAL ⓐ 📖 🚻 ♿ **B**

CHURCH OF THE GOOD SHEPHERD

431 ST MARK'S CHURCH

NT 237 691

29 Oxgangs Avenue

Opened by Archbishop Gordon Gray in 1962. Designed by Peter Whiston with a slated roof above walls made of cobbles and a rich interior. Stained glass by Dom Basil Robinson, OSB. Stations of the Cross by Vincent Butler (Saltire Award, 1971). Statues of Our Lady and St Mark by Norman Forrest. Services: Saturday Vigil 6.00pm, Sunday Masses 9.00am and 11.00am

Open Wednesdays and Saturdays 11.00am to 1.00pm

ROMAN CATHOLIC ♿ 🚻 ⓐ

432 PILRIG ST PAUL'S CHURCH

NT 266 752

Junction of Pilrig Street and Leith Walk

Splendidly bold French Gothic by Peddie & Kinnear, 1861-63. A spectacular interior with leafy stone capitals carrying a diagonal arch-braced roof of laminated timber. Gothic spire with chiming clock at the south corner. Windows by Ballantine and Field & Allen. The chancel furnishings make an impressive pitch-pine Gothic display beneath the organ by Forster & Andrews, 1903.

Sunday Service: 11.00am

Open by arrangement with Dr Sime, 0131 552 9652

CHURCH OF SCOTLAND 🦽 wc ② ☕ 🏠 B

433 POLWARTH PARISH CHURCH

NT 750 495

36-38 Polwarth Terrace, Edinburgh

Splendid example of late 19th and early 20th-century architecture by Sydney Mitchell and Wilson 1901, with the tower by James Jerdan & Sons 1913. The architecture shows pre-Reformation influences, including stone carvings of the face of Mary, the mother of Christ, and several 'Green men'. Marble chancel augmented by one of the finest pulpits in the country, sculpted by William Beveridge in 1903. Ascension window at the east end of the chancel by Clayton & Bell. Pipe organ by Forster & Andrews, 1903. On local bus routes 10, 27, 38.

Sunday Service: 11.00am and other Services as advertised

Church website: www.polwarth.org.uk

Open by arrangement with the Minister, telephone 0131 667 4055. Church office open 9.30-12.30pm Tuesday, Wednesday and Thursday, telephone 0131 346 2711

CHURCH OF SCOTLAND ② 🦽 wc 🏠 B

434 PORTOBELLO OLD PARISH CHURCH

NT 309 738

Bellfield Street, off Portobello High Street

The oldest church in Portobello, built 1809 by William Sibbald, in classical style with a pediment. The clock tower was added in 1839. Organ by Peter Conacher 1873, rebuilt by Henry Willis 1984. Furniture of Austrian oak. Mort safe and interesting memorials in graveyard. Public swimming baths and safe, sandy beach at end of the street. Good bus service (26) from city centre.

Sunday Service: 11.00am

Open 10.00am-2.00pm Monday to Friday all year

CHURCH OF SCOTLAND 🦽 ② 🏠 wc ☕ B

PORTOBELLO OLD PARISH CHURCH

435 PRIESTFIELD PARISH CHURCH

NT 271 721

Dalkeith Road, Edinburgh

Built in 1879, Sutherland & Walker, in the Italian Lombardic style. Beautiful stained glass windows designed by three young artists in 1921. Other features of note are the handsome pulpit and organ gallery and a most unusual baptismal font. On Dalkeith Road, A68. City buses 2, 2a, 14, 21, 33, 85, 86.

Sunday Service: 11.00am

Church website: www.priestfield.org.uk

Open by arrangement, contact the Minister 0131 668 1620

CHURCH OF SCOTLAND ⓘ 📖 ② wc A

436 QUEENSFERRY PARISH CHURCH, SOUTH QUEENSFERRY

NT 130 782

The Loan, South Queensferry, Edinburgh

Well-used and well-loved Burgh Church, built in 1894 and extended in 1993. Of special interest is the display of banners and the wrought iron railings which incorporate a burning bush motif. Centre of village.

Sunday Services: 10.00am and 11.30am

Church website: www.qpc.freeuk.com

Open all year, Monday to Friday 10.00-11.30am. Access to historic graveyard

(1635-early 1900s) can be arranged in advance, telephone 0131 331 1100

CHURCH OF SCOTLAND ♿ ⓘ 📖 ② ☕ A

QUEENSFERRY PARISH CHURCH, SOUTH QUEENSFERRY

437 PRIORY CHURCH OF ST MARY OF MT CARMEL, SOUTH QUEENSFERRY

NT 129 784

Hopetoun Road, South Queensferry, Edinburgh

Originally a Carmelite Friary founded in 1330, the church fell into disrepair during the 16th century. It was restored for the use of the Episcopal church in 1890, the work being begun by John Kinross. Later work was carried out in the 1960s by Ian Lindsay. Church extensively refurbished in 2000, new

PRIORY CHURCH OF ST MARY OF
MT CARMEL, SOUTH QUEENSFERRY

floor (with underfloor heating), and a glass engraved screen to side chapel. Font cover designed by Lorimer. Fourteenth-century aumbry. Mass dial on outside south wall. Sunday Services: 9.30 and 11.00am; Thursday: 10.00am

Church website: www.priorychurch.co.uk

Open by arrangement, telephone the church office 0131 331 5540.

Also open during Ferry Fair Week in August

SCOTTISH EPISCOPAL   🦽 📖 wc **A**

438 RATHO PARISH CHURCH

NT 138 710

Baird Road, Ratho, Edinburgh

An interesting medieval cruciform church, with later aisles. The east aisle dated 1683, the south 1830. To the west of the south aisle is a 12th-century doorway, partially visible, with scalloped capitals and decorated hoodmould. Twentieth-century refurbishment revealed a Celtic cross stone which might suggest early worship on this site. In the south porch a 13th-century tomb slab belonging to one of the Knights Templar who owned Ratho in the Middle Ages. In the graveyard are several interesting headstones and a panelled coffin formed of a single stone. Organ by Smethurst of Manchester 1964. Sunday Service: 11.00am

Church website:

www.rathoparishchurch.org.uk

Open by arrangement, telephone

Mrs Watson 0131 333 1732

CHURCH OF SCOTLAND

🦽 ♨ 📖 wc **A**

RATHO PARISH CHURCH

439 ST MARGARET'S PARISH CHURCH

NT 284 745

27 Restalrig Road South, Edinburgh

Rebuilt by William Burn 1836 on the foundations
of the previous 15th-century church. The flowing
window tracery follows the original design,
stained glass by William Wilson 1966. Attached
to the south-west corner is the hexagonal St
Triduana's Chapel, once the lower storey of a
two-tier chapel built for James III about 1477.
The vault springs from a central pier, its six
shafts topped by capitals with crinkly foliage.
Notable 17th and 18th-century monuments in the
graveyard. Sunday Service: 10.30am

Church website: www.st-margarets-church.com

Open Tuesday to Friday 11.30am-1.00pm, or by

arrangement, contact Mr Skakle 0131 661 2510,

or the church office 0131 554 7400

CHURCH OF SCOTLAND ♿ ⊘ 🚾 ⏇ **A**

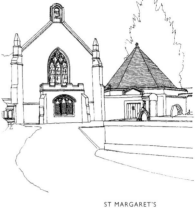

ST MARGARET'S
PARISH CHURCH

440 ST MICHAEL'S CHURCH

NT 234 722

1 Slateford Road, Edinburgh

One of architect John Honeyman's most notable
buildings, completed 1883. Square 135ft tower and
longest aisle in the city. Sanctuary illuminated by
clerestoried nave beneath dark-timbered roof. Unusual
reredos bearing Ten Commandments, Beatitudes and
the Creed. Pulpit and lectern decorated with biblical
fruits by Gertrude Hope. Communion table, fall and
Bible markers by Hannah Frew Paterson, dedicated in
April 2001. Organ by Brindley and Foster 1895.
Stained glass, including work by Douglas Strachan
(1895-1925). The building was extensively restored in
1998 and provides for a variety of worship, cultural
and outreach activities. Bus routes 4, 28, 34 and 44.
Sunday Services: 11.00am; June to August 10.00am
and 11.00am. Occasional Evening Services

Church website: www.stmichaels-kirk.co.uk

Open Edinburgh Doors Open Day, and by arrangement,

telephone 0131 478 9675

CHURCH OF SCOTLAND ♿ ⊘ 🚾

ST MICHAEL'S CHURCH

441 ST CUTHBERT'S CHURCH

NT 227 715
104 Slateford Road
Built to a design by J B Bennett and opened in 1896. Major renovation 1969.
Significant works of art including original stained glass windows and several
tapestries by the Edinburgh Tapestry Company at the Dovecot Studios, the most
recent being of 1996 to mark the centenary. Services: weekdays 9.00am, Saturday
10.00am, Vigil Mass 6.00pm, Sunday Mass 10.00am
Open during and after services every day or by arrangement with the
Parish Priest, telephone 0131 443 1317
ROMAN CATHOLIC 🔲 🚻 (in hall) ② 🖵 (after Sunday Mass)

442 STOCKBRIDGE PARISH CHURCH

NT 247 748
Saxe Coburg Street, Edinburgh
Classical church by James Milne 1823 with an
Ionic pilastered and pedimented front and a small
domed steeple. The interior contains the original
U-plan gallery. In 1888 Hardy & Wight added the
apse which was decorated in 1987 with war
memorial murals by the German artist Reinhardt
Behrens depicting the Lothian coastline 'at the
going down of the sun and in the morning ...'.
Historic 2-manual organ by August Gern 1883,
installed 1995. Services: Sunday 11.00am;
Wednesday 1.00pm
Telephone the administrator, 0131 332 0122
CHURCH OF SCOTLAND 🔲 ② 🚻 **A/B**

STOCKBRIDGE PARISH CHURCH

443 VIEWFORTH ST DAVID AND ST OSWALD

NT 244 725
104 Gilmour Place, Edinburgh
Originally a Free Church. Built by Pilkington and Bell 1871 to an orthodox four-
square plan with restrained detail. The massive upward growth contrasts with the
fragile shafted geometric window in the central gable. Octagonal belfry, truncated
in 1976. Powerful interior, rebuilt after a fire in 1898, with very thin cast-iron
columns supporting huge transverse beams over the side galleries. Organ
reconstructed 1976 from two instruments by Blackett & Howden 1899 and Forster
& Andrews 1904. Sunday Service: 10.30am. Shared by Associated Presbyterian
congregation. Services: Sunday 12.00 noon; Wednesday 7.00pm
Church website: www.viewforth.org
Telephone the Church Administrator 0131 229 1917
CHURCH OF SCOTLAND ② 🚻 **B**

444 WARDIE PARISH CHURCH

NT 246 768

Primrose Bank Road, Trinity

A jolly Gothic church with Francophile detail, by John McLachlan 1892.
Distinctive silhouette with central lantern and conical pinnacles. Inside, a clear-span
tunnel roof. A complete and perfect set of Gothic oak furnishings by Scott Morton
& Co 1935 including the organ case (organ by Rushworth & Dreaper).

Sunday Services: 11.00am, 10.30am, July and August

Open Tuesday, Thursday and Friday 9.00am-12.00 noon, telephone the church office

0131 551 3847

CHURCH OF SCOTLAND 🔕 ⓓ 🚻

WARDIE PARISH CHURCH

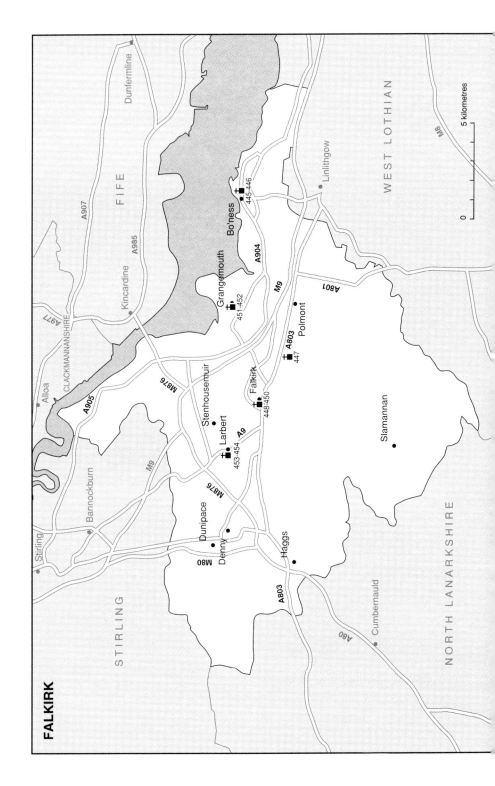

FALKIRK

STIRLING

Stirling ●

Bannockburn ●

M9

A905

A977

CLACKMANNANSHIRE

Alloa ●

A905

Kincardine ●

A985

A907

FIFE

Dunfermline ●

M9

Grangemouth

451-452 ⊞✝

Bo'ness

445-446 ⊞✝

Linlithgow ●

WEST LOTHIAN

A904

M9

A803

Polmont ●

447 ■

A801

Stenhousemuir ●

Larbert ●
453-454 ✝■

A9

Falkirk
448-450 ■✝

M876

M876

Dunipace ●

Denny ●

M80

Haggs ●

A803

Slamannan ●

NORTH LANARKSHIRE

Cumbernauld ●

A80

M8

0 — 5 kilometres

FALKIRK

Local Representative: Mr Alan Naylor, Candiehill, Candie, Avonbridge, Falkirk (*telephone* 01324 861583)

445 ST CATHERINE'S CHURCH, BO'NESS

NS 999 812
Cadzow Crescent, Bo'ness
The congregation was formed in 1888 and moved to the present building in 1921. The hall was added in 1928. The sanctuary windows depict the children of the Bible. Organ by Miller of Dundee. Off Dean Road, adjacent to Douglas Park. Services: Sunday: 11.30am (Sung Eucharist); Wednesday: 10.15 (Said Eucharist)
Open by arrangement, telephone the Rector 01324 482438
SCOTTISH EPISCOPAL ♿ wc

ST CATHERINE'S CHURCH, BO'NESS

446 CARRIDEN PARISH CHURCH, BO'NESS

NT 019 812
Carriden Brae, Carriden, Bo'ness
The first church of Carriden was consecrated in 1243 by Bishop David de Bernam, although it is believed that the parish goes back to the time of St Ninian, AD c.396. The present church is the third. Designed by P MacGregor Chalmers, 1909, in simple Romanesque style with a west tower and stone spire. The bell was cast in Rotterdam, Peter Oostens 1674. Inside a wooden sailing ship 'The Ranger' hangs from the barrel-shaped pitch pine roof. Six-bay nave. Baptistry chapel with a wall painting thought to be of the Scottish School. Sounding board on north wall 1655. A fine stone arcaded baptismal font, 2-manual pipe organ moved from the John Knox Church, Gorbals after the Blitz of 1941.
Sunday Service: 11.15am
Open (April to September) Wednesday 12.00 noon-1.00pm, or by arrangement, telephone 01324 631008
CHURCH OF SCOTLAND ♿ ⓘ wc **B**

CARRIDEN PARISH CHURCH, BO'NESS

447 BRIGHTONS PARISH CHURCH

NS 928 778
Main Street, Brightons
Built in 1847. Local quarry owner Alexander
Lawrie gifted the stone to build the church
to a design by Brown & Carrick of
Glasgow. T-plan church with small steeple
with bell. Side galleries added in 1893.
Chancel area modernised 1935. Windows
1993 by Ruth Golliwaws of New Orleans,
USA. B805, four miles south of Falkirk; or
B810, half a mile from Polmont Station.
Sunday Services: 11.00am and 1st Sunday;
September to May 6.00pm
Church website: www.brightonsparishchurch.org.uk
Open for prayer September to June, Thursday 10.00am-12.00 noon
CHURCH OF SCOTLAND   🔠 ⊘ wc

BRIGHTONS PARISH CHURCH

448 FALKIRK FREE CHURCH

Beaumont Drive, Newcarron, Falkirk
The present congregation began in 1991 and moved into its new building in 1998.
The building reflects modern architecture but maintains a spiritual and practical
ambience. Sunday Services: 11.00am and 6.30pm; Prayers: Wednesday and Saturday
7.30pm, Saturday 7.00pm. Other activities contact the Minister
Church website: www.falkirkfreechurch.com
Open by arrangement, telephone the Rev R MacLeod 01324 631008
FREE CHURCH OF SCOTLAND 🔠 wc ⊘ 🏠 🖥

449 FALKIRK OLD AND ST MODAN'S PARISH CHURCH

NS 887 800
Manse Place, off High Street, Falkirk
Dating from 1811, although 12th-century pillars remain in the vestibule. There has
been a Christian church on this site for 1200 years; local legend links the earliest
foundation with the Celtic St Modan in the 6th century. The square tower dates
from the 16th century, and the gable marks of the earlier nave and chancel are
visible. Above the tower an 18th-century bell-tower with 13 bells. Two late 19th-
century stained glass windows; pipe organ 1892 Foster and Andrews. Twelfth-
century sanctuary cross. Stained glass windows by Christopher Whall. Major
refurbishment in the 1960s. Sunday Services: winter 11.15am and 6.30pm; summer
9.30am and 11.15am
Church website: http://fkoldstm.webspace.fish.co.uk
Open Monday to Friday 12.00 noon-2.00pm. Lunches served
CHURCH OF SCOTLAND 🔠 ⊘ 🍴 🖥 wc **B**

FALKIRK OLD AND ST MODAN'S PARISH CHURCH

450 ST FRANCIS XAVIER, FALKIRK

NS 886 812

Hope Street

Opened in 1961 replacing 1843 building destroyed by fire 1955. Architect A R
Conlin. 12-ft statue of St Francis by Maxwell Allan and of the Four Evangelists by
Miss E Dempster. Stations of the Cross on laminated glass panels by Felix
McCullough, mosaics by Casa Group, painting of St John the Baptist by Peter
Brady. Services: Sunday 10.00am, 12.00 noon, 7.00pm; Monday-Friday 10.00am,
Saturday 10.00am; and Vigil Mass 7.00pm

Church website: www.saintfrancis.org.uk

Open 8.00am-6.00pm

ROMAN CATHOLIC ♿ [wc] ☺ ☕ (after 10.00 am Mass)

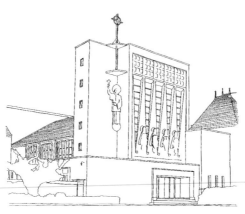

ST FRANCIS XAVIER, FALKIRK

451 ST MARY'S CHURCH, GRANGEMOUTH

NS 932 818

Ronaldshay Crescent, Grangemouth

The present church was built in 1938
to replace a 'tin kirk' of 1901; the
architect was Maxton Craig of
Edinburgh. A small hall was added in
1978. The west window, 1962, depicts
the industries of Grangemouth. Altar
cross, candlesticks and vases by
Edward Spencer, the Artificers' Guild,
his last work. Services: Sunday: 8.30am
(Said Eucharist), 10.00am (Sung
Eucharist); Tuesday: 10am (Said
Eucharist)

Open first Saturday of month,
12.00 noon-2.00pm. Or by arrangement,
telephone the Rector 01324 482438

SCOTTISH EPISCOPAL [♿] [wc]

ST MARY'S CHURCH, GRANGEMOUTH

452 GRANGEMOUTH: ZETLAND CHURCH, GRANGEMOUTH

NS 931 818

Ronaldshay Crescent, Grangemouth

Building by Wilson & Tait completed 1911. Cruciform in plan with a south aisle and
north and south transepts. Four arches support a timber barrel roof and there is a
small gallery at the end of the nave. Second World War memorial stained glass
window by Douglas Hamilton, Glasgow, with four lights depicting Peace, Victory,
Willingness to Lay Down Life and The Glory of the King of Heaven. Willis organ
of 1890 installed 1983. Memorial Chapel furnished in the south transept 1990 used
for private prayer and small services. Grounds have won Falkirk Council's Church
Gardens award for past eight years. Sunday Service: 11.15am

Open Wednesday mornings 9.30-11.30am, March to October

CHURCH OF SCOTLAND [♿] [wc] **B**

453 LARBERT OLD CHURCH

NS 856 822

Denny Road, Larbert

Near site of earlier chapel – 12th-century dependency of Eccles Kirkton of St
Ninian's and Cambuskenneth Abbey. The present church was built in 1820,
architect David Hamilton, replacing a pre-Reformation church which was located
within the adjacent churchyard. The chancel was added in 1911. The fine oak
panelling dates from 1887. There are good memorial windows including Gordon
Webster and Stephen Adam. The apsidal triptych of the Transfiguration is believed

to be the only example of Frank Howard's work (1805-66) in Scotland and was executed by Edmundson of Manchester. There are some interesting memorial plaques. The graveyard includes the burial place of James Bruce, Abyssinian explorer, and Master Robert Bruce, the post-Reformation divine, as well as the early partners of the Carron Company. The bell-tower has a carillon of chimes dating from 1985.

Sunday Services: 11.30am and 6.30pm

Open by arrangement,

telephone 01324 562955

CHURCH OF SCOTLAND

LARBERT OLD CHURCH

454 OUR LADY OF LOURDES AND ST BERNADETTE, LARBERT

NS 865 829

323 Main Street, Larbert

The present building designed by J N Scott & A Lorne 1934, was intended to be a hall but was used for worship until a permanent church could be built. When this plan was abandoned in the 1950s the building was adapted to become exclusively the place of worship. Entrance porch by Sam Sweeney added 1995. Wall hangings by Maison Bouvrier 2002. Marian Grotto in grounds 1983 to mark the Golden Jubilee, recently embellished and decorated by local talent from within the church community. Sunday Services: 11.30am and 6.30pm Mass

Open 9.00am-dusk, or apply to Presbytery adjacent to Church

ROMAN CATHOLIC

OUR LADY OF LOURDES AND ST BERNADETTE, LARBERT

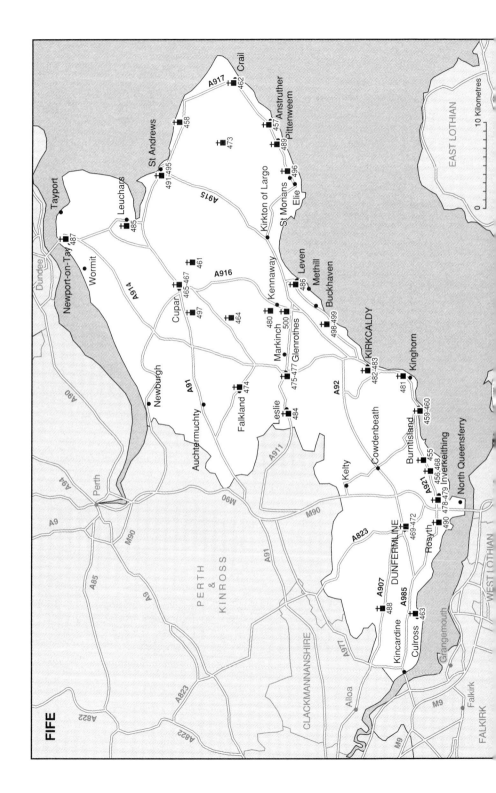

FIFE

Tayport

Newport-on-Tay 487

Wormit

Leuchars 485

St Andrews 491-495

A917 Crail 462

458

473

Anstruther 457
Pittenweem 489

St Monans
Elie 496

Kirkton of Largo

A915

Newburgh

Cupar 465-467

A916 461

497

464

Kennaway

480
Markinch 500

Glenrothes 475-477

Leven 486
Methill
Buckhaven 498-499

Falkland 474

Leslie 484

A91

Auchtermuchty

A92

KIRKCALDY 482-483

Kinghorn 481

459-460

Kelty

Cowdenbeath

Burntisland

Inverkeithing 455
456-468

A911

A90

M90

A823

A907

Kincardine 488

A985

Culross 463

DUNFERMLINE

Rosyth 490
469-472

A921 478-479
North Queensferry

PERTH
&
KINROSS

CLACKMANNANSHIRE

Alloa

EAST LOTHIAN

WEST LOTHIAN

Grangemouth

FALKIRK

Falkirk

Dundee

Perth

A90

A94

A9

A85

A822

A823

A822

A9

A977

M90

M9

0   10 Kilometres

FIFE

Local Representative: The Rev Malcolm Trew, 155 Park Road West, Rosyth (*telephone* 01383 420949)

455 ST COLUMBA'S CHURCH, ABERDOUR

NT 186 851

Inverkeithing Road, Aberdour

Built in 1843 for the Earl of Moray as a private chapel for his employees in Aberdour. It was transferred to the Scottish Episcopal Church in 1918. A cruciform plan, tall and light with lancet windows. The west window blocked off by the addition of a balcony, which has recently been enclosed. A921 from Dalgety Bay, in the village on the right. Linked with St Peter's, Inverkeithing and St Serf's, Burntisland. Sunday Service: 11.00am

Open by arrangement, telephone Mrs Clifford 01383 860521, or Mrs Wallington 01383 860795

SCOTTISH EPISCOPAL

ST COLUMBA'S CHURCH, ABERDOUR

456 ST FILLAN'S, ABERDOUR

NT 193 855

Hawkcraig Road, Aberdour

One of the finest examples of Norman architecture in Scotland, this 'miniature Cathedral' sits in its own graveyard overlooking Aberdour harbour. The early church, standing in 1123, consisted of the nave and chancel, lit by deep splayed windows which still exist. The church was enlarged in the 15th century by the addition of a side aisle, and in the 17th by the small transeptual aisle, now used by the choir. The church fell into disrepair in the 18th century and was restored in 1925. 'Even to enter St Fillan's is to worship.' Sunday Service: 10.30am

Open by arrangement, telephone 01383 860611

CHURCH OF SCOTLAND

ST FILLAN'S, ABERDOUR

457 ANSTRUTHER PARISH CHURCH

NO 567 037

Burial Brae (off Crail Road), Anstruther

James Melville (brother of Andrew, the leading
Covenanter) inspired the purchase of land in
1590 for a new church, but he was exiled by
James VI and the church was not built until
1634. Described in 1837 as 'one of the most
elegant country churches anywhere to be seen'.
Tahitian Princess buried outside the south wall.
Many interesting features. Anstruther is the

ANSTRUTHER PARISH CHURCH

birthplace of Thomas Chalmers. A917 Crail, 400 yards east of St Andrews cross
road. Bus services: Fife Scottish 95 and 57, Minibus M1 and M611, Stagecoach x23.
Sunday Service: 11.00am; Healing Service second Sunday of month 2.00pm

Open April to September, Tuesday 2.00-3.00pm, Thursday 11.00am-12.00 noon.

All year coffee morning, Tuesday 10.00am-12.00 noon in Hew Scott Hall

(converted 13th-century West Anstruther Church)

CHURCH OF SCOTLAND ♿ **B**

458 BOARHILLS CHURCH

NO 562 137

On A917 west of Boarhills

Church built 1866/7, although there has been a
burial ground here considerably longer. The architect
was George Rae. Original oil lamps, now converted
to electricity. Sunday Service: 10.00am in February,
April, June, August, October and December

BOARHILLS CHURCH

Open by arrangement with the Minister, telephone 01334 472948

CHURCH OF SCOTLAND ♿ (back door) **C**

459 BURNTISLAND PARISH CHURCH

NT 234 857

East Leven Street, Burntisland

Built in 1592 to an unusual square plan. One of the first post-Reformation
churches built in Scotland, still in use. The General Assembly of the Church of
Scotland met in Burntisland in May 1601 in the
presence of James VI when a new translation of
the Bible was approved. Organ originally by
Cousans, 1909. Information available on the
churchyard. Extensive refurbishment completed
in 1999. Sunday Services: 11.00am

Open June to August, 10.00am-12.00 noon and
2.00-4.00pm. Other times key from Curator,
telephone 01592 873275

CHURCH OF SCOTLAND ♿ 🚹 📖 🅿 ♿ wc **A**

BURNTISLAND PARISH CHURCH

460 ST SERF'S CHURCH, BURNTISLAND

NT 230 864

Ferguson Place x Cromwell Road, Burntisland

Built in 1905 to a design by Truro Cathedral architect J L Pearson, the stone is from the local Grange quarry. The chancel is divided from the nave by a fine Gothic arch. The east end of the chancel is semi-octagonal behind a tri-form arch springing from slender columns, surmounted by a Gothic arch. Linked with St Peter's, Inverkeithing and St Columba's, Aberdour.

Services: Sunday 9.30am; Tuesday: 11.00am

Open by arrangement, telephone Mrs M McQuarrie 01592 873117

SCOTTISH EPISCOPAL   ♿ 🗋 wc ☕ **B**

461 CERES CHURCH

NO 399 117

Kirk Brae, Ceres

Built 1806 to a design by Alexander Leslie, with a battlemented tower, its spire added in 1852, the building has the original box pews and long communion tables running the full length of the church. Crenellated tower with obelisk corner pinnacles. The 17th-century stone-slated Lindsay vault in the kirkyard was possibly attached to the medieval church. Linked with Springfield Church.

Sunday Service: 11.00am

Open on September Doors Open Day, and by arrangement, telephone the Minister 01334 828233

CHURCH OF SCOTLAND   ⊘ 🚹 wc **B**

CERES CHURCH

462 CRAIL PARISH CHURCH

NO 613 080

Marketgate, Crail

Consecrated 1243 with alterations 1526, 1796. Restored 1963. Judith Campbell windows (1970 and 1975). Pictish cross slab. Seventeenth-century carving. Pipe organ by Harrison & Harrison 1892, rebuilt and installed here 1936. Graveyard (with dead house). Hourly bus service, Leven–St Andrews (some to Dundee). Sunday Service: 11.15am; also 17 June to 2 September at 9.30am (informal)

Open 2.00-4.00pm, 18 June to 1 September.

In 2004 – 15 June to 2 September (Tuesday, Wednesday and Thursday). Also on Doors Open Day – first Sunday in September

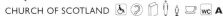

CHURCH OF SCOTLAND   ♿ ⊘ 🗋 🚹 🚻 ☕ wc **A**

CRAIL PARISH CHURCH

463 CULROSS ABBEY

NS 989 863
Kirk Street, Culross
Built on the site of a Celtic Christian Culdee church. Abbey founded in 1217 by
Malcolm, 7th Earl of Fife; dedicated to St Mary and St Serf. Much of the original
building remains, although a great deal of it is in ruins. The monks' choir forms
the present parish church, in continuous use since 1633. Modernised in 1824 and
restored in 1905 by Sir R Rowand Anderson. Many features of interest. Situated in
16th-century small town of Culross. Seven and a half miles west of Dunfermline.
Sunday Service: 11.30am
Church website: www.culrossandtorryburnchurch.org.uk
Open daily, summer 10.00am-dusk, winter 10.00am-4.00pm
CHURCH OF SCOTLAND ⌂ wc **A**

464 CULTS KIRK

NO 347 099
*Kirkton of Cults, south side of A914, half a mile from
Pitlessie, four miles south-west of Cupar*
A place of worship since the 12th century, the present
kirk built 1793. Bell inscribed 'John Meikle, Edinburg,
fecit for the Kirk of Cults, 1699'. Lepers window,
Laird's Pew, memorials, one by Chantry of Sir David
Wilkie RA, the most famous son of the manse, one by
Samuel Joseph of his father and mother. Wilkie Hall,

CULTS KIRK

Pitlessie village, collection of etchings and engravings by Wilkie, viewing by
appointment 01337 830491. Sunday Service: 11.30am until July 2002, then 10.00am
Open 8.00am-8.00pm
CHURCH OF SCOTLAND ♿ ⚲ ⌂ **B**

465 CUPAR OLD AND ST MICHAEL OF TARVIT
PARISH CHURCH

NO 380 146
Kirkgate, Cupar
The tower dates from 1415; its spire and belfry (containing
two bells 1485 and 1689) were added in 1620 and the four-
face clock in 1910. The church itself was rebuilt in 1785.
Inside are war memorials on the east and south walls and
the guidon of the Fife and Forfar Yeomanry. A recess in the
west wall contains the 15th-century recumbent figure of a
knight ('Muckle Fernie'). Adjacent graveyard contains hand
of David Hackston, a Covenanter from Rathillet.
Sunday Service: 11.00am, and September to April 6.30pm
Open Saturdays 10.00am-12.00 noon, June to August,
or by appointment, telephone 01334 653036
CHURCH OF SCOTLAND ◉ ⌂ wc **A**

CUPAR OLD AND ST MICHAEL
OF TARVIT PARISH CHURCH

466   ST JAMES THE GREAT CHURCH, CUPAR

NO 376 146
St Catherine Street, Cupar
Built in 1866 to a design by Sir R Rowand Anderson. Fine choir screen, reredos
and panelling, Lorimer 1920. Organ originally by D & T Hamilton of Edinburgh
1875. Town centre, A91 Stirling to St Andrews. By rail from Edinburgh and
Dundee. By coach from Kirkcaldy, Dundee, St Andrews and Stirling.
Services: Sunday 8.00am and 11.00am; Wednesday 10.00am
Open weekdays, 10.00am-3.00pm
SCOTTISH EPISCOPAL [wc] **B**

467   ST JOHN'S PARISH CHURCH, CUPAR

NO 373 147
Bonnygate, Cupar
The 150ft spire with belfry dominates the view of
Cupar from the many approaches. Built 1878,
Campbell Douglas & Sellars, Glasgow, when first
Cupar Free Church became too small. Galleried
interior. Set on a raised area in stepped gardens.
The inside of the church was re-decorated in
February 2001. Sunday Service: 11.00am. Mid-
week half hour service every Wednesday 9.30am
Church website:
www.churchofscotland/congregations/stjohn's
Open all year, Wednesday 9.30am-11.30am.
Other times by arrangement 01334 655851
CHURCH OF SCOTLAND [♿] [♨] [ ] [ ] [ ] [wc] **B**

ST JOHN'S PARISH CHURCH, CUPAR

468   DALGETY PARISH CHURCH, DALGETY BAY

NT 155 836
Regents Way, Dalgety Bay
A hall church designed by Marcus
Johnston, built in 1981 and extended in
1991. Worship area and suite of halls
which are used by congregation and local
community groups. War memorial in
grounds. Sunday Services: 9.30am and
11.00am, all year; also second Sunday of
the month, September to June
Church website: www.dalgety-church.co.uk
Open by arrangement, telephone Mr W Wood,
13 Doune Park, Dalgety Bay 01383 822 529
CHURCH OF SCOTLAND [♿]

DALGETY PARISH CHURCH, DALGETY BAY

469 DUNFERMLINE ABBEY

NT 090 873
St Margaret Street, Dunfermline
Founded in 1072. Consists today of the nave of
medieval monastic church (1150) and the modern
parish church (1821) erected over foundations of
original Choir. Burial place of King Robert the
Bruce and numerous other Scottish royals
including Malcolm III (Canmore) and his Queen,
St Margaret of Scotland. Exquisitely carved
pulpit by William Paterson, Edinburgh 1890.
Fine pipe organ of 1882, rebuilt Walker in 1966.
Signposted from outskirts of city.
Sunday Services: 9.30am and 11.00am

DUNFERMLINE ABBEY

Open April to October, Monday to Saturday 10.00am-4.30pm, and Sunday 2.00-4.30pm.
Abbey shop also open as above. Groups by arrangement, telephone Mr F Tait 01383 872242
CHURCH OF SCOTLAND ⊘ ⌷ ⌷ ⌷ wc **A**

470 ST LEONARD'S, DUNFERMLINE

NT 096 869
Brucefield Avenue
The most striking feature of the church,
P McGregor Chalmers 1904, is a round Celtic tower. Inside,
the semi-circular apse has a dramatic painting of the Risen
Christ surrounded by Gospel characters, designed by the
architect and painted by Mr A Samuel 1927. Heraldic
gallery dedicated to the Scottish Wars of Independence led
by Wallace and Bruce. Sunday Service: June to August
10.00am; September to May 9.30am and 11.00am
Open Tuesday and Thursday mornings (church office)
CHURCH OF SCOTLAND ♿ wc ⊘ **B**

ST LEONARD'S,
DUNFERMLINE

471 ST MARGARET'S MEMORIAL CHURCH, DUNFERMLINE

NY 096 876
Holyrood Place, Dunfermline
A commanding building forming part of the ancient gateway
to the town at the East Port. Built in 1896 to a design by Sir
R Rowand Anderson in 12th-century Transitional style.
Stained glass circular window by John Blyth, stone reredos
by Hew Lorimer, wood carving by Steven Foster and
historical prints by Jurek Pütter. Three new stained glass
windows by Douglas Hogg. Services: Saturday 6.30pm;
Sunday 9.00am and 11.00am; weekdays 10.00am
Open by arrangement, telephone Father Barr 01383 625611
ROMAN CATHOLIC ♿ ⊘ ⌷ wc **B**

ST MARGARET'S MEMORIAL
CHURCH, DUNFERMLINE

472 VIEWFIELD BAPTIST CHURCH, DUNFERMLINE

NT 095 875

East Port, Dunfermline

Gothic design by Peter L Henderson, 1882-84.
Front façade skewed giving a vestibule narrower at
one side than the other and making necessary the
cylindrical addition for the east gallery staircase.
Wood vaulted ceiling upheld by laminated wood
arches, supported internally by six cast-iron pillars.
Pipe organ. Sunday Services: 11.00am and 6.30pm

Church website: www.viewfield.org.uk

Church office open 9.30am-2.30pm every weekday, telephone 01383 620465

BAPTIST ⬚ⓌⒸ ⓓ ⬚ (open 10.00am-2.00pm Monday-Friday, in adjacent Viewfield Centre)

VIEWFIELD BAPTIST
CHURCH, DUNFERMLINE

473 DUNINO CHURCH

NO 541 109

In woods up farm road off B9131,
between St Andrews and Anstruther

There has been a church at Dunino since 1240. The
present building is 1827 by James Gillespie Graham
with the chancel and porch 1928 by J Jeffrey Waddell &
Young. Font by Sir Robert Lorimer, stained glass by J
Jennings of London and W Wilson. Early Celtic carved
stone in the churchyard. Sunday Service: 10.00am in
January, March, May, July, September and November

Open daily

CHURCH OF SCOTLAND ♿ 🚪 ⬚ⓌⒸ **B**

DUNINO CHURCH

474 FALKLAND PARISH CHURCH

NO 252 074

The Square, Falkland

On the site of an earlier building, the present church was
completed in 1850 to a design by David Bryce and gifted
to the people of Falkland by Onesiphorus Tyndall Bruce,
of the family of Bruce of Earlshall. The style is Victorian
Gothic. Centre pews convert to long communion tables.
Stained glass 1897. Organ by Hill, Norman & Beard,
1923. A912 Perth–Kirkcaldy. Bus service: 36 from Perth.
Sunday Service: 2004 – 10.00am; 2005 – 11.30am

Open 7 June to 3 September, Monday to Friday 2.00-4.00pm
(2004). Open 6 June to 2 September, Monday to Friday
2.00-4.00pm (2005). Teas/coffee, bookstall. Contact
Robert M Herd, Session Clerk, telephone 01337 857732

CHURCH OF SCOTLAND ♿ ⓓ 🚻 🚪 ⬚ ⬚ⓌⒸ **B**

FALKLAND PARISH CHURCH

475 ST COLUMBA'S PARISH CHURCH, GLENROTHES

NO 270 009

Rothes Road, Glenrothes

Built in 1960 and designed in conjunction with the
theologians at St Mary's College of St Andrews
University with the emphasis on how the Scottish
Reformation could be best expressed in a church building.
The sanctuary features seating around three sides, with the
Lord's table in the centre. Mural by Alberto Morocco
measuring 59ft by 9ft of scenes from the last days of
Christ. Iron bell-tower is a landmark in the centre of the
town. Sunday Service: 11.00am September to June, July to
August 10.00am

Open by arrangement, telephone Carol Gibson 01592 754320

CHURCH OF SCOTLAND [⎿] [wc]

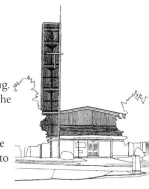

ST COLUMBA'S PARISH
CHURCH, GLENROTHES

476 ST LUKE THE EVANGELIST, GLENROTHES

NO 273 008

Ninian Quadrant, Glenrothes

By J Cassells 1960, the church is in a Perpendicular style, set alongside a playpark
in the earliest and most central part of the new town of Glenrothes. Furnished
with the warmth of pine, its interior is light and airy with an unusual layout, and
houses several items of interest. Sunday Services: 9.30 and 11.00am

Open Monday and Thursday 10.00am-1.00pm, Tuesday 9.00-10.30am,

Sunday 9.15am-1.00pm

SCOTTISH EPISCOPAL [⎿] [▭] [wc] **A**

477 ST PAUL'S CHURCH, GLENROTHES

NO 281 005

Warout Road, Glenrothes

Completed 1957 from design by Isi Metzstein and Andy McMillan of Gillespie,
Kidd & Coia. Described by *The Scotsman* as 'the most significant piece of
architecture north of the English Channel' and in *The Twentieth Century Church* as
'a homage to architecture's liberating function'. Interior contains the 'Catalonian'
altar crucifix 1957 and 'The Madonna' or 'Lady
Piece' by Benno Schotz 1960. Carved Stations
of the Cross and figure of St Paul by Harry
Bain 1983. Follow Woodside Road from town
centre, corner of Woodside Road/Warout Road.
Sunday Services: 11.30am

Church website: www.stpaulsandstmarys.co.uk

Open first Saturday of the month,

11.00am-6.00pm

ROMAN CATHOLIC [⎿] **B**

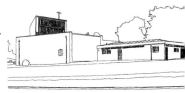

ST PAUL'S CHURCH, GLENROTHES

478 ST PETER'S PARISH CHURCH, INVERKEITHING

NT 131 830

Church Street, Inverkeithing

A Norman foundation, church dedicated to St Peter 1244. The present building is a nave and aisles church by Gillespie Graham 1827 attached to a 14th-century tower. Refurbished 1900, P MacGregor Chalmers. Fourteenth-century stone font, one of the finest in Scotland, thought to have been gifted by Robert III for the baptism of his son the Duke of Rothesay. Sunday Service: 11.15am

Open July to August, Friday 2.00-4.00pm,

Saturday 10.00am-12.00 noon, 2.00-4.00pm

CHURCH OF SCOTLAND

ST PETER'S PARISH
CHURCH, INVERKEITHING

479 ST PETER'S EPISCOPAL CHURCH, INVERKEITHING

NT 128 827

Hope Street, Inverkeithing

The church was built to serve the Scottish Episcopal community in Jamestown, at one time outside the Royal Burgh of Inverkeithing. The nave was built in 1903 to a design by Henry F Kerr and the chancel added in 1910. The interior was altered in 1980 to form a worship area and hall. Set in well-kept gardens on the southern approach to the town from the Forth Road Bridge. Linked with St Columba's, Aberdour and St Serf's, Burntisland.

Sunday Service: Holy Communion 11.00am

Open by arrangement, telephone D Macdonald 01383 414194

SCOTTISH EPISCOPAL

ST PETER'S EPISCOPAL
CHURCH, INVERKEITHING

480 ST KENNETH'S PARISH CHURCH, KENNOWAY

No 350 023

Cupar Road, Kennoway

The church in Kennoway dates back to St Kenneth, who preached in the 6th century. The present Romanesque church was built in 1850 and was designed by Thomas Hamilton. Six stained glass windows by Marjorie Kemp, 1950. Monuments to past ministers. Sunday Services: 11.15am and, during term-time, 7.00pm

Church website: www.st-kenneths.freeserve.co.uk

Open Monday to Friday 9.30am-12.30pm,

plus Tuesday 1.00-3.00pm and Thursday 5.00-7.00pm

CHURCH OF SCOTLAND   B

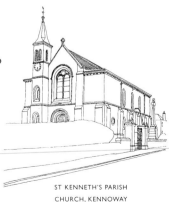

ST KENNETH'S PARISH
CHURCH, KENNOWAY

481 KINGHORN PARISH CHURCH

NT 272 869

St James Place, Kinghorn

The Kirk by the Sea for over 750 years has an
unrivalled view across the beach to the Firth of
Forth and Edinburgh. It has a historic bell-tower
and a 'Sailors' Aisle' built in 1609 celebrating the
naval connection and a model of the first Unicorn.
Sunday Services: 9.30am and 11.00am (except first
Sunday of month; 10.30am in church hall)

Open every Tuesday 6.00pm-8.00pm

CHURCH OF SCOTLAND ⊘

KINGHORN PARISH CHURCH

482 ST BRYCE KIRK
(formerly Kirkcaldy Old Parish Church)

NT 280 917

Kirk Wynd, Kirkcaldy

Consecrated in 1244 by the Bishop of St Andrews, the
ancient tower offers excellent views of Kirkcaldy. The body
of the church is by James Elliot 1808. Good stained glass
windows, some by Morris & Co from Burne-Jones designs
of 1886. United with St Brycedale. Historic graveyard.
Sunday Service: 11.00am

Church website: www.stbrycekirk.fsnet.co.uk

Open during August, Friday and Saturday 10.00am-4.00pm

CHURCH OF SCOTLAND 🦽 ⊘ 👤 👤 wc B

ST BRYCE KIRK, KIRKCALDY

483 ST BRYCE KIRK (formerly St Brycedale)

NT 279 917

St Brycedale Avenue, Kirkcaldy

Built as a Free Church 1877-81 by James Matthews of
Aberdeen. A 197ft tower and spire and associated pyramid-
roofed twin towers lift the church out of the ordinary. In
1988, a transformed church at first-floor level was created
above a multi-purpose ground-floor. Organ by Brindley &
Foster 1893. Stained glass includes windows by Adam &
Small 1881, Douglas Strachan 1923, and Edward Burne-
Jones (executed by William Morris & Co) 1889. Now united
with Kirkcaldy Old. On junction of Kirk Wynd and
St Brycedale Avenue. Sunday Service: 11.00am

Church website: www.stbrycekirk.fsnet.co.uk

Open Monday to Thursday 9.00am-10.00pm, Friday 9.00am-
3.00pm. Coffee Bar open Monday to Thursday 10.00am-9.00pm,
Friday 10.00am-3.00pm

CHURCH OF SCOTLAND 🦽 ⊘ 👤 👤 ☕ wc B

ST BRYCE KIRK, KIRKCALDY

484 ST MARY, MOTHER OF GOD, LESLIE

NO 251 018
High Street, Leslie
Originally Leslie Free Church by R Thornton Shiells
1879. In 1900 it was renamed the Logan United Free
Church after the Minister at that time. Closed as a Free
Church in 1956 and opened as Roman Catholic in 1959.
Tower 120ft and spire. Stained glass by John Blyth,
painting of the Crucifixion by Geoffrey Houghton-
Brown. Sunday Service: 9.30am and 6.30pm
Church website: www.stpaulsandstmarys.co.uk
Open first Saturday of each month 11.00am-6.00pm
ROMAN CATHOLIC 👨‍🦽 ⑦ wc **B**

ST MARY, MOTHER OF GOD, LESLIE

485 ST ATHERNASE CHURCH, LEUCHARS

NO 455 214
Main Street, Leuchars
Twelfth-century Norman church in a historic
conservation setting. The belfry was added c.1700, and
nave restored in 1858. Chancel and apse of outstanding
architectural interest. Sunday Service: 11.00am
Open March to October daily 9.30am-6.00pm. Teas,
Tuesdays 10.00am-4.00pm. Tours for groups, telephone
Church Officer, 18 Schoolhill, Leuchars 01334 838884
CHURCH OF SCOTLAND ⑦ 📖 wc **A**

ST ATHERNASE
CHURCH, LEUCHARS

486 LEVEN PARISH CHURCH (formerly Scoonie Kirk)

NO 383 017
Durie Street, Leven
Scoonie Kirk is the original Parish Church of Leven
with its roots going back over 16 centuries. The
church moved to its present site in 1775.
In 1904 the building was extended following
a design by the eminent church architect
P MacGregor Chalmers which incorporated some of
the earlier building. The unique pipe organ was built
by the French organ builder August Gern 1884 and
was restored 1992. The building also has some very
striking stained glass windows.
Sunday Service: 11.00am
Church website: www.leven@fish.co.uk
Open Easter to September, Tuesdays 11.00am-1.00pm
CHURCH OF SCOTLAND 👨‍🦽 ⑦ 📖 💻 wc **B**

LEVEN PARISH CHURCH

487 ST MARY'S EPISCOPAL, NEWPORT ON TAY

NO 420 278
10 High Street
Simple but picturesque church by architect T M Cappon, consecrated 1887. A plain
interior, beautified from 1920 onwards with panelling, pulpit and windows – all
donated as memorials. The rood screen of 1940 is by William Lamb. Refurbished
2000 by Alex Edmonstone of Perth. Organ 1903/4 by John Miller of Dundee.
Sunday Service: Eucharist 10.45am
Open by arrangement telephone Frank Smith 01382 542109
SCOTTISH EPISCOPAL ② ⓘ ☕ (after service) **B**

488 CHURCH OF THE HOLY NAME, OAKLEY

NT 025 885
Station Road, Oakley
Built by the Smith-Sligo family of Inzievar House
to a design by Charles Gray. Consecrated October
1965. Outstanding features include stained glass
windows by Gabriel Loire of Chartres. Carved
Stations of the Cross also by Gabriel Loire.
Services: Vigil Mass Saturday 6.30pm;
Sunday Mass 10.15am
Open by arrangement, telephone the Parish Priest at
Priest's House (adjacent via grass path to right of church)
ROMAN CATHOLIC

CHURCH OF THE
HOLY NAME, OAKLEY

489 PITTENWEEM PARISH CHURCH

NO 549 026
Kirkgate, Pittenweem
This ancient monument has developed over a
long time. The earliest work is around 1200.
The Church was extended in 1532 with an
entrance from Cove Wynd and the addition of
the Tolbooth Tower with Bailies Loft. The
interior was refurbished in 1883 in Victorian
style with new entrance, galleries and stairs. The
bell dates from 1662, while the clock in the
tower is a fine example by John Smith. Stained
glass by William Wilson and John Blyth of the
1950s and 1960s. Sunday Service: 11.30am
Open weekdays 8.00am-6.00pm. Keys from the Post
Office (C & A Campbell's) in Market Place
CHURCH OF SCOTLAND ♿ ② 🏛 wc **A**

PITTENWEEM PARISH CHURCH

490 ROSYTH METHODIST CHURCH

NT 114 842

Queensferry Road x Woodside Avenue, Rosyth
Founded in 1916, the present building
was opened in 1970. A sanctuary of A-
frame design with single-storey hall and
ancillary rooms adjoining by Alan
Mercer, architect. Striking 30ft-high
mural, painted in Byzantine style by
Derek Seymour. Sunday Services: 9.30am
(Scottish Episcopal), 11.00am (Methodist)
Open by arrangement, telephone Mr Martin
Rogers 01383 415458
METHODIST 🦽 ⍰

ROSYTH METHODIST CHURCH

491 ALL SAINTS', ST ANDREWS

NO 512 168

North Castle Street, St Andrews
Complex of church hall, rectory and club in Scottish vernacular with an Italian
flavour. Orange pantiled roofs and lots of crowsteps. Slated chancel and bell-tower
by John Douglas of Chester 1906-9; the rest is by Paul Waterhouse 1919-24.
Woodwork of rood, chapel altarpiece and front canopy by Nathaniel Hitch, stone
Madonna and Child by Hew Lorimer 1945, marble font and wrought iron screen by
Farmer & Brindley. Three windows by Herbert Hendrie, Louis Davis and Douglas
Strachan. Sunday Services: 8.00am, 10.00am and 6.00pm
Open daily 10.00am-4.30pm
SCOTTISH EPISCOPAL 🦽 📖 ☕ (Ladyhead book and coffee shop) WC B

ALL SAINTS', ST ANDREWS

492 PARISH CHURCH OF THE HOLY TRINITY, ST ANDREWS

NO 509 167

South Street, St Andrews
Tower and occasional pillars
1412, completely rebuilt on
original ground-plan in 1909,
architect McGregor Chalmers.
South porch commemorates John
Knox preaching here. Much fine
stained glass by Strachan, Davis,
Hendrie, Wilson and others:
clerestory windows have badges
of all Scottish regiments of First

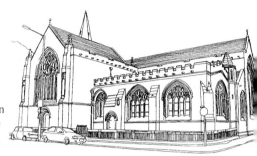

PARISH CHURCH OF THE HOLY TRINITY, ST ANDREWS

World War. Elaborate memorial pulpit of Iona marble, alabaster and onyx.
Decorated font of Caen stone. Memorial tomb of Archbishop Sharp. Oak barrel
roof. Hunter and Memorial Aisle has much fine wood-carving. Seventeenth-century
sacramental silver. Harrison and Harrison organ. Twenty-seven-bell Taylor of
Loughborough carillon. Sunday Services: 11.00am and 6.00pm

Open Tuesday and Saturday 10.00am-12.00 noon, as advertised, or by arrangement,
telephone 01334 474494

CHURCH OF SCOTLAND 🦽 WC 🅿 🛈 ☕ **A**

493 HOPE PARK CHURCH, ST ANDREWS

NO 505 167

St Mary's Place, St Andrews
Completed in 1865, Peddie & Kinnear.
Unusual canopy pulpit. Stained glass. Pewter
communion ware, pulpit falls. A91 St
Andrews, turn right at first mini roundabout,
300 yards on left opposite bus station.
Rail service to Leuchars.
Sunday Services: 9.30am and 11.00am

Church website: www.hopeparkchurch.co.uk
Open Holy Week and Christmas week,
Monday to Friday 10.00am-4.00pm,
July to August, Wednesday 10.00am-4.00pm

CHURCH OF SCOTLAND 🦽 🅿 🛈 📖 WC **A**

HOPE PARK CHURCH, ST ANDREWS

494 MARTYRS CHURCH, ST ANDREWS

NO 510 168

North Street (opposite University Chapel)
Originally United Free Church, 1926-28 by
Gillespie & Scott. Woodwork by Andrew
Thom & Sons of St Andrews. Stained glass
by Douglas Strachan, Herbert Hendrie,
William Wilson, Sadie McLellan and Marjorie
Kemp. Roll of Honour designed and painted
by J D Macgregor. Sunday Service: 11.15am
Open by arrangement with the
Minister 01334 472948
CHURCH OF SCOTLAND
[♿] (side door) ⊘ [▯] [wc] **B**

MARTYRS CHURCH, ST ANDREWS

495 ST ANDREW'S CHURCH, ST ANDREWS

NO 509 164

Queen's Terrace, St Andrews
Sir R Rowand Anderson Church 1869. Fine 19th-century stained glass in the east
and west walls. Two bays of excellent modern stained glass work. An open church
policy and friendly welcome are a stable mission of this vibrant and enthusiastic
congregation. Sunday Services: Holy Communion 8.00am and 10.00am, Choral
Evensong 6.00pm (not Sundays after Christmas, Easter, nor in July and August);
Monday to Friday Morning Prayer 8.30am, Friday Holy Communion 11.00am
SCOTTISH EPISCOPAL [♿] ⊘ [▯] [wc] **B**

496 ST MONANS PARISH CHURCH

NO 523 014

Braehead, St Monans
Occupying a striking position close to the sea,
the church was built by Sir William Dishington
1370, with alterations by William Burn 1828
and Ian G Lindsay 1961. Fourteenth-century
sedilia, piscina and aumbry. Medieval
consecration crosses. Early 19th-century votive
model ship of the line, heraldic bosses. Organ
from Saughtonhall Congregational Church,
Edinburgh, installed here 1995. External
angled buttresses and 'buckle' corbels. A917 to
St Monans, signposted.
Sunday Service: 10.30am
Open April to October during daylight hours
CHURCH OF SCOTLAND  **A**

ST MONANS PARISH CHURCH

SPRINGFIELD CHURCH

497 SPRINGFIELD CHURCH

NO 342 119

Manse Road, Springfield near Cupar, Fife

Built in 1861 to a plain, rectangular design. It contains notable late Victorian
stained glass windows. The building was refurbished in 1970. Linked with Ceres
Church. Sunday Service: 9.45am

Open by arrangement, telephone the Minister 01334 828233

CHURCH OF SCOTLAND [&] [i] [wc]

498 WEMYSS PARISH CHURCH

NT 340 968

Main Road, East Wemyss

Red sandstone church 1937, Peter Sinclair. United with West Wemyss and Lower
Wemyss in 1976, now known as Wemyss Parish Church. Light oak furnishings,
pipe organ, memorial stained glass. Surrounded by gardens with lovely views.
A915 Kirkcaldy–Leven. Sunday Service: 11.00am

Open by arrangement, telephone Mr Barker 01592 714874, or Miss Tod 01592 651495.
Open in conjunction with Wemyss Environmental Centre Open Day. Second Sunday each
summer month until September 2.00-4.30pm. SWACS barbeque 2.00pm, Sunday 3 August.
Guided parties to famous caves, some with Pictish and Viking markings, and Macduff Castle

CHURCH OF SCOTLAND [&] [?] [i]

WEMYSS PARISH CHURCH

THE CHURCH AT WEST WEMYSS

499 THE CHURCH AT WEST WEMYSS

NT 328 949

Main Street, West Wemyss

Built in 1890, Alexander Tod, simple crow-stepped cruciform church of pink sandstone. Spiral tracery in the gable's big rose window. Repurchased from the Church of Scotland in 1972 by Captain Michael Wemyss, who agreed to maintain the building externally if the church continued to be used for worship. The congregation of Wemyss Parish Church is responsible for the interior and continuing worship. Beautiful mural by William McLaren on the inner wall of the transept which now accommodates halls, vestry and kitchen. New wall hangings 2001, sewn by members on the theme 'Jesus, Light of the World'. Old graveyard. Signed off A915 Kirkcaldy–Leven. Sunday Service: 9.30am

Open by arrangement, telephone A Tod, Corner Cottage, 40 South Row,

Coaltown of Wemyss 01592 651498

CHURCH OF SCOTLAND A

500 ST KENNETH'S PARISH CHURCH, WINDYGATES

No 346 006

Originally the United Free Church built by James McIntosh in 1926. Sunday Service: 9.45am

Church website: www.stkenneths.freeserve.co.uk

Open by arrangement with St Kenneth's, Kennoway, telephone 01333 351372

CHURCH OF SCOTLAND ⓘ WC

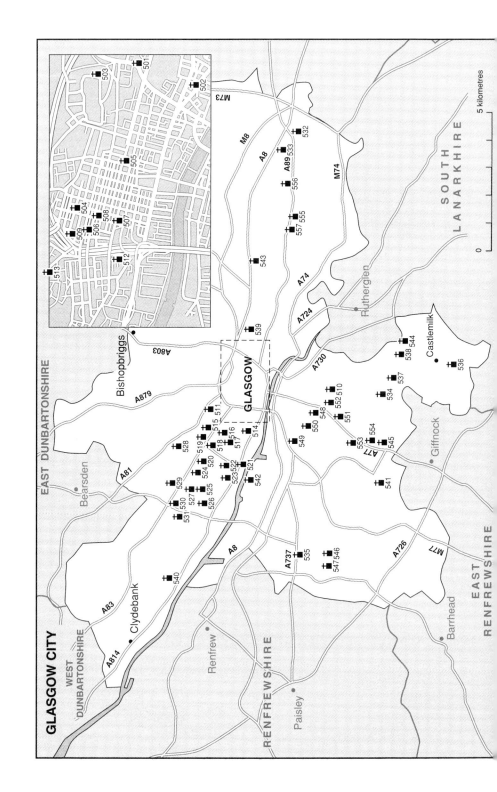

GLASGOW CITY

WEST DUNBARTONSHIRE

EAST DUNBARTONSHIRE

SOUTH LANARKSHIRE

RENFREWSHIRE

EAST RENFREWSHIRE

Bearsden
Clydebank
Bishopbriggs
GLASGOW
Rutherglen
Castlemilk
Giffnock
Barrhead
Renfrew
Paisley

M73
M8
A8
A89
M74
A74
A724
A730
A803
A879
A81
A8
A83
A814
A737
A726
M77
A77

5 kilometres
0   5

GLASGOW

Local Representatives: Mrs Jane Boyd, Manager, Renfield St Stephen's Church Centre, 260 Bath Street, Glasgow G2 4JP (*telephone:* 0141 332 4293)
Mrs Mary Canavan, Flat 10, 9 Victoria Circus, Glasgow G12 9LB (*telephone:* 0141 334 5462)

501 CATHEDRAL CHURCH OF ST MUNGO

NS 603 656
Castle Street, Glasgow
Dedicated in 1136, the largest and most complete of Scotland's medieval cathedrals still in use. Medieval stone screen. Crypt with shrine of St Mungo. Modern tapestry. Organ by Willis 1879, last rebuilt by Harrison & Harrison 1996. Sunday Services: 11.00am and 6.30pm
Open daily, April to September, 9.30am-6.00pm, Sunday 1.00-5.00pm; October to March, 9.30am-4.00pm, Sunday 1.00pm-4.00pm. Light lunches, etc, in adjacent St Mungo's Museum
CHURCH OF SCOTLAND 🚻 ② 🚻 (May to September) 📗 **A**

CATHEDRAL CHURCH
OF ST MUNGO

502 ST ALPHONSUS CHURCH

NS 600 646
217 London Road, Glasgow
A late work by Peter Paul Pugin 1905. Rock-faced sandstone screen façade. The tracery in the gable window formalised into a saltire cross. Inside, the nave arcades have polished granite piers. One hundred and fiftieth anniversary commemorative window 1996 by Lorraine Lamond. Church is in the middle of the 'Barras', 500 metres east of Glasgow Cross. Services: Saturday 4.30pm (Vigil); Sundays 10am, 11.00am, 12.00 noon, 4.45pm
Church website: www.alphonsus.fsbusiness.co.uk / home.htm
Open Monday to Friday 12.00 noon-2.00pm, Saturday and Sunday 9.00am-6.00pm
ROMAN CATHOLIC ② 🚽 **B**

503 ST MUNGO'S CHURCH

NS 600 659
Parson Street, Glasgow
Designed by the London architect George Goldie 1869 in French Gothic style. High altar by Gillespie, Kidd and Coia 1952. The church is in the care of the Passionist congregation. Five apsidal chapels include St Paul of the Cross – founder of the Passionists – St Margaret of Scotland, and Our Lady of Sorrows which has a Portuguese polychrome wood statue. Late 19th-century stained glass by Mayer of Munich.

ST MUNGO'S CHURCH

Gothic-style timber confessionals. Opposite Charles Rennie Mackintosh's Martyrs
School, and five minutes walk from Glasgow Cathedral and the St Mungo Museum.
Sunday Services: 10.00am, 12.00 noon and 7.00pm
Open Monday to Friday 9.30am-1.00pm, 5.30-6.30pm; Saturday 9.30am-1.00pm,
4.30-8.00pm; Sunday 9.30am-1.00pm, 6.30-8.00pm
ROMAN CATHOLIC ② wc **B**

504 ST ALOYSIUS CHURCH

NS 586 660
25 Rose Street, Glasgow
Fine late-Renaissance style church, designed in 1910 by
Belgian-born architect Charles Menart, with a 150ft
campanile, domed crossing and ornate marble-lined
interior. The church is in the care of the Jesuit Order, and
Jesuit saints figure in the stained glass. The shrine of St
John Ogilvie SJ is in the east transept, with mosaics
depicting his martyrdom in Glasgow in 1615. Near
Glasgow School of Art and Sauchiehall Street. Sunday
Services: 9.00am, 10.30am, 12.00 noon (Sung), and 9.00pm
website: www.aloyius-glasgow.org
Open daily 7.30am to 6.30pm and on Sunday until 10.00pm.
Full details of services on the website
ROMAN CATHOLIC 🚻 ② wc 🛈 **A**

ST ALOYSIUS CHURCH

505 ST GEORGE'S – TRON PARISH CHURCH

NS 590 655
165 Buchanan Street, Glasgow
Designed by William Stark and completed 1808. Originally
St George's Parish Church and the eighth burgh church to
be built in Glasgow in what was then the extreme west-end
of the city. St George's united with Tron St Anne's in 1940.
Baroque-style tower with five stages capped by a ribbed
dome and obelisk. Plain, galleried interior with flat ceiling.
The Christ-centred life and ministry of the Rev Tom Allan
(1955-64) was instrumental in the awakening of the
evangelical Christian church in Glasgow and beyond. Sunday
Services: 11.00am and 6.30pm; The 30 Minute Service each
Wednesday 1.10-1.40pm. Wednesday Prayer Meeting 1st and
3rd Wednesday of each month. House Groups 2nd and 4th
Wednesday of each month.
Church website: www.thetron.com
The church is open for prayer and meditation Tuesday to Friday
12.00-2.00pm and Saturday and Sunday 2.00-4.00pm. Other times
by arrangement, telephone Mr William Bradford 0141 332 0187
CHURCH OF SCOTLAND 🚻 ② **A**

ST GEORGE'S –
TRON PARISH CHURCH

506 RENFIELD ST STEPHEN'S PARISH CHURCH AND CENTRE

NS 582 659

260 Bath Street, Glasgow

Designed as an Independent Chapel by London
architect J T Emmett in 1852 in Decorated Gothic
style. Built in beautiful polished Kenmure sandstone
with tall clerestoried nave supported on clustered
columns with finely moulded capitals and arches,
each with carved musical angels. The main stained
glass windows are by Norman Macdougall 1905
depicting the four evangelists, and representations of
Christian vertues, flanking Christ in Glory. There is
also a window by John Clark. A Church Centre with
Side Chapel, offices, extensive halls and restaurant
were added in the 1960s. Patio with fountain from
Glasgow garden festival. Following the collapse of
the steeple during a storm on St Stephens Day 1998,
the church and basement have been sensitively
restored and modernised by Hunter and Clark,
architects CRGP. Sunday Service: 11.00am

Open daily 9.00am-10.00pm.

Oasis Restaurant open 9.00am-4.00pm

CHURCH OF SCOTLAND ♿ ⓘ ☕ wc

RENFIELD ST STEPHEN'S
PARISH CHURCH AND CENTRE

507 ST VINCENT STREET – MILTON FREE CHURCH

NS 583 656

265 St Vincent Street, Glasgow

Alexander Thomson's masterpiece,
distinctive Victorian Presbyterian church,
designed in the classical style, and
embellished by a unique Thomsonian
combination of Egyptian, Indian and
Assyrian influences 1859. Owned by
Glasgow City Council.

Sunday Services: 11.00am and 6.30pm

Open by appointment. Also Doors Open Day,
telephone Mr Sieczowski 0141 649 1563

FREE CHURCH OF SCOTLAND ♿ wc **A**

ST VINCENT STREET –
MILTON FREE CHURCH

ADELAIDE PLACE BAPTIST CHURCH

508 ADELAIDE PLACE BAPTIST CHURCH

NS 584 658

209 Bath Street, Glasgow (corner of Bath Street and Pitt Street)
Built 1877, T L Watson. Stunning redevelopment 1995 of decaying building
creating a multi-functional centre including sanctuary, guest house and nursery.
Sunday Services: 11.00am; Monthly Evening Services
Church website: www.adelaides.co.uk
Open daily 8.00am-8.00pm. Takes part in Glasgow Doors Open Day/Churches Open Day.
Also wide variety of concerts and other events; telephone 0141 248 4970 for details
BAPTIST 👤 ⓘ 🚻 **B**

509 GARNETHILL SYNAGOGUE

NS 502 661

129 Hill Street, Glasgow
Opened in 1879, the first purpose-built
synagogue in Scotland. It was designed by
John McLeod of Glasgow in Romanesque-
cum-Byzantine style. A round-arched portal
with highly decorated orders leads to the
body of the synagogue. Ladies' gallery is
carried on octagonal piers with ornate
Byzantine capitals. Stained glass by J B
Bennet & Sons. Refurbished in 1996. From
Sauchiehall Street walk up Garnet Street to
Hill Street. Services: Saturday 10.00am,
Jewish Festivals 9.30am
Open by arrangement. Contact the caretaker,
Mr Harry McNeill, preferable by letter, or telephone
0141 332 4151. Scottish Jewish Archives open by
arrangement, telephone 0141 332 4911
JEWISH 👤 (three steps) ⓘ **B**

GARNETHILL SYNAGOGUE

510 HOLY CROSS

NS 586 624

113 Dixon Avenue/Belleisle Street

Romanesque style church designed by
Pugin and Pugin and opened in 1911.
Rich interior with marble carvings.
Stained glass windows above the
sanctuary by Hardman, representing St
John the Evangelist and St Margaret of
Scotland, and above the gallery
depicting the Exultation of the Holy
Cross, St Peter, St Andrew, St Helen and
St Sylvester. Mosaic of 1961 of Christ
Triumphant above the altar. Organ by

HOLY CROSS

Forster & Andrews, built 1895 for Alva Parish Church and installed 1983. Stations
of the Cross by Beyeart. Services: Saturday Vigil 6.00pm; Sunday Masses 9.30am,
11.00am, 12.15pm, 8.00pm

Open Monday to Saturday 7.30am-7.00pm

ROMAN CATHOLIC ♿ wc ② **B**

511 ST COLUMBA'S CHURCH

NS 583 671

74 Hopehill Road, Glasgow

By Gillespie, Kidd & Coia, completed in 1941, the year of the Clydebank and
Govan blitz, and the cost met by the families of the area, each of whom paid 6d
per brick. Italian Romanesque style with an imposing west front. Sculpture of the
Paschal Lamb over central door. Painted panels of the Stations of the Cross by
Hugh Adam Crawford, from the Catholic Pavilion at the Glasgow Empire
Exhibition 1938. In the sanctuary a marble reredos with a carved crucifix by Benno
Schotz. North of St George's Cross, via Maryhill Road. Services: Saturday Vigil
Mass 6.00pm; Sunday Mass 11.00am and 5.00pm

Open at any time, by contacting the Priest in the house adjacent

ROMAN CATHOLIC ♿ ② **A**

ST COLUMBA'S CHURCH

512 ST PATRICK'S

NS 580 655
137 William Street
Designed by Messrs Pugin of London in early Decorated style,
the church was opened for worship in 1898. One of the most
striking of the many features within the church is the High
Altar of white marble, supported on six columns of Connemara
marble with floreated capitals. The throne is surmounted by a
magnificent cupola of Caen stone. Services: Saturday 6.00pm;
Sunday 10.00am and 12.00 noon; various daily services
Open daily dawn to dusk
ROMAN CATHOLIC [♿] [wc] (?) ☕ **B**

ST PATRICK'S

513 WOODLANDS METHODIST CHURCH

NS 576 665
229 Woodlands Road, Glasgow
Built for Swedenborgians by David Barclay 1909 in use
by Methodists since 1977. A wide stair leads to the
church. Organ 1876 from Cathedral Street Swedenborgian Church, originally built by Foster & Andrews
and augmented with pipes from Willis organ at St John's,
Sauchiehall Street. Windows by Guthrie & Wells and
George Benson, and war memorial window from
St John's. Nearest rail station Charing Cross; nearest
underground Kelvinside. Services: Sunday 11.00am
Open by arrangement, telephone the church office 0141 332 7779
METHODIST [♿] (?) [wc]

WOODLANDS
METHODIST CHURCH

514 SANDYFORD HENDERSON CHURCH

NS 570 659
13 Kelvinhaugh Street
Early Gothic style 1855 by J T Emmett, completed by John Honeyman. Fine stained
glass aisle windows in geometric/floral patterns by Ballantine & Allan, Edinburgh,
1857, and three pictorial west windows by William Wailes,
Newcastle 1859-60. 3-manual 'Father' Willis organ 1866
moved into First World War memorial chancel, added in
1922. Exterior stonework restored in 2000. Closed for
interior refurbishment from August 2003 to July 2004.
Sunday Services: to be held in Kelvin Park Lorne Hotel, 923
Sauchiehall Street, Glasgow (close to the church) 11.00am
and 6.00pm; Wednesday: 7.30pm Prayer and Bible Study at
Finnieston Evangelical Church, Minerva Street, Glasgow
For information about services or refurbishment,
telephone Professor A Nash 0141 886 5871
CHURCH OF SCOTLAND **B**

SANDYFORD
HENDERSON CHURCH

515 ST MARY'S CATHEDRAL

NS 578 668

300 Great Western Road, Glasgow
Fine Gothic revival church by Sir George Gilbert Scott with
outstanding contemporary murals by Gwyneth Leech and
newly restored Phoebe Traquair reredos. 3-manual pipe
organ. Glasgow's only full peal of bells. Major restoration
2001. A82, three-quarters of a mile west of St George's
Cross. Two minutes walk Kelvinbridge Underground.
Sunday Services: Eucharist 8.00am, Sung Eucharist
10.00am, Eucharist 12.00 noon, Choral Evensong 6.30pm
Open daily, 9.30am-5.00pm
SCOTTISH EPISCOPAL 🦽 📖 ⊘ wc wc **A**

ST MARY'S CATHEDRAL

516 WELLINGTON CHURCH

NS 570 667

University Avenue, Glasgow
T L Watson's Roman Classical church with mighty
Corinthian columned portico 1884. Renaissance style
interior with fine plaster ceilings. Pipe organ Forster &
Andrews. Refectory situated in crypt. City buses 11 and
44. Underground to Hillhead or Kelvinbridge, ten
minutes walk. Sunday Services: 11.00am and 7.00pm
Church website: www.wellingtonchurch.co.uk
Access to church via crypt, open Monday to Friday, during
University term. Also Glasgow Doors Open Day
CHURCH OF SCOTLAND 🦽 ⌑ 📖 ⊘ ☕ (and lunch during term time) wc **A**

WELLINGTON CHURCH

517 UNIVERSITY MEMORIAL CHAPEL

NS 568 666

The Square, Glasgow University, Glasgow
1923-27 by Sir J J Burnet in Scots Gothic and in harmony
with the University buildings of Sir George Gilbert Scott.
The structure is reinforced concrete, faced with stone. Tall
interior with sculpture by Archibald Dawson. Ten of the
stained glass windows are by Douglas Strachan in a cycle
depicting the whole of human life as a spiritual enterprise.
Other windows by Gordon Webster and Lawrence Lee.
The chapel incorporates the Lion and Unicorn Stair
salvaged from the Old College. Sunday Service: 11.00am;
Monday to Friday: 8.45am during term time
Open 9.00am-5.00pm Monday to Friday, 9.00am-12.00 noon
Saturday. Chapel Choir Service December.
Tours available from visitors' centre
ECUMENICAL 🦽 ⊘ ⌑ 📖 ☕ (all in visitors' centre) **A**

UNIVERSITY
MEMORIAL CHAPEL

518 HILLHEAD BAPTIST CHURCH

NS 568 671
Cresswell Street, off Byres Road, Glasgow
Designed by T L Watson 1883, in Greek
Revival style. The impressive harmony and
richness of the original dark woodwork
and pews gives an intimacy to this interior
where sunlight is filtered through delicately
coloured glass. Fine Lewis pipe organ.
Near to Botanic Gardens.
Sunday Services: 11.00am and 6.30pm
Open by arrangement, telephone 0141 339 3254
BAPTIST ⓘ ☕ wc **B**

HILLHEAD BAPTIST CHURCH

519 LANSDOWNE PARISH CHURCH

NS 576 669
416 Great Western Road, Glasgow
Built 1863 to a design by John Honeyman. Spire 218 feet, one of the slimmest in
Europe, a powerful landmark on Great Western Road. Box pews. Beautiful stained
glass by Alfred and Gordon Webster, and war memorial frieze by Evelyn Beale.
Pipe organ 1911, Norman & Beard, said to have the finest tuba rank in Glasgow
with some wonderful flutes. On corner with Park Road, opposite Kelvinbridge
underground. City buses 20, 41, 59, 66, from city centre.
Sunday Service: 11.00am (creche available)
*Open by arrangement, 0141 339 2794, or Mr J Stuart 0141 339 2678. Also Glasgow Doors
Open Day, telephone the Minister*
CHURCH OF SCOTLAND ⓘ 🏠 ☕ wc **A**

520 KELVINSIDE HILLHEAD PARISH CHURCH

NS 567 673
Saltoun Street, Observatory Road, Dowanhill, Glasgow
1876 by James Sellars, the design is said to have been
much influenced by William Leiper. A tall apsed church,
the west front is full of carving. The interior was recast
in 1921 by P MacGregor Chalmers. Communion table of
Rochette marble. Good stained glass by Burne-Jones for
William Morris & Co 1893 and Sadie McLellan 1958.
Organ by H Willis & Son 1876, restored in 1930. At
junction of Saltoun Street with Observatory Road. City
buses and underground to Hillhead. Sunday Services:
11.00am; also October to May 6.30pm
*Open Saturday 10.30am-12.30pm all year. Other times,
telephone the Minister 0141 339 2865. Venue for many concerts*
CHURCH OF SCOTLAND ♿ 🏠 ⓘ ☕ wc **A**

KELVINSIDE HILLHEAD
PARISH CHURCH

521 ST SIMON

NS 562 659

33 Partick Bridge Street

Founded by Daniel Gallagher, famous as
'the priest who taught David Livingstone
Latin'. Built 1858 by Charles O'Neill as St
Peter's, renovated in 1956 by Gillespie, Kidd
& Coia. Marble altar has a panel by
Mortimer depicting Christ comforted by
His Mother. Used by the Polish Community
since World War II. Services: Sunday
10.00am, 11.00am (in Polish), 12.15pm and
6.30pm; Monday to Saturday 12.30pm
Church website: www.stsimonspartick.org.uk
Open daily 10.00am-2.00pm
ROMAN CATHOLIC ♿ wc ? ☕

ST SIMON

522 ST PETER'S

NS 561 668

46-50 Hyndland Street

Substantial church by Peter Paul Pugin 1903 in revived Gothic style. Bright interior
lit by clerestory windows. Elaborate reredos. Pipe organ 1916, restored 1999. Good
stained glass 1903 and 1937. Redecorated for Centenary celebrations 2003.
Services: Vigil Saturday 6.00pm; Sunday 10.00am, 12.00 noon and 6.00pm;
weekdays 8.00am and 10.00am
Church website: http://peelcom.com/partickchurches/stpeters
Open daily Wednesday, Thursday and Friday 7.00am-11.00am; Saturday, Sunday,
Monday and Tuesday 9.00am-7.00pm
ROMAN CATHOLIC wc ? **B**

523 PARTICK METHODIST CHURCH

NS 553 666

524 Dumbarton Road, G11 6SN

Church and halls by W F McGibbon,
opened in 1881. Good stained glass by
Abbot & Co 1957. Fine organ by Forster
& Andrews 1886. Organ recitals most
Saturday afternoons (contact church to
confirm times). Public transport by bus,
underground and train. Sunday Service:
11.00am; occasional evening services
Open by arrangement, telephone 0141 334 1181
METHODIST ♿ wc

PARTICK METHODIST CHURCH

524 CATHEDRAL CHURCH OF ST LUKE

NS 563 675

27 Dundonald Road, Dowanhill, Glasgow
Formerly Belhaven United Presbyterian
Church by James Sellars 1877, powerfully
vertical Normandy Gothic. The
congregation of St Luke's relocated here
in 1960. The main front is inspired by
Dunblane Cathedral. Marvellous display of
stained glass, Stephen Adam 1877, richly
stencilled roof timbers, and original light
fittings and furniture. Modern iconostasis
featuring icons, some of which were
painted on Mount Athos in the traditional
Byzantine style.
Sunday Service: 10.30am-1.00pm
Open by arrangement, telephone
Mr N Pitticas 0141 339 7368
GREEK ORTHODOX **B**

CATHEDRAL CHURCH OF ST LUKE

525 ST BRIDE'S CHURCH, HYNDLAND

NS 559 676

69 Hyndland Road, Glasgow
Designed by G F Bodley, who built the
chancel 1904, the nave 1907 and part of the
north aisle. H O Tarbolton completed the
church (1913-16), including rebuilding part of
the nave and adding two north aisles and the
tower. The interior scheme is mainly
Bodley's. Carved woodwork by Scott Morton
& Co. Sculpture of Our Lady and Child by
Eric Gill 1915. Very fine 2-manual organ by
Hill 1865, installed here 1972. Sunday
Services: Sung Eucharist 10.30am; daily
Eucharist, times vary
Open by arrangement, telephone Mr Rae 0141 332
8430 and Rev R F Jones 0141 334 1401.
Occasional Choral Evensong, usually with visiting
choirs and concerts as advertised
SCOTTISH EPISCOPAL wc **B**

ST BRIDE'S CHURCH, HYNDLAND

526 BROOMHILL CHURCH

NS 549 674
Randolph Road, Glasgow
Red sandstone church 1902, and hall
1899, designed by Stewart & Paterson.
Stained glass by Guthrie & Wells,
Glasgow, Abbey Studio, Edinburgh
and Brian Hutchison. Pipe organ
refurbished by Harrison and Harrison
1997. Located at corner of Randolph
Road/Marlborough Avenue.
City buses: 16, 44. Sunday Services:
11.00am and 6.30pm
Church website: www.broomhillchurch.co.uk
Open by arrangement, telephone
Mr J Boyle 0141 339 2552
CHURCH OF SCOTLAND   **B**

BROOMHILL CHURCH

527 HYNDLAND PARISH CHURCH

NS 559 675
79 Hyndland Road, Glasgow
William Leiper 1887 in red Ballochmyle sandstone. Floodlit timber vaulted interior
roof, columns with richly carved capitals. Gleaming original terrazzo floor.
Original furnishings beautiful marble pulpit and common table, Henry Willis pipe
organ, the whole building complemented by a collection of stained glass with
windows by Norman Macdougall 1889, Douglas Stachan 1921, Douglas Hamilton
1930, Gordon Webster 1961, William Wilson 1962, Sax Shaw 1968, Paul Lucky
1984, Rab MacInnes 1999. Additionally three windows by Oscar Paterson 1897
salvaged from St Bride's Church, Partick. Travel by Underground to Hillhead or
Partick from the city centre, or by
train from Queen Street Low Level to
Hyndland. Bus from city centre, 44 to
top Clarence Drive, or 11 to Church
itself. Sunday Service: 11.00am 1st
Sunday in October until Palm
Sunday; 10.30am Easter Day until last
Sunday in September; 6.30pm 1st
Sunday in October to Easter Day
website: www.hyndlandparishchurch.org
Open by arrangement with church officer,
telephone 0141 338 6637
CHURCH OF SCOTLAND

 A

HYNDLAND PARISH CHURCH

528 ST GREGORY BARBARIGO

NS 565 686

130 Kelvindale Road

The church, dedicated to St Gregory Barbarigo, is strategically placed in the centre of the parish. The parish was founded in 1965 and the church, designed by Borthwick & Watson, was opened in 1971. The Kelvin walkway, which runs along the west side of the church, enhances the complex of buildings. One of the many attractive features of the church is the stained glass Stations of the Cross. Mass times: Saturday Vigil 6.00pm, Sunday 9.30am and 11.00am

Parish Feast Day 17 June 2004, Summer Fête 19 June 2004, Christmas Fayre 5 December 2004. Open by arrangement with Parish Clergy, telephone 0141 946 3009. Library open after Mass every day and 10.00am-2.00pm Saturday

ROMAN CATHOLIC ♿ wc ♪ ☕

529 ST JOHN'S RENFIELD, KELVINDALE

NS 558 683

Beaconsfield Road, Kelvindale, Glasgow

Bold and striking church in a commanding position. Topped by an openwork flèche, the stonework has the understated detail characteristic of its time, 1931 (architect James Taylor Thomson). Light and lofty interior, complete with original fitments, and stained glass by Douglas Strachan and Gordon Webster. Turn off Great Western Road to Kelvindale. Sunday Service: 11.00am all year; 8.30pm September to Easter, and first Sunday of month, Easter to August

Open Wednesday, Thursday, Friday 9.30am-12.30pm

CHURCH OF SCOTLAND ♿ ♪ wc **B**

ST JOHN'S RENFIELD, KELVINDALE

530 TEMPLE-ANNIESLAND CHURCH

NS 547 699

869 Crow Road, Glasgow

Red sandstone Gothic-style church built by Badenoch & Bruce 1905. Adjoining hall was original United Presbyterian church built in 1899 by Alexander Petrie. U-plan interior with red pine panelled gallery and pews. War memorial, from Temple Parish Church (united with Temple-Anniesland 1984 and now demolished) with unique clock designed and built 1921 by first minister, Rev J Carswell. Sunday Services: 11.00am and 6.30pm, July to August 11.00am only; Thursday: 11.00am

Open Thursdays 10.00am-12.00 noon (not July)

CHURCH OF SCOTLAND ♿ ♪ ⚴ ☕ **B**

TEMPLE-ANNIESLAND CHURCH

531   JORDANHILL PARISH CHURCH

NS 544 682

28 Woodend Drive, Glasgow
Church 1905 and hall, west aisle and gallery 1923 by
James Miller in Perpendicular style. Battlemented and
pinnacled tower. Mock hammerbeam roof spans the
broad interior. Further extensions to hall 1971 and
sanctuary refurbishment 1980 by Wylie Shanks. Organ
by Lewis 1923. Woodend Drive is off Crow Road (A739
Clyde Tunnel to Bearsden). Sunday Services: 10.30am
and 6.30pm, 1st Sunday of the month; Wednesday:
10.00am, September to June

JORDANHILL
PARISH CHURCH

Open Monday to Friday 8.30am-12.30pm and 1.30pm-5.00pm
CHURCH OF SCOTLAND   ♿ ⓓ 🍴 📖 wc **B**

532   BAILLIESTON ST ANDREW'S CHURCH

NS 681 639

Church Street, Baillieston, Glasgow
Present church completed 1974 following the union of
Baillieston Old and Rhinsdale Churches in 1966.
Sexagonal design with slim spire, by James Houston &
Sons of Kilbirnie. Allen organ installed. Sunday
Services: 11.00am and 6.30pm

BAILLIESTON
ST ANDREW'S CHURCH

Open Monday, Wednesday and Friday 9.30am-12.00 noon
CHURCH OF SCOTLAND   ♿ ⓓ

533   ST BRIDGET'S CHURCH, BAILLIESTON

NS 680 642

15 Swinton Road, Baillieston, Glasgow
Built 1893 by Pugin & Pugin in light sandstone. Notable 'Creation' rose window
above sanctuary area and carved 'Christ Triumphant' below. Mosaic work 'Suffer
the Children', 'Nativity', 'Glories of Mary',
'Annunciation', and stained glass windows
'Christ with Saints' and 'Sacred Heart' 1945-
49 by the John Hardman Studios. 'St Bridget'
and 'St Colmcille' windows by Shona McInnes
1999. Located 200 yards west of Edinburgh
Road/Coatbridge Road A8/A89.
Sunday Services: 9.00am and 10.30am, 12.00
noon and 6.00pm; daily Service 9.30am;
Saturday 5.30pm

Open for some hours each day.
Otherwise contact Church House adjacent
ROMAN CATHOLIC ⓓ

ST BRIDGET'S CHURCH, BAILLIESTON

534 BATTLEFIELD EAST PARISH CHURCH

NS 586 613

1220 Cathcart Road

The first church on this site was by
John Honeyman 1865 in Early English
style. It became the hall in 1912 when
the adjacent red sandstone church by
John Galt was opened. Spacious
interior with galleries supported on
cast-iron columns and a fine timber
wagon roof. Stained glass includes
windows by Abbey Studios 1937,
Sadie McLellan 1972 and Susan Laidler
1980. Pipe organ by Ingram of
Edinburgh. Near Mount Florida
railway station. Sunday Service: 11.00am; and occasional Evening Service 6.30pm

Open Monday to Friday 9.45am-11.45am. Ring bell on door of glass corridor for the Beadle

CHURCH OF SCOTLAND ♿ ⊘ 🏠 wc ☕ **B**

BATTLEFIELD EAST PARISH CHURCH

535 CARDONALD PARISH CHURCH

NS 526 639

2155 Paisley Road West, Glasgow

Opened 1889 as a mission church. This is the first church designed by
P MacGregor Chalmers. Early English Gothic of Ballochmyle red sandstone.
Stained timber roofs open to the top. Chancel has alabaster and stone pulpit by
Jackson Brown & Co and fine workmanship in its oak communion table, reading
desk and elders' benches. North wall screen by Ross & Manson. Rich and varied
collection of stained glass windows
including three-light chancel
window by J & W Guthrie, series
of six windows by Sadie McLellan,
Millennium window (2000) by
Roland Mitton. Sunday Services:
11.15am, Communion Sundays
11.15am and 6.30pm

Open Tuesday mornings January to
May, September to December
10.00am-11.00am. Viewing by
arrangement 11.00am-12.00 noon
0141 882 1051. Open daily
Christmas week 10.00am-12.00 noon

CHURCH OF SCOTLAND

♿ ⊘ ☕ 🏠 ⚲ wc **B**

CARDONALD PARISH CHURCH

CARMUNNOCK PARISH CHURCH, 'THE KIRK IN THE BRAES'

536 CARMUNNOCK PARISH CHURCH, 'THE KIRK IN THE BRAES'

NS 599 575
Kirk Road, Carmunnock
Rebuilt 1767 on pre-Reformation site and repaired in 1840. External stone staircases to three galleries. Laird's gallery. Stained glass by Norman Macleod MacDougall. Ancient graveyard has watch-house with original instructions for grave watchers 1828, and burial vault of Stirling-Stuart family, Lairds of Castlemilk. City bus 31. Sunday Service: 11.00am
Open April to September, Saturday 2.00-4.00pm. Other times by arrangement, telephone 0141 644 1578. Conducted tours, Saturday 2.00pm on Glasgow Doors Open Day
CHURCH OF SCOTLAND ♿ ⊘ ⌇ ⬚ ⬚ ⬚ (in village) **B**

537 CATHCART OLD PARISH CHURCH

NS 587 606
119 Carmunnock Road
Original design 1923 by Clifford & Lunan, but completed 1928 by Watson, Salmon & Gray. The size is enhanced by the low porch and range of vestries. South transept contains a display of the Church's history over 800 years; the north transept was converted in 1962 to the McKellar Memorial Chapel. Tapestry of The Last Supper by Charles Marshall, stained glass by R Douglas McLundie. Organ by John R Miller 1890, restored and converted to electro-mechanical action 1994. Services: Sunday 11.00am
Church website: www.glasgowthecaringcity.org
Open Monday to Friday 10.00am-2.00pm
CHURCH OF SCOTLAND 🚾 ⊘ ⬚ **B**

CATHCART OLD PARISH CHURCH

538 CROFTFOOT PARISH CHURCH

NS 603 602

318 Croftpark Avenue, Glasgow

Keppie & Henderson 1936. A neat Byzantine
design in red brick with ashlar facings.
Carved patterns, symbolising scriptural
themes, decorate the main door portico, nave
and chancel columns and chancel furnishings.
The bell is the Second World War memorial.
Ten minute walk from Croftfoot railway
station. Sunday Services: 11.00am and 6.30pm

Open Monday to Friday, 9.00am-12.00 noon,
and 1.30pm-4.00pm, except public holidays.

Tours, telephone Mr W Yule 0141 637 7613

CHURCH OF SCOTLAND

CROFTFOOT PARISH CHURCH

♿ ⓒ 🍵 (Wednesday am) wc **B**

539 OUR LADY OF GOOD COUNSEL

NS 610 655

73 Craigpark, Dennistoun

Designed by Glasgow Architects, Gillespie, Kidd & Coia, and opened in 1965.
Features a dramatic tapering and sloping copper-clad roof with deep eaves. Inside
there is outstanding brickwork and a high wooden ceiling. Imposing altar. Services:
daily 10.00am; Saturday Vigil 5.30pm; Sunday 10.00am, 12.00 noon, 5.30pm

Church website: www.olgc.org.uk

Open 9.00am-11.00am weekdays, 9.00am-1.00pm and 5.00pm-6.00pm Sundays

ROMAN CATHOLIC ♿ wc ⓒ 📖 **A**

540 DRUMRY ST MARY

NS 515 709

Drumry Road East, Drumchapel

Simple church (Ross, Doak & Whitelaw,
1955-57) with shallow-pitched roof,
linked to hall by a vestibule with a bell
turret. Contains a 120-year old marble
font from Old Partick Parish Church.
Main feature is the Garden of
Remembrance for Bereaved Parents as
designed by and featured in BBC's
'Beechgrove Garden'. Stones in the
garden from the 'Peel of Drumry'.
Sunday Service: 11.00am

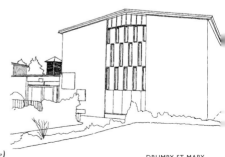

DRUMRY ST MARY

Church open weeknights evenings;
Garden open at all times (access via rear gate)

CHURCH OF SCOTLAND ⓒ wc 🍵

541 EASTWOOD PARISH CHURCH

NS 558 607

5 Mansewood Road, Glasgow

Built 1863, in transitional Gothic, arranged on a
cruciform plan. Designed by Charles Wilson,
who died before its completion, assisted by
David Thomson. Its stained glass windows
include examples by the Königliche
Glasmalerei-Anstalt, München (Royal Glass
Painting Establishment, Munich) and by
Gordon Webster. The family church of the
Maxwells of Pollock. Sunday Service: 11.15am
Open by arrangement, telephone 0141 586 6684
or 0141 632 0724

CHURCH OF SCOTLAND [WC] [ ] **B**

EASTWOOD PARISH CHURCH

542 GOVAN OLD PARISH CHURCH (ST CONSTANTINE'S)

NS 554 659

866 Govan Road, Glasgow

Affectionately called 'the people's cathedral'. Set well back in a churchyard of
great antiquity. The present building stands in a long series of churches on this site
dating back to Celtic times. Completed 1888, the design by Robert Rowand
Anderson proved very influential for the next 50 years. Its style is Early English in
the Scottish manner, with details based on Pluscarden Priory near Elgin. A set of
twelve windows by Charles E Kempe. Good stained glass by Burlison & Grylls and
Clayton & Bell in the Steven Chapel and by Shrigley & Hunt in the baptistry.
Archaeological excavation has provided a fresh context for the large collection of
early medieval sculpture including hogback stones, cross shafts, cross slabs and the
richly ornamented and recently conserved Govan Sarcophagus. Fine pipe organ
originally built by Brindley and
Foster. City buses and
underground to Govan Station.
Sunday Service: 11.00am; daily
Service: Monday to Friday
10.00am

Open 1st Wednesday in June to 3rd
Saturday in September, Wednesdays
10.30am-12.30pm, and
Wednesdays, Thursdays and
Saturdays 1.00-4.00pm.
Also open by arrangement,
telephone 0141 440 2466

CHURCH OF SCOTLAND

[ ] [ ] [ ] [WC] [ ] **A**

GOVAN OLD PARISH CHURCH (ST CONSTANTINE'S)

543 HIGH CARNTYNE PARISH CHURCH

NS 636 653
358 Carntynehall Road, Glasgow
First church extension charge of Church of Scotland. Congregation met in 'the
hut' until building was completed by J Taylor Thomson 1932. Original single bell
still in use. Extensive suite of halls built alongside the church in 1955. Buses 33,
41, 42, 43, 51. Sunday Service: 11.00am; Wednesday 9.30am
Open Wednesday and Saturday 10.00am-12.00 noon
CHURCH OF SCOTLAND 🛆 ⑨ 🖵 (by arrangement) 🆆ᴄ **B**

544 KING'S PARK PARISH CHURCH

NS 601 608
242 Castlemilk Road, Glasgow
Red brick with stone dressings, Romanesque
in style by Hutton & Taylor 1932, an
innovation in church design specially
evolved by the Presbytery of Glasgow.
The commission was the result of an
architectural competition. Notable collection
of stained glass windows by Sadie
McLellan, Gordon Webster, David Hamilton

KING'S PARK PARISH CHURCH

and others. Set in a pleasant small garden. Ample parking. By rail to King's Park or
Croftfoot, ten minute walk. First Bus number 7 to Castlemilk Road.
Sunday Services: 11.00am, 6.30pm; 11.00am only July to August
Open Monday to Friday 9.30am-12.00 noon, all year except public holidays.
Tours, telephone Mr Ian Henderson 0141 589 5603
CHURCH OF SCOTLAND 🛆 ⑨ (on request) 📖 ⑨ 🖵 (Tues am) 🆆ᴄ

545 ST MARGARET'S, NEWLANDS

NS 569 610
Kilmarnock Road, Newlands, Glasgow
The church, a 'classic of the Romanesque Revival', was designed by Dr Peter
MacGregor Chalmers and built in stages between 1910 and 1935. A basilica with
double apse, it is splendid in size and simple
beauty. The stained glass windows include
examples by Morris & Co, the St Enoch Studio
and Gordon Webster. With three new windows
by John Clark. Sunday Services: Said Eucharist
9.00am, Sung Eucharist 10.30am, Evensong
6.30pm; Tuesdays 10.30am Said Eucharist
Church website: www.gn.afc.org/st-margarets
Open 9.00-12.30pm, Monday to Friday. Other details
from church office 0141 636 1131
SCOTTISH EPISCOPAL (Anglican) 🛆 ⑨ **B**

ST MARGARET'S, NEWLANDS

546 ST JAMES'S PARISH CHURCH, POLLOK

NS 530 626

183 Meiklerig Crescent, Pollok, Glasgow

Church built 1895 as Pollokshields Titwood Church, and moved stone by stone from its original site four miles away by Thomson, McCrae & Sanders, and rededicated in 1953. Congregation worshipped in a school hall and then in a wooden hut until the building was completed. Good stained glass. Within the Sanctuary there is a storytelling centre – 'The Village' – which provides programmes of events for the community. Bus service 3 from Glasgow city centre. M8, Junction for Paisley Road West. Sunday Service: 11.00am

Open Saturdays 10.00am-12.00 noon. Close to Pollok House, the Burrell Collection, Crookston Castle and Ross Hall

CHURCH OF SCOTLAND   🔲 🔲 🔲 🔲 🔲 **B**

547 ST JAMES THE GREAT

NS 525 625

20 Beltrees Road (junction with Crosstobs Road)

Parish established in 1949 and the present building by Alexander McAnally was opened in 1968. The external walls are of pink Accrington brick with stone dressings and a stone façade. Inside the walls are of cream brick and the ceiling is of cedarwood. Wrought-iron work by Thomas Bogie and Sons of Edinburgh. The circular nave can seat 544. The high altar is of various marbles. Services: Saturday 10.00am, Vigil 5.30pm; Sunday 10.00am and 12.00 noon, daily Mass 10.00am

Open daily from 8.00am-11.00am, Tuesdays and Wednesdays 8.00am-8.00pm

ROMAN CATHOLIC   🔲 🔲 🔲 🔲 🔲 🔲

548 ST NINIAN'S CHURCH, POLLOKSHIELDS

NS 582 632

1 Albert Drive, Pollokshields, Glasgow

The foundation stone of St Ninian's was laid on 16 September 1872, and building commenced to a design by David Thomson. Completed in 1877, and extended west in 1887. The apse is decorated with frescoes painted by William Hole 1901, and the charming little sacristy designed by H D Wilson, a member of the congregation, in 1914. Good stained glass including windows by Heaton, Butler & Bayne. The windows in the chancel represent The Gospel Story, by Stephen Adam. Sunday Services: Holy Communion (Said) 8.30am, Sung Eucharist and Sermon 10.15am, Evening Prayer (Said) 6.30pm

Open by arrangement, telephone Mrs Y Grieve

0141 638 7254

SCOTTISH EPISCOPAL

🔲 (from rear of church, notification needed) 🔲 🔲 🔲 🔲 **B**

ST NINIAN'S CHURCH,
POLLOKSHIELDS

549 SHERBROOKE ST GILBERT'S CHURCH, POLLOKSHIELDS

NS 561 636

240 Nithsdale Road, Pollokshields, Glasgow
The original building by William Forsyth
McGibbon was ravaged by fire in 1994, its
centenary year. Now the church is restored
by James Cuthbertson, architect. The interior
features the work of Scottish craftsmen:
stained glass windows, inspired by the
themes of creation, the Cross and rebirth, by
Stained Glass Design Partnership, Kilmaurs;
3-manual pipe organ by Lammermuir Pipe
Organs; pulpit, tables and font by Bill
Nimmo, East Lothian. Close to Dumbreck
railway station, and on 59 bus route.

SHERBROOKE ST GILBERT'S
CHURCH, POLLOKSHIELDS

Sunday Service: 10.30am

Open by arrangement, telephone the Church Officer 0141 427 1968

CHURCH OF SCOTLAND ♿ ② ⚲ 📖 wc **B**

550 POLLOKSHIELDS PARISH CHURCH

NS 569 615

Junction of Shields Road and Albert Drive
Large Gothic church with a tall spire by Robert Baldie, 1877-78, the chancel was
remodelled 1911-14. White marble pulpit by Peter McGregor Chalmers. Stained
glass by Stephen Adam, W & J J Keir and Robert Anning Bell. Organ by Harrison
& Harrison 1913. At the rear of the church are four needlework panels by Sally
Moodie Harkness representing the Sun, Moon, Earth and Sea.
Services: Sunday 11.00am; Wednesday 9.45am.

Open Wednesday 10.00am-12.00 noon; or by arrangement, telephone the
Church Officer 07855 288801

CHURCH OF SCOTLAND ♿ wc ② 🖥 (Wednesday) **B**

551 QUEEN'S PARK BAPTIST CHURCH

NS 579 266

180 Queen's Drive and Balvicar Drive, Glasgow
'QP', an evangelical-charismatic church, is a changing church and recent years have
seen significant growth which parallels spiritual renewal in the fellowship,
preaching, ministry, outreach and worship. Since October 1995 the church occupies
two nearby sites: a Romanesque building (Camphill), McKissack & Rowan 1887;
and a French Gothic building (Queen's Drive), William Leiper 1876. The interiors
of both buildings have been significantly modernised and renovated to make them
relevant places for Christian worship and work in the 21st century. The Camphill
building was fully stone cleaned and repaired during 1998-99. Queen's

QUEEN'S PARK BAPTIST CHURCH (BALVICAR DRIVE, LEFT, AND QUEEN'S DRIVE, RIGHT)

Drive/Pollokshaws Road, two minutes from Queen's Park Station.
Sunday Services: 10.30am and 6.30pm
Open Sundays, and other times by arrangement, telephone Dr J Brooks 0141 423 3962
BAPTIST ♿ ② 🚻 📖 👤 **A** (Camphill) **B** (Queen's Drive) 🚾

552 QUEEN'S PARK CHURCH

NS 579 625
170 Queen's Drive, on junction with Albert Avenue
Nave and aisles Gothic church with spire on corner site by James Thomson 1873-75. Halls added 1879. Galleried interior with two tiers of cast-iron columns and a barrel-vaulted roof. Stained glass window by Daniel Cottier and some exposed wall decoration. Organ by Lewis & Co 1903. War memorial plaques for Queens Park West, Strathbungo, Queens Park High and Crosshill Queens Park Church.
Sunday Services 11.00am and 6.30pm
Church website: www.qpp.org.uk
Open by arrangement, telephone 0141 637 9605 or 0141 423 2302
CHURCH OF SCOTLAND 🚾 **B**

553 SHAWLANDS UNITED REFORMED CHURCH, GLASGOW

NS 570 622
111 Moss-side Road, Shawlands, Glasgow
Formerly a Churches of Christ church, by Miller & Black 1908, in red sandstone. Open baptistry. From Shawlands Cross 300 yards.
Sunday Service: 11.00am
Church website: www.shawlands-urc.co.uk
Open by arrangement, telephone 0141 638 2442
UNITED REFORMED ♿ ☕ 🚾 🚻

SHAWLANDS UNITED REFORMED CHURCH, GLASGOW

SOUTH SHAWLANDS CHURCH

554 SOUTH SHAWLANDS CHURCH

NS 569 615

Regwood Street/Deanston Drive

Perpendicular Gothic by Miller and Black, dedicated in 1913. An unusual feature of
the interior is the cantilevered gallery. Beautiful stained glass including a window
in the chancel by Douglas Hamilton 1959. Sunday Services: 11.00am (10.00am in
school holidays) and 6.30pm on 2nd Sunday

Open by arrangement, telephone 0141 632 0013

CHURCH OF SCOTLAND [wc] ⍭ (by arrangement) ⏾ ⬜ **B**

555 SHETTLESTON OLD PARISH CHURCH

NS 649 370

111 Killin Street, Shettleston, Glasgow

Church by W F McGibbon, opened in 1903. Fine collection of stained glass,
including windows by Alfred Webster and Gordon Webster. Fine 2-manual organ.
Train to Shettleston. City buses 30, 61. Sunday Service: 11.00am

Open by arrangement, telephone the Church Officer 0141 778 2484

CHURCH OF SCOTLAND ♿ ⏾ ⬜ [wc] **B**

SHETTLESTON OLD PARISH CHURCH

556 ST PAUL THE APOSTLE, SHETTLESTON

NS 653 641
1653 Shettleston Road
Basilican church by Jack Coia 1959.
Exterior copper calvary and stations of
the cross by Jack Mortimer. Spacious
interior with much marble and slate,
re-ordered for modern liturgy. Interesting
baptistry and a rebuilt organ from
Greenlaw Parish Church, Paisley.
Services: daily 9.30am; Saturday 5.30pm;
Sunday 9.00am, 10.30am; Family Service
12.00 noon, Youth Mass 6.30pm;
Morning Prayer 9.10am weekdays;
Evening prayer 5.30pm weekdays
Church website:
www16.brinkster.com/saintpauls/index.htm

ST PAUL THE APOSTLE, SHETTLESTON

Parish Feast Day Conversion of St Paul,
25 January. Open 8.00am-7.30pm; access to Blessed Sacrament Chapel 8.00am-7.30pm
ROMAN CATHOLIC ♿ wc (adapted in Hall) wc **B**

557 SHETTLESTON METHODIST CHURCH

NS 643 642
1104 Shettleston Road, Glasgow
Former Primitive Methodist Church of
1902 which replaced a tin tabernacle of
1889. The Church incorporates
windows from the former Parkhead
Methodist Church. Opposite
Shettleston Police Station. Services:
Sunday 11.00am; Tuesday 10.30am
Church website:
zyworld.com/shettlestonmethodist
Open by arrangement, telephone the
Church Office 0141 778 5063
METHODIST ♿ wc

SHETTLESTON METHODIST CHURCH

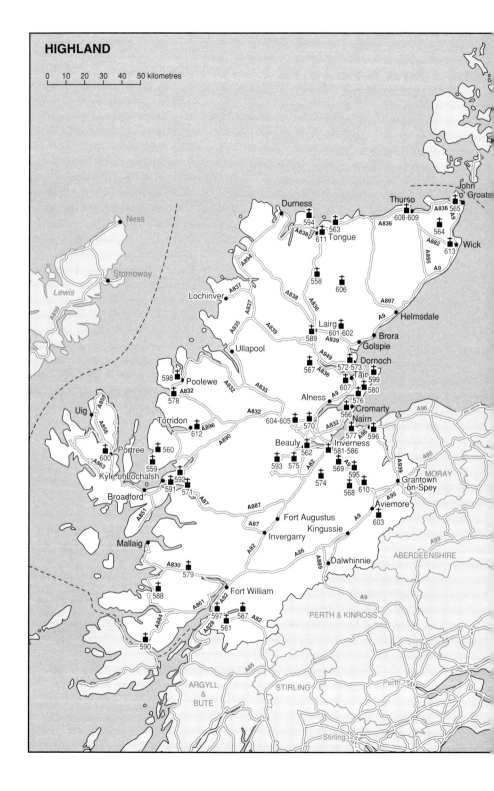

HIGHLAND

0 10 20 30 40 50 kilometres

Ness

Stornoway

Lewis

John o' Groats

Thurso
A836 565
608-609
564
A882
613 Wick
A836
A895
Durness
594
A838
563
611 Tongue
A9

558
606
A897
A894
Lochinver
A837
A9 Helmsdale
A837
A838
A836
Lairg
601-602
A835
589 A839
Brora
Ullapool
A839
Golspie
567 Dornoch
A949
572-573
A836 Tain
599
598
607 580
Poolewe
A832
A9 576
578
A832 A835
566 Cromarty
Alness Nairn
Torridon
A832 604-605 A96
612 A896
570 A832 577 596
A890
560
Beauly Inverness
559
593 562 581-586
600 Portree
575 569 595
Kyle of Lochalsh 592
A82 574 568 610 Grantown-on-Spey
591 571 A87
MORAY
Broadford
A939
A96 A95
A851
A887
Aviemore
A87 Fort Augustus 603
Kingussie
Invergarry
Mallaig
A82 A86
Dalwhinnie ABERDEENSHIRE
A830
579
A889
A9
588
Fort William
A861
A82
597 587 A82
A828 561
A884
590
PERTH & KINROSS
A85
ARGYLL
&
BUTE STIRLING Perth
Stirling

HIGHLAND

Local Representatives: Lyndall Leet, 8 Burnside, Thurso, Caithness (*telephone* 01847 896989) and Dr Judith Spenceley, 22 Beaufort Road, Inverness (*telephone* 01463 231669)

558 ALTNAHARRA PARISH CHURCH, SUTHERLAND

NC 568 355

Half-way between the school and the Telford bridge, the church was built 1854-37 by Hugh Mackay as a Free Church. Fine stonework and interior woodwork. Oil lamps now converted to electricity. Long communion tables between front pews for Communicants to sit at. Stained glass window in memory of Kathleen Joan Kimball. Sunday Service: 3.00pm on 1st and 3rd Sundays of each month

Open at all times

CHURCH OF SCOTLAND

ALTNAHARRA PARISH
CHURCH, CAITHNESS

559 APPLECROSS CHURCH, ROSS-SHIRE

NG 711 417

Camusterrach, Applecross (two miles towards Toscaig from Post Office)

Plain harled church built 1855 for the Free Church. Became United Free Church in 1900 and Church of Scotland in 1929. Clachan Church (see below) at head of Applecross Bay is also open to visitors. Applecross has connections with 7th-century St Maelrubha. Sunday Services: 12.00 noon in hall, 6.00pm in church

Open by arrangement with the Minister, telephone 01520 744263

CHURCH OF SCOTLAND   🚻

560 CLACHAN CHURCH, APPLECROSS, ROSS-SHIRE

NG 712 459

Standing on the ancient site of St Maelrubha's church (AD 673), the present church was built in 1817. The beauty and tranquillity of the surroundings complement the quiet simplicity of the plain stone building. To the left of the gate stands a tall, plain slab with an incised Celtic cross, said to mark the grave of Ruairidh Mor MacAogan, abbot of Applecross, who died in AD 801. The remains of carved Celtic crosses, dating from the 8th century, are in glass cases in Heritage Centre opposite. The church is recommended for its simplicity and peace, a fitting heritor of the old Gaelic name of '*A'Chomraich*' – the Sanctuary. SCS St Maelrubha Millennium Pilgrimage to this church. No regular services, but used for weddings, funerals and memorial services

Open daily

INTERDENOMINATIONAL **B**

CLACHAN CHURCH,
APPLECROSS, ROSS-SHIRE

561 ST MUN'S, BALLACHULISH, ARGYLL

NN 083 579

Built 1837 by Bishop Scott, Vicar-Apostolic for West of Scotland. Simple Highland
church in good condition. Adjacent building was originally the priest's house.
Sunday Service: 11.00am; daily as announced

Open at all times

ROMAN CATHOLIC wc

562 ST MARY'S CHURCH, BEAULY,
INVERNESS-SHIRE

NH 528 467

High Street, Beauly

Nave, chancel and north aisle, and adjoining
house, built as a unit in red sandstone 1864,
probably by Joseph A Hansom. Nearby the ruins
of Beauly Priory, founded for Valliscaulian
monks in 1230, maintained by Historic Scotland.
Also serves St Mary's, Eskadale.

Sunday Mass: 11.00am

Open Easter to September. Other times,
call at Priest's house adjoining

ROMAN CATHOLIC ♿ ⊘ wc **B**

ST MARY'S CHURCH,
BEAULY, INVERNESS-SHIRE

563 FARR PARISH CHURCH, BETTYHILL, SUTHERLAND

NC 708 622

Built 1909 to a standard design used for United Free Churches in the Highlands.
Nearby, at Clachan, stands the old Parish Church, built 1774, now a museum of
the Clearances and Clan Mackay. Amongst the gravestones is the Farr Stone, a
Christianised Pictish stone. Strathnaver Trail of 29 sites of archaeological,
historical and natural heritage interest runs from the museum to Altnaharra.

Sunday Service: 11.30am

Open at all times

CHURCH OF SCOTLAND wc

FARR PARISH CHURCH, BETTYHILL, SUTHERLAND

564 BOWER PARISH CHURCH, CAITHNESS

ND 238 622

Midway between Thurso and Wick on B876

Built 1847, architect William Davidson. Re-casting and alterations, architect Donald Leed 1902. Finialled and panelled Gothic screen flanks pulpit. Unusual in that two long windows which formerly flanked the pulpit are in the north, not south, wall. Stained glass window dedicated to Sir John Sinclair, 7th Baronet of Dunbeath. Mural memorials to members of Henderson and Sinclair families and plaque in memory of Zachary Pont, minister 1605-13, and his wife Margaret, daughter of John Knox. Ongoing restoration work has uncovered bronze bell from pre-Reformation church. Sunday Service: 12.15pm

Open by arrangement, telephone Mrs McAdie 01955 661252

CHURCH OF SCOTLAND [wc] **B**

565 CANISBAY CHURCH

ND 343 728

Most northerly place of worship on the Scottish mainland, the site occupied by the chapel of St Drostan, who headed a mission to Pictland in the 6th century. The present cruciform church is largely 17th century, but the nave incorporates walling from the medieval church and a worn 17th-century monument flanked by pairs of Corinthian pilasters. John de Groat stone of 1568 stands in the vestibule. Sunday Service: 12.15pm

Open daily 9.00am-9.00pm, Easter to end October.

In winter, key from Mrs Cormack (next to church)

CHURCH OF SCOTLAND [&] **A**

CANISBAY CHURCH

566 EAST CHURCH, CROMARTY, ROSS-SHIRE

NH 791 673

Church Street, Cromarty

Described by John Hume as 'unquestionably one of the finest 18th century parish churches in Scotland'. Starting as a simple east-west rectangle in the late 16th century, the north aisle was added 1739 to create a T-plan church. Further alterations in 1756 and 1798. The interior dates principally from the 18th century with galleries added to accommodate the growing congregation, the most elaborate being the Cromartie loft of 1756. Several fine monuments. Owned and maintained by the Scottish Redundant Churches Trust. Four Sunday services during summer months, telephone the SRCT 01334 472032 for dates and times. Occasional services, including weddings, by arrangement

Open 8.30am-5.00pm (4.00pm in winter)

FORMER CHURCH OF SCOTLAND [wc] **A**

EAST CHURCH, CROMARTY, ROSS-SHIRE

567   CROICK CHURCH, ARDGAY, SUTHERLAND

NH 457 915

Ardgay, Strathcarron

Harled T-plan 'Parliamentary' church built by James
Smith 1827 from a Thomas Telford design. One of the
few Parliamentary churches still in use in its original
form. Furnishings virtually unchanged since first built;
old-style long communion table and original pulpit. East
window has messages scratched in 1845 by evicted
inhabitants of Glencalvie. Pictish broch in church glebe.
Ardgay is ten miles west of A9/A836 (signposted).
Sunday Services: 2nd Sunday, May to September, 3.00pm;
Communion 2nd Sunday in July, 3.00pm

Open during daylight hours

CHURCH OF SCOTLAND  **A**

CROICK CHURCH,
ARDGAY, SUTHERLAND

568   DALAROSSIE CHURCH, INVERNESS-SHIRE

NH 767 242

3 miles from old A9

Dalarossie Church, on the River Findhorn, is an
ancient place of worship dating back to the 8th
century at the time of St Fergus. The present
building, set within the walled graveyard, dates
from 1790 and features an ancient baptismal font as
well as a 'covenant stone'. Services: April to
October, 1st and 3rd Sundays 10.30am; November
to March, 1st Sunday 10.30am

Open by arrangement, telephone 01463 772242

or Mrs Vivian Roden 01808 511355

CHURCH OF SCOTLAND (by arrangement) **B**

DALAROSSIE CHURCH,
INVERNESS-SHIRE

569   DAVIOT CHURCH, INVERNESS-SHIRE

NH 722 394

On A9, 6 miles south of Inverness

Built in 1826 and restored 1991. There has been a
place of worship on the site since early times, long
before its charter was granted in the 13th century.
The surrounding graveyard tells of the changing
history of this interesting parish.

Sunday Service: 12.00 noon

Open by arrangement, telephone 01463 772242

CHURCH OF SCOTLAND (guides by arrangement) **B**

DAVIOT CHURCH, INVERNESS-SHIRE

570 ST JAMES THE GREAT CHURCH, DINGWALL, ROSS-SHIRE

NH 552 588

Castle Street, Dingwall

The building is on the site of an earlier chapel, 1806, which was demolished in 1851 and the new building erected to a New Gothic design by J L Pearson. It was consecrated in 1854 but gutted by fire in 1871. Restoration, by Alexander Ross, Inverness, began immediately, following the original design. Services: 9.30am or 11.00am on alternate Sundays. Wednesdays: Morning Prayer and Eucharist 10.30am. Please check notice board for details

Open daily during daylight hours

SCOTTISH EPISCOPAL 🚻 wc

ST JAMES THE GREAT CHURCH,
DINGWALL, ROSS-SHIRE

571 ST DUTHAC'S CHURCH, DORNIE, ROSS-SHIRE

NG 884 268

Dornie, by Kyle of Lochalsh (beside Eilean Donan Castle)

The first Catholic church on the site was built in 1703. The present building dates from 1860; architect Joseph A Hansom. It is in simple Gothic style with nave and chancel. The stone reredos has polished granite shafts, while similar columns support the altar. The simplicity continues with the demi-octagonal stone pulpit and braced rafter roof. Sunday Service: 10.30am; Saturday Vigil 7.30pm

Open daily

ROMAN CATHOLIC 🛏 **B**

ST DUTHAC'S CHURCH,
DORNIE, ROSS-SHIRE

572 DORNOCH CATHEDRAL, DORNOCH, SUTHERLAND

NH 797 897

High Street, Dornoch

Cathedral founded by Bishop Gilbert de Moravia in the 13th century; the first service in the building was held in 1239. The medieval masonry of the chancel and the crossing piers remains mostly intact today. The nave was destroyed by fire in 1570, the transepts and choir were reroofed 1616, and the nave rebuilt 1837. In 1924 the interior stonework was exposed. Lavish display of stained glass, including several windows by James Ballantine, others by Percy Bacon, and the St Gilbert window by Crear McCartney 1989.

Sunday Services: all year 11.00am, summer months 8.30pm

Open during daylight hours

CHURCH OF SCOTLAND 🚻 ⊘ 🛏 **A**

573 ST FINNBARR'S, DORNOCH, SUTHERLAND

NH 799 898

Schoolhill, Dornoch

Simple but picturesque Gothic by Alexander Ross 1912-13. Stained glass triple
lancet east window by Percy Bacon. Of special note are the 70 tapestry kneelers
with highland themes executed by 14 members of the congregation between 1981
and 1993. Sunday Services: Holy Eucharist 10.00am every week, subject to change.
Check with Vestry Secretary

Open April to October 10.00am-4.00pm; at other times by arrangement with Vestry
Secretary, telephone 01862 810877

SCOTTISH EPISCOPAL

574 DUNLICHITY CHURCH, DUNLICHITY, INVERNESS-SHIRE

NH 659 327

near Loch Duntelchaig

An ancient place of worship, much
earlier than the present building
which dates back in part to the 16th
century. Many interesting features,
including a 1702 handbell, and
surrounded by a graveyard of much
historical interest, with its own 1759
watch-house.

Services: April to October 1st Sunday
7.00pm; November to March, 1st
Sunday, 10.45am

Open by arrangement, telephone
01463 772242

DUNLICHITY CHURCH,
DUNLICHITY, INVERNESS-SHIRE

CHURCH OF SCOTLAND ⓘ (guides by arrangement) **B**

575 ST MARY'S CHURCH, ESKADALE, INVERNESS-SHIRE

NH 453 399

A spacious white harled church in a picturesque woodland setting. Built 1826 by
the 14th Lord Lovat. Alterations and additions by Peter Paul Pugin 1881. Founder's
tomb in the chancel. Lovat family graveyard to the west of the church. The
contemporary stable to accommodate horses ridden by those attending Mass,
50 metres to the west of the church, is an unusual feature. On a minor road on the
south east side of the River Beauly. Served by St Mary's, Beauly.

Sunday Mass: 9.00am alternate Sundays

Open by arrangement, telephone Mr James Christie 01463 741536

ROMAN CATHOLIC **B**

576 FEARN ABBEY, ROSS-SHIRE

NH 837 773
Hill of Fearn
Known as 'The Lamp of the North', it is one of
the oldest pre-Reformation Scottish churches still
in use for worship. Rebuilt 1772 by James Rich
and restored by Ian G Lindsay & Partners 1972.
Further restoration in summer 2001. Originally a
monastery of Premonstratensian monks of the
Order of St Augustine. Patrick Hamilton, burnt
for heresy at St Andrews in 1528, was the
Commendatory Abbot from 1517 to 1528. A9,
Hill of Fearn Village. Sunday Service: 11.30am
Open daily Easter to September, 10.00am-4.30pm;
or by appointment, telephone Mr J Maxwell
01862 871247
CHURCH OF SCOTLAND 📖 WC A

FEARN ABBEY, ROSS-SHIRE

577 FORT GEORGE CHAPEL, INVERNESS-SHIRE

NH 761 567
Fort George, Ardersier
The garrison chapel built in 1767, probably
to a design by William Skinner. Interior,
two-tiered arcade on three sides supported
by Roman Doric columns. Eighteenth-
century three-decker pulpit. Working
garrison. Visitor displays, Historic Scotland.
Off A96, north-east of Inverness
Open April to September, Monday to Saturday
9.30am-6.30pm; Sunday 9.30am-6.30pm;
October to March; Monday to Saturday 9.30am-
4.30pm; Sunday 2.00-4.30pm
NON-DENOMINATIONAL ♿ 📖 ☕ A

FORT GEORGE CHAPEL, INVERNESS-SHIRE

578 GAIRLOCH FREE CHURCH, GAIRLOCH, ROSS-SHIRE

NG 804 761
On a commanding site overlooking Loch Gairloch. Gothic in style, to a design by
Matthews & Lawrie 1881. Simple interior with original fittings and Gothic
panelled gallery across east end. Spandrels of roof trusses with cusped decoration.
Fabric appeal. A832 to Gairloch. Sunday Services: 11.00am and 5.00pm.
Gaelic Service: 12.00 noon alternate Sunday
Open by arrangement, telephone the Minister 01445 712371
FREE CHURCH OF SCOTLAND ♿ 📖 WC C

579 ST MARY AND ST FINNAN CHURCH, GLENFINNAN, INVERNESS-SHIRE

NM 904 808

The church was consecrated in 1873. Designed by E Welby Pugin in the Gothic style, the church enjoys an elevated and commanding position overlooking Loch Shiel with a spectacular view of the loch and surrounding hills. The church is a memorial chapel to the MacDonalds of Glenaladale, the family with whom Bonnie Prince Charlie stayed prior to the raising of the Jacobite standard at Glenfinnan in August 1745. The church contains memorial stones to the Prince and to members of the MacDonald family. Located in the village, 15 miles west of Fort William on A830 to Mallaig. Sunday Mass: 1.00pm

ST MARY AND ST FINNAN CHURCH, GLENFINNAN, INVERNESS-SHIRE

Open daily sunrise to sunset

ROMAN CATHOLIC **B**

580 INVER MEETING HOUSE, INVER, ROSS-SHIRE

NH 863 828

New Street, Inver

A meeting house in the style of cottages. Inver, largely in original form, originates as a settlement of persons displaced during clearances. Memorial, to north of village on the shore, marks common grave of cholera victims, a large proportion of the population. Sunday Service: 10.00am

Open by appointment, telephone Mr Skinner 01862 871522

CHURCH OF SCOTLAND 🦽

581 OLD HIGH CHURCH, INVERNESS

NH665 455

Church Street, Inverness

Present building completed 1772 to a plan by George Fraser of Edinburgh on site of medieval church. Traditionally thought to be the site where St Columba converted Brude, King of the Picts, to Christianity. Porches, apse and chancel arch date from 1891, to designs by Ross & Macbeth. Lowest portion of the west bell-tower is 15th or 16th century. The colours of the Queen's Own Cameron Highlanders are hung and the Regiment's Books of Remembrance are housed in

OLD HIGH CHURCH, INVERNESS

the church. 2-manual organ by Henry Willis & Sons 1895, rebuilt by H Hilsdon 1923. Stained glass by, amongst others, Douglas Strachan 1925, Stephen Adam & Co 1893, and A Ballantine & Gardiner 1899. Sunday Service: 11.15am all year; mid-June to mid-September Fridays 1.00pm-1.15pm

Open June, July and August, Fridays 12.00 noon-2.00pm. Guided tour at 12.30pm

CHURCH OF SCOTLAND ⛪ 📖 **A**

582 ST ANDREW'S CATHEDRAL, INVERNESS

NH 664 450

Ardross Street, Inverness

One of the first new cathedrals completed 1869 in Great Britain after the Reformation, by local architect Alexander Ross. Polished granite pillars, stained glass, fine furnishings. Angel font after Thorvaldsen. Founder's memorial, ikons presented by Tsar of Russia. Peal of bells. Fine choir. On west bank of River Ness, just above Ness Bridge, A862, close to town centre.

Sunday Services: Eucharist 8.15am, Family Eucharist 9.30am, Sung Eucharist 11.00am, Choral Evensong 6.30pm; Matins, Eucharist and Evensong daily

Open daily 8.30am-6.00pm (later June to September)

SCOTTISH EPISCOPAL ⟨⟩ ⟨⟩ May to September ⟨⟩ wc **A**

583 ST MARY'S CHURCH, INVERNESS

NH 662 455

30 Huntly Street, Inverness

On the west bank of the River Ness, very close to the city centre. Built 1837 by William Robertson in Gothic Revival manner. Re-decorated recently and new stained-glass window installed to mark the Millennium and the Great Year of Jubilee. Sunday Services: Mass 10am and 6.30pm; Vigil Mass Saturday 7.00pm, June to September

ST MARY'S CHURCH, INVERNESS

Open daily, summer 9.00am-6.00pm, winter 9.00am-3.00pm

ROMAN CATHOLIC ⟨⟩ ⟨⟩ **A**

584 ST MICHAEL & ALL ANGELS, INVERNESS

NH 659 457

Abban Street/Lochalsh Road, Inverness

In 1877 Canon Edward Medley established a mission in a thatched cottage on the Maggot Green, close to River Ness; a church was built in 1886 to a design by Alexander Ross. As the site proved liable to flooding, it was re-built in extended form in Abban Street in 1903-4, also by Ross. Many interior fittings, altar with gilded angels and tester, and font with lofty steeple cover were designed by Sir Ninian Comper and installed in 1904. Between 1924-28 a major reconstruction, to a design by Comper, saw six new tracery windows, including a magnificent stained glass window of the four archangels, being created. The church was completely restored during 2002. Situated close to the town centre, by the riverside, to the north-west of Friar's Bridge. Sunday Services: Sunday Low Mass 8.00am, Parish Mass 11.00am, Low Mass daily

Church website: www.angelforce.co.uk/stmichael

Open daily 9.00am-4.00pm. Other times, telephone Canon Black 01463 233797

SCOTTISH EPISCOPAL ⟨⟩ ⟨⟩ wc ⟨⟩ ⟨⟩ ⟨⟩ **B**

ST MICHAEL & ALL ANGELS, INVERNESS

585 ST STEPHEN'S, INVERNESS

NH 672 449

Southside Road, Inverness

By W L Carruthers 1897 in Arts & Crafts Gothic, the hall added later. The church consists of a nave, single north transept and an apsidal chancel. Square tower with a delicate needle spire. High open roof, pulpit of locally grown native oak. Noteworthy stained glass of 1897 and 1906 by A Ballantine & Son. 2-manual organ by Wadsworth Bros 1902. Substantially renovated in 2000 by Sandy Edmonstone. At junction of Old Edinburgh Road and Southside Road. Sunday Service: 10.00am; Evening Communion 8.00pm Easter Sunday, 4th Sunday of June and last Sunday of January and September

Open by arrangement, telephone the Minister 01463 237129

CHURCH OF SCOTLAND ⟨♿⟩ ⟨☞⟩ ⟨♀⟩ ⟨wc⟩ **B**

586 TWEEDMOUTH MEMORIAL CHAPEL, INVERNESS

NM 663 445

Royal Northern Infirmary,
Ness Walk, Inverness

Earliest example of purpose-built ecumenical worship space in Scotland, built in 1898, architect A Ross and R B MacBeth. Three sanctuary areas for Reformed, Roman Catholic and Episcopalian worship. Occasional services, weddings and baptisms

Keys available from Hospital Porters

INTERDENOMINATIONAL

 ⟨♿⟩ ⟨wc⟩ ⟨☞⟩ **B**

TWEEDMOUTH MEMORIAL CHAPEL, INVERNESS

587 KINLOCHLEVEN PARISH CHURCH, INVERNESS-SHIRE

NS 187 621

Riverside Road, Kinlochleven

Built 1930 to a simple but elegant design by
J Jeffrey Waddell with a high arch at the chancel
end. Chancel area is a round bell-shape with
stained glass windows depicting biblical scenes.
Two stained glass windows in the south wall of
the nave depicting St Andrew and St George.
Linked with Nether Lochaber in 1981. A82 from
Glencoe. Sunday Services: 10.00am and 6.30pm
Open by arrangement, telephone 01855 831227
CHURCH OF SCOTLAND ♿ ⑦

KINLOCHLEVEN PARISH CHURCH,
INVERNESS-SHIRE

588 ST FINAN'S CHURCH, KINLOCHMOIDART, INVERNESS-SHIRE

NM 710 728

The church stands on a ledge of level ground in woodland above the mouth of
the River Moidart and below an impressively steep hillside. It was built in 1857 to
a design by Alexander Ross in simple Early English style, with crow stepped
gables, a small belfry and a porch. There are two unusual stained glass windows by
the Victorian artist Jemima Blackburn. Up a track leading off the A861, half-mile
north of the bridge over the River Moidart.

Services: Christmas, Easter and Sundays, May to September 5.30pm

Open daily

SCOTTISH EPISCOPAL **C**

589 LAIRG PARISH CHURCH, SUTHERLAND

NC 583 065

Church Hill Road, Lairg

A simple Gothic church, built of local
granite 1847, designed by William Leslie.
Renovated 2001, disabled access. The
graveyard, one and a half miles away, served
the original church and contains some
interesting monuments, including a large
marble monument to Sir James Matheson of
Achany. Linked with Rogart (St Callan's)
and Pitfure. Sunday Service: 10.45am; also
6.30pm on 1st Sunday of month
*Open by arrangement, telephone Rev J Goskirk
01549 402373. Adjacent church hall (built
1998) has level access and adapted toilets*
CHURCH OF SCOTLAND ♿ ⑦ wc

LAIRG PARISH CHURCH, SUTHERLAND

590 KIEL CHURCH, LOCHALINE, INVERNESS-SHIRE

NM 972 538
Lochaline, Morvern
The present church is the third on
this site. Ruins of a medieval church
are on the site of the original and
much earlier building which,
according to legend, was erected at
the command of St Columba.
Today's church was designed by
P MacGregor Chalmers 1898.
Interesting stained glass. Memorial

KIEL CHURCH, LOCHALINE, INVERNESS-SHIRE

plaque to the MacLeods, father and son, whose ministry here spanned more than a
century. Fifteenth-century cross outside the front of the church. The nearby 18th-
century Session House contains a collection of carved stones 8th to 16th centuries.
One mile out of the village on the Drimnin road. Sunday Service: 11.00am
Open daily all year
CHURCH OF SCOTLAND ⊘ ⏽ **c**

591 ST DONNAN'S, LOCHALSH, ROSS-SHIRE

NG 855 272
Nostie, by Lochalsh
Unassuming, simple church by Stevenson & Dunworth 1962-64. East wall inside is
patterned with panels inset with stones from the Nostie Burn. The angels on the
altar pedestal were carved by F R Stevenson. Sunday Service: 10.30am
If church is locked, key obtainable from Mrs C Dodds, Fernfield, Nostie (opposite the church)
SCOTTISH EPISCOPAL ⏽ wc

592 LOCHCARRON PARISH CHURCH (WEST CHURCH), ROSS-SHIRE

NG 893 391
Former United Free Church designed by William Mackenzie 1910, sited in centre of
Lochcarron. Crisply painted; standard UF layout. Also of interest the burial ground
one mile east of the village with roof-
less former parish church 1751,
superseded by neighbouring big,
white-harled East Church 1834-36,
James Smith, architect. Open during
summer months. Services (West church
only): every Sunday 11.00am, and 2nd
and 4th Sunday 6.00pm
Open during daylight hours
CHURCH OF SCOTLAND
♿ 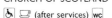 (after services) wc

LOCHCARRON PARISH CHURCH
(WEST CHURCH), ROSS-SHIRE

593 OUR LADY AND ST BEAN, MARYDALE, CANNICH, INVERNESS-SHIRE

NH 342 317

OUR LADY AND ST BEAN,
MARYDALE, CANNICH, INVERNESS-SHIRE

Simple stone church in Gothic style, with adjoining presbytery, walled garden, school and schoolhouse, built as a unit by Joseph A Hansom 1868. The church has nave and apse with a porch and circular bell-tower. St Bean is said to have been a monk of Iona, a cousin of St Columba, and the first to evangelise Strathglass. Sputan Bhain (NH 334 305) was the spring at which he baptised. On the other side of the road is Clachan Comair, a walled graveyard with the ruins of a small 17th-century church, on the site of an early 10th-century chapel dedicated to St Bean. In 1998 a new altar was installed made from solid 300-year-old oak, designed by local artist Alistair MacPherson. The former presbytery is being developed as a monastic retreat, with an icon painting workshop. On the north side of the A831, between Cannich Bridge and Comar Bridge. Mass 5.00pm Saturdays (Vigil)

Church website: www.sanctiangeli.org

Open daily

ROMAN CATHOLIC wc **B**

594 MELNESS CHURCH, SUTHERLAND

NC 586 634

Near Talmine, 4 miles from junction with A838 (Tongue–Durness)

Built at the turn of the 20th century by local craftsmen to replace an earlier building at an adjacent site. Interior totally wood lined. Local feeling was that it should have been called the 'Kerr Memorial Church' as it was due to the Minister at the time, Rev Cathel Kerr, that the church was completed.

Sunday Service: 12.30pm (Holy Communion held twice yearly)

Open at all times

CHURCH OF SCOTLAND wc (image)

595 MOY CHURCH, INVERNESS-SHIRE

NH 772 342

On old A9, 13 miles south of Inverness

Built in 1765, on a previous site, and surrounded by an interesting graveyard with its own watch-house. Memorial stone to Donald Fraser, the hero of the 'Rout of Moy', just before the Battle of Culloden in 1746. Services: April to October, 4th Sunday 10.45am; November to March, 3rd and 5th Sunday, 10.45am

Open by arrangement, telephone 01463 772242 or Mrs Vivian Roden 01808 511355

CHURCH OF SCOTLAND (image) (by arrangement) **B**

MOY CHURCH, INVERNESS-SHIRE

596 NAIRN OLD PARISH CHURCH, NAIRN

NH 879 564

Academy Street / Inverness Road, Nairn

Considered the finest structure in the area, 1897 by John Starforth. Architecture of Early English Transition period; Gothic reminiscences are abundant. Transeptal in form but almost circular in shape. Square tower is almost 100ft high. Lovely light interior. Glorious stained glass. Sunday Service: 10.30am

Open weekdays 9.30am-12.30pm

CHURCH OF SCOTLAND [♿] [②] [🚻] [📖] [wc] **A**

597 NETHER LOCHABER PARISH CHURCH, ONICH, INVERNESS-SHIRE

NN 031 614

Onich, near Fort William

Built in 1911 to replace original Telford church at Creag Mhor, using some of the original stone. Known as one of the finest rural churches in the Highlands. Most illustrious minister was Dr Alexander Stewart 1851-1901, known as 'Nether Lochaber' and renowned throughout the Celtic world for his wide-ranging learning and writing. Celtic cross, 20ft, erected by the Stewart Society at Innis-na-Bhirlin cemetery off A82 five miles north of Onich. Linked with Kinlochleven 1981. Church located on A82 in Onich village eleven miles south of Fort William.

Sunday Service: 12.00 noon

Keys available from Tigh-na-Mara, Onich

CHURCH OF SCOTLAND [♿] [②]

NETHER LOCHABER PARISH
CHURCH, ONICH, INVERNESS-SHIRE

598 ST MAELRUBHA'S, POOLEWE, ROSS-SHIRE

NG 857 807

St Maelrubha's Close, Poolewe

The first Episcopal church to be built on the north-west coast of Scotland since the Jacobite rebellion of 1745, St Maelrubha's (a former cow byre) was dedicated in 1965. Tiny, simple and made of local stone, it houses a fragment of the Celtic cross erected as a monument to the Saint and brought from Applecross. Memorial to the Highland Fieldcraft Training Centre. Visiting clergy take Sunday Services during the summer. Close to Inverewe Garden (National Trust for Scotland).

Sunday Service: 11.00am; Wednesday 10.00am

Open during daylight hours

SCOTTISH EPISCOPAL ♿ wc ⚱ 📖 ☕

599 PORTMAHOMACK CHURCH, ROSS-SHIRE

NH 917 846

Off Main Street

Simple rectangular former United Free Church building, architects Andrew Maitland & Sons 1908. Flower Festival during Gala Week (last in July). Tarbat Discovery Centre (former Tarbat Old Parish Church) has displays of church and archaeology, including Pictish stones, and place for private prayer in crypt. Adjacent archaeological dig ongoing.

Sunday Service: 11.30am

Please ask for key at Village Shop (50m), shop hours only

CHURCH OF SCOTLAND wc

PORTMAHOMACK CHURCH, ROSS-SHIRE

600 PORTREE PARISH CHURCH

NG 482 436

Somerled Square

St Columba brought Christianity to Skye and the ruins of earlier churches are to be seen in and around Portree. The present building, designed by John Hay of Liverpool, was built as a Free Church in 1854, became the United Free Church in 1900 and the Church of Scotland in 1929. St Columba and St Taraglen are depicted in stained glass windows. Other windows by Douglas Hamilton and Thomas Webster. Sunday Services: 11.00am and 6.30pm

Open throughout the summer 11.00am-4.00pm

CHURCH OF SCOTLAND ♿ wc ② ⚱ Gaelic services **C**

601 PITFURE CHURCH, ROGART, SUTHERLAND

NC 710 038

A simple, pleasant place to worship. Built by
the United Free congregation in 1910,
architect Robert J Macbeth, Inverness.
Linked with Lairg. Sunday Service: 1st, 3rd
and 5th Sundays of month, October to May
12.15pm; June to September 11.30am (check
locally or telephone the number below);
2nd Sunday of month 6.30pm

Open by arrangement, telephone
Rev J Goskirk 01549 402373

CHURCH OF SCOTLAND 👤 ⟳ 📖 wc

PITFURE CHURCH, ROGART, SUTHERLAND

602 ST CALLAN'S CHURCH, ROGART, SUTHERLAND

NC 715 038

Rebuilt in 1777 on the site of a medieval church. The austere whitewashed exterior
with its plain sash windows gives little hint of the warm, gleaming interior. A high
canopied pulpit stands against the east wall. Long communion table and pews. Other
pews are tiered from the entrance to the west end. Two small stained glass memorial
windows on either side of the pulpit: 'Nativity' and 'Penitence' by Margaret Chilton
and Marjorie Kemp 1929. Modern vestry wing built in 1984. From crossroads at
Pittentrail, take Rhilochan/Balnacoil road. Church on right approximately two miles.
Linked with Lairg. Sunday Service: 2nd and 4th Sundays of month, October to May
12.15pm; June to September (check locally or telephone the number below).

Open by arrangement, telephone Rev J Goskirk 01549 402373

CHURCH OF SCOTLAND ⟳ 📖 wc B

603 ST JOHN THE BAPTIST CHURCH, ROTHIEMURCHUS INVERNESS-SHIRE

NH 900 111

Church founded by John Peter Grant, 11th
Laird of Rothiemurchus 1930. Architect,
Sir Ninian Comper. A simple white interior
with a groin vaulted ceiling and a rose
damask baldacchino. Simple burial ground
surrounds the church. Approximately one
mile from the centre of Aviemore, 'the
little white church on the ski road'.
Sunday Service: Holy Eucharist 10.30am

Open by arrangement, contact the Parish
Administrator 01540 661875

SCOTTISH EPISCOPAL 👤 B

ST JOHN THE BAPTIST CHURCH,
ROTHIEMURCHUS INVERNESS-SHIRE

604 FODDERTY & STRATHPEFFER PARISH CHURCH, ROSS-SHIRE

NH 482 480

Strathpeffer

Designed by William C Joass and built 1888-90 as part of the development of Strathpeffer as Britain's most northerly Spa. A rectangular building with side aisles and balcony to the rear; the chancel extends from the nave under a low roof. Services: Sunday 11.00am; also last Sunday in the month, April to October 8.00pm

Open by arrangement, telephone the Minister on 01997 421398

CHURCH OF SCOTLAND wc ⊘

FODDERTY & STRATHPEFFER
PARISH CHURCH, ROSS-SHIRE

605 ST ANNE'S CHURCH, STRATHPEFFER, ROSS-SHIRE

NH 483 580

Designed by John Robertson as a memorial to Anne, Duchess of Sutherland and Countess of Cromartie, it was constructed between 1890 and 1892 with the chancel added in 1899. The pulpit is of Caen stone and alabaster, the altar and reredos of marble and alabaster showing carved reliefs. Stained glass windows are by J Powell & Sons 1891 and Heaton, Butler & Bayne 1892-c.1910.

Sunday Service: 9.30am or 11.00am. Please check notice board for details

Open daily, Easter to September

SCOTTISH EPISCOPAL ♿ ⊘ 📖 **B**

ST ANNE'S CHURCH, STRATHPEFFER, ROSS-SHIRE

606 STRATHNAVER PARISH CHURCH, SYRE, SUTHERLAND

NC 694 439

Junction of Kinbrace and Syre roads

Built 1901 as a mission station from
Altnaharra. Pre-fabricated by Speirs and
Co, Glasgow and erected on site. Neat and
tiny corrugated iron church lined with
wood. Plaque in memory of the Rev
Robert Sloan, Minister 1969-74. Modern
cemetery and car park across the road.
Nearby is the Rossal clearance village,
maintained by the Forestry Commission,
and Patrick Sellar's House.
Sunday Service: on the 2nd, 4th and 5th
Sundays of each month 3.00pm

Open at all times

CHURCH OF SCOTLAND **C**

STRATHNAVER PARISH CHURCH,
SYRE, SUTHERLAND

607 ST ANDREW'S CHURCH, TAIN, ROSS-SHIRE

NH 777 822

Manse Street, Tain

Designed 1887 by Ross & Macbeth, replacing an earlier corrugated iron structure.
The earliest stained glass, by Ballantyne and Gardner, was moved from the earlier
church. Other glass by A L Ward 1910, and W Wilson 1955 and 1961. Fine organ
by Hamilton & Muller, restored 1986. Forward altar designed and carved from
American oak by Peter Bailey of Skye 1995. Services: Sunday Eucharist 11.15am;
1st Sunday of every month Matins 10.00am; Thursday Eucharist 6.00pm

Church website: www.moray.anglican.org

Open 10.00am-4.00pm

SCOTTISH EPISCOPAL [wc] **B**

ST ANDREW'S CHURCH, TAIN, ROSS-SHIRE

608 ST PETER'S & ST ANDREW'S CHURCH, THURSO, CAITHNESS

ND 115 684

Princes Street, Thurso

Built in 1832 to a design by William Burn, the church is the centre point of the town, fronted by town square garden and war memorial. U-plan gallery. Pipe organ, Norman & Beard 1914. Stained glass includes 'The Sower' by Oscar Paterson 1922. Sunday Services: 11.00am and 6.30pm

Open July to August daily,
2.00-4.00pm, 7.00-8.00pm

CHURCH OF SCOTLAND

ST PETER'S & ST ANDREW'S CHURCH, THURSO, CAITHNESS

609 ST PETER & THE HOLY ROOD, THURSO

ND 117 682

Sir George's Street

The church was built in 1885 to the design of Alexander Ross, the chancel being added in 1905 in memory of Mr Norman Sinclair. The stained glass depicting 'The Good Samaritan' is in memory of Sir George Sinclair of Ulbster. The 2-manual organ by George Benson 1894, built for a Lancashire Chapel, was dismantled and moved here in 1973 by members of the congregation. The carved oak reredos depicts the Ascension and the first Pentecost. Services: Sunday Communion 8.00am and 9.30am, Choral Evensong 6.30pm; Tuesday Communion 10.30am; Friday Compline 7.00pm

Open Wednesday 10.30am-4.00pm
May to September at other times by
arrangement with Mr Southwick
01847 821295

SCOTTISH EPISCOPAL

ST PETER & THE HOLY ROOD, THURSO

610 TOMATIN CHURCH, INVERNESS-SHIRE

NH 803 290
*On east side of old A9 in
village of Tomatin*
A fine example of the 'tin churches'
erected c.1910 by the United Free
Church to serve as mission churches
and halls in areas of new
population. Services: April to
October, 2nd and 5th Sundays
10.30am; November to March, 2nd
and 4th Sundays 10.30am
*Open by arrangement, telephone
01463 772242 or Mrs Vivian Roden
01808 511355*
CHURCH OF SCOTLAND
⋔ (by arrangement)

TOMATIN CHURCH, INVERNESS-SHIRE

611 ST ANDREW'S PARISH CHURCH, TONGUE, SUTHERLAND

NC 591 570
Tongue
Rebuilt by Donald Mackay, Master of Reay, in 1680 following the Reay family's
conversion to Protestantism (c.1600). The site was that of the ancient Celtic and
latterly Roman Catholic Church (St Peter's Chapel). During a renovation in 1729 a
vault was built covering the graves of earlier members of the MacKay family.
Information leaflets are available free in the church. The church is on the Durness
road (A838) past Tongue Hotel. Sunday Service: 11.00am
Open all year, daylight hours
CHURCH OF SCOTLAND ⌇ 📖 **A**

ST ANDREW'S PARISH CHURCH, TONGUE, SUTHERLAND

612 CORRY CHURCH, TORRIDON, ROSS-SHIRE

The architect for Corry Church was Alexander Ross. The church was built in 1887, originally as a Free Church. Situated near the head of Loch Torridon, it is constructed with the local red sandstone inside and out. Splendid views all around of the majestic Torridon mountains.

Sunday Service: May to September 12.15pm

Open May to September. At other times, contact keyholder, telephone 01445 791323

CHURCH OF SCOTLAND

613 ST JOHN THE EVANGELIST, WICK, CAITHNESS

ND 363 505

Francis Street / Moray Street

Built 1870 to a design Alexander Ross of Inverness, St John's is especially attractive with a warm friendly atmosphere. Four-light windows known affectionately as the 'I am' windows ('I am the Good Shepherd, … the Resurrection and the Life, … the True Vine, … the Bread of Life'), by David Gulland, a former member of the vestry of St John's and a recognised expert in glass.

Sunday Service: Sung Eucharist 11.30am

Open by arrangement with Peter MacDougall, telephone 01955 602914

SCOTTISH EPISCOPAL

ST JOHN THE EVANGELIST, WICK, CAITHNESS

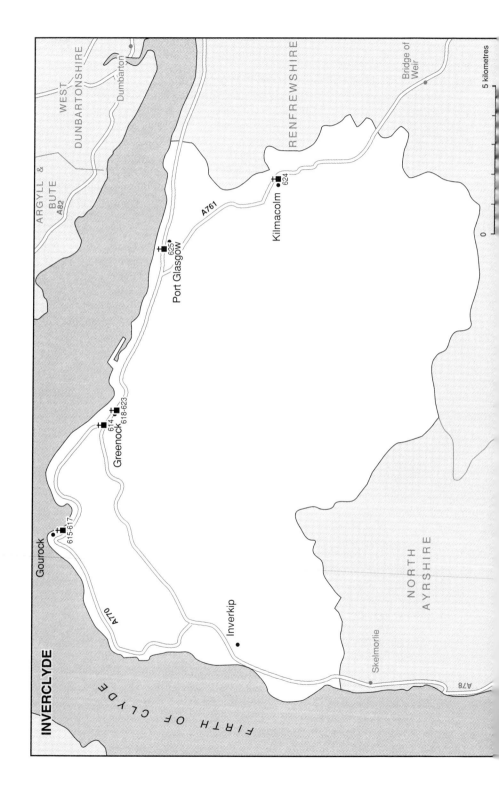

INVERCLYDE

Gourock
615-617

Greenock
614
618-623

Port Glasgow
625

Kilmacolm
624

Inverkip

Dumbarton

WEST DUNBARTONSHIRE

ARGYLL & BUTE

A82

RENFREWSHIRE

Bridge of Weir

NORTH AYRSHIRE

Skelmorlie

A78

A761

A770

A82

FIRTH OF CLYDE

0   5 kilometres

INVERCLYDE

Local Representative: Mr Ian Milne, 39 Union Street, Greenock
(*telephone* 01475 796331)

614 ARDGOWAN PARISH CHURCH

NS 271 768
31 Union Street, Greenock
Built as Trinity United Presbyterian Church 1871, and designed by John Starforth
in Gothic style. Became St Andrews in 1967 when united with St Andrews, and
became Ardgowan in 1992 when united with Union Church. Refurbished 2002
after the ceiling collapsed. Sunday Service: 11.00am
Open by arrangement with the Minister, telephone 01475 790849
CHURCH OF SCOTLAND 🦽 wc ② **B**

615 ST BARTHOLOMEW'S, GOUROCK

NS 239 777
Barrhill Road, Gourock
This beautiful little church sits on a cliff
overlooking the River Clyde. Designed by J C
Sharp of Gourock 1867. Chancel extension
enhanced by a beautiful window depicting the
Ascension designed by George Walton. Mural
of the Nativity on the west wall. Memorial
lectern and font. Plaque of Dutch tiles in

ST BARTHOLOMEW'S, GOUROCK

remembrance of the hospitality given to Dutch soldiers, sailors and airmen during
the Second World War. Sunday Service: Sung Eucharist 10.30am; Wednesday and
Saints' Days Holy Eucharist 10.30am
Open by arrangement, telephone Mrs Boeker telephone 01475 521411
SCOTTISH EPISCOPAL wc ② 📖 **B**

616 ST JOHN'S, GOUROCK

NS 246 778
Bath Street
Gothic style church built 1857 (J J and W H Hay) and tower with open-work
crown added 1878 (Bruce and Sturrock). Interior whitewashed with tall arch-
braced timber roof. The sanctuary underwent major renovations in 1998 when
wooden flooring was laid and the pews replaced by chairs to give greater
flexibility. Makin Organ. Number of stained glass windows. Lively and quiet
worship when we can come together to praise and glorify God. The church is used
daily by many organisations. Sunday Service: 11.00am and evenings as arranged
Church website: www.gourockweb.com/st_johns/
Open by arrangement, telephone 01475 630879
CHURCH OF SCOTLAND ② ☕ 👶 (Sunday Surfers and crèche) 📖 **C**

ST NINIAN'S CHURCH, GOUROCK

617 ST NINIAN'S CHURCH, GOUROCK

NS 242 777
18 Royal Street, Gourock
Gourock formed part of the pre-Reformation parish of Inverkip, mentioned in
Papal registers of 1216-27. In 1878 Archbishop Eyre of Glasgow arranged for the
construction of a chapel-school to be dedicated to St Ninian. The foundation stone
was laid in 1879. Extension carried out in 1982 for the visit to Scotland of Pope
John Paul II. The altar contains marble from the papal altar at Bellahouston.
Mosaics by Frank Tritschler, stained glass by Dom Ninian Sloan of Pluscarden
Abbey, and a chasuble fashioned from an original Paisley shawl by Debbie Gonet.
Small museum.
Sunday Mass: 9.30am and 11.30am; daily 10.00am and Vigil Mass Saturday 5.30pm
Church website: www.st-ninians-gourock.org
Open daily 9.00am-6.00pm. Information leaflets in French, Spanish, Italian and
German – children's worksheets also available. For access to museum, telephone Parish Priest
01475 632078 or fax 01475 631984
ROMAN CATHOLIC   🔊 📖 wc 🕯

618 ST PATRICK, GREENOCK

NS 271 761
5 Orangefield Place
Unique and striking example of the work of G Antonio Coia 1935. The soaring
gable characterises a church of great strength. A framework of steel is encased in
reinforced concrete and enveloped in red Lancashire brick with a backing of Scots
clay cement bricks. Exquisite stone sculpture by Archibald Dawson including bas
relief of St Patrick blessing a child rising from between the two doors.
Services: Saturday Vigil 7.00pm; Sunday Masses 8.00, 10.00, 11.30am and 7.00pm
Open daily 8.00am-7.30pm
ROMAN CATHOLIC 🔊 **A**

619 FINNART ST PAUL'S, GREENOCK

NS 265 774
Newark Street
Finely detailed late-Gothic church designed by Sir Robert Rowand Anderson.
Opened for public worship in 1893 it has just undergone a major programme of
restoration. Stained glass by Burne-Jones, Douglas Strachan and William Wilson.
3-manual and pedal pipe organ by Father Willis 1894.
Sunday Service: 11.00am
Open by arrangement with Minister 01475 639602 or Session Clerk 01475 722232
CHURCH OF SCOTLAND 🦽 wc ⊘ 🍴 (by arrangement) ☕ (by arrangement) **A**

620 THE OLD WEST KIRK, GREENOCK

NS 279 765
Esplanade, Greenock
Cruciform church first built 1591 at Westburn, but rebuilt here 1926-28 with a new
tower designed by James Miller. The masonry, window tracery and balustraded
forestair are all original. Also brought from the old site are the surrounding
headstones and graveslabs, some bearing trade emblems or coats of arms. Inside
the church are galleries originally intended to be occupied by the laird, the sailors
and the farmers of the parish. Notable collection of stained glass including
windows by Morris & Co and Daniel Cottier. Behind the octagonal pulpit is a
mural panel by the local artist Ian Philips 1991. Sunday Service: 11.00am
Church website:www.greenockoldwestkirk.freeserve.co.uk
Open Wednesdays mid-May to mid-September from 10.30am-12.00 noon, 2nd Saturday,
September 10.00am-4.00pm (Inverclyde Doors Open Day). Other times by contacting Rev
Ian Johnson, telephone 01475 888277
CHURCH OF SCOTLAND 🦽 ⊘ 🍴 ☕ 🍴 wc **B**

THE OLD WEST KIRK, GREENOCK

621 ST JOHN'S EPISCOPAL, GREENOCK

NS 274 766

Union Street (opposite Watt Library)
The present building was consecrated in 1878,
designed by Paley and Austin of Lancaster –
their only Scottish church. The intricately carved
rood screen, based on a medieval screen in
Gloucestershire and designed by H O Tarbolton,
was given by the family of Sir John Kerr, one-
time Governor of Bengal. The font is a copy of
a 15th-century font in Suffolk. Organ by Mirrlees
of Glasgow. Services: Sunday 9.00am Eucharist,
11.00am Sung Eucharist (1st Sunday Matins
and Eucharist), 6.30pm Evensong (2nd and
last Sundays)
Open by arrangement with Ian Milne,
telephone 01475 796331
SCOTTISH EPISCOPAL wc ⊘ **B**

ST JOHN'S EPISCOPAL,
GREENOCK

622 ST LUKE'S, GREENOCK

NS 273 763

Nelson Street
Designed by David Cousin and built in 1840, with the spire being added in 1855.
The clock 1856 was the gift of Miss Frances Ann Wood. The interior was
completely gutted by fire in 1912 and replaced by a new chancel, designed by John
Keppie, with four stained glass windows, a new organ and seating for 1144.
Services: Sunday 11.00am; Wednesday Advent and Lenten lunches and
service 12.00 noon
Open by arrangement with Mr Mitchell 01475 726916 or Mr Robertson 01475 725451
CHURCH OF SCOTLAND ♿ wc ⊘ ⊑ (after morning service) ⓘ 📖 **A**

623 ST MARY'S, GREENOCK

NS 274 768

14 Patrick Street
Designed in Early French Gothic style by George Goldie and opened in 1862. The
tower was left incomplete. Major alterations 1914, including a new Lady Chapel.
The sanctuary was remodelled in 1960s and 1970s. Stained glass windows
depicting Our Lady and various saints by Wailes of Newcastle. 'Lourdes' window
by Patrick Feeny installed 1965. Organ by Joseph Brook of Busby 1886, moved
here 1949; the casing is German. Services: daily 10.00am; Saturday Vigil 6.30pm;
Sunday 10.00am and 12.00 noon
Church website: www.stmarysgreenock.org
Open daily 9.00am-5.00pm (Friday 2.00pm); Sunday 9.00am-4.00pm
ROMAN CATHOLIC ♿ wc ⊘ ⊑ 📖 **B**

624 KILMACOLM OLD KIRK

NS 359 670
Built in 1830 James Dempster, Greenock,
on the site of 13th- and 16th-century
churches. Thirteenth-century chancel is
incorporated as the Murray Chapel. South
aisle, J B Wilson, Glasgow, added 1903.
early 20th-century stained glass windows
by C E Moira, Norman Macdougall and
Horace Wilkinson. Modern examples by
John K Clark and Lorraine Lamond. Near
centre of village, west of junction of B786
with A761. Sunday Service: 11.00am, July
and August 10.00am
Open daily 10.00am-4.00pm
CHURCH OF SCOTLAND 🦽 📖 ⊘ wc **B**

KILMACOLM OLD KIRK

625 ST JOHN THE BAPTIST, PORT GLASGOW

NS 319 746
Shore Street, Port Glasgow
Built 1854 with pinnacles rising from the buttressed gable front. Refurbished 2000.
Stained glass including 'The Risen Christ' above the main door by Edward
Harkness. Fresco of St Thérèse above Sacristy door by George Duffy. Services:
Sunday 9.30 and 11.00 am; Monday Mass 9.30 am; Tuesday Mass 6.30 pm;
Wednesday to Friday Mass 9.30am; Saturday Mass 10.00am, Vigil Mass 6.00pm
Church website: www.johnthebaptist.portglasgow@btinternet.com
Open by arrangement with Housekeeper, telephone 01475 741139
ROMAN CATHOLIC 🦽 ⊘ wc

ST JOHN THE BAPTIST, PORT GLASGOW

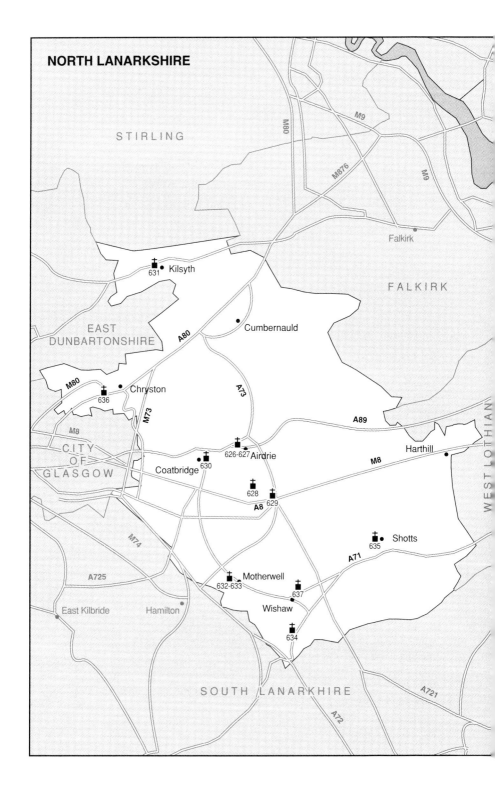

NORTH LANARKSHIRE

STIRLING

M9

M80

M876

M9

Falkirk

FALKIRK

631 Kilsyth

EAST
DUNBARTONSHIRE

A80

Cumbernauld

A73

M80

636 Chryston

M73

A89

M8

CITY
OF
GLASGOW

626-627 Airdrie

Coatbridge 630

Harthill

M8

628

A8 629

WEST LOTHIAN

M74

635 Shotts

A71

A725

632-633 Motherwell

637

East Kilbride   Hamilton

Wishaw

634

SOUTH LANARKSHIRE

A721

A72

NORTH LANARKSHIRE

Local Representative: Mrs Mary Canavan, Flat 10, 9 Victoria Circus, Glasgow
G12 9LB (*telephone* 0141 334 5462)

626 NEW MONKLAND PARISH CHURCH, AIRDRIE
NS 753 678
Condorrat Road, Glenmavis, Airdrie
A fine old Scots plain kirk which hides an attractive interior, by Andrew Bell of
Airdrie 1776. It holds a commanding position at the highest point in the village,
and incorporates the bell-tower of an earlier church (1698) which housed a cell for
minor offenders. The old church was replaced when it 'suffered so badly from
overcrowding that youthful members of the congregation colonised the exposed
joists to roost!' The apse was added in 1904 by John Arthur. Extensive restoration
1997. Simple watchhouse by the cemetery. Sunday Service: 10.30am
Open by arrangement, telephone Mr John Blades 01236 766511
CHURCH OF SCOTLAND ② wc **B**

627 ST MARGARET'S, AIRDRIE
NS 765 656
96 Hillcraig Street, Airdrie
Parish founded in 1836, this simple neo-classical church
by Wilkie & Gray, 1839, has a square tower and spire
rising above the pedimented front. Before it was built,
adherents had to travel to Glasgow for services, many on
foot. Services: weekdays 10.00am, Saturday 5.00pm Vigil,
Sunday 10.00am, 12.00 noon and 4.00pm
*Open during summer 9.00am-6.00pm, winter 9.00am-4.00pm,
or by arrangement with Parish Priest, telephone 01236 763370*
ROMAN CATHOLIC ♿ ② wc

ST MARGARET'S, AIRDRIE

628 CORPUS CHRISTI, CALDERBANK
NS 768 630
In the middle of Calderbank village
The parish was founded in 1948 and the church was
opened in 1952. It has undergone several renovations
inside to accommodate liturgical changes. Stained glass
window of the Sacraments 1985, designed by Shona
McInnis. New church furnishings by J McNally, made by
a local craftsman. Sunday Services: 9.00am, 11.00am;
weekdays: 10.00am; Saturday: 8.45am and Vigil 6.00pm
*Open 8.00am-8.00pm (if main door closed,
use right-hand side door)*
ROMAN CATHOLIC ②

CORPUS CHRISTI, CALDERBANK

629 ST ALOYSIUS, CHAPELHALL

NS 7829 6257
Main Street, Chapelhall
Opened in 1894, built to a design by
Pugin and Pugin. Sanctuary completely
renewed 1941-52. Marble reredos with
gold mosaic panels depicting scenes
from the life of St Aloysius. Stained
glass installed in rose window 1984, by
Shonna McInnes of Orkney who also
designed the remaining four windows
in the Sanctuary, installed in 1994 to
celebrate the church centenary.
Beautiful gardens behind the church
with excellent presbytery house
designed by McInally. Services:
Saturday Vigil 6.30pm, Sunday
10.00am, 12.00 noon and 5.30pm
Open daily 9.00am-7.30pm
ROMAN CATHOLIC 🔧 ⊘ 📖 wc

ST ALOYSIUS, CHAPELHALL

630 ST PATRICK, COATBRIDGE

NS 733 651
Main Street, Coatbridge
Built for the many Irish labourers
fleeing the potato famine, and
dispossessed Highlanders. Designed by
Pugin and Pugin 1896, in elegant
Gothic with a finely composed gable
frontage. Services: weekdays 10.00am,
Saturday Vigil 6.00pm, Sunday
10.00am, 12.00 noon and 6.00pm;
Holidays 10.00am, 1.00pm, 5.30pm
(Vigil) and 7.30pm
Church website: www.stpatricks-online.com
Open 10.00am-4.30pm
ROMAN CATHOLIC 🔧 ⊘ 📖 wc ☕ **B**

ST PATRICK, COATBRIDGE

631   ST PATRICK'S, KILSYTH

NS 720 777
30 Low Craigends, Kilsyth
Large-scale one-box brick structure
surmounted by a clerestory and unusual
roof by Gillespie, Kidd & Coia 1965.
One of only four Gillespie, Kidd &
Coia churches with all its original
features intact. Recent (2000) Historic
Scotland and Heritage Lottery Funded
restoration. Services: Saturday Vigil
6.30pm; Sunday 9.30am and 12.00
noon; weekdays 10.00am

ST PATRICK'S, KILSYTH

Open by arrangement with the Parish Priest, telephone 01236 822136
ROMAN CATHOLIC ♿ ⊘ wc **A**

632   DALZIEL ST ANDREW'S, MOTHERWELL

NS 752 571
Motherwell Cross
Union of the former Dalziel and St Andrew's
Church of Scotland congregations in 1996. The
parish of Dalziel has a history stretching back
to the 12th century, while St Andrew's was a
daughter church of Dalziel. Erected in 1874, the
building houses an organ by the German firm of
Walcker 1900, recently restored. Worship is a
sensitive mixture of traditional and modern
with a warm welcome for all ages. Sunday
Services: 11.00am in the Main Sanctuary;
Evening worship 6.30pm in the Mission Hall,
Jupiter Street (except July and August)
Open Saturday 10.00am-12.00 noon, or by
arrangement with the Church Officer,
telephone 01698 266 284
CHURCH OF SCOTLAND ♿ wc ⊘ 🧍 📖 ☕

DALZIEL ST ANDREW'S, MOTHERWELL

633   ST LUKE'S, MOTHERWELL

NS 746 599
Davaar Drive
A recently renovated church whose intimate setting serves well the Liturgy of the
Second Vatican Council. Services: Saturday 9.30am, 5.15pm; Sunday 10.30am,
5.15pm; weekdays 9.30am
Open by arrangement with Chapel House 01698 230402
ROMAN CATHOLIC ♿ wc ⊘

634 OVERTOWN PARISH CHURCH

NS 801 527

Main Street, Overtown, by Wishaw
Village church built in 1876. Near
picturesque Clyde Valley, Strathclyde
Country Park and many other places
of interest. A71, Edinburgh to
Kilmarnock (35 miles from
Edinburgh), just off M74
(20 miles from Glasgow)
Church website:
www.overtownparishchurch.org.uk
Open early May for sale of plants, with
guided tours and café, third Saturday
in September – Church Open Day,
guided tours and café
CHURCH OF SCOTLAND ⓘ 🍴 ☕ wc

OVERTOWN PARISH CHURCH

635 ST PATRICK, SHOTTS

NS 876 599

84 Station Road, Shotts
The church, designed by P P Pugin, is a
classic example of his work. White Carrara
marble altars and reredos added 1930s.
Stained glass depicts Crucifixion and scenes
of the local pits and iron works, as well as
St Barbara (patron saint of miners), St
Joseph, St Cecilia, St John Ogilvie and the
Baptism of The Lord. Stations of the Cross
are from Germany. The church has been
adapted to changing liturgical practice while
retaining its original character and quality.
Services: Saturday 9.30am, 6.30pm (Vigil);
Sunday 10.45am (Sung Mass with Choir),
6.00pm; Monday to Friday 10.00am
Church website: www.saintpatrick.org.uk
Open Monday to Thursday 9.00am-1.00pm,
Friday 9.00am-6.00pm
ROMAN CATHOLIC ♿ ⓘ wc

ST PATRICK, SHOTTS

636 STEPPS PARISH CHURCH

NS 657 686
17 Whitehill Avenue, Stepps
Fine example of the neo-Gothic style favoured by ecclesiastical architect
P MacGregor Chalmers 1900. Designed to reflect scale and simplicity of a village
church. Interesting stained glass including works by Stephen Adam (1900). Pipe
organ, Joseph Brook 1884, rebuilt James MacKenzie 1976. On rail and bus routes
Glasgow–Cumbernauld. Sunday Service: 10.00am mid-June to mid-August,
11.00am mid-August to mid-June
Open Tuesday, Thursday 10.00am-12.00 noon all year. Other times, telephone 0141 779 9556
CHURCH OF SCOTLAND

637 ST IGNATIUS OF LOYOLA, WISHAW

NS 799 551
74 Young Street
Designed by George Goldie and opened in 1865, enlarged by Bruce & Hay, 1883.
Built in Basilica form with two aisles and a bell tower which is the most prominent
landmark in Wishaw. The tower houses a bell (tone E) which is rung every day at
12.00 noon and 6.00pm for the Angelus prayer and also 30 minutes before the
main Sunday services and during weekday services. Stained glass windows based
on paintings by Jessie McGeechan of Coatbridge. Services: Sunday 10.15am, 12.00
noon, 6.00pm with Saturday Vigil 5.30pm, Monday-Friday 9.30am, Saturday
10.00am
Church website: www.saintignatiuswishaw.org.uk
Open Sunday 9.30am-1.30pm and 5.30-7.30pm, Monday-Friday 8.30am-1.30pm
(Thursday 4.30pm), Saturday 9.00am-12.00 noon and 5.00-7.00pm
ROMAN CATHOLIC   **A**

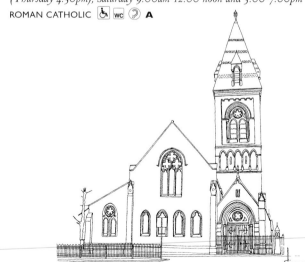

ST IGNATIUS OF LOYOLA, WISHAW

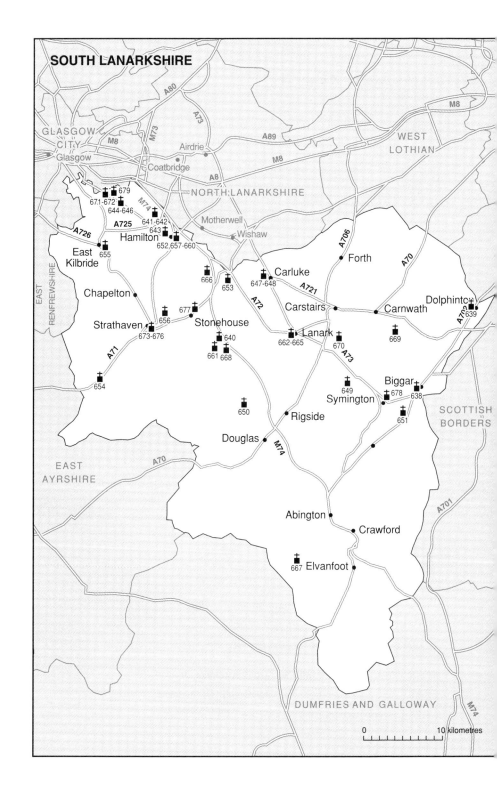

SOUTH LANARKSHIRE

GLASGOW CITY
Glasgow
Airdrie
Coatbridge
NORTH LANARKSHIRE
WEST LOTHIAN
M8
M8
A80
A73
A89
A8
M73

679
671-672
644-646
641-642
643
652,657-660
Hamilton
655
East Kilbride
A726
A725
M74

EAST RENFREWSHIRE

Chapelton
666
653
647-648
Carluke
A721
Forth
A706
A70
Carstairs
Carnwath
Dolphinton
639
A702

656
677
Stonehouse
Strathaven
673-676
662-665
Lanark
670
A73
669
A72

654
A71

640
661 668

650
649
Symington
Rigside
678
638
Biggar
651

Douglas
M74

SCOTTISH BORDERS

EAST AYRSHIRE
A70

Abington
Crawford
A701

667 Elvanfoot

DUMFRIES AND GALLOWAY
M74

0   10 kilometres

SOUTH LANARKSHIRE

Local Representative: Mr Sandy Gilchrist, 11 Mercat Loan, Biggar
(*telephone* 01899 221350)

638 BIGGAR KIRK

NT 040 379
Kirkstyle, Biggar
Rebuilt 1546, the last collegiate church
to be founded before the Reformation
in Scotland. A cruciform building with
fine stained glass, including work by
William Wilson and Crear McCartney.
In the kirkyard are memorials to the
forebears of William Ewart Gladstone

BIGGAR KIRK

and also Thomas Blackwood Murray, the Scottish motor pioneer of 'Albion'.
From M74, A702, twelve miles from Abington. Sunday Services: 11.00am;
also 9.30am June, July and August
Open daily in summer 9.00am-5.00pm. In winter,
key from Moat Park Heritage Centre opposite
CHURCH OF SCOTLAND **B**

639 BLACK MOUNT PARISH CHURCH

NT 101 464
Just off A702 at Dolphinton (turning signposted to Dunsyre)
Originally a parsonage in the 13th century, it appears to have always occupied the
same site, undergoing a complete rebuild in 1789, with late 19th-century additions.
A typical T-plan church, built so the preacher has the light behind him and the
congregation can hear him. The bell dates from c.1800. Sunday Service: 9.30am,
10.45am and 12.00 noon on a quarterly rotation with Culter and Libberton
Open by arrangement, telephone Mrs E Dickson 01968 682265
CHURCH OF SCOTLAND ♿ wc

640 OUR LADY AND ST JOHN, BLACKWOOD

NS 790 439
Carlisle Road, Blackwood, Kirkmuirhill
Stone building in Gothic style, opened 1880. The
grounds for the church were donated by the Hope-Vere
family. The Sanctuary extended in 1881 to accommodate
the altar donated by Mrs Lancaster. Stained glass
windows were also added at this time. The first two
parish priests were Benedictines from Ampleforth.
Services: Saturday 6.00pm; Sunday 10.00am and 6.00pm
Open by arrangement, telephone 01555 893459
ROMAN CATHOLIC

OUR LADY AND ST JOHN,
BLACKWOOD

641 BOTHWELL PARISH CHURCH

NS 705 586
Main Street, Bothwell
Scotland's oldest collegiate church still in use for worship and dedicated to St
Bride, occupies the site of a former 6th-century church. Medieval choir. Nave and
tower 1833, David Hamilton, altered 1933. Monuments to the Earls of Douglas and
the Duke of Hamilton. Stained glass by Gordon Webster, Douglas Strachan and Sir
Edward Burne-Jones. Fascinating tales of an outstanding royal wedding and link
with Bothwell Castle. Graveyard. Off A725 near Hamilton.
Sunday Service: 10.30am
Open daily Easter to September. Bus parties welcome by arrangement, telephone 01698 853189
CHURCH OF SCOTLAND ♿ ⏲ 🚻 📖 🚻 wc **A**

642 ST BRIDE'S, BOTHWELL

NS 706 550
Fallside Road
This impressive and striking building
was opened in 1973. The concrete block
walls are rendered externally to
harmonise with the surrounding
buildings. The red knotty pine ceiling
and quarry tile floor bring warmth to
the interior and coloured blocks of glass
have been used to contrast with the
white walls. Superb pipe organ, striking

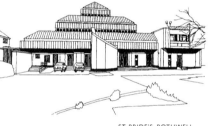

ST BRIDE'S, BOTHWELL

modern statute of Mary, and a modern sculpture of the Last Supper. Convent of
Poor Clares next door to church can also be visited. Masses: Monday-Friday
9.30am, Saturday Vigil 5.30pm, Sunday 10.00am, 12.00 noon and 6.00pm, Advent
and Lent Prayer Service at 5.15pm
Open Tuesday and Wednesday 10.00am-8.00pm or by arrangement with the Housekeeper,
Parish House, Fallside Road
ROMAN CATHOLIC ♿ ⏲ 🍽 📖 **B**

643 CADZOW PARISH CHURCH

NS 723 550
Woodside Walk, Hamilton
This Gothic style church, designed by R A Bryden, was opened in 1877 for coal
miners and their families. Halls designed by Cullen, Lochhead and Brown added in
1925 and 1961. Pipe organ by Forster and Andrew of Hull installed in 1889.
Communion table, chairs and eagle lectern are by Thomas Wilson of Glasgow.
Stained glass windows by Stephen Adam, Douglas Hamilton, John Blyth and Sadie
McLellan. There is a Mission Church in Ferniegair Village. Sunday Services: June to
August 9.30am and 10.45am, September to May 10.45am and 6.30pm
Open by arrangement with Session Clerk, telephone 01698 425512
CHURCH OF SCOTLAND wc ⏲ **C**

644 CAMBUSLANG OLD PARISH CHURCH

NS 646 600

3 Cairns Road, Kirkhill, Cambuslang

St Cadoc is believed to have had a holy site here AD
c.550, and early buildings have been recorded from
12th century. The present building is by David Cousin
1841. Steeple with clock and bell. The chancel is by
P MacGregor Chalmers 1922. Stained glass and
tapestries by Sadie McLellan 1957. Millennium wall-
hanging in vestibule 2001. Heraldic shields of
heritors decorate the ceiling. Interesting gravestones
in churchyard including one to Rev William
McCulloch, Minister at Scotland's largest ever revival
'The Cambuslang Wark' in 1742. Near Greenlees Road
B759. Sunday Services: September to June 11.00am
and 6.30pm; July and August 9.30am and 11.00am

Church website: www.cambuslang-old-parish-church.com

Open by arrangement, telephone Mrs F McQueen

0141 641 4845

CHURCH OF SCOTLAND   ⊘   ⟨♿⟩   wc   **B**

CAMBUSLANG OLD
PARISH CHURCH

645 ST BRIDE'S, CAMBUSLANG

NS 643 604

21 Greenlees Road, Cambuslang (opposite Police Station)

The church, which opened in 1900, has a
Crucifixion window, an example of the early work
of stained glass artist Gordon M Webster, and
another free-standing window also by Webster.
Services: Saturday Vigil 5.30pm; Sunday 10.00am,
12.00 noon and 6.00pm

Open 7.00am-8.00pm every day

ROMAN CATHOLIC   ⟨♿⟩   wc   ⊘

ST BRIDE'S, CAMBUSLANG

646 ST CUTHBERT'S, CAMBUSLANG

NS 643 604

3 Brownside Road

Towards the end of the 19th century Cambuslang became an increasingly
residential area and the need arose for an Episcopal church. In 1899, Bishop W T
Harrison opened a hall on Bushley Hill for worship dedicated to St Cuthbert.
Subsequently, the Duke of Hamilton offered land and the present church was
dedicated in 1909, the architect being W D Walton of Glasgow. Services: Sunday
9.30am (Sung Eucharist), Wednesday 10.00am (Said Eucharist)

Open every morning during term-time, otherwise key in Rectory next door

SCOTTISH EPISCOPAL   wc

647 ST ANDREW'S PARISH CHURCH, CARLUKE

NS 843 508

Mount Stewart Street, Carluke

The original church was replaced by the present building in
1799 following designs by Henry Bell (of the steamship
'Comet' fame). It incorporates an arch inside the porch and a
window with slender fluted pillars in the front of tower from
the old church. The tower of the old church has been retained
as a monument in its original site in the old graveyard at the
bottom of the town. Within the church are an organ made by
H Willis and Sons and installed in 1903, stained glass windows
including one made by Gordon McWhirter Webster 1932 and a
pulpit fall and companion communion table runner by Marilyn
E W McGregor DA 1999. Memorial garden 'Garden of Hope'
2001. Sunday Service: 11.00am

Open by arrangement, telephone Mrs Jennifer Johnstone 01555 750155
CHURCH OF SCOTLAND 🦽 ⊘ 📖 🚾 B

ST ANDREW'S PARISH
CHURCH, CARLUKE

648 ST ATHANASIUS, CARLUKE

NS 844 508

21 Mount Stewart Street, Carluke

The present church was erected in 1857, but a larger
building was required by the 1980s when the building
was extended as far as the grounds allowed. The
marriage of old and new buildings in 1984 has given a
modern and attractive church while still retaining much
of the original character. The architects were Cullen,
Lochhead and Brown. Services: Saturday Vigil 6.00pm;
Sunday 9.00am and 11.15am; weekdays 10.00am

Open 9.00am-4.00pm daily
ROMAN CATHOLIC 🦽 ⊘ 🚾

ST ATHANASIUS, CARLUKE

649 CAIRNGRYFFE KIRK

NS 923 384

Carmichael Crossroads, Carmichael

Known as 'The Little Cathedral of the Upper Ward', due to the quality of the
decoration, this church was built 1750 and extensively remodelled 1904 by Sir
Robert Lorimer. The staircase to the gallery and several headstones were brought
from the site of the 12th-century church a mile away. Magnificent stained glass
window, 1904. Other glass by Crear McCartney. Many memorials to the
Carmichael family and clan. Sunday Service: 9.30 or 11.00am as indicated on
notice board. Communion: first Sunday of November, March and June

Open Sunday before Christmas and Easter, 2.00-4.00pm,

otherwise by arrangement with the Minister 01899 308838
CHURCH OF SCOTLAND 🦽 🚾 ⊘ ☕ 📖 B

650 COALBURN PARISH CHURCH

NS 813 345
25/1 Bellfield Road
Built as a Mission Station in 1893 and a fully sanctioned charge 1895. Totally destroyed by fire 1918 and rebuilt 1922. Linked with Lesmahagow 1998. Church renovated and reordered 2001 to become all-purpose. Six Ministers have served during the 110 years. Sunday Service: 12.00 noon
Open by arrangement with Miss Lundie 01555 820730 or Mrs Nicol 01555 820647
CHURCH OF SCOTLAND 🦽 wc ☕ (by arrangement)

651 CULTER PARISH CHURCH

NT 027 342
200 yards off Birthwood Road, Culter
Appropriated by Kelso Abbey in 1170, the church is dedicated to St Michael. Rebuilt about 1810, being made shorter and wider. The interior was recast 1910, two of the galleries being removed, leaving only the west one. Refurnished 1938. Ornamental gates. Chancel burial ground for Culter Allers and Culter Mains. Bertram (of Nisbet) burial aisle next to vestry. Sunday Service: 9.30am, 10.45am and 12.00 noon on a quarterly rotation with Black Mount and Libberton
Open by arrangement with Mr E Cosh 01899 220221
CHURCH OF SCOTLAND wc 👂 **B**

652 ST JOHN'S CHURCH, HAMILTON

NS 724 523
Duke Street, Hamilton
Idiosyncratic classical building (originally a chapel-of-ease) 1835. The interior was renovated in 1971 by Cullen Lochhead & Brown who also completed the St John's Centre, opened 1970, and incorporating the former St John's Grammar School of 1836 and the Centenary Hall of 1934. In October 2000 the firm Cullen Lochhead & Brown also completed a Millennium Project which involved the re-fashioning of most of the existing suite of halls and the erection of an extension. Two works in stained glass by Susan Bradbury feature in the St John's Centre. In the Chapel ('Wings') and in the coffee room ('Giving and Receiving'). Located at the 'Top Cross' opposite Marks & Spencer. Sunday Services: 10.45am and 6.30pm (summer 10.00am and 9.00pm)
Church website: www.stjohnshamilton.org.uk
St John's Centre open to the public Monday to Friday 10.00am-12.00 noon and 2.00 4.00pm, and on Saturday from 10.00am-4.00pm
CHURCH OF SCOTLAND 🦽 👂 🍴 📖 ☕ **C**

ST JOHN'S CHURCH, HAMILTON

653 DALSERF PARISH CHURCH

NS 800 507

Built 1655, centre transept added 1892. Oblong
building with pulpit on long side. Outside stairs
to three galleries. Belfry. Two large memorial
windows on either side of pulpit by Douglas
Hogg. The graveyard contains a pre-Norman
hogback stone and an outstanding Covenanting
memorial 1753, to Rev John MacMillan, founder
of the Reformed Presbyterian Church. Off A72
between Garrion Bridge and Rosebank.
Sunday Service: 12.00 noon
Open by arrangement, telephone Church Officer,
Mr W Knox 01698 883770
CHURCH OF SCOTLAND 🦽 📖 ☕ wc **A**

DALSERF PARISH CHURCH

654 DRUMCLOG MEMORIAL KIRK

NS 640 389

J McLellan Fairley 1912. The church has strong
associations with the covenanters. A71, five
miles west on Darvel road. Part of Avendale
Old Church. Sunday Service: 9.30am. All-age
communion on the third Sunday of each
month, except July and August. There is also
an open-air Conventicle Service at the Battle
of Drumclog Monument on the first Sunday
of June. Details of special services to be found
on church website
Church website: www.avendale-drumclog.com
Open by arrangement, telephone
Mr J Spence 01357 521939
CHURCH OF SCOTLAND

DRUMCLOG MEMORIAL KIRK

655 ST BRIDE, EAST KILBRIDE

NS 641 544

Whitemoss Avenue

Built 1963-64 by Gillespie, Kidd & Coia to a radical modernist design. The original
150ft campanile had to be demolished in 1966 due to the deterioration of the
brickwork. This is one of the busiest churches in South Lanarkshire with a
congregation of over 8000. Services: Sunday 9.00am, 10.30am, 12.00 noon,
6.00pm; Monday-Friday 10.00am and 1.00pm; Saturday 10.00am and 6.00pm
Open by arrangement with Father Ryan, telephone 01355 220005
ROMAN CATHOLIC

🦽 wc ☕ ☕ (after noon Mass on Sunday and 10.00am Mass Monday-Thursday) **A**

656 GLASFORD PARISH CHURCH, GLASSFORD

NS 726 470

Jackson Street, Glassford

Built 1820. Memorial stained glass windows to Rev Gavin
Lang, grandfather of Cosmo Lang, Archbishop of Canterbury.
Ruins of 1633 church and Covenanter's stone. Off A71
Stonehouse–Strathaven or A723 Hamilton– Strathaven.
Linked with Strathaven East. Sunday Service: 10.00am

Open by arrangement. Also Doors Open Day,

telephone Rev W Stewart 01357 521138

CHURCH OF SCOTLAND   🅰 📖 wc **B**

GLASFORD PARISH
CHURCH, GLASSFORD

657 HAMILTON OLD PARISH CHURCH

NS 723 555

Strathmore Road, Hamilton

The present building is a Georgian gem. The only
church designed and built by William Adam, 1734.
Samples from the roof timbers found to be full of
lead shot – Adam used wood from an old man-of-
war! Chancel furnishings include embroidery by
Hannah Frew Paterson. Exceptionally detailed

HAMILTON OLD PARISH CHURCH

engraved glass windows by Anita Pate depict the history of the church back to the
6th century. Memorial stained glass window of African animals to John Stevenson
Hamilton, founder of Kruger National Park. Eleventh-century Netherton Cross and
Covenanting memorials in graveyard. In centre of town. Sunday Service: 10.45am

Church website: www.hopc.fsnet.co.uk

Open Monday to Friday, 10.30am-3.30pm. Or by arrangement, telephone 01698 281905,
Monday to Friday 9.00am-2.00pm. Easter Sunday, church decorated with thousands of
daffodils

CHURCH OF SCOTLAND   ⓘ (by arrangement on weekdays) wc **A**

658 HAMILTON WEST PARISH CHURCH

NS 712 558

Peacock Cross, Burnbank Road, Hamilton

The church was originally founded in 1874 as the 'Burnbank Mission Station' of
St John's Free Church. Having been raised to full status in 1875, the church was
rebuilt in 1880 and the Glasgow architect John Hutchison was commissioned. The
result is the present building, whose design exhibits many features in the 13th-
century Gothic style. The interior has one of the best examples in Scotland of a
wooden hammerbeam roof. The organ was built by Hill & Son of London 1902
and is still in use today. The exterior is floodlit, highlighting the stonework which
was restored in 1988. Sunday Service: 10.45am, except July 10.00am

Open by arrangement, telephone Mr James Murdie 01698 425237

CHURCH OF SCOTLAND   ⓘ wc **B**

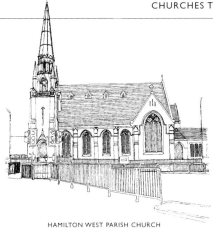

HAMILTON WEST PARISH CHURCH

659   ST MARY THE VIRGIN, HAMILTON

NS 721 567

Auchingramont Road, Hamilton

The building designed by John Henderson was
opened for worship in 1847 and is Early
English in style. Chancel ceiling panels were
painted by Mabel Royds (1874-1941). There are
fine stained glass commemorative windows
with several memorials in marble and stone
reflecting the links with the town's military
history. Organ, Foster & Andrews 1890. Sunday
Services: 8.30 and 10.00am, first and third
Sunday 6.00pm; Wednesday 10.00am

Church website: www.stmarysepiscopalhamilton.co.uk

Open daily during March to September

(key at Rectory)

SCOTTISH EPISCOPAL ⏵ wc ⏺ **B**

ST MARY THE VIRGIN, HAMILTON

660   HILLHOUSE PARISH CHURCH

NS 696 554

Clarkwell Road, Hamilton

Established 1955, the church has warmly welcomed many visitors from this country
and abroad during its relatively short history. We are a lively, go-ahead church,
who believe in challenging people with the Gospel of Christ in a way that is
relevant today. We promise you one thing, whatever your age, you wan't be bored
in Hillhouse. Events are intimated on the website.

Sunday Services: September to April 10.45am and 7.00pm; May to August 10.45am

Church website: www.hillhousechurch.co.uk

Open by arrangement with the Session Clerk, telephone 01698 425194

CHURCH OF SCOTLAND ♿ wc ⏵ ⏷ (by arrangement) ⏺ (by arrangement)

661 KIRKMUIRHILL PARISH CHURCH

NS 799 429
Carlisle Road, Kirkmuirhill
Built in 1868 by the United Presyterian Church,
Architect Robert Baldie. Early English Gothic
Revival style, the most prominent feature being the
spire which dominates the surroundings. Four
stained glass windows by Robert Paterson 1941,
Douglas Hamilton 1954, and Linda Fraser 1986.
Embroidered pew and chair cushions designed
by Pat Hodgson of Hawksland Lesmahagow and
worked by members of the congregation.
Sunday Services: 11.00am and 6.30pm
Open by arrangement with Session Clerk,
telephone 01555 892305
CHURCH OF SCOTLAND 👤 🔊 📖 wc

KIRKMUIRHILL PARISH CHURCH

662 GREYFRIARS PARISH CHURCH, LANARK

NS 880 437
Bloomgate, Lanark
William Leiper designed this, his smallest church,
in 1875 for the Bloomgate United Presbyterian
Congregation. Its simple gothic interior is
enlivenend by a slender bellcote inspired by
Andrew Heiton's Findlater Church in Dublin.
2-manual pipe organ by Ingram, recently
fully refurbished. Pulpit fall and welcome
banner by local artist Myra Gibson.
Sunday Service: 11.00am
Church website: www.webartz.com/greyfriars
Open on Doors Open Day and by arrangement
with the Minister, telephone 01555 663363
CHURCH OF SCOTLAND 👤 🔊 wc B

GREYFRIARS PARISH CHURCH, LANARK

663 CHRIST CHURCH, LANARK

NS 881 439
Hope Street
Gothic church of a simple rectangle with aisles of 1853 by John Henderson.
Carving by Major General Stevenson. Modern stained glass by Pauline Payne,
Art Teacher of Lanark Grammar School in the 1960s and 1970s.
Sunday Service: 10.30am
Open by arrangement with the Minister 01555 663065
SCOTTISH EPISCOPAL   B

664 ST MARY'S, LANARK

NS 886 435

70 Bannatyne Street, Lanark

Gothic revival cruciform church by Dublin architects Ashlin & Coleman 1908.
Graceful 144ft spire. Remarkable interior decoration including imposing reredos of
Caen stone and marble, statues of St Mungo, St Margaret and St Columba and fine
stained glass. Services: weekdays 9.30am; Saturday Vigil 6.30pm; Sunday 9.30am,
11.00am and 6.30pm

Open during daylight hours

ROMAN CATHOLIC 🔲 🔲 🔲 🔲 🔲 **A**

665 ST NICHOLAS PARISH CHURCH, LANARK

NS 881 437

The Cross, Lanark

By John Reid of Nemphlar 1774.
Stained glass, baptismal font in Caen
stone. Fine pipe organ. On A73, 30
miles south of Glasgow, follow signs
for New Lanark.

Sunday Service: 11.00am;
Wednesday 10.15am

*Open during Doors Open Day and by
arrangement, telephone 01555 662600.*

CHURCH OF SCOTLAND

🔲 🔲 🔲 🔲 🔲 **B**

ST NICHOLAS PARISH CHURCH, LANARK

666 ST MARY'S, LARKHALL

NS 757 509

Raploch Road

Founded as a mission in 1861, the present church was built 1872. Rectangular Free-
style church with over-hanging eaves and harled walls with painted surrounds to
doors and windows. Inside, pointed arches divide the nave from the aisles.
Services: Saturday Mass 6.30pm; Sunday 8.00am, 10.45am, 4.30pm (winter),
6.00pm (summer)

Open by arrangement, telephone 01698 882564

ROMAN CATHOLIC 🔲 🔲 (hall) **C**

667 LOWTHER PARISH CHURCH, LEADHILLS

NS 885 148

On B797 near south end of village

Built in 1883 as the United Free Church, it amalgamated with the Parish Church in 1937. Double manual pedal organ and an electronic organ. Memorial window depicting 'Dorcas'. Sunday Service: 11.30am

Open 1st Sunday or by arrangement, telephone 01659 74326

CHURCH OF SCOTLAND [wc] [access icon]

668 LESMAHAGOW OLD PARISH CHURCH

NS 814 399

David I granted a church and lands to the Tironensian monks in 1144. He also granted the right of sanctuary, violated in 1335 when the church was burned, with villagers inside, by John Eltham, brother of Edward I. The present church was built in 1803 and the apse added in the 1890s. Pipe organ 1889. Several stained glass windows including one whose central panel, 'The Descent from the Cross', is a copy of that in Antwerp Cathedral. The bell is dated 1625. Display in the Chapter House. Lesmahagow on M74, 23 miles south of Glasgow. A conservation village. Sunday Service: 10.00am

Church website: www.lopc.org.uk

Open by arrangement, telephone Rev Sheila Mitchell 01555 892425, or Church Officer Mr Alex McInnes 01555 892697

CHURCH OF SCOTLAND [access] [hearing] [book] [access] [wc]

LESMAHAGOW OLD
PARISH CHURCH

669 LIBBERTON & QUOTHQUAN PARISH CHURCH

NS 992 428

On B7016 from Biggar to Carnwath

Carnwath was separated from Libberton in 1186 and Quothquan Parish was joined to Libberton in 1660. Quothquan Church (about 2 miles from Libberton) is now a ruin; its aisle is the burial place of the Chancellor family. The new church was built on an ancient site of worship at Libberton in 1812, and restored in 1902. It has fine woodwork and memorials of distinction. Sunday Service: 9.30am, 10.45am and 12.00 noon on a quarterly rotation with Black Mount and Culter

Open by arrangement, telephone Miss J Gibson 01899 308107

CHURCH OF SCOTLAND [access] [wc] **B**

670 PETTINAIN CHURCH

NS 955 429

7 miles east of Lanark, between A73 and A70
Fine example of a rural parish kirk, with
outstanding views across open countryside.
The site has been a place of worship since
the early 12th century when David I
established the chapel of 'Pedynane'. The
present church dates principally from the
18th century with an earlier belfry of 1692
and an incised cross slab re-used as a
relieving lintel. Interesting walled burial
ground. Acquired by the Scottish Redundant
Churches Trust in 2000 with the generous
support of local people. Occasional services,
plus weddings and funerals by arrangement

PETTINAIN CHURCH

*Open July and August, Sundays, 1.00-4.00pm or by arrangement with the SRCT, telephone
01334 472032*

FORMER CHURCH OF SCOTLAND ♿ 🚻 **B**

671 RUTHERGLEN OLD PARISH CHURCH

NS 613 617

Main Street x Queen Street, Rutherglen
The present church was designed by the architect J J Burnet 1902 in Gothic style,
the fourth on this site since the original foundation in the 6th century. The gable
end of an 11th-century church still stands in the graveyard supporting St Mary's
steeple (15th century). It contains the church bell 1635. Stained glass including a
First World War memorial. Communion cups dated 1665 are still in use. The
churchyard occupies an ancient site, at its gateway two stone offertory shelters,
and a sundial set above its entrance dated 1679.
Sunday Service: 11.00am

Church website:www.rutherglen.clara.co.uk/index.htm

Open second Saturday of every month, 10.00am-12.00 noon

CHURCH OF SCOTLAND ⓘ wc 🍽 B

672 ST COLUMBKILLE'S CHURCH, RUTHERGLEN

NS 614 616

Main Street, Rutherglen
Magnificent church, Coia 1940, replacing original church founded in 1851. Modern
adaptation of an Italian basilica. Between A724 and A731. Trains and city buses.
Sunday Masses 9.00am, 10.30am, 12.00 noon and 7.00pm; Vigil Mass Saturday
5.30pm

Open Monday to Thursday 9.00am-5.00pm, Friday 9.00am-2.00pm

ROMAN CATHOLIC ♿ ⓘ 🏛 🍽 wc

ST COLUMBKILLE'S CHURCH, RUTHERGLEN

673 AVENDALE OLD PARISH CHURCH, STRATHAVEN

NS 701 443

59a Kirk Street, Strathaven

Records show a church in Strathaven in 1288. This church was built in 1772 and the interior renovated 1879. The centre section of the south gallery was reserved for the family and tenants of the Duke of Hamilton and is known as 'The Duke's Gallery'. Stained glass window of the Last Supper, Crear McCartney 1996. In town centre A71. Sunday Service: 11.00am. All-age communion is celebrated at the 11.00am service on the third Sunday of each month, except July and August. Details of evening services to be found on church website

Church website: www.avendale-drumclog.com

Open Monday to Friday 9.00am-12.00 noon (not school holidays).

Other times, telephone Session Clerk 01357 521939

CHURCH OF SCOTLAND ♿ ☺ 👤 📖 👤 wc **B**

AVENDALE OLD PARISH CHURCH, STRATHAVEN

674 STRATHAVEN EAST PARISH CHURCH

NS 702 446

Green Street, Strathaven

The white painted exterior is a local landmark. Built 1777 with clock tower added 1843. Major rebuilding 1877. Prominent pulpit and memorial windows. Linked with Glasford Church. Sunday Service: 11.30am

Open by arrangement, telephone Rev W Stewart 01357 521138

CHURCH OF SCOTLAND ⊘ wc **A** (tower) **B** (church)

675 STRATHAVEN WEST

NS 700 444

Townhead Street

Originally a Relief Church out of Strathaven East, dedicated 1835, it was conceived with enthusiasm, built and dedicated within nine months. Design based on Carluke Church. Pipe organ 1930. Two major refurbishments, for centenary and sesquicentenary, resulting in a surprising warm, attractive interior. War memorial in vestibule. Two memorial stained glass windows. Sunday Service: 11.00am

Open by arrangement, telephone Mr Hendry 01357 520300

CHURCH OF SCOTLAND ♿ wc ⊘ ☕ 🛈 **B**

STRATHAVEN WEST

676 ST PATRICK'S CHURCH, STRATHAVEN

NS 70 44

52 Stonehouse Road

Built 1901 and paid for by Archbishop Charles Eyre of Glasgow. A sanctuary extension and porch were added in 1953. It was built to serve the growing Catholic population of Strathaven following immigration from Ireland and the Highlands. The original smaller church, built in 1853, stands besides the church and is now a parish hall. Services: Monday-Friday 9.30am; Saturday 10.00am, Vigil 6.00pm; Sunday 9.00am and 11.00am

Open by arrangement, telephone 01357 520104

ROMAN CATHOLIC ♿ wc ⊘

677 PATERSON CHURCH, STONEHOUSE

NS 755 469
Lawrie Street
The current building, named for the Rev Henry Angus Paterson who ministered to
the congregation for over 60 years, dates from 1879. Remained a United Free
Church at the Union of 1929. Refurbished following a fire in 1977. Fine collection
of stained glass windows by Crear McCartney. Sunday Service: 10.00am
Open Tuesday mid-June to end of August 10.00am-12.00 noon
UNITED FREE ② ☕ 📖

678 SYMINGTON KIRK

NS 999 352
Kirk Bauk
The original church was established c.1160. The present building is largely 18th
and 19th century though the belfry is 1734. Watchtower in graveyard. A feature of
the interior is the scissorbeam roof. Sunday Service: 9.30am or 11.00am as
indicated on notice board; Communion: 1st Sunday of November, March and June
Open by arrangement with the Minister, telephone 01899 308838
CHURCH OF SCOTLAND ♿ wc (in hall) ② **B**

SYMINGTON KIRK

679 ST ANDREW'S, UDDINGSTON

NS 697 601
4 Bothwell Road
Built 1890, architect Miles Septimus Gibson, the foundation stone laid by Lady
Mary Alice Douglas Home, aunt of the later Prime Minister Sir Alec Douglas
Home. After a fire in 1993 the chancel was restored by Alex Braidwood of
Blantyre. Stained glass by J T & C E Stewart of Glasgow and Peter Berry of
Malmesbury. The Blackett & Howden pipe organ, damaged in the fire, awaits
restoration. Painting of Bothwell Castle by architect and local historian J Jeffrey
Waddell. Sunday Service: 11.15am
Open by arrangement, telephone Miss Lyth 01698 812536
SCOTTISH EPISCOPAL wc

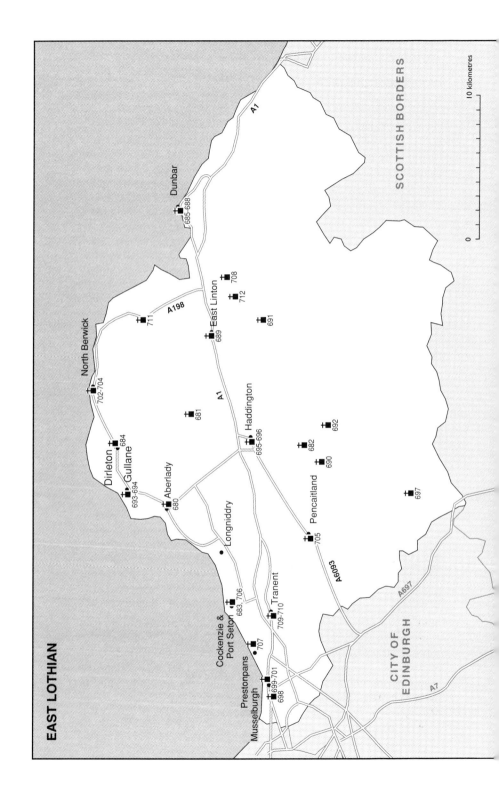

EAST LOTHIAN

Dunbar 685-688

East Linton
708
712

691

A198

711

North Berwick
702-704

A1

681

Haddington
695-696

Dirleton
684

Gullane
693-694

Aberlady
680

682
692

690

Pencaitland
697

Longniddry

705

A6093

Cockenzie &
Port Seton
683,706

707

Tranent
709-710

A697

Prestonpans
699-701

698

Musselburgh

SCOTTISH BORDERS

CITY OF
EDINBURGH

A7

0   10 kilometres

EAST LOTHIAN

Local Representative: Mrs Margaret Beveridge, St Andrews, Duns Road, Gifford EH41 4QW (*telephone* 01620 810694)

680 ABERLADY PARISH CHURCH

NT 462 799
Main Street, Aberlady

Fifteenth-century tower, the body of the church recast in 1886 by William Young. Stained glass by Edward Frampton, London 1889. Eighth-century cross. Marble monument attributed to Canova. Tour guide boards in English, French, German, Spanish, Swedish. A198 Edinburgh–North Berwick. Sunday Service: 11.15am

Open 1 May to 30 September, 8.00am to dusk. Other times, telephone B White 01875 853137, or F Burnett, 14 Rig Street, Aberlady 01875 870237

CHURCH OF SCOTLAND  **A**

ABERLADY PARISH CHURCH

681 ATHELSTANEFORD PARISH CHURCH

NT 533 774

The original church 'Ecclesia de Elstaneford' on this site is said to have been founded in 1176 by the Countess Ada, mother of William the Lion. The present church dates from 1780. Cruciform design with central aisle, transepts and semi-octagonal chancel. Bellcote on the west gable. Three stained glass windows by C E Kempe. Doocot 1583. Church has historic link with the Scottish Saltire: commemorative plaque and Saltire floodlit. Heritage Centre to rear of church opened in 1997 with audio visual display (entry free). From A1, B1347. Sunday Service: 10.00am

Open daily, dawn to dusk

CHURCH OF SCOTLAND **B**

ATHELSTANEFORD PARISH CHURCH

682 BOLTON PARISH CHURCH

NT 507 701

There has been a church on this site since before
1244. The present building dates from 1809 and
remains structurally unchanged since that time. The
architect was probably Archibald Elliot. The interior
is plain and unspoiled, complete with carpenter's
Gothic pulpit, and gallery on clustered iron posts.
Robert Burns's mother, brother and sisters are buried
in the churchyard. Graveguard and other items
dating from the time of the 'Resurrection Men'
displayed in the porch. Linked with Saltoun,
Humbie and Yester. B6368 from Haddington.
Sunday Service: 10.00am, alternating with Saltoun
Church website: www.lbes.demon.co.uk
Open daily
CHURCH OF SCOTLAND 📖 **B**

BOLTON PARISH CHURCH

683 COCKENZIE METHODIST CHURCH

NT 398 756

28 Edinburgh Road, Cockenzie
The third of East Lothian's three Primitive
Methodist Chapels, 1878. Simple and attractive.
Original interior. South side of main road at
west end of village. Sunday Service: 2.30pm
Open by arrangement, telephone
Christine Thomson 01875 811137
METHODIST ♿

COCKENZIE METHODIST CHURCH

684 DIRLETON KIRK

NT 513 842

Attractive stone building erected in 1612 to
replace 12th-century kirk in Gullane which
was 'continewallie overblawin with sand'.
Archerfield Aisle added 1650, first example
of neo-classical design in Scotland. Tower
crowned with Gothic pinnacles 1836.
Interesting examples of stained glass,
including 'St Francis and the Animals',
Margaret Chilton 1936.
Sunday Service: 11.30am
Open daily 10.00am to dusk. Light lunches,
snacks in adjacent Dirleton Gallery
CHURCH OF SCOTLAND ♿ 🔊 📖 ☕ wc **A**

DIRLETON KIRK

685 CHURCH OF OUR LADY OF THE WAVES, DUNBAR

NT 678 791

Westgate, Dunbar

Built in 1877, the church has stained glass behind the altar and wood carvings showing the Way of the Cross. Sunday Service: 10.30am; Saturday Vigil: 6.30pm; Mass: Monday, Tuesday, Wednesday and Friday 9.30am; Thursday 7.00am

Open by arrangement,

telephone 01368 862701

ROMAN CATHOLIC 🚻 ② 📖 ⚱ ☕

CHURCH OF OUR LADY
OF THE WAVES, DUNBAR

686 DUNBAR METHODIST CHURCH

NT 679 791

10 Victoria Street, Dunbar

Scotland's oldest Methodist Church, built in 1764. John and Charles Wesley were trustees and John often preached here. Enlarged 1857, renovated 1890. Fine interior, unexpected from plain exterior. Oak pulpit. Stained glass windows from St Giles, Edinburgh. South side of road leading from High Street to Harbour. Sunday Service: 11.00am

Open by arrangement, telephone David Hancock 01368 862052

METHODIST ⚱ ⚱ 📖 **A**

DUNBAR METHODIST CHURCH

687 DUNBAR PARISH CHURCH

NT 682 786

Queen's Road, Dunbar

The building, designed by Gillespie Graham in 1821, has been beautifully reconstructed by Campbell & Arnott 1990 following a devastating fire in 1987. The colourful and modern interior includes the early 17th-century monument to the Earl of Dunbar and some fine stained glass by Shona McInnes and Douglas Hogg 1990. Two hundred yards south of High Street, south end. Intercity trains to Dunbar. Sunday Service: 11.00am

Open daily 2.00-4.00pm Wednesday and Friday, June to September,

or telephone Mrs D Brunton 01368 862903

Various exhibitions during season

CHURCH OF SCOTLAND 🚻 ⚱ 📖 ② ☕ 🚾 **A**

688   ST ANNE'S CHURCH, DUNBAR

NT 678 791
Westgate, Dunbar
The church is by H M Wardrop and Sir R
Rowand Anderson 1890. Built in the Gothic
revival style and decorated with some Scots detail.
Carved oak furnishings, Henry Willis organ,
stained glass by Ballantine & Gardiner, Heaton,
Butler & Bayne, and the Abbey Studio. North end
of Dunbar High Street. Sunday Service: 9.30am
(except 1st Sunday of month), and 11.00am

ST ANNE'S CHURCH, DUNBAR

Open by arrangement, telephone Rev P Allen 01368 865711, or S Bunyan 01368 863335
SCOTTISH EPISCOPAL   🦽 🚻 **B**

689   PARISH OF TRAPRAIN, PRESTONKIRK, EAST LINTON

NT 592 778
Preston Road, East Linton
Dedicated to St Baldred, the church possesses in its former
chancel the best fragment of 13th-century church architecture
in East Lothian. The tower dates from 1631, the main building
from 1770, enlarged 1824, redesigned internally 1892 by James
Jerdan. Organ by Vincent of Sutherland. St Baldred window
1959 and two Second World War memorial windows by
William Wilson. Among the gravestones are those of Andrew
Meikle, inventor of the threshing machine, and George
Rennie, agriculturalist and brother of John Rennie, the civil
engineer. Off A1, follow signs to Preston Mill. Sunday
Service: 11.00am; 25 December 10.00am. Please note times
of services may be changed

PARISH OF TRAPRAIN,
PRESTONKIRK,
EAST LINTON

Open by arrangement, telephone 01620 860598
CHURCH OF SCOTLAND   🦽 🚻 (by arrangement) 🚻 (in Church Hall) **A**

690   SALTOUN PARISH CHURCH, EAST SALTOUN

NT 474 678
There has been a church on this site since before 1244. The
present building is a T-plan Gothic kirk of 1805 which John
Fletcher Campbell built 'as a monument to the virtues of his
ancestors'. The actual designer is most likely to have been
Robert Burn. The interior was recast in 1885; the architect was
John Lessels. Beneath the church lies the Fletcher Vault,
containing the remains of Andrew Fletcher, 'The Patriot', and
members of his family. Linked with Bolton, Humbie and
Yester. Sunday Service: 10.00am, alternating with Bolton
Church website: www.lbes.demon.co.uk
Open daily
CHURCH OF SCOTLAND 🦽 **A**

SALTOUN PARISH CHURCH,
EAST SALTOUN

691   NUNRAW ABBEY

NT 593 700

Garvald, by Haddington

Modern Monastery of Cistercian Monks built 1952-70 (but unfinished), architect
Peter Whiston. Nunraw House is a historic building and functions as the Abbey
guest house where people may stay for a few days of retreat in the monastic
atmosphere. Sunday Services: Mass 11.00am, Vespers 4pm, Compline 7.30pm;
weekday Services: Lauds and Mass 6.45am, Vespers 6.00pm, Compline 7.30pm

Reception area and Abbey open at all times

ROMAN CATHOLIC ♿ wc ② 👤 📖

692   YESTER PARISH CHURCH, GIFFORD

NT 535 681

Main Street, Gifford

By James Smith, finished 1710. A white harled
T-plan church with square staged tower and slated
spire. Weather vane in the form of a heron, William
Brown, Edinburgh 1709. Church bell from the old
Church of Bothans 1492. Pulpit 17th-century with
bracket for baptismal basin. Memorial in village
wall opposite to Rev John Witherspoon, son of the
Manse, who signed the American Declaration of
Independence 1784. B6369 from Haddington.
Hourly bus service. Sunday Service: 11.30am

Open daily, April to October, 9.00am to sunset.

Village gala day June. Flower show August

CHURCH OF SCOTLAND 📖 ② wc A

YESTER PARISH CHURCH, GIFFORD

693   GULLANE PARISH CHURCH (ST ANDREW'S)

NT 480 827

East Links Road, Gullane

The church, designed by Glasgow architect John Honeyman and completed in
1888, replaced an earlier 12th-century building vacated in 1612 when the
congregation was rehoused in a new kirk at Dirleton. The Kirk Session of Dirleton
decided to build the present parish church for the
benefit of 'the large number of summer visitors
annually residing in the village'. Simple Norman
style with east apse. The zig-zagged chancel arch
is derived from the old parish church, as is the
south doorway whose tympanum has a low relief
of St Andrew. A198 to North Berwick.
Sunday Service: 9.45am

Open daily all year. Coffee on Tuesdays 10.00-11.30am

CHURCH OF SCOTLAND ♿ 👤 📖 ② A

GULLANE PARISH CHURCH
(ST ANDREW'S)

694 ST ADRIAN'S CHURCH, GULLANE

NT 480 838
Sandy Loan, Gullane
A simple aisleless church in Arts & Crafts
style by Reginald Fairlie 1926. Built of
stone from the Rattlebag quarry, with a low
tower and slated pyramidal spire. Three-
light chancel window by Douglas Strachan
1934. Sandy Loan is the beach road at the
west end of the village. Sunday Services:
Sung Eucharist 9.30; Said Eucharist first
and third Sundays 8.00am
Open 10.00am-5.00pm, April to September
SCOTTISH EPISCOPAL 🦽 ⓐ 🛈 **B**

ST ADRIAN'S CHURCH, GULLANE

695 HOLY TRINITY CHURCH, HADDINGTON

NT 518 739
Church Street, Haddington
Built 1770 on site of original 'Lamp of
Lothian'. Chancel added 1930. 'Stations
of the Cross', Bowman. 'Christ
Crucified', Sutherland. Medieval walls
of former priory and town defences.
Sunday Services: 8.30am, Sung
Eucharist 10.00am, Evensong 6.00pm
(except July and August); Wednesday
Eucharist 10.00am

HOLY TRINITY CHURCH, HADDINGTON

Open Wednesday 10.00am-4.00pm, and in summer Saturday 10.00am-4.00pm.
Other times, contact the Rectory adjacent or office in Church halls
SCOTTISH EPISCOPAL 🛈 ⓐ wc **B**

696 ST MARY'S COLLEGIATE CHURCH, HADDINGTON

NT 519 736
Sidegate, Haddington
Dating back to the 14th century, one of the three great pre-Reformation churches
of the Lothians, known as 'The Lamp of Lothian', largest parish church in
Scotland, with fascinating history. Nave repaired for John Knox and the reformers
after Siege of Haddington 1548 and used as the parish church for almost 400
years. Transepts and choir restored, Ian G Lindsay & Partners 1973. Lauderdale
Aisle, now The Chapel of the Three Kings, in regular ecumenical use. Fine stone
carvings, especially west door. Notable stained glass by Sir Edward Burne-Jones
and Sax Shaw. Modern tapestries. Fine pipe organ by Lammermuir Pipe Organs

ST MARY'S COLLEGIATE CHURCH, HADDINGTON

1990. A peal of eight bells installed in the tower (and dedicated by the Moderator) in 1999. Sunday Services: All Age Worship 9.30am and Worship 11.00am
Church website: www.kylemore.btinternet.co.uk/stmarys.htm
Open Good Friday to 30 September, daily, 11.00am-4.00pm, Sunday 2.00-4.30pm.
Annual ecumenical Whitekirk/Haddington Pilgrimage second Saturday in May.
Regular concerts and recitals of international repute
CHURCH OF SCOTLAND **A**

697 HUMBIE KIRK

NT 461 637
On the site of a pre-Reformation church, set in an ox-bow of Humbie Burn, a T-plan Gothic church by James Tod dated 1800. Vestry added 1846, and alterations by David Bryce 1866. The chancel added 1930, probably W J Walker Todd. Open scissor-braced timber roof. East window stained glass by Douglas Strachan. Organ c.1850, probably the work of an Edinburgh builder with decorative Gothic dark wood case, from the Norwegian Seamen's Chapel at Granton. Fine gravestones with classical detail dating from earlier church. Broun Aisle, Bryce 1864, sited at west gate, erected by Archibald Broun of Johnstonburn 'in lieu of the burial place of his family within the church, which in deference to the feelings of the parishioners, he has now closed'! Linked with Bolton, Saltoun and Yester.
Sunday Service: 10.00am
Open daily
CHURCH OF SCOTLAND **B**

698 PARISH CHURCH OF
ST MICHAEL'S, INVERESK

NT 344 721
Musselburgh
There has been a church on the site since the
6th century. The present church was built in
1805 to the design of Robert Nisbet, the
steeple by William Sibbald. The interior was
reorientated and remodelled in 1893 by J
MacIntyre Henry and again in 2002 by
Simpson & Brown. Known as the 'visible Kirk'
because of its prominent position, it stands on
the site of a Roman praetorium and replaces a
medieval church. Fine Adam-style ceiling and
some excellent stained glass. Magnificent pipe
organ by Lewis 1892, originally built with
early form of electric action. Surrounded by a
fine graveyard with many interesting old
stones. Sunday Service: 11.15am
Open by arrangement, telephone Mr G Burnet
0131 665 2689. Village gardens open under
Scotland's Gardens Scheme, 5-6 June 2004
CHURCH OF SCOTLAND & (ramp) ⊘ ⎕ ⎕ wc **A**

PARISH CHURCH OF
ST MICHAEL'S, INVERESK

699 MUSSELBURGH CONGREGATIONAL CHURCH

NT 341 729
6 Links Street, Musselburgh
Simple but charming Georgian
building completed in 1801, built with
stone carried by fishermen and sailors
from the shores of the Forth at
Fisherrow. Oldest church in
Musselburgh and one of first
Congregational churches in Scotland.
Pipe organ, fine example of the work
of George Holdich built 1860 for
St Michael's, Appleby. Rebuilt for
Musselburgh Congregational Church
1977. Church sits behind Brunton
Hall. Sunday Service: 11.00am
Open by arrangement, telephone Mrs Doris
Brown, 11 Links Street 0131 665 3768
CONGREGATIONAL & ⎕ ⎕ wc **C**

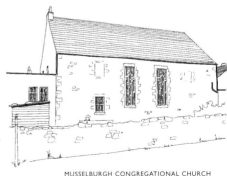

MUSSELBURGH CONGREGATIONAL CHURCH

700 OUR LADY OF LORETTO AND ST MICHAEL, MUSSELBURGH

NT 346 753

17 Newbigging, Musselburgh

Stone building opened in 1905. Sanctuary recently modernised. All windows are of stained glass and the walls of the sanctuary are covered in fine artwork, in gold leaf, depicting the events in the life of our Lord, corresponding to the Joyful Mysteries of the Rosary. Sunday Services: 9.00 and 11.30 am; Saturday Vigil 6.00pm

Open daily

ROMAN CATHOLIC 🦽 ✍ 📖 **B**

OUR LADY OF LORETTO
AND ST MICHAEL, MUSSELBURGH

701 ST PETER'S EPISCOPAL, MUSSELBURGH

NT 348 723

High Street, Musselburgh

Anglican church, near the site of the Battle of Pinkie (1547), in a traditional French Gothic style by Paterson & Shiells 1865. Narrow chancel and semi-circular apse and steeply pitched roof. Fine, older stained glass windows and 17th-century character wooden panelling in St Michael's Chapel. Sunday Services follow biblical themes and are friendly, relaxed and relevant. Kids' club during services. Sunday 11.15am; Wednesday 10.00am

Open by arrangement with Mr Alan Stevens, telephone 0131 665 6697

SCOTTISH EPISCOPAL 🦽 ✍ WC **B**

702 ABBEY CHURCH, NORTH BERWICK

NT 551 853

High Street, North Berwick

Built 1868 as United Presbyterian by Robert R Raeburn in Early English style. A complete early 20th-century scheme of stained glass with, superimposed on one window, an arrangement of suspended planes representing an ascent of doves, by Sax Shaw 1972. Sunday Services: 10.15am and 6.00pm

Open 9.00am-6.00pm, Mondays to Fridays, July and August

CHURCH OF SCOTLAND

🦽 ✍ 📖 WC

ABBEY CHURCH, NORTH BERWICK

703 CHURCH OF OUR LADY STAR OF THE SEA, NORTH BERWICK

NT 553 850

Law Road, North Berwick

Built in 1879, it is a simple Victorian church by Dunn & Hansom with seating for
200 people. The chancel was added by Basil Champreys in 1889 and the Lady
Chapel by Sir Robert Lorimer in 1901. The interior contains a number of pictures
after Benozzo Gozzoli and Botticelli and a Della Robbia (probably a copy).
Services: Monday to Friday 10.00am; Saturday Vigil 6.00pm; Sunday 10.00am

Church website: www.nbstar.org.uk

Open daily, 8.00am-dusk

ROMAN CATHOLIC   🦽 ⓐ **B**

704 ST BALDRED'S CHURCH, NORTH BERWICK

NT 556 853

Dirleton Avenue, North Berwick

The original Norman-style church by John Henderson 1861 was cleverly extended
in 1863 incorporating the old masonry by Seymour & Kinross, who also designed
the altar. The porch with its magnificent carved doors was added by Robert
Lorimer in 1916. Choir stalls by H O Tarbolton, porch doors by Mrs Meredith-
Williams. Stained glass by Ballantine & Son. Convenient for North Berwick
railway station. Sunday Services: Sung Eucharist 11.00am; Said Eucharist second
and fourth Sunday, 8.00am

Open all year, 10.00am-4.00pm

SCOTTISH EPISCOPAL 🦽 ⓐ 📖 ⓘ **B**

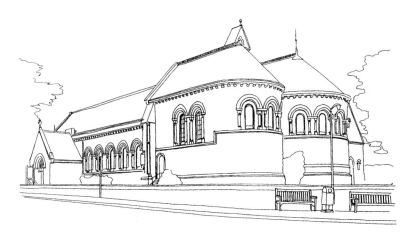

ST BALDRED'S CHURCH, NORTH BERWICK

705 PENCAITLAND PARISH CHURCH

NT 443 690

Consecrated in 1242, the earliest part of the church dates from the
12th century. The present building consists of nave, with a gallery
at the west end, and two aisles on the north side, the older called
the Winton Aisle and the other the Saltoun Aisle. Churchyard
with many interesting gravestones, offering houses, renovated
carriage house, stables, harness room and cottage. Coffee shop on
Thursdays from 2.00-4.00pm in Carriage House, except the first
Thursday of the month. A1 from Edinburgh to Tranent, B6355 to
Pencaitland. Bus 113 from Edinburgh. Sunday Service: 10.00am;
Sunday Evening Service 6.30pm, every fortnight

Church website: www.ppclink.co.uk

Open by arrangement, telephone Rev Mark Malcolm 01875 340208,
or e-mail: minister@ppclink.co.uk

CHURCH OF SCOTLAND 🧑‍🦽 ⚲ ⌂ 📖 ☕ wc A

PENCAITLAND
PARISH CHURCH

706 CHALMERS MEMORIAL CHURCH, PORT SETON

NT 403 757

Edinburgh Road, Port Seton

Built to a design by Sydney Mitchell for the United Free
Church, the foundation stone was laid in 1904. It has a very
elegant spire and bell-tower and unique stencilled interior.
Stained glass windows by Margaret Chilton and Marjorie
Kemp 1924-50. Sunday Services: 11.15am and 6.15pm all year
The Church is open to visitors and for coffee at the end of both
services every Sunday.

CHURCH OF SCOTLAND 🧑‍🦽 ⓘ wc ⌂ ☕ A

CHALMERS MEMORIAL
CHURCH, PORT SETON

707 ST ANDREW'S EPISCOPAL, PRESTONPANS

NT 392 749

West Loan, Prestonpans

Stone-built simple hall church, built as a Free
Kirk in 1843, with slender cast-iron columns
supporting the roof. Light spacious interior.
Former gallery now enclosed to form upper
room over kitchen and toilets. Fine stained
glass including a recent window by Sax
Shaw. Sunday Service: Sung Eucharist 9.30am
Open by arrangement with Mr John Busby,
telephone 01875 340512

SCOTTISH EPISCOPAL  🧑‍🦽 wc

ST ANDREW'S EPISCOPAL, PRESTONPANS

708   STENTON PARISH CHURCH

NT 641 753

Main Street, Stenton

By William Burn 1829, a T-plan kirk with a
splendid east tower. Redesigned internally by
James Jerdan in 1892. Stained glass by E C
Kempe and Ballantine & Gardiner. In the
graveyard is a fragment of the 16th-century kirk
and a fine selection of monuments. Rood well
in village. Follow signs to Stenton off A1.
Sunday Service: 9.30am. Please note time
of service may be changed

Open daily dawn to dusk

CHURCH OF SCOTLAND

ⓓ wc (only available at services) **B**

STENTON PARISH CHURCH

709   TRANENT METHODIST CHURCH

NT 403 729

63 Bridge Street, Tranent

Built 1870, second of East Lothian's three
Primitive Methodist Chapels. Subdivided 1958
to create church hall. Simple interior. Monument
to Barnabas Wild, minister 1890s. North side of
main road at west end of town.

Sunday Service: 11.00am

Open first Saturday of month for coffee morning

METHODIST 🖵 **A**

TRANENT METHODIST CHURCH

710   ST MARTIN OF TOURS, TRANENT

NT 410 727

East end of High Street (opposite supermarket)

This is the third church building on the site in one hundred years and was built in
1969 in an octagonal shape using the Scandinavian compressed timber girder
design. Contains two rough stained glass windows
and an early 20th-century Italian crucifix above the
altar. Irish limestone statue of classical design of St
Martin as a Roman soldier and an original icon of
St Martin in orthodox style. Sunday Mass: Saturday
Vigil 6.00pm; Sunday 10.30pm; weekdays, Tuesday
to Friday 9.00am; other Masses and Services
advertised in the weekly newsletter

Open by arrangement, telephone 01875 610232

ROMAN CATHOLIC

ST MARTIN OF TOURS, TRANENT

711 ST MARY'S PARISH CHURCH, WHITEKIRK

NT 596 815

Dating from 12th century, the original
building was reconstructed during the
15th century starting with the vaulted
stone choir, built in 1439 by Adam
Hepburn of Hailes. In medieval times
Whitekirk was an important place of
pilgrimage. The church was set on fire
in 1914 by suffragettes. Restored by
Robert Lorimer. Ceiled wagon roof over
nave and transepts, communion table,
pulpit, lectern and font all by Lorimer.

ST MARY'S PARISH CHURCH, WHITEKIRK

Stained glass by C E Kempe 1889 and Karl Parsons 1916. Tithe barn and historic
graveyard. On A198. Sunday Service: 11.30am

Open daily dawn to dusk

CHURCH OF SCOTLAND 📖 wc **A**

712 WHITTINGEHAME PARISH CHURCH

NT 603 737

Main Street

Spiky battlemented Gothic T-plan
church built 1722, and added to by
Barclay and Lamb in 1820 for James
Balfour, grandfather of A J Balfour,
Prime Minister 1902-5. Eighteenth-
century burial enclosure of Buchan
Sydserfs of Ruchlaw and good late
17th-century headstones show that
there was an earlier church on the site.
Follow signs to Whittingehame off A1.
No regular Church Services

Open by arrangement,

telephone 01620 860598

CHURCH OF SCOTLAND ♿ **B**

WHITTINGEHAME PARISH CHURCH

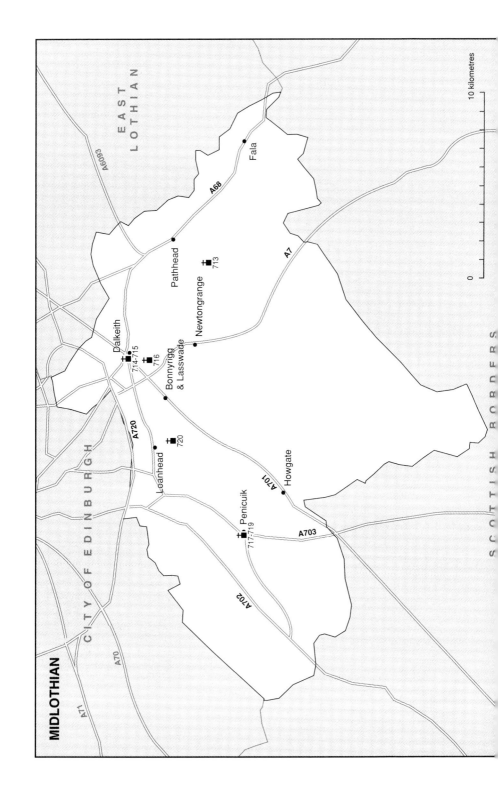

MIDLOTHIAN

CITY OF EDINBURGH

EAST LOTHIAN

SCOTTISH BORDERS

A1
A70
A720
A6093
A68
A7
A701
A702
A703

Dalkeith
Loanhead
Bonnyrigg & Lasswade
Newtongrange
Pathhead
Fala
Penicuik
Howgate

714-715
716
713
720
717-719

0   10 kilometres

MIDLOTHIAN

CRICHTON COLLEGIATE CHURCH

713 CRICHTON COLLEGIATE CHURCH

NT 381 616

Crichton, Pathhead

Collegiate church rebuilt in 1449 by William Crichton, Lord Chancellor of Scotland. Restored by Hardy & White 1898 and Benjamin Tindall 1998. Fine pointed barrel vaults over choir and transepts and splendid square tower over crossing. Organ by Joseph Brook & Co. Magnificent position at head of Tyne valley close to Crichton Castle. Signed road B6367 from A68 at Pathhead. Programme available of occasional services and concerts in summer months

Open May to September, Sunday 2.00-5.00pm. Or by appointment,
telephone Mrs Tindall 01875 320341. Crichton Castle open 1 April to 30 September

NON-DENOMINATIONAL 🚻 wc ☕ A

714 ST MARY'S CHURCH, DALKEITH

NT 335 677

Dalkeith Country Park, Dalkeith

Built as the chapel for Dalkeith Palace in 1843 by William Burn and David Bryce. Early English style with splendid features: double hammerbeam roof, stained glass windows, heraldic floor tiles by Minton, and water-powered organ by David Hamilton of Edinburgh, installed 1845. Sunday Service: 9.45am

Open on Sunday 2.00-4.00pm from May to August; on Midlothian Doors Open Day in September, and at other times by arrangement, telephone Mr Grieve 0131 663 4817.
Summer concerts. Charity fun day in September

SCOTTISH EPISCOPAL 🚻 wc A

ST MARY'S CHURCH, DALKEITH

715 ST NICHOLAS BUCCLEUCH PARISH CHURCH, DALKEITH

NT 333 674

121 High Street, Dalkeith

Medieval church, became collegiate in 1406. Nave
and transepts 1854 by David Bryce. James, 1st Earl
of Morton and his wife Princess Joanna (the
profoundly deaf third daughter of James I) are
buried within the choir, c.1498. Memorial
monument with their effigies mark the burial site.
Organ by Binns, 1906. Two hundred yards east of
A68/A6094 junction. Sunday Services: Family
Worship 9.30am, Parish Worship 11.00am

Church website: www.stnicholasbuccleugh.org.uk

Open 14 April to 30 September, Monday to Saturday 10.00am-4.00pm

CHURCH OF SCOTLAND   🦽 ② ⍾ 🗂 ⍾ ☕ wc **A**

ST NICHOLAS BUCCLEUCH
PARISH CHURCH, DALKEITH

716 NEWBATTLE CHURCH

NT 331 661

Newbattle Road, Newbattle

Harled, T-plan church with belfry
by Alexander McGill 1727. Two galleries added
1851. A remarkable number of the original
fittings survive including the upper part of the
17th-century pulpit and the pilastered wooden
frame of the Lothian Loft. Organ by Eustace
Ingram, 1895. Good 17th-century gravestones
including the amazing, ornamented Welsh family
monument. Sunday Service: 10.00am

Open by arrangement, telephone Mr Iain McCarter
0131 663 3896

CHURCH OF SCOTLAND wc ② 🗂 **B**

NEWBATTLE CHURCH

717 PENICUIK SOUTH CHURCH

NT 236 595

Peebles Road, Penicuik

Designed in 1863 by Frederick T Pilkington. Open
timber roof. Stained glass. Organ by C & F Hamilton,
1901. Fully restored 1991. Short history available.
Sunday Services: 11.15am and 7.00pm

Church website: http://come.to/penicuiksouthkirk

Open by arrangement, telephone 01968 674692,
or 01968 674276

CHURCH OF SCOTLAND 🦽 ② ⍾ wc **B**

PENICUIK SOUTH CHURCH

718 ST JAMES SCOTTISH EPISCOPAL CHURCH, PENICUIK

NT 232 597

Broomhill Road, Penicuik

The original church which now forms the nave was designed by H Seymour of Seymour & Kinross 1882. The chancel, vestries, tower and bell were added by H O Tarbolton 1899. An excellent lot of stained glass, including one light by Shrigley & Hunt of Lancaster and four magnificent lights by C E Kempe. Rood screen designed by Tarbolton and carved by T Good; communion rails also designed by Tarbolton and carved by Scott Morton & Co. Reredos designed and executed by Mrs Meredith-Williams 1921. Sunday Services: 8.00am and 10.15am; first Sundays Choral Evensong 6.30pm

ST JAMES SCOTTISH
EPISCOPAL CHURCH, PENICUIK

Open by arrangement, telephone the Rector 01968 672862

SCOTTISH EPISCOPAL ♿ ⊘ 👤 ♿ ☕ wc **B**

719 CHURCH OF THE SACRED HEART, PENICUIK

NT 234 601

56 Crown Street

Built in a plain Gothic style in 1882 as a chapel school; it may be the only (Catholic) chapel school still in use. Extended 1982 by Gilbert Gray, the ceiling connecting the old and new is quite a feature. Original Stations of the Cross by Vampoulles. Services: Saturday Vigil 6.00pm; Sunday 10.30am also weekday services

Open daily 8.30am-8.00pm

ROMAN CATHOLIC ♿ wc ⊘

720 ROSSLYN CHAPEL (ST MATTHEW'S)

NT 275 631

Chapel Loan, Roslin

Built 1450 as the church of a college established by William Sinclair, 3rd Earl of Orkney. Intended to be cruciform but only the choir was completed. Famous for its decorative stone carving that covers almost every part of the building. The 'Prentice Pillar' has spectacular decoration. Sunday Services: 10.30am and 4.45pm

Open all year, Monday to Saturday 10.00am-5.00pm, Sunday 12.00 noon-4.45pm

SCOTTISH EPISCOPAL ♿ 👤 🏠 ☕ wc **A**

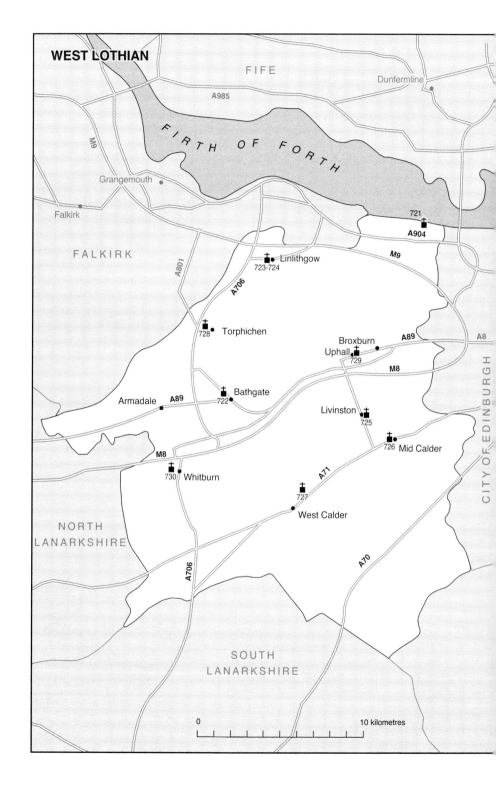

WEST LOTHIAN

Local Representative: Mr Alan Naylor, Candiehill, Candie, Avonbridge, Falkirk (*telephone* 01324 861583)

721 ABERCORN KIRK

NT 082 792
½ mile east of Hopetoun House
The Kirk probably occupies the site of a 7th-century monastery founded by Lindisfarne Priory. The building dates from 11th century and has a fine 12th-century south door. The Duddingston burial aisle 1603, Binns aisle 1618, Philipstoun burial enclosure 1723 and Hopetoun aisle 1707 have fine mural monuments. Interior remodelled by Peter McGregor Chalmers 1893 except for the splendid Hopetoun Loft of 1707 designed by William Bruce with carving by William Eizat and a heraldic ceiling by Richard Waitt. Sunday Service 10.00am
Open at all times
CHURCH OF SCOTLAND 🦽 wc **A**

722 ST COLUMBA'S, BATHGATE

NS 967 688
79 Glasgow Road
Design by W J Walker Todd and Millar in 1915, the Church is of rectangular plan with reduced chancel with organ recess off. The principal elevation is a pitched roof swept down over ancillary accommodation. Square tower over the vestry and a stone gabled and arched entrance to the west. Alterations and extension in 1998 provided a more flexible building. Triptych in the apse by local artist, Mabel Dawson, said to be presented by Lady Baillie. Sunday Service: 11.15am. Café last Saturday of the month 12.00 noon-2.00pm
Church website: www.sstpeterslinlithgow.co.uk
Open Wednesday mornings 10.00am-12.00 noon or by
arrangement with the Priest-in-Charge 01506 842384
SCOTTISH EPISCOPAL 🦽 wc ☕

723 ST MICHAEL'S PARISH CHURCH, LINLITHGOW

NT 002 773
Kirkgate, Linlithgow
One of the finest examples of a large medieval burgh church. Consecrated in 1242 on the site of an earlier church, most of the present building dates from the 15th century with some 19th-and 20th-century restoration. Situated beside Linlithgow Palace, its history is intertwined with that of the royal house of Stewart. The modern aluminium crown 1964 symbolises the

ST MICHAEL'S PARISH
CHURCH, LINLITHGOW

Church's continuing witness to Christ's Kingship. Window commemorating 750th anniversary of the church 1992 by Crear McCartney. Carving of Queen by John Donaldson added to Queen's pulpit in 2003. New organ installed by Matthew Copley 2001 from Queen Ethelburga's College, Harrogate. The Peel, Linlithgow Palace and Loch adjacent. Sunday Services: 9.30am and 11.00am

Church website: www.stmichaels-parish.org.uk

Open all year, May to September, Monday to Saturday 10.00am-4.00pm; Sunday 12.30pm-4.00pm; October to April, Monday to Friday 10.00am-3.00pm

CHURCH OF SCOTLAND ② ⓘ (on request) 📖 **A**

724 ST PETER'S EPISCOPAL CHURCH, LINLITHGOW

NS 000 770

High Street, Linlithgow

Built in 1928 as a memorial to George Walpole, Bishop of Edinburgh and his wife Mildred, with assistance from missions in England and USA. Design by J Walker Todd of Dick Peddie & Todd is a Byzantine basilica with a 'cross in the square' plan form, a high central dome and half dome over the sanctuary apse. It is a small church located on south side of High Street, and is popular as a refuge from the main shopping area. Sunday Services: 9.30am Sung Eucahrist, 6.30pm Evensong on 1st Sunday of month; and Tuesday: Said Eucharist 10.30am

Church website: www.stpeterslinlithgow.co.uk

Open Tuesday and Saturday, from May to September 2.00-4.00pm, or telephone Rev Stuart Bonney 01506 842384

SCOTTISH EPISCOPAL ⓘ 📖 wc

ST PETER'S EPISCOPAL
CHURCH, LINLITHGOW

725 LIVINGSTON VILLAGE KIRK

NT 037 669

Kirk Lane, Livingston

There has been a church on the site since 12th century. The present building was rebuilt 1732. Late 18th-century pews and pulpit with Gothic sounding board and a pretty stair. Pewter communion vessels and old collecting shovels on display. Plaque in entrance commemorates Covenanters from village drowned off Orkney. Kirkyard has some fine monuments from 17th and 18th centuries, including some lively headstones featuring phoenixes and leafy cartouches. Close to Heritage Centre. Sunday Service: 10.00am. Other services as advertised on notice board

Church website: www.livoldpar.org.uk

Open by arrangement, telephone the Minister 01506 420227

CHURCH OF SCOTLAND ♿ ② wc **B**

LIVINGSTON VILLAGE KIRK

726 KIRK OF CALDER, MID CALDER

NT 074 673

Main Street, Mid Calder

This 16th-century parish church, recently restored, won the West Lothian Award for Conservation in 1992. John Knox, James 'Paraffin' Young, David Livingstone and Frederick Chopin have already visited here – we look forward to meeting you too! Admission free, donations welcome. Organ by James Conacher, 1888. Restoration of stained glass windows 1995. Off A71 on B7015 in village of Mid Calder.

Sunday Service: 10.30am

Church website: www.kirkofcalder.com

Open May to September, Sunday 2-4pm. Near to Almondell Country Park, open all year

CHURCH OF SCOTLAND

KIRK OF CALDER, MID CALDER

727 POLBETH HARWOOD PARISH CHURCH

NT 017 628

Chapelton Drive, Polbeth, West Calder

The congregation was formed in 1795 and the church completed in 1796 as Burgher Kirk. Congregation translated from West Calder to Polbeth in 1962. A71 between Livingston New Town and West Calder. Fifteen minutes walk from West Calder station. Sunday Service: 11.00am

Open Monday and Wednesday during school term time, 10.00am-12.00 noon; Thursday 6.00-8.00pm during summer

CHURCH OF SCOTLAND

POLBETH HARWOOD PARISH CHURCH

728 TORPHICHEN KIRK

NS 969 725
The Bowyett, Torphichen
Built in 1756 on the site of the nave
of the 12th-century preceptory, it is a
T-shaped building with three
galleries including a laird's loft. Two
centre pews can be tipped back to
form extended communion tables.
Sanctuary stone in the graveyard.
Preceptory church adjoining in the
care of Historic Scotland.
Sunday Service: 11.15am
Open parish church and preceptory
Easter to end October, Saturday
11.00am-5.00pm, Sunday 2.00-5.00pm.
Exhibition. Charge for entry to preceptory.
Groups welcome for guided tours of
both buildings, telephone
Mrs Mary Wilson 01506 653475
CHURCH OF SCOTLAND   📖 🍴 wc **A**

TORPHICHEN KIRK

729 ST NICHOLAS, UPHALL

NT 060 722
Ecclesmachan Road, Uphall
Tower and nave with Romanesque
doorway of 1187, Buchan stairs of the
17th century, aisles added 1590 and
1878. A picture shows the balconies
that existed before the restoration of
1938. Buried in the tower are Erskines,
Earls of Buchan and sons. Mixture of
old and modern stained glass windows.
The bell, one of the oldest in West
Lothian, is inscribed '*in onore sancte*
nicolae campana ecclegie de strabork anno
dni mviii'. 'Judas' Bible of 1613.
Sunday Service: 11.00am
Church website: www.strathbrockparish.net
Open by arrangement, telephone the
Minister 01506 852550
CHURCH OF SCOTLAND   ♿ wc ❓ 📖 **B**

ST NICHOLAS, UPHALL

730 WHITBURN SOUTH PARISH CHURCH

NS 947 646

Manse Road, Whitburn

In its present form dating from 1729, the walls house a modern interior of the 1950s, the result of a fire. Cruciform and typically Georgian, though some earlier architectural features are evident. The graveyard is host to several local notables and is the last resting place of Robert Burns' eldest daughter, Elizabeth Paton (dear 'Bought' Bess) who married John Bishop, the overseer at Polkemmet Estate.

Sunday Service: 11.00am all year; 1st Sunday September to May 6.00pm; 1st Sunday in June 3.00pm; Christmas Day 10.00am, Maundy Thursday 7.00pm

Open by arrangement with the Church Officer, telephone

Mr John Tennant 01501 741627

CHURCH OF SCOTLAND   ♿ ᴡᴄ ② **B**

WHITBURN SOUTH PARISH CHURCH

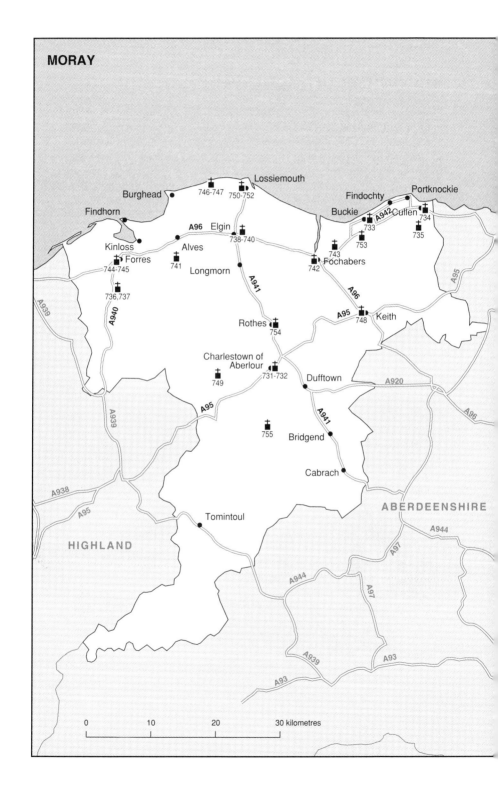

MORAY

Findhorn

Burghead ●   746-747 750-752
746-747   Lossiemouth

Kinloss   A96 Elgin
Forres   Alves   738-740
744-745   741 Longmorn

736,737
A940

A939   Rothes
                 754

A941

Charlestown of
Aberlour
749   731-732
                 Dufftown

A95

755 Bridgend

Cabrach

A938
A95   Tomintoul

HIGHLAND

Findochty Portknockie
Buckie   A942 Cullen
          733   734
743   753   735
742 Fochabers

A96
A95 Keith
748

A95

A920

A941

ABERDEENSHIRE

A944

A97

A944   A97

A939 A93

A93

A95

A939

A96

A95

0   10   20   30 kilometres

MORAY

Local Representative: Mrs Elizabeth Beaton, Keam Schoolhouse, Hopeman, Moray (*telephone* 01343 830301)

731 ABERLOUR PARISH CHURCH

NJ 264 428
The Square, Aberlour
Originally dedicated to St Drostan, the
church was built in 1812. The Norman
tower 1840 by William Robertson,
architect, Elgin, was the sole survivor of
a disastrous fire in 1861. George Petrie,
architect, rebuilt the church in neo-
Norman style. Choir added 1933 by
J Wittet in memory of Sir James Ritchie
Findlay. First organ by Brindley & Foster
1900, rebuilt by Ernest Lawton 1932, and
present organ rebuilt by Sandy
Edmonstone 1991.
Sunday Service: 11.00am
Key available, telephone 01340 871027
CHURCH OF SCOTLAND   👤   ⏰   wc   **B**

ABERLOUR PARISH CHURCH

732 ST MARGARET OF SCOTLAND, ABERLOUR

NJ 272 431
High Street, Aberlour
Designed by Alexander Ross and
consecrated in 1879, the tall Gothic
church retains its splendid original
interior. Built for local episcopal
congregation and the orphanage 120
years ago, the feet of hundreds of
children have worn down the Victorian
tiled floor. Lovely carvings of flowers,
birds and squirrels on pillar capitals and
screen arch. Organ originally built by
Harrison 1879. Sunday Services:
11.00am, 1st Sunday in the month;
9.15am other Sundays
*Key from Aberlour Hotel
(must be signed for)*

ST MARGARET OF SCOTLAND, ABERLOUR

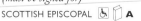
SCOTTISH EPISCOPAL   👤   📖   **A**

733 ST PETER'S CHURCH, BUCKIE

NJ 419 653

St Andrew's Square, Buckie

To plans donated by Bishop Kyle and supervised
by A and W Reid of Elgin. Dedicated on a site
donated by Sir William Gordon. Rose window.
Recent art work includes six murals of excellent
quality in church hall and two canvases of David
and Saul and of the 'Death of St Joseph' in the
church, by local artist Lynn Thain. High altar of
Italian marble surrounded by murals depicting
'The Calming of the Storm' and 'The Walking
on the Water'. Reredos and baptistry, C J Menart
1907. Statue of Our Lady of Aberdeen, copy of
original in Brussels. Organ originally by
Bryceson 1875, recently installed here from Fort
Augustus Abbey. Services: Saturday Vigil Mass
6.30pm; Sunday 10.00am; weekdays 9.30am
Church website: www.stpetersbuckie.eboard.com
Open daily, 9.00am-6.00pm
ROMAN CATHOLIC 📖 ☖ **A**

ST PETER'S CHURCH, BUCKIE

734 OLD KIRK OF CULLEN

NJ 507 664

Cullen

This 13th-century church was originally dedicated to St Mary the Virgin and is the
burial place of the 'interior parts' of Queen Elizabeth de Burgh 1327. A chaplainry
was endowed here by Robert I in 1327 and the church acquired collegiate status in
1543. Later additions include the St Anne's Aisle of 1539, while there is a fine
example of a laird's loft 1602. Other features include a pre-Reformation aumbry or
sacrament house, tombs and monuments including one to James, 1st Earl of

Seafield, Chancellor of Scotland at
the Treaty of Union of 1707, and
17th-century box pews. The
churchyard has many interesting and
imposing tombs, monuments and
gravestones. The Church is at Old
Cullen, three-quarters of a mile
south-west of the town centre.
Sunday Service: 10.30am
Open summer 2.00-4.00pm Tuesday
and Friday, and by arrangement,
telephone the Minister 01542 841851
CHURCH OF SCOTLAND ♿ 📖 ☖ 🚻 **A**

OLD KIRK OF CULLEN

735 ST JOHN'S CHURCH, DESKFORD

NJ 509 617

Built in 1871 in the Victorian Gothic style, architect John Miller (architect and master of works to Seafield Estates, Cullen). It has unusual tracery detail in the transept window. Inside there is stencil work on the walls. The Old St John's Church (ruined) at Kirkton of Deskford incorporates a fine aumbry 1551 with inscriptions in English and Latin and carvings of angels supporting monstrance. B9018, three miles south of Cullen. Sunday Service: 2nd and 4th of every month, 12.00 noon

Open by arrangement, telephone the Minister 01542 841851

CHURCH OF SCOTLAND ♿ **B**

736 EDINKILLIE PARISH CHURCH

NJ 020 466

Edinkillie, Dunphail, near Forres

Small church built 1741 in traditional 18th-century style. Central pulpit and galleries on three sides. Fine pipe organ. Beautifully situated on the banks of the River Divie, nine miles south of Forres on the A940 from Forres to Grantown-on-Spey. Linked with Dyke. Sunday Service: 12.00 noon

Open by arrangement, telephone Mr C J Falconer (Beadle) 01309 611220 or Mr W Reid 01309 611279

CHURCH OF SCOTLAND ♿ wc

EDINKILLIE PARISH CHURCH

737 DYKE PARISH CHURCH

NH 990 584

Dyke, near Forres, Moray

Built 1781 in centre of village. Interesting crypt and triple pulpit (one of the only two in Scotland). Follow road to Brodie Castle, turning right to village before castle entrance. Linked with Edinkillie. Sunday Service: 10.30am

Open by arrangement, key in village, telephone 01309 641257

CHURCH OF SCOTLAND ♿ **A**

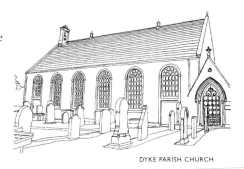

DYKE PARISH CHURCH

738 GREYFRIARS CONVENT OF MERCY, ELGIN

NJ 219 628
Abbey Street, Elgin
Beautiful and careful restoration, 1891-1908, by architect John Kinross for the 3rd
Marquess of Bute, of a 15th-century Franciscan friary. Magnificently carved oak
screen divides the choir from the nave and a splendid barrel-vaulted ceiling
stretches unbroken to the stained glass window above the altar. Fine cloister with
original medieval well. Services: Masses Tuesday 10.00am and Fridays 7.00pm
Open by arrangement with the Sisters of Mercy, telephone 01343 547806.
Rose garden open May to September (entrance in Institution Road)
ROMAN CATHOLIC   📖 wc **A**

739 HOLY TRINITY, ELGIN

NJ 214 630
Trinity Place, Elgin
Gothic style on a Greek cross ground-plan
to a design by William Robertson 1826.
The crenellated and pinacled south entrance
gable intended as an architectural feature
visible from the High Street is now blocked
by the ring-road. Chancel added 1852 and
interior recast; nave lengthened 1879. Plain
dignified interior with late 19th-century
stained glass. Services: Sunday Holy
Communion 8.00am, Family Eucharist
11.00am, Evensong 6.30pm; Holy
Communion Tuesday 7.00pm, Wednesday
8.00am, Friday 11.00am, Saturday 9.00am
Open 9.00am-5.00pm
SCOTTISH EPISCOPAL wc ⑨ **B**

HOLY TRINITY, ELGIN

740 ST SYLVESTER'S, ELGIN

NJ 219 626
Institution Road, Elgin
The church and presbytery were designed and completed in 1844, architect
Thomas Mackenzie of Elgin. Dedication in recognition of the financial support by
the younger brother of Sir William Drummond of Grantully who took the name
Sylvester on converting to Catholicism. Lady Altar 1915, by R B Pratt. Sanctuary
altered 1968 in keeping with the new liturgy. Major alterations to church and
adjoining school 2000 to form sacristy and meeting rooms, by Ashley Bartlam
Partnership. Large cross by the monks of Pluscarden.
Services: Saturday 6.00pm Vigil; Sunday 11.15am
Open 9.00am-8.00pm daily except Tuesdays
ROMAN CATHOLIC ♿ ⑨ wc **B**

PLUSCARDEN ABBEY, ELGIN

741 PLUSCARDEN ABBEY, ELGIN

NJ 143 576

Pluscarden, near Elgin

Founded in 1230 by Alexander II for Valiscaulian monks, it became Benedictine in 1454. Following the Reformation it was the property of various local families, culminating in the Dukes of Fife from whom it was bought by the Marquess of Bute, and whose son, Lord Colum, gave it to the monks in 1943. The buildings were eventually re-occupied in 1948. There are a number of interesting works by prominent artists and architects following the restoration. Abbey is signposted from A96 and B9010. Member of Moray Church trail. The Abbey offers retreat accommodation for men and women. Full details of this, together with Services and opening times, may be obtained by telephoning 01343 890257 (fax 01343 890258).

Church website: www.pluscardenabbey.org

Annual Pluscarden Pentecost lectures: Tuesday, Wednesday and Thursday after Pentecost.

Open daily 4.45am-8.45pm

ROMAN CATHOLIC A

742 GORDON CHAPEL, FOCHABERS

NJ 346 589

Castle Street, Fochabers

Built in 1834 to a design by Archibald Simpson, restored in 1874. Stained glass includes designs by Sir Edward Burne-Jones. Fine organ by Hill 1874. The church is upstairs with the rectory (originally a school) below. Services: Sunday 8.30am Holy Communion 10.30am Eucharist with hymns; 1st Sunday of the month 6.30pm Sung Evensong

Church website: www.gordonchapel.org.uk

Open daily during daylight hours.

SCOTTISH EPISCOPAL A

GORDON CHAPEL, FOCHABERS

ST NINIAN'S, TYNET

743   ST NINIAN'S, TYNET

NJ 379 613

Mill of Tynet, Fochabers

The oldest post-Reformation Catholic church still in use in Scotland. At the request of the Duke of Gordon 1755, built to resemble a sheep-cot in days when it was still an offence to celebrate Mass. Renovated 1957, Ian Lindsay, architect, the long low whitewashed building is still 'a church in disguise'.

Sunday Service: 8.30am

Open by arrangement, telephone Mr P Cromar, 'Golar',

Newlands of Tynet (opposite church)

ROMAN CATHOLIC   **A**

744   ST LAURENCE PARISH CHURCH, FORRES

NJ 035 588

High Street, Forres

Built on a site of Christian worship dating from mid-13th century, today's neo-Gothic building – designed by John Robertson and dedicated in 1906 – is a fine example of the stonemason's craft. The pitch-pine ceiling and the stained glass windows by Douglas Strachan and Percy Bacon help to create the special atmosphere of peace and beauty. Font replica of one in Dryburgh Abbey. Information leaflets in English, French, German, Spanish and Italian are free. Welcomers on duty. Sunday Service: 10.00am

Open May to September, Monday to Friday 10.00am-12.00 noon, 2.00-4.00pm.

Other times by arrangement, telephone 01309 672260

CHURCH OF SCOTLAND   ♿ ⊘ ⛪ 📖 WC **B**

745 ST JOHN'S CHURCH, FORRES

NJ 041 592

Victoria Road, Forres

Built 1830-40, to a design by Patrick Wilson, substantially remodelled in Italianate manner by Thomas Mackenzie, Elgin, 1844. The building has been beautified over the years including the laying of mosaic tiles throughout the chancel and aisles. The frontage is adorned with a wheel window, the entrance sheltered by an arcaded logia and flanked by a campanile. A large canvas in the apse 1906 and mural behind the font 1911 are the work of William Hole RSA. Sunday Services: 8.00am, 10.00am and 6.00pm

Open daylight hours (or key at Rectory)

SCOTTISH EPISCOPAL ♿ ⏰ 📖 **A**

ST JOHN'S CHURCH, FORRES

746 THE MICHAEL KIRK, GORDONSTOUN

NJ 193 689

Duffus, by Elgin

Reached by footpath from Gordonstoun (the 'silent' walk), this dignified little church was built in 1705 as a mausoleum for 'the Wizard Laird', Sir Robert Gordon, on the site of the ancient Kirk of Ogstoun. Roofed, furnished and fitted by John Kinross in 1900 for Lady Gordon-Cumming. Gothic Survival with remarkable window tracery enhanced by flower carvings.

Services: Holy Communion 8.40am most Sundays during the academic year; candlelit Compline 9.00pm, Thursdays during winter term

Church website: www.gordonstoun.org.uk

Key by the door, or contact the Chaplain at Gordonstoun School reception,

telephone 01343 835804

INTERDENOMINATIONAL 📖 (school shop) **A**

747 ST CHRISTOPHER'S, GORDONSTOUN

NJ 184 690

Duffus, by Elgin

Gordonstoun School was founded in 1934 by Kurt Hahn, with the aim of encouraging self-reliance and independence. St Christopher's is the main school chapel, built 1965-66 to designs by former pupil Patrick Huggins, to complement the Michael Kirk (see above). Seating is 'gathered about the lectern pulpit and the Communion Table' whose positions emphasise the equal importance of Word and Sacrament, while giving space for orchestral or dramatic performances. Main school service: Sunday 10.45am during term time

Church website: www.gordonstoun.org.uk

Report to Gordonstoun School reception

INTERDENOMINATIONAL ♿ 📖 (school shop) 🚾

748 ST THOMAS' CHURCH, KEITH

NJ 430 502
Chapel Street, Keith
Built 1831, architect William Robertson,
Elgin. Successor to 1785 chapel and cottage
at Kempcairn, following planning and
fundraising by Father Lovi. Roman Doric
pilastered exterior and 'plain' interior with
nave and sanctuary. Enlarged with copper-
clad dome, altar, communion rails, pulpit
and oak pews 1915. Altarpiece painting
'The Incredulity of St Thomas',
commissioned by Charles X of France
1828. Fine stained glass windows 1970s. St
John Ogilvie Chapel commemorating saint
born nearby. Extensive restoration 1996
Open daily, dawn to dusk
ROMAN CATHOLIC ♿ ♿ ♿ wc **A**

ST THOMAS' CHURCH, KEITH

749 KNOCKANDO PARISH CHURCH

NJ 186 429
Award-winning design for new church by the Law & Dunbar-Nasmith Partnership
1993 on the site of an earlier building destroyed by fire in 1990. Sympathetic with
the building which it has replaced. The Creation is symbolised in a new stained
glass window by Andrew Lawson-Johnson. Watch-house in the kirkyard. From A95
Aviemore–Elgin or A941 Dufftown–Elgin, take B9102 Archiestown Knockando. At
Cardhu turn right. Church is signposted. Linked with Rothes.
Sunday Service: 10.30am
Open Wednesday only, 2.00pm–4.00pm July and August
CHURCH OF SCOTLAND ♿ ♿ ♿ ♿

KNOCKANDO PARISH CHURCH

750 ST COLUMBA'S, LOSSIEMOUTH

NJ 232 711

Union Street, Lossiemouth

Small church in the shape of a Latin Cross, designed by Arthur Harrison of Stockton-on-Tees and paid for by the Bute family. The building materials were all shipped from Teesside. The sanctuary lamp is in the form of a ship's lamp. Stained glass window by Fr Ninian Sloan of 'Our Lady Star of the Sea' dedicated to the memory of the Royal and Allied navies stationed at Lossiemouth 1946-72 and donated by them. Sunday Mass: 6.30pm

Open by arrangement with Mrs Margaret Kinnaird, telephone 01343 813539

ROMAN CATHOLIC & wc

751 ST GERARDINE'S HIGH, LOSSIEMOUTH

NJ 233 706

St Gerardine's Road, Lossiemouth

The foundation stone was laid in 1898 and the building is of Norman design by Sir J J Burnet. The plainness of the Norman Tower, white harled walls and red roof belie the magnificent interior. The features include many items of stained glass depicting various Biblical themes. Sunday Service: 11.00am and 6.00pm

Open by arrangement, telephone the Minister 01343 813146, or Mr James Cumming 01343 812194

CHURCH OF SCOTLAND & ? | B

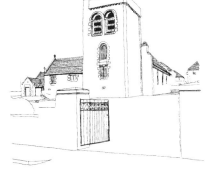

ST GERARDINE'S HIGH, LOSSIEMOUTH

752 ST MARGARET OF SCOTLAND, LOSSIEMOUTH

NJ 227 706

Stotfield Road, Lossiemouth

Small church of 1922 with Gothic detailing built to a design by Alexander Ross of Inverness, responsible for Episcopal churches great and small throughout the north, including Inverness Cathedral. Simple interior with open timber vaulted ceiling. Sunday Service: Parish Eucharist 9.30am; Thursday Eucharist 10.00am and Eventide Prayer 5.00pm

Open May to September, Fridays 2.00pm–5.00pm

SCOTTISH EPISCOPAL

ST MARGARET OF SCOTLAND, LOSSIEMOUTH

753 ST GREGORY'S CHURCH, PRESHOME

NJ 409 615

Preshome, Clochan

Built in 1788. A wide rectangular church
with harled walls and freestone dressing.
The church is adorned with urn finials; its
west end is a charming product of 18th-
century taste, in which Italian Baroque has
been skilfully naturalised to a Banffshire
setting. Copy of a painting of St Gregory
the Great by Annibale Caracci.
Oustanding survival of pipe organ by
James Bruce of Edinburgh 1820, with
carved Gothic case. Two holy water stoups
of Portsoy marble. Services: Sunday Mass
occasionally at 6.00pm

Open by arrangement, telephone

Mr G Gordon, St Gregory's Chapel House

ROMAN CATHOLIC **A**

ST GREGORY'S CHURCH, PRESHOME

754 ROTHES PARISH CHURCH

NJ 278 492

High Street / Seafield Square, Rothes

Built in 1781 with a steeple added in 1870. A traditional Scottish design of the
Reformed tradition with the pulpit on the long wall, a three-sided gallery and apse.
Linked with Knockando. Sunday Service: 12.00 noon

Open July to August, Tuesday to Thursday 2.00-4.00pm

CHURCH OF SCOTLAND ♿ 📖 ⚲

ROTHES PARISH CHURCH

755 OLD SEMINARY, SCALAN

NJ 246 195

Braes of Glenlivet, Ballindalloch, Banffshire

Scalan (Gaelic for hut), probably turf shelter serving sheiling during summer grazing. First home for remote, recusant Catholic seminary established in 1716 for the training of priests. The improved College was built 1762-67, becoming a farmhouse after the Seminary moved to Aquhorthies, Aberdeenshire in 1799. Association for the Protection of Rural Scotland award 1995.

Turn off B9008 Tomintoul–Dufftown at Pole Inn (signposted).

Services: Annual Mass, 1st Sunday July 4.00pm

Open all year

ROMAN CATHOLIC **A**

OLD SEMINARY, SCALAN

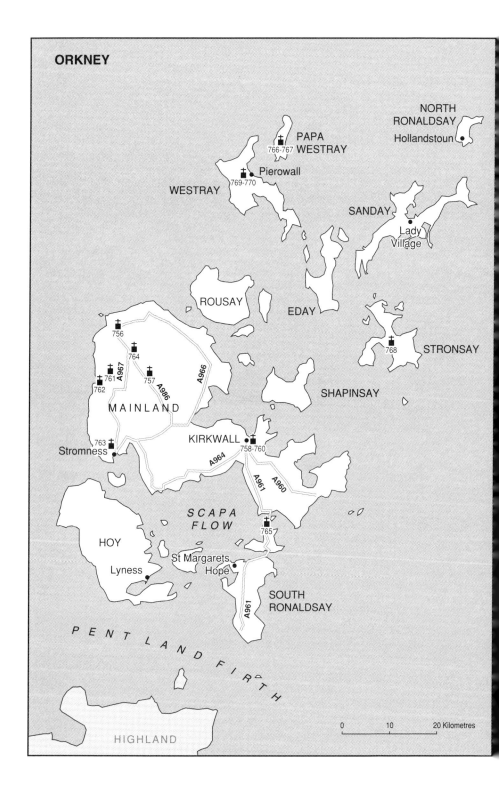

ORKNEY

NORTH
RONALDSAY
Hollandstoun

PAPA
WESTRAY
766-767

Pierowall
769-770

WESTRAY

SANDAY

Lady
Village

ROUSAY

EDAY

STRONSAY
768

756

764

A966

SHAPINSAY

761
762
A967
757
A986

MAINLAND

KIRKWALL
758-760

763
Stromness

A964

A961
A960

SCAPA
FLOW
765

HOY

Lyness

St Margarets
Hope

A961

SOUTH
RONALDSAY

P E N T L A N D   F I R T H

0   10   20 Kilometres

HIGHLAND

ORKNEY

Local Representative: Mr R L B Cormack, Westness House, Rousay, Orkney (*telephone* 01856 821286)

ST MAGNUS CHURCH, BIRSAY

756 ST MAGNUS CHURCH, BIRSAY

HY 248 277

The original church was built by Earl Thorfinn c.1060 and has been altered and restored several times, most recently in 1986. Stained glass window by Alex Strachan showing scenes from the life of St Magnus. Inside the church are two 16th- and 17th-century tombstones. Seventeenth-century belfry. The Mons Bellus stone is probably from the nearby Bishop's Palace. The church is now maintained by the St Magnus Church Birsay Trust. Twenty miles from Kirkwall, across the road from the Earl's Palace. Occasional Services: details locally.

Open daily, April to September. Key available all year from village shop. St Magnus Day Service of Praise at 7.30pm 16 April 2003; Jazz Festival Praise Service 5.30pm, last Sunday of April 2003

NON-DENOMINATIONAL 🏠 wc (nearby) **B**

757 ST MICHAEL'S, HARRAY

HY 314 179

Mainland

Plain white rendered church of 1836 with Caithness slate roof and round-headed windows. Pulpit with sounding board with pews and galleries round three sides. Five stained glass windows. Refurbished 1980s and extension of 1984 houses the vestry, meeting room, kitchen and toilets. The bell, dated 1724, was gifted by the Earl of Morton. Services 11.00am every 3rd Sunday in rotation with Quoyloo and Twatt; check locally

Open by arrangement with Mary Bichan, telephone 01856 771273

CHURCH OF SCOTLAND ♿ wc ☯ **B**

ST MICHAEL'S, HARRAY

ST MAGNUS CATHEDRAL, KIRKWALL

758 ST MAGNUS CATHEDRAL, KIRKWALL

HY 449 108

Broad Street, Kirkwall

The Cathedral Church of St Magnus the Martyr was founded in 1137 by Earl
Rognvald Kolson and dedicated to his uncle, Earl Magnus Erlendson. Completed
c.1500. It contains many items of interest and ranks as one of the finest cathedrals in
Scotland. Organ by Willis 1926. Owned and maintained by Orkney Islands Council.
Custodian on duty. Tours on application; tours of upper floors and tower must be
booked – over 12s only and under 16s must be accompanied – £5 per person. St
Magnus Centre in Palace Road open Monday to Saturday 8.30am-6.30pm. Sunday
1.30-6.30pm (reduced hours in winter); heritage centre, study library, refreshments and
souvenirs; free entry, disabled access/toilets. Sunday Service: 11.15am

Church website: www.orkney.gov.uk/heritage

Open April to September, Monday to Saturday 9.00am-6.00pm, Sunday 2.00-6.00pm;
October to March, Monday to Saturday 9.00am-1.00pm and 2.00-5.00pm.
Closed public holidays and Christmas festive season, except for Church Services

CHURCH OF SCOTLAND

🏛 (side entrance) ｗｃ (public nearby) 📖 (braille and audio tape versions of guidebook available) **A**

759 KIRKWALL EAST CHURCH

HY 451 110

King Street

Built 1892, Architect S Blaikie Jr. In 2002 the interior was completely renovated to
provide a functional suite of rooms on two floors for church and community use.
Services are held in the Upper Room in a bright and friendly atmosphere.
Furnishings by Sui Generis, Eday, Orkney. Eustace Ingram organ.
Sunday Service: 11.15am

Open by arrangement, telephone the Minister 01856 875469

CHURCH OF SCOTLAND 🏛 ｗｃ 📖 ☕ **c**

760 ST OLAF'S, KIRKWALL

HY 452 106

Dundas Crescent

St Olaf's was opened by Bishop Suthers on St Olaf's Day (29 July) 1876. It is an imposing building of dressed stone, compact and with high timbered ceilings like a ship. Complete scheme of stained glass with windows by Heaton, Butler & Bayne, James Ballantine & Son and Ballantine & Gardiner, with the east window of the Ascension being the centrepiece. Stone credence and aumbry taken from the first St Olaf's church built in the 9th century. Organ by G M Holdich 1881. Services: Sunday 9.30am Family Communion; Wednesday 10.30am Holy Communion

Open in summer 10.00am–5.00pm; at other times by arrangement with the Rector, telephone 01856 872024

SCOTTISH EPISCOPAL wc ☕

761 QUOYLOO CHURCH

HY 246 207

Mainland

Built in 1828 as a United Free Church and united with St Peter's in 1935. New hall, built mainly by voluntary labour, completed 1994. Wall hangings made by Guild and helpers, one for union of Harray and Sandwick in 1997. Photographs of previous ministers. Services 11.00am every 3rd Sunday in rotation with Harray and Twatt; check locally

Open at all times

CHURCH OF SCOTLAND ♿ wc ⌚ ☕ (after service)

QUOYLOO CHURCH

762 ST PETER'S, SANDWICK

HY 235 199
One mile north of Skara Brae, Mainland
A rare survival of a quite exceptional unaltered
Scots Parish Kirk of 1836. Situated on a rugged
and exposed site, commanding views over the Bay
of Skaill with Skara Brae in the distance.
Dominated by a towering pulpit reaching to gallery
height, the austere interior powerfully evokes the
experience of Presbyterian worship in the 19th
century when over 500 packed the building – each
allowed a mere 18 inches of pew. Acquired by the
Scottish Redundant Churches Trust in 1998 and
restored in 2002-3. Officially re-opened by HRH
Duke of Gloucester in May 2003

ST PETER'S, SANDWICK

For opening and service arrangements, telephone the SRCT 01334 472032
FORMER CHURCH OF SCOTLAND ♿ **A**

763 ST MARY'S, STROMNESS

HY 253 091
Church Road
Established as a mission church in July 1885, St Mary's became an independent
charge, moving into the present building, in 1888. The font and ciborium were
given by the Earl of Zetland. Joined with St Olaf's in Kirkwall in 1943. Two
beautiful modern stained glass windows. Services: Sunday 11.30am Family
Communion, Thursday 11.00am Holy Communion
*Open by arrangement with Mr George Walker, Tostigan, Downies Lane, Stromness,
telephone 01856 850534*
SCOTTISH EPISCOPAL [wc] ☕

764 TWATT CHURCH

HY 268 244
Mainland
Tall stone United Free Church of 1874 with front
elevation of dressed local stone with freestone
corners and window facings. Inside, a gallery
occupies three walls. In the vestibule a memorial
tablet commemorates the first Minister: John
Garson. Extension of 1974. The building is also
used as the local Post Office. Services 11.00am
every 3rd Sunday in rotation with Quoyloo and
Harray; check locally
*Open by arrangement with the Minister,
telephone 01856 771803*
CHURCH OF SCOTLAND ♿ [wc] ⏀ ☕ (after service)

TWATT CHURCH

THE ITALIAN CHAPEL

765 THE ITALIAN CHAPEL

HY 488 006

Lambholm, Orkney

All that remains of the Italian Prisoner of War Camp 60, the famous Italian Chapel was created from two Nissen huts in 1943, using material from sunken blockships in Scapa Flow. Wonderful testimony to the artistic skills of Domenico Chiocchetti and his fellow prisoners who came to Orkney to work on the construction of the Churchill Barriers. Beautifully designed chancel, altar, altar-rail and Holy water stoup. Painted glass windows depicting St Francis of Assisi and St Catherine of Siena. Restored 1960. A Preservation Committee is dedicated to the upkeep of the Chapel. Service: on 1st Sunday of summer months 3.00pm

Open daily

ROMAN CATHOLIC ♿ 📖 **B**

766 ST ANN'S, PAPA WESTRAY

HY 496 516

Next to school in centre of island

Built in 1842, this was the first kirk in Scotland to be given to the Free Church by the proprietor. Rectangular building with rubble masonry walls and harled exterior. Restoration 2001 by Orkney Islands Council, Health Board and congregation, St Ann's is now home to the Island's surgery, a small flat and community facilities. Several beautiful locally made felt hangings. Sunday Service: 2.30pm

Open at all times

CHURCH OF SCOTLAND ♿ 📖 🚾 **C**

ST ANN'S, PAPA WESTRAY

ST BONIFACE, PAPA WESTRAY

767 ST BONIFACE, PAPA WESTRAY

HY 488 527

Kirkhouse, Papa Westray

Founded in the 8th century, St Boniface was an important church in the early
Middle Ages, possibly the seat of Orkney's first Bishopric. The present building is
12th century, enlarged early 1700s and furnished with box pews, gallery and high
pulpit. Restored 1993. Viking age hog-backed tombstone in the kirkyard; Pictish
cross-slab now in the Orkney Museum, Kirkwall. Services: Wednesdays 8.00pm
mid-June to end-August; also Christmas, Holy Week and occasional services in
winter

Open at all times

NON-DENOMINATIONAL 🦽 📖

768 MONCUR MEMORIAL CHURCH, STRONSAY

HY 654 252

In centre of Stronsay

Stronsay's only church, built in 1955 to a design by Edinburgh architect Leslie
Grahame MacDougall using a legacy from jute manufacturer Alexander Moncur
whose maternal grandfather was Minister in Stronsay 1825-60. A large, harled,
cruciform building, retaining many traditional Orcadian features in its construction.
Red sandstone and blue whinstone blend with the wooden floor and large roof
trusses to give a quiet dignified appearance. Beautiful stained glass window of
Christ as the Good Shepherd by Marjorie Kemp 1935 enhances the chancel.
Services: Sunday 11.00am

Open daily 9.00am-9.00pm May to September; at other times by arrangement
with the Mininster 01857 616311

CHURCH OF SCOTLAND

WESTRAY PARISH KIRK

769 WESTRAY PARISH KIRK

HY 457 462

Kirkbrae, Westray

Oblong barn-style building, built 1846, with part-piended roof of local flagstone slates. Original pulpit with canopy, topped by a dove. Whole building refurbished in 2002/03. Renewable energy (ground-source heat pump and wind turbine) meet energy needs. Pipe organ by Solway Organs 1967. Sunday Service: 11.30am; Evening Services shared with Baptist and United Free Kirks; see local notices

Open by arrangement, telephone the Minister 01857 677357

CHURCH OF SCOTLAND ♿ wc 📖 **C**

770 WESTRAY UNITED FREE CHURCH (NEW KIRK)

NY 446 473

The first minister, the Rev George Reid, did pioneering work of education, both sacred and secular, of the young people of Westray and the adjacent islands (which then worshipped in a much smaller building). The present church was built 1866-67 to seat 550. In 1899 the Reid Memorial Hall was erected, seating 2-300. This is now used for worship since, with a dwindling population, the church is now too big. Sunday Services 11.30am; Evening as advertised locally

Open by arrangement with the Minister, telephone 01857 677232

UNITED FREE wc 🚻 ☕ (after services) **C**

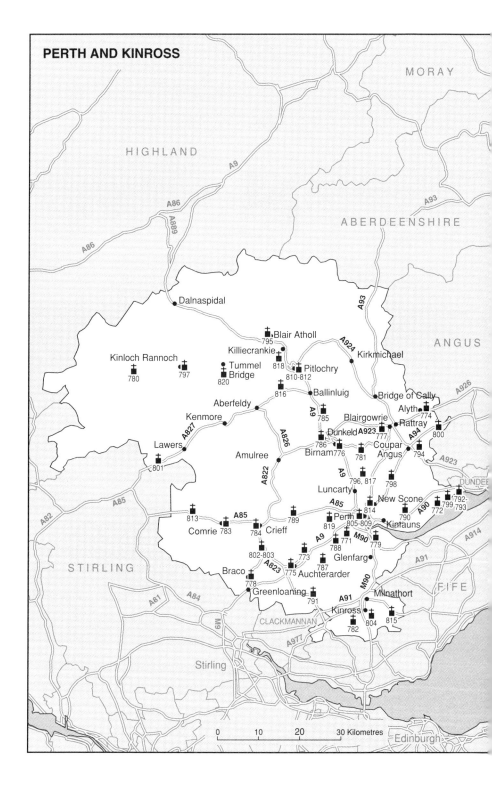

PERTH AND KINROSS

MORAY

HIGHLAND

ABERDEENSHIRE

ANGUS

Dalnaspidal

Blair Atholl
795

Killiecrankie
818

Kinloch Rannoch
780   797

Tummel
Bridge
820

Pitlochry
810-812

Ballinluig

Kirkmichael

Bridge of Cally

Aberfeldy
816

Alyth
774

Kenmore

785

Blairgowrie

Rattray
800

Dunkeld
786

A923
777

Coupar
Angus
781

794

Lawers
801

Amulree

Birnam
776

798

796, 817

Luncarty

New Scone
814

792-
793

772 799

813

A85
789

790

Comrie 783

784 Crieff

Perth
819
805-809

Kinfauns
790

802-803

773

788
771
779

Braco
778

775 Auchterarder

Glenfarg

787

Greenloaning
791

STIRLING

DUNDEE

FIFE

Minathort

CLACKMANNAN

Kinross
782

804 815

Stirling

0   10   20   30 Kilometres

Edinburgh

PERTH & KINROSS

771 ABERDALGIE AND DUPPLIN CHURCH

NO 064 194

Aberdalgie

Nestling in the Earn Valley on a site of
enduring worship for centuries, the present
church was built by the Earl of Kinnoull in
1773. A T-plan church of local sandstone
features a fine laird's loft and Georgian
retiring room. Fourteenth-century Tournai
marble Oliphant monument. Sir Robert
Lorimer remodelled the interior in 1929.
Extensive use of Austrian oak gives the
church a sense of peace and simple dignity.
Renovations 1994. Signed off B9112, south
of Aberdalgie village. One of the four
churches of the Stewartry of Strathearn.
Sunday Service: 11.15am

Open by arrangement, telephone
Rev Colin Williamson 01738 625854

CHURCH OF SCOTLAND [WC] **B**

ABERDALGIE AND DUPPLIN CHURCH

772 ABERNYTE PARISH CHURCH

NO 267 311

Abernyte, by Inchture

The present church was built in 1736 to
replace a building of pre-1400, although
there may have been a Celtic church here
much earlier. Major renovations in 1837
when the present cruciform shape was
established. Intricate beams, stained glass
and a modern wall hanging of 1992.
Signposted from village. Linked with
Longforgan and Inchture with Kinnaird.
Sunday Service: 11.00am

Open during daylight hours

CHURCH OF SCOTLAND **B**

ABERNYTE PARISH CHURCH

773 ABERUTHVEN CHURCH

NN 979 155
2 miles from Auchterarder on A824
The present modest church was built in 1991. The remains of the medieval parish
church of St Kattan are to the west of the village with the beautifully detailed
classical Montrose Mausoleum by William Adam of the 1730s.
Services: Sunday 12.00 noon
Open by arrangement, telephone Mrs S Peterson 01738 629682
or Mrs Lockhart 01764 662201
CHURCH OF SCOTLAND ♿ Montrose Mausoleum **A**

774 ALYTH PARISH CHURCH

NO 243 488
Kirk Brae, Alyth
In a prominent position overlooking the town, Alyth
Parish Church was completed in 1839 to a design by
Thomas Hamilton. Gothic, with Romanesque
influences, and an unusually high spire. Eighth or
9th century Pictish stone stands four feet high in the
vestibule. All windows are stained glass and include
work by Alf Webster. Large funeral escutcheon
marks the death of Sir George Ramsay in a duel in
1790. 3-manual organ by Harrison & Harrison 1890.
Sunday Service: 11.00am
Open July and August, Saturday 10.00am-12.00 noon,
Sunday 2.00-4.00pm
CHURCH OF SCOTLAND ♿ wc wc ② ⑂ 📖 **B**

ALYTH PARISH CHURCH

775 ST KESSOG'S CHURCH, AUCHTERARDER

NN 942 128
High Street, Auchterarder
Built 1897, architect Alexander Ross of Inverness.
Beautiful altar and reredos of Caen stone, both
richly decorated with Florentine mosaic. Rood
screen of white stone. East and west windows by
Kempe of London. In quiet grounds and garden
50 yards off High Street. Linked with St James,
Muthill. Sunday Service: January to June 9.30am,
July to December 11.00am
Open July and August, Monday to Friday
2.00-4.00pm, or by arrangement,
telephone the Very Rev Randal MacAlister
01764 662525
SCOTTISH EPISCOPAL ⑂ wc **C**

ST KESSOG'S CHURCH, AUCHTERARDER

776 ST MARY'S CHURCH, BIRNAM

NO 032 418

Perth Road, Birnam

The main church and clock tower to a design by William Slater 1858, with north aisle by Norman & Beddoe 1883. Slater font and cover, Kempe east window, William Morris windows to Burne-Jones designs. Organ originally by Foster & Andrews 1874. Three-bell chime, clock by James Ramsay of Dundee 1882. Beautifully kept churchyard. On old A9 in centre of village.

Sunday Service: 9.45am; Wednesday 9.30am

Open by arrangement, telephone 01350 727329

SCOTTISH EPISCOPAL   🐕 (via Rectory) 📖 wc **B**

777 BLAIRGOWRIE PARISH CHURCH

NO 177 454

James Street, Blairgowrie

The present building was completed in 1904 in Early English Gothic style with transepts, aisles, apse and a small back gallery. Five stained glass windows in the apse depict scenes from the life of Moses. Norman & Beard organ 1907, rebuilt 1989 by Mr A F Edmondstone. The first Free Church of Blairgowrie 1843 is now the hall and back vestibule.

Sunday Service: 11.15am.

Open June to August, Thursday and Saturday 2.00-4.00pm

CHURCH OF SCOTLAND   wc 🎧 👤

BLAIRGOWRIE PARISH CHURCH

778 ARDOCH PARISH CHURCH, BRACO

NO 839 098

Feddal Road, Braco

Officially opened for worship in 1781 as a 'chapel-of-ease', the church was originally a rectangular building. The bellcote was added in 1836 and a chancel built on the east end by William Simpson of Stirling in 1890. The most recent addition is the church hall, built 1985. Ardoch Church sits close by the famous Roman camp. Directions: A9 north of Dunblane, take A822 to Braco, turn onto B8033 to Kinbuck and church is on right. Sunday Service: 11.30am in 2004; 10.00am in 2005.

Open by arrangement, telephone
01786 880589

CHURCH OF SCOTLAND   🐕 🎧 wc **C**

ARDOCH PARISH CHURCH, BRACO

779 DUNBARNEY PARISH CHURCH, BRIDGE OF EARN

NO 130 185
Manse Road, Bridge of Earn
Built 1787. Pedimented bellcote added, interior
recast and other alterations 1880. Rectangular plan
with bow-ended west porch. Off the main street
of Bridge of Earn. Sunday Service: 9.30am
Open June to August by arrangement, telephone 01738
812463. Annual Flower Festival, last weekend in
September (Friday, Saturday and Sunday)
CHURCH OF SCOTLAND wc 🦻 **C**

DUNBARNEY PARISH CHURCH,
BRIDGE OF EARN

780 BRAES OF RANNOCH PARISH CHURCH, BRIDGE OF GAUR

NN 507 566
South Loch Road, Bridge of Gaur
Built in 1907, Peter MacGregor Chalmers. The
bellcote is from an earlier building of 1776 and
also borne by a church built in 1855 on this site.
Granite-walled interior, unusual chancel and lovely
woodwork give a special atmosphere of peace and
beauty. Rothwell pipe organ from Urquhart
Church, Elgin, rebuilt 1991 David Loosley. This
was the only charge of Rev Archibald Eneas
Robertson (1907-20), first ascender of all 'Munros'
in Scotland (283 peaks over 3000ft). B846
Aberfeldy to Bridge of Gaur, and south Loch
Rannoch road to Finnart. Sunday Service: 9.45am
Open daily
CHURCH OF SCOTLAND 📖 **B**

BRAES OF RANNOCH PARISH
CHURCH, BRIDGE OF GAUR

781 CAPUTH PARISH CHURCH

NO 088 401
Caputh, near Dunkeld
Now into its 3rd century, Caputh Church was built
in 1798. There has been a church in Caputh since
the 9th century, the present one being a fine stone
building. The interior has oak furnishings, stained
glass windows. Organ by James Bruce of
Edinburgh, c.1830. On A984, four miles east of
Dunkeld, Perthshire. Sunday Service: 11.15am
Open by arrangement, telephone
Mrs Easton 01738 710389
CHURCH OF SCOTLAND 🦻 wc

CAPUTH PARISH CHURCH

782 CLEISH CHURCH

NT 095 981

Built on 13th-century site in 1832
with additions 1897. Organ and
lights from St Giles, Edinburgh.
The hymn 'Jesus, tender Shepherd,
hear me' was written by former
minister's wife in the manse.
Interesting wall chart and
graveyard. Exit 5 M90, Cleish two
miles. Sunday Service: 11.15am
Open daily, 10.00am-5.00pm
CHURCH OF SCOTLAND 🕭 **B**

CLEISH CHURCH

783 COMRIE PARISH CHURCH

NN 770 221

Burrell Street, Comrie
Designed and built in 1881 by
George T Ewing on a site
surrounded by attractive grounds
overlooking the River Earn. Organ
by T C Lewis, built 1910 for the
London Exhibition. A85. Regular
bus service from Perth. Linked
with Dundurn. Sunday Service:
10.00am June to September;
10.30am October to May
Open daily
CHURCH OF SCOTLAND
♿ 🕭 📖 wc **C**

COMRIE PARISH CHURCH

784 CRIEFF PARISH CHURCH

NN 867 219

Strathearn Terrace
St Michael's tall saddle-backed tower dominates the skyline of Crieff. Designed by
local architect George T Ewing and built of Alloa stone. The organ, originally
1882 by Forster & Andrews, was reconstructed 1964. Brilliant stained glass
windows including some by Alfred Webster and Stephen Adam.
Sunday Services: 9.40am Informal Service with church band; 11.00am Morning
Worship; 6.30pm Evening Worship
Open by arrangement with the Minister, telephone 01765 653907
CHURCH OF SCOTLAND ♿ wc 🕭 **B**

785   ST ANNE'S, DOWALLY

NO 001 480

Built in 1818 on the site of a 16th-century building, St Anne's is a small country church with a bright interior. The designer was probably John Stewart, although the church has been much altered since. Dates on the bell (which is still in use) and belfry suggest that they came from the earlier church. The chancel has carved screens which were originally in Dunkeld Cathedral. One of the memorials is to John Robb, a minister of the parish who perished in the shipwreck in which Grace Darling became a national heroine. The Church is situated on the right hand side of the A9, three and a half miles north of Dunkeld.

Sunday Service: 2.00pm, 2nd, 4th and 5th Sundays of the month

Church website: www.dunkeldcathedral.org.uk

Open by arrangement, telephone Mrs Jim Kirk 01796 482407

CHURCH OF SCOTLAND   ⑦ 🗋 ☕ wc **B**

786   DUNKELD CATHEDRAL

NO 024 426

Cathedral Street, Dunkeld

The Cathedral lies in a superb setting on the banks of the Tay. The restored choir, now used as the parish church, was completed in 1350. Chapter house 1469, adjacent to choir, contains a small museum. The tower, ruined nave and south porch are in the care of Historic Scotland. Just off A9, at west end of Dunkeld.

Sunday Service: Easter to Remembrance Sunday, 10.00am and 11.00am

Church website: www.dunkeldcathedral.org.uk

Open daily, summer 9.30am-7.00pm, winter 9.30am-4.00pm. Flower Festival 20-22 May 2004, Concerts at 8.00pm 16 May, 6 June, 18 July, 1 and 22 August, 12 September 2004. Arts Festival 24-27 June 2004

CHURCH OF SCOTLAND   ♿ ⑦ 🗋 wc ⚲ (July and August) ⚲ **A**

787   DUNNING CHURCH

NO 019 145

Perth Road

Built for the United Free Church in plain Gothic style, the foundation stone was laid in 1908. The church became Church of Scotland in 1929, replacing the old St Serf's. The church features an open timber roof and a chancel and has simple well-crafted furnishings. Fine stained glass, including the west window of the Evangelists and a new window to mark the second Christian Millennium. Services: Sunday 10.30am

Open by arrangement, telephone R Nicol 01764 684203

Monday to Saturday 7.00am-5.00pm

CHURCH OF SCOTLAND   ♿ wc ⑦ ☕   DUNNING CHURCH

788   FORTEVIOT CHURCH (ST ANDREW'S), FORTEVIOT

NO 050 174

In an area of historical importance – in the 9th century Kenneth MacAlpin had his palace here, and a basilica existed from the first half of the 8th century – this church, the third, was erected in 1778. It was remodelled in the mid-19th century. Celtic bell dated AD 900, one of five Scottish bronze bells. Medieval carved stones. The font is from the pre-Reformation church of Muckersie united with Forteviot in 1618. Organ by Hamilton of Edinburgh. Extensively renovated 1994. One of the four churches of the Stewartry of Strathearn. Sunday Service: 10.00am

FORTEVIOT CHURCH
(ST ANDREW'S), FORTEVIOT

Open by arrangement, telephone Rev C Williamson 01738 625854

CHURCH OF SCOTLAND   **C**

789   FOWLIS WESTER PARISH CHURCH

NN 928 241

The church is a 13th-century building renovated in 1927 by Jeffrey Waddell of Glasgow with much Celtic ornament. It retains many of the original features including a 'lepers' squint'. The Pictish cross under the north wall is evidence of over 1000 years of Christian worship in the area. Turn off A85, five miles from Crieff to Fowlis Wester (signed). Sunday Service: 10.30am for 2003 and 10.00am for 2004

FOWLIS WESTER PARISH CHURCH

Open by arrangement, telephone Mrs McColl 01764 683205

CHURCH OF SCOTLAND   ♿ ② **B**

790   ST MADOES AND KINFAUNS CHURCH, GLENCARSE

NO 167 223

Glencarse, near Perth

Built 1799 on the site of earlier churches and refurbished in 1923. T-plan church with laird's gallery. New vestry and entrance hall by David Murdoch of Methven 1996. Interesting historic graveyard with 18th-century gravestones of sculptural merit. Pictish St Madoes Stone now on display in Perth Museum and Art Gallery. Contemporary embroidered pulpit falls. Sunday Service: September to May 11.00am; June to August 10.00am

Open 1st Sunday of month, June to September 1.00-4.00pm

CHURCH OF SCOTLAND   ♿ ② ⚲ WC **B**

ST MADOES AND KINFAUNS
CHURCH, GLENCARSE

791 GLENDEVON PARISH CHURCH

NN 979 051

West side of A823, one mile north of
Tormaukin Hotel

Seventeenth-century church with large
stained glass window by Alf Webster of
Glasgow 1913 and small stained glass window
in memory of Rev Alexander Taylor 1872-
1949. Various memorial plaques. Pulpit and
Communion table and chair carved by Mr
Philips of Tormaukin. Large gravestone to
Jane Rutherford. Sunday Service: 11.15am
Open at all times

CHURCH OF SCOTLAND wc **B**

GLENDEVON PARISH CHURCH

792 ALL SOULS' CHURCH, INVERGOWRIE

NO 347 303

59 Main Street, Invergowrie

Red sandstone church with 140ft spire, designed by Hippolyte Blanc 1890. High
altar has beautiful Italian marble reredos and crucifix. Lady Chapel contains altar
from Rossie Priory Chapel. Sculptured Stations of the Cross. Embroidered wall-
hanging to celebrate centenary of consecration 1996. Church hall used for
community activities. Services: Sunday 10am Sung Eucharist; Wednesday Said
Eucharist 10.15am

Open weekdays during school terms, 9.00am-4.00pm

SCOTTISH EPISCOPAL wc (only available if hall is in use) **A**

793 INVERGOWRIE PARISH CHURCH

NO 346 304

Main Street, Invergowrie

Building opened 1909. Architect John
Robertson. Early Gothic with square tower
and fine open timber roof. Pulpit and
Communion Table of Austrian oak with
carvings by local branch of YWCA. War
memorial bell 1924. Stained glass window
depicting Disruption minister Rev R S
Walker conducting open-air Communion.
Sunday Service: 11.00am

Church website: www.invergowrie.f9.co.uk
Open last Wednesday in July and August, 7.00-
8.00pm. Keyholder Mr G Grant 01382 562251

CHURCH OF SCOTLAND wc ♿ ⚲ **B**

INVERGOWRIE PARISH CHURCH

794 KETTINS PARISH CHURCH

NO 238 390

Kettins, by Coupar Angus

On the site of one of six chapels established by a nearby Columban monastery, the present church dates from 1768, with the north wing added in 1870 and the tower in 1891. Sixteen stained glass windows dating from 1878 onwards. Belgian bell of 1519 now rests, complete with belfry, close to the west gable it once surmounted. Celtic stone. Off A923, Dundee–Coupar Angus, one and a quarter miles south-east of Coupar. Linked with Meigle. Sunday Service: 11.30am

Open by arrangement, telephone 01828 640278

CHURCH OF SCOTLAND   🖐 ② 👤 **B**

KETTINS PARISH CHURCH

795 KILMAVEONAIG CHURCH

NN 874 658

Kilmaveonaig, Blair Atholl

An Episcopal Chapel rebuilt in 1794 by John Stewart on the site of the old parish church of Kilmaveonaig 1591, and having belonged to the Episcopal Communion without a break since the Revolution. Enlarged 1899. Lorimer reredos added 1912. Old bell 1629, from Little Dunkeld church. Off A9 to Blair Atholl, opposite Tilt Hotel. Sunday Service: 10.00am; spring and summer Evensong, 1st Sunday of the month April to September 6.30pm

Open by arrangement. Key available from Tilt Hotel

SCOTTISH EPISCOPAL 🖐 **B**

KILMAVEONAIG CHURCH

796 KINCLAVEN PARISH CHURCH

NO 151 385

By Stanley, near Perth

Built 1848 on site of previous church. Mixed Romanesque and Tudor with a narthex at the west end and bellcote at the east end. Churchyard contains the war memorial lychgate 1919 by Reginald Fairlie, and some table tombs of the 17th century and later. Built into the churchyard wall is the monument to Alexander Cabel (Campbell), Bishop of Brechin 1608. Sunday Service: 9.45am

Open by arrangement, telephone

Mr Gordon 01738 710548,

CHURCH OF SCOTLAND ② 📖 👤 🚻 🚻 **B**

KINCLAVEN PARISH CHURCH

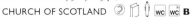

797 THE OLD CHURCH OF RANNOCH, KINLOCH RANNOCH

NN 663 585

South Loch Road, Kinloch Rannoch

A Thomas Telford church of 1829, extensively altered and enlarged 1893. Wooden beamed roof, stained glass window, hour-glass by pulpit. B846 from Aberfeldy, B8019 from Pitlochry. Sunday Service: 11.30am

Open daily 10.00am-dusk. Other times, key from Mrs D MacDonald,
Bridgend Cottage, telephone 01882 632359

CHURCH OF SCOTLAND   ♿ ⓘ ▣ wc **C**

798 COLLACE PARISH CHURCH, KINROSSIE

NO 197 320

Kinrossie, by Perth

Early 19th century on site of an earlier church dedicated in 1242. Stained glass window 1919. Remains of medieval building. Important 17th- and 18th-century gravestones. A94 from Perth, signposted from village smithy. Sunday Service: 11.15am

Open by arrangement, contact Miss E Miller
01821 650236 or Mr W Ewing 01821 650235

CHURCH OF SCOTLAND ⓘ ♔ ▣ ♟ wc **B**

COLLACE PARISH CHURCH, KINROSSIE

799 LONGFORGAN PARISH CHURCH

NO 309 300

Main Street, Longforgan

Church of 1795 in traditional Scottish box shape. Tower 1690 with eight-sided steeple and unusual clock. Apse added 1900. Several stained glass windows. Wood carving by Sir Robert Lorimer and remains of medieval font. Unique pipe organ. Interesting tombstones preserved. Graveyard with lychgate. New modern stained glass window. Adjacent to A90, 16 miles from Perth and 7 miles from Dundee.

Sunday Service: summer months 9.15am; winter 11.30am

Open Wednesdays 2.00-4.00pm, May to
September, or by arrangement, telephone
Mrs Hulbert 01382 360294

CHURCH OF SCOTLAND ♿ ⓘ ♔ ▣ wc **B**

LONGFORGAN PARISH CHURCH

800 MEIGLE PARISH CHURCH

NO 287 446

The Square, Meigle

Re-built in 1870 by John Carver after fire
destroyed the pre-Reformation stone
church of 1431. Stands on the ancient site
of a turf church erected by Columban
missionaries around AD 606. Fine stone
font. Interesting graveyard. Pictish stones
in adjacent museum (Historic Scotland).
Linked with Kettins. Sunday Service:
10.00am

Open by arrangement, telephone
01828 640278

CHURCH OF SCOTLAND   ⓑ ② 🚻 wc **B**

MEIGLE PARISH CHURCH

801 MORENISH CHAPEL

NO 607 356

By Killin

Built in 1902 by Aline White Todd in memory of her daughter Elvira who died in
childbirth. The central piece of the chapel is the magnificent east window by
Tiffany in heavily leaded tracery, and sumptuous stained glass showing Moses
receiving the ten commandments on Mount Sinai. On A827 Killin–Kenmore.
Served by Killin and Ardeonaig. Sunday Service: 3.00pm, 1st Sunday of month
during the summer

CHURCH OF SCOTLAND

802 MUTHILL PARISH CHURCH

NN 868 171

Station Road, Muthill, by Crieff

Replacing the 12th-century church (still existing).
Built in 1826 in Gothic style to a design by
Gillespie Graham, nicknamed 'Pinnacle' Graham
by those less enthusiastic for the sprockets of
19th-century Gothic. Pulpit canopy similarly
sprocketed. A822, three miles south of Crieff.
Buses from Stirling to Crieff.
Sunday Service: 11.30am (coffee 11.00am),
except August and September 10.00am

Open 1st Sunday in August. Coincides with opening
of nearby Drummond Castle Gardens
(Scotland's Gardens Scheme)

CHURCH OF SCOTLAND   ⓑ 🚻 **B**

MUTHILL PARISH CHURCH

803 ST JAMES CHURCH, MUTHILL

NN 869 170
Station Road, Muthill
Built 1836, designed by R & R Dickson of Edinburgh.
Oldest Episcopal church in the area. Numerous family
crests of historic interest and memorial tablets. Fifty
yards from village centre opposite primary school.
Linked with St Kessog's, Auchterarder. Sunday Service:
11.00am January to June; 9.30am July to December
Open by arrangement, telephone
the Very Rev Randal MacAlister 01764 662525
SCOTTISH EPISCOPAL   ♿ **B**

ST JAMES CHURCH, MUTHILL

804 ORWELL PARISH CHURCH

NO 121 051
Church constructed 1729 using stone from the Old
Kirk of Orwell on the banks of Loch Leven. The
roof was raised and the present windows, floor and
seating installed and galleries added in 1769. The
interior is enhanced by embroidered banners and
kneelers crafted by members of the Church. Number

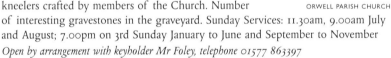

ORWELL PARISH CHURCH

of interesting gravestones in the graveyard. Sunday Services: 11.30am, 9.00am July
and August; 7.00pm on 3rd Sunday January to June and September to November
Open by arrangement with keyholder Mr Foley, telephone 01577 863397
CHURCH OF SCOTLAND ♿ ② wc **B**

805 ST JOHN'S KIRK OF PERTH

NO 119 235
St John Place, Perth
Burgh Church of Perth dedicated to John the Baptist and
consecrated in 1242 on site of earlier church. Divided into three
churches after the Reformation and restored 1923-26 by Sir
Robert Lorimer. Good examples of modern stained glass
including window of Knox Chapel by Douglas Strachan. Statue
of John the Baptist by Indian sculptor Fanindra Bose, and
tapestry opposite Shrine (part of the 1926 restoration) by Archie
Brennan of Dovecote Studios Edinburgh. Nave with barrel
vaulting has carvings of events in the life of Christ. Glass screen
at west door installed 1988. Organ by Rothwell 1926, rebuilt
1986 by Edmonstone. Sunday Services: 9.30am and 11.00am
Church website: www.st-johns-kirk.co.uk

ST JOHN'S KIRK
OF PERTH

Open May to September, 10.00am-4.00pm weekdays, 12.00-2.00pm Sundays; October to
April, when Church Officer is present, usually Wednesday to Saturday from 10.00am.
Guided tours by arrangement, telephone Mrs M Howat 01738 626520
CHURCH OF SCOTLAND ♿ ② 🏠 👤 wc **A**

806 ST NINIAN'S CATHEDRAL, PERTH

NO 116 237
North Methven Street
First Cathedral to be built after the
Reformation, being consecrated in
1850. The architect was William
Butterfield. Baldachino in Cornish
granite, fine wooden statue of the
Risen Christ and interesting stained
glass. Founder's window, the font and
one of the banners by Sir Ninian
Comper. Services: Sunday: Holy
Communion 8.00am, Sung Eucharist
11.00am; Monday to Friday: Morning Prayer 9.00am;
Wednesday: Holy Communion 11.00am; Thursday: Holy Communion 9.00am
Open Monday to Friday 9.00am-5.00pm
SCOTTISH EPISCOPAL ♿ wc ⑨ **B**

ST NINIAN'S CATHEDRAL, PERTH

807 NORTH CHURCH, PERTH

NO 116 237
Mill Street, Perth
A pleasant city centre church built in 1880 by T L Watson of Glasgow in Italian
Romanesque style. Sunday Services: 9.30am, 11.00am and 6.30pm; Thursday
lunchtime 1.00pm
Open by arrangement, telephone Mr G Weaks 01738 444033
CHURCH OF SCOTLAND ⑨ ⌷ wc **B**

808 ST LEONARD'S-IN-THE-FIELDS & TRINITY, PERTH

NO 117 232
Marshall Place, Perth
Fine example of the late Gothic revival by
John L Stevenson of London, opened in
1885. Outstanding architectural features are
the crown tower and the heavy buttresses.
The organ, Bryceson 1881, which came
from North Morningside Church in
Edinburgh, was installed in the centenary
year 1985. Sunday Services: 11.00am
Open on Doors Open Day (September)
CHURCH OF SCOTLAND **A**

ST LEONARD'S-IN-THE-FIELDS
& TRINITY, PERTH

809 ST JOHN'S EPISCOPAL, PERTH

NO 119 233

Princes Street, Perth

The present site has been used for worship since 1800. Present building designed by John Hay of Liverpool 1850-51. Many stained glass windows, sculptures by Miss Mary Grant, chancel arch carved by Heiton. Fine Harrison & Harrison organ 1971. Services: Sunday: Holy Communion 8.00am, Sung Eucharist 10.30am; Thursday: Holy Communion 11.00am

Open by arrangement, telephone

Mr T Mason 01738 627870

SCOTTISH EPISCOPAL [wc] (?) ⌂ **B**

ST JOHN'S EPISCOPAL, PERTH

810 PITLOCHRY CHURCH

NO 942 581

Church Road, Pitlochry

Built in 1884 by C & L Ower, Dundee. The porch was added in 1995, built of stone from Pitlochry East Church, the East and West congregations having united in 1992. Seating arranged in a part circle around the communion table. Monument to Alexander Duff, 19th-century missionary. Identifiable as 'the church with the clock' 100 yards from main street. Sunday Services: 9.30am All Age Worship, and 11.00am Traditional form of service

Open mid-June to mid-September,

Monday to Friday 10.00am-12.00 noon

CHURCH OF SCOTLAND [&] (?) ⌂ [wc] **B**

PITLOCHRY CHURCH

811 HOLY TRINITY EPISCOPAL, PITLOCHRY

NN 946 578

Atholl Road

Opened 1858, architect C Buckeridge of Oxford, nave extended 1890. Organ by Hele (1903). Reredos by Sir Ninian Comper, pulpit panels by pupils of Miss Kinderslay of Cliffe, Dorchester. Stained glass windows by various artists including E Kempe, donated between 1877 and 1956. Lychgate built about 1923. Services: Sunday Holy Communion 8.00am; 1st and 3rd Sundays Holy Communion 11.30am with hymns; 2nd and 4th Sundays Matins 11.30am; 5th Sunday see notice in church porch

Open by arrangement, telephone 01796 472176, or see notice in church porch

SCOTTISH EPISCOPAL [wc] ⌂ ⌂ **B**

812 PITLOCHRY BAPTIST CHURCH

NO 942 580

Atholl Road, next to Tourist Information Centre

Founded 1878 and originally meeting in a joiner's shop, the Pitlochry Fellowship built this church in 1884 to a design by Crombie of Edinburgh. Today's congregation welcomes visitors from across the world all year round. Sunday Services: 11.00am and 6.30pm

Open by arrangement with Atholl Centre, a Christian holiday and conference centre, situated behind church, telephone 01796 473044

BAPTIST & wc ✷ (Shop with Christian books and fair trade goods in adjoining Atholl Centre) **C**

PITLOCHRY BAPTIST CHURCH

813 DUNDURN PARISH CHURCH, ST FILLANS

NN 697 241

Built 1878. Of particular interest is the medieval stone font. Oak panelling, pulpit and communion table with Celtic knotwork. Set in grounds with striking view across Loch Earn. Linked with Comrie Parish Church. Sunday Service: 11.30am June to September; 12.00 noon October to May

Open daily, Easter to October

CHURCH OF SCOTLAND 📕 ✷

DUNDURN PARISH CHURCH, ST FILLANS

814 SCONE OLD PARISH CHURCH

NO 134 256

Burnside, Scone

Church built in 1286 near to Scone Palace. Moved to present site in 1806 using stone from original building. Mansfield pew presented by Queen Anne of Denmark 1615. Memorial to David Douglas, botanist, in graveyard. A94 from Perth. Number 7 bus from Perth. Sunday Service: 11.00am

Open various Saturdays in 2004, 10.00am-12.00 noon. For details, telephone Mr Moir 01738 551549

CHURCH OF SCOTLAND & 📕 ☕ wc **B**

SCONE OLD PARISH CHURCH

815 PORTMOAK PARISH CHURCH, SCOTLANDWELL

NO 183 019

One mile west of Scotlandwell

The present building, dated 1832, is the third
on the site. The bell is dated 1642 and the
Celtic crosses are of the 10th or 11th centuries.
Memorial stone in the graveyard to Michael
Bruce (1746-67), author of several of the
scripture paraphrases used in Church of
Scotland worship. Annual commemorative
service in evening of first Sunday in July.
Sunday Service: 10.00am

Open by arrangement with Mrs Crighton,
telephone 01592 840550

CHURCH OF SCOTLAND 🦽 ⒟ **B**

PORTMOAK PARISH CHURCH,
SCOTLANDWELL

816 ST ANDREW'S CHURCH, STRATHTAY

NN 910 534

The chancel was built in 1888 and the nave added in 1919. A vestibule and hall
were added in 1982. Heavily carved woodwork on pulpit, lectern and priest's
prayer desk. Lovely stained glass. A free-standing belfry was provided in 1995. In
village, over River Tay from Grandtully on A827 between Ballinluig and Aberfeldy.
Linked with St Mary's, Birnam. Sunday Service: 11.30am

Open by arrangement. Key from village shop

SCOTTISH EPISCOPAL 🗋 wc **A**

817 STANLEY PARISH CHURCH

NO 108 330

Built in 1828 by local mill owners the
Buchanan family for mill workers, the
church seated 1000. It was adapted in
1962 and incorporated a new pew
arrangement. The halls which are
below the sanctuary were refurbished
in 1997. The vestibule houses the war
memorial. The site is floodlit by night
and the extensive church grounds
hold an annual outdoor fête on the
first Saturday of September.
Sunday Service: 11.30am

CHURCH OF SCOTLAND 🦽 ⒟ **B**

STANLEY PARISH CHURCH

818 TENANDRY CHURCH

NN 911 615
Tenandry, Pitlochry
Small country church built in 1836 of stone and
slate and of traditional design. Fine view of the
Pass of Killiecrankie from the road above the
church. Turn north from B8019 at Garry Bridge
two miles north of Pitlochry (signed).
Sunday Service: 10.00am
Open daily
CHURCH OF SCOTLAND ♿ 🏠 wc **B**

TENANDRY CHURCH

819 TIBBERMORE CHURCH

NO 052 234
Quarter mile south of Tibbermore crossroads
The present church dates from 1632, though the site
has been a place of worship from the Middle Ages
onwards. The church was remodelled and enlarged in
1789 to designs by James Scobie, made T-plan in
1808 and the interior refurnished in 1874. The
present interior is little altered since that date. The
graveyard contains many monuments of interest, in
particular the exceptional memorial to James Ritchie,
displaying his curling equipment and the recumbent
figure of his bull. Transferred to the ownership of
the Scottish Redundant Churches Trust in 2001
For opening and service arrangements, contact the SRCT,
telephone 01334 472032
FORMER CHURCH OF SCOTLAND ♿ **B**

TIBBERMORE CHURCH

820 FOSS KIRK, TUMMEL BRIDGE

NN 790 581
South Loch Tummel Road, Foss
Founded AD 625 by St Chad and used until
the Reformation. Fell into disrepair 1580,
restored 1821. Perth bell 1824. Ancient
graveyard behind the church with view of
Loch Tummel. Linked with Braes of Rannoch
and Rannoch. B8019 from Pitlochry to
Tummel Bridge, then B846 to Foss or B846
from Aberfeldy to Foss. Sunday Services: May
to September, 1st and 3rd Sundays 7.00pm;
October to April, 1st Sunday 2.30pm
Open daily
CHURCH OF SCOTLAND 🏠 **C**

FOSS KIRK, TUMMEL BRIDGE

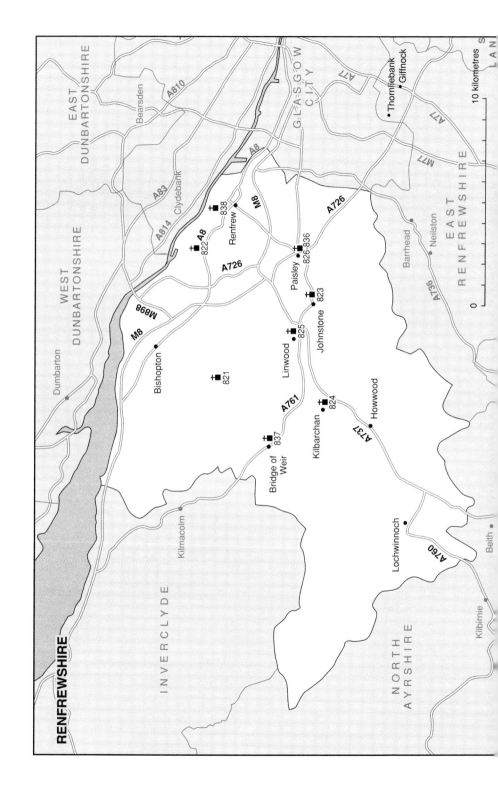

RENFREWSHIRE

EAST DUNBARTONSHIRE

Bearsden

A810

WEST DUNBARTONSHIRE

Clydebank

A814

A83

Dumbarton

INVERCLYDE

Kilmacolm

GLASGOW CITY

A8

M8

838 Renfrew

822 A8

A726

M868W

M8

Bishopton

821

Linwood

A726

826-836 Paisley

823

825

Johnstone

Howwood

A761

824 Kilbarchan

837 Bridge of Weir

A737

Lochwinnoch

A760

NORTH AYRSHIRE

Kilbirnie

Beith

EAST RENFREWSHIRE

Barrhead

Neilston

A736

A77

M77

Thornliebank

Giffnock

A77

LAN

0   10 kilometres

RENFREWSHIRE

Local Representative: Mr Norman MacGilvray, 20 Well Street, West Kilbride
(*telephone* 01294 829221)

821 HOUSTON & KILLELLAN PARISH CHURCH

NS 410 671
Kirk Road, Houston
Gothic, by David Thomson 1874, this
building is the third on this ancient
site. Very good stained glass.
Interesting organ. Between Bridge of
Weir and Inchinnan.
Sunday Service: 11.00am
Open Sundays 11.00am-1.00pm
CHURCH OF SCOTLAND **B**

HOUSTON & KILLELLAN PARISH CHURCH

822 INCHINNAN PARISH CHURCH (ST CONVAL'S KIRK)

NS 479 689
Old Greenock Road, Inchinnan
Sir R Rowand Anderson's Church
of 1904 was razed to make way for
Glasgow Airport, and the present
building by Miller and Black,
consecrated in 1968, incorporates
much of interest and beauty from
the earlier church. Foundation by St
Conval in 597. King David I gave
patronage of first stone church to
Knights Templar, succeeded by
Knights of St John. Celtic and
medieval stones. Two miles west of
Renfrew on A8.
Sunday Service: 10.45am
*Open Thursday during term-time,
12.00 noon-1.30pm. Light lunches
available*
CHURCH OF SCOTLAND

INCHINNAN PARISH CHURCH
(ST CONVAL'S KIRK)

823 JOHNSTONE HIGH PARISH CHURCH

NS 426 630

Quarry Street, Johnstone

An octagonal building of grey sandstone
built in 1792. Clock tower with spire.
Stained glass. Historic graveyard. In the town
centre, trains from Glasgow every 15 minutes.
Sunday Service: 11.00am; Songs
of Praise first Sunday 6.30pm

*Open Thursday to Saturday 10.00am-12 noon,
all year. Tours by arrangement at church hall
coffee shop*

CHURCH OF SCOTLAND   **B**

JOHNSTONE HIGH PARISH CHURCH

824 KILBARCHAN WEST CHURCH

NS 401 632

Church Street, Kilbarchan

Hall built as the church in 1724 on the site
of an earlier church. Present church
completed 1901, architect W H Howie. Some
fine stained glass resited from old church and
glass from early 20th century. 3-manual organ
built 1904 by William Hill & Sons.
At Kilbarchan Cross next to NTS Weaver's
Cottage. Sunday Services: 11.00am;
Wednesdays: 10.30am, October to May

Open by arrangement 01505 342930

CHURCH OF SCOTLAND **B**

KILBARCHAN WEST CHURCH

825 LINWOOD PARISH CHURCH

NS 432 645

Blackwood Avenue, at Clippens Road, Linwood

A spacious red brick building dating from 1965. An earlier church of 1860 existed
on another site, demolished in 1976. The furniture and communion silver are from
the earlier church. Contemporary art-
work includes a large aluminium cross
presented by the former Rootes Vehicle
Plant. Fine pipe organ 1957. Sunday
Services: 9.30am and 11.00am

*Open Friday 11.30am-1.30pm during school
term, and by arrangement, telephone
Mrs F Dooley 01505 331 065*

CHURCH OF SCOTLAND

LINWOOD PARISH CHURCH

826 PAISLEY ABBEY

NS 486 640

Founded in 1163. Early 20th-century
restoration of the choir by P MacGregor
Chalmers and Lorimer. Medieval architecture,
royal tombs of Marjory Bruce and Robert III,
the 10th-century Barochan Cross.
Exceptionally fine woodwork including organ
case by Lorimer, stained glass by Burne-Jones
and others. Organ by Cavaille-Coll 1872,
rebuilt Walker 1968. M8, junction 27, follow
signs to Paisley town centre. By train to
Paisley, Gilmour Street. Sunday Services:
11.00am, 12.15pm, Holy Communion, 6.30pm
Open daily, Monday to Saturday 10.00am-
3.30pm. Flower Festival 10-12 June 2004 'Vision
of St Mirin'. Other details from Abbey Office,
telephone 0141 889 7654
CHURCH OF SCOTLAND ② 🍴 🍷 📖 ☕ 🚾 **A**

PAISLEY ABBEY

827 ST MIRIN'S CATHEDRAL, PAISLEY

NS 488 642

Incle Street

St Mirin's Cathedral was built in 1931 to replace the old church in East Buchanan
Street. Constituted Cathedral Church of the Diocese of Paisley in 1947. The
architect was Thomas Baird and the building is neo-Romanesque in style with an
airy arched interior. Visitors should note the sculpted pulpit and Art Deco Stations
of the Cross. Services: daily 10.00am and 1.00pm; Saturday Vigil 6.30pm; Sunday
8.00am, 10.00am, 12.00 noon and 4.00pm

Open daily 8.00am-8.00pm

ROMAN CATHOLIC ♿ 🚾 ② **B**

ST MIRIN'S CATHEDRAL, PAISLEY

828 CASTLEHEAD PARISH CHURCH, PAISLEY

NS 476 636
Main Road, Castlehead, Paisley
Built 1781 as the first Relief church in Paisley.
Interior renovated 1881. Bishop organ 1898.
Graveyard has graves of Robert Tannahill (local
poet), past ministers, merchants and the mass
graves of the cholera epidemic. At west end of
town, at junction of Castlehead Main Road and
Canal Street. Sunday Service: 11.00am
*Open May to September, Monday, Wednesday
and Friday 2.00-4.00pm*
CHURCH OF SCOTLAND ♿ ♿ **B**

CASTLEHEAD PARISH CHURCH, PAISLEY

829 MARTYRS' CHURCH, PAISLEY

NS 474 639
Broomlands Street, Paisley
The church is named after the Paisley martyrs
who were executed in 1685. Built 1847 with
additions and alterations, including tower and
south front in neo-Norman style 1905, T G
Abercrombie, architect. Inside are galleries on
three sides on cast-iron colonnettes. The pulpit,
18ft long, has been likened to the bridge of a
ship. Close to A761, west of Paisley centre.
Sunday Service: 11.00am
Open Friday 10.00am-1.00pm
CHURCH OF SCOTLAND ☕ ♿ **B**

MARTYRS' CHURCH, PAISLEY

830 NEW JERUSALEM CHURCH, PAISLEY

NS 481 637
17 George Street, Paisley
Built for Wesleyan Methodists in 1810, and in use
by Swedenborgians since 1860, this is an unusual
building with halls on the ground floor and the
church upstairs. Three striking stained glass windows
by W & J J Keir, including one designed by Sir Noel
Paton. Fine pulpit, communion table, and ceiling
rose. Nearest railway stations Paisley Canal and
Paisley Gilmour Street. Sunday Service: 11.00am
*Open by arrangement, and on Doors Open Day,
September 11.00am-4.00pm, telephone
Rev Robert Gill 0141 887 4119*
SWEDENBORGIAN

NEW JERUSALEM CHURCH, PAISLEY

831 ST MARY'S (OUR LADY HELP OF CHRISTIANS), PAISLEY

NS 471 636
167 George Street
Designed by Pugin & Pugin in Decorated style and built 1891, the apse was added 1905. Organ by Andrew of Glasgow. Recent refurbishment has included redecoration of the interior. The church contains works of Austrian and Bavarian origin. Services: daily 9.15am and 9.30am; Saturday Vigil 6.30pm; Sunday 9.30am and 11.00am
Church website: www.stmaryspaisley.fsnet.co.uk
Open daily 8.30am-5.30pm
ROMAN CATHOLIC B

832 ST JAMES'S CHURCH, PAISLEY

NS 477 644
Underwood Road, Paisley
Early French Gothic style to a design by Hippolyte Blanc, largely gifted by Sir Peter Coats 1884. Spire 200ft. Full peal of bells, rung every Sunday. 'Father' Willis pipe organ, rebuilt J Walker 1967. Stained glass windows 1904. Landscaped grounds. M8, junction 29, St James interchange. Sunday Service: 11.00am
Open Monday, Wednesday and Friday, 10.00am-4.00pm. Also Doors Open Day, September 10.00am-4.00pm. Contact day centre at rear of church for access
CHURCH OF SCOTLAND B

833 ST PETER'S, PAISLEY

NS 474 613
154 Braehead Road
The church with its brick tower is a dominant feature on the hill at Glenburn. It was completed in 1958 and a new church hall opened in 2003. The parish celebrates the 50th anniversary of its foundation in 2003.
Services: Sunday 10.00am, 12.00 noon (includes a Children's Liturgy), 5.15pm; Saturday 9.30am and Vigil 6.30pm; Monday-Friday 9.30am; Wednesday 7.00pm
Church website: www.st-peters-paisley.co.uk
Open by arrangement with the Parish Priest, telephone 0141 884 2435
ROMAN CATHOLIC

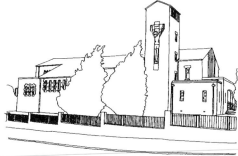

ST PETER'S, PAISLEY

834 THOMAS COATS MEMORIAL BAPTIST CHURCH, PAISLEY

NS 478 640

High Street, Paisley

Built by the Coats Family as a memorial
to Thomas Coats. Hippolyte Blanc
Gothic, opened May 1894. Beautiful
interior, 'by far the grandest of the
Paisley churches' (*Groome's Gazetteer*) with
carved marble and alabaster. Famous Hill
4-manual pipe organ. On main street
going west from Paisley Cross.

Sunday Service: 11.00am

Church website: www.fenet.co.uk/coats

Open by arrangement, telephone

Mr L Irvine 0141 887 2773.

Doors Open Day 11 September 2004

BAPTIST   🦽 ⌀ ⌀ ⌀ wc **A**

THOMAS COATS MEMORIAL BAPTIST CHURCH, PAISLEY

835 WALLNEUK NORTH CHURCH, PAISLEY

NS 486 643

Abercorn Street, Paisley

Built 1915. Architect T G Abercrombie.
Pipe organ by Abbott & Smith of Leeds
1931, dedicated to Peter Coats, donor of
this church. Its fine oak case was carved
and built by Wylie & Lochead, Glasgow.
Near town centre.

Sunday Service: 11.00am; Wednesday:
12.30pm

Doors Open Day, September

CHURCH OF SCOTLAND   🦽 ⌀ ⌀ ⌀ ☕ **A**

WALLNEUK NORTH CHURCH, PAISLEY

836 GLASGOW INTERNATIONAL AIRPORT CHAPEL, PAISLEY

NS 478 663

Second Floor, Terminal Building, Glasgow Airport

A recent addition to Glasgow Airport, open to passengers and staff of all faiths and
creeds. Christian Services are announced 30 minutes in advance by public address.

Open at all times

NON-DENOMINATIONAL   🦽 ☕

837 ST MACHAR'S, RANFURLY

NS 392 653

Kilbarchan Road, Ranfurly, Bridge of Weir
Early Gothic 1878 by Lewis Shanks,
brother of one of the local millowners.
The chancel was added in 1910 by
Alexander Hislop. Stained glass by J S
Melville & J Stewart 1900, Herbert
Hendrie 1931, William Wilson 1946,
Gordon Webster 1956. Descriptive booklet
by Maurice L Gaine 1996. A761 at east
end of village. Sunday Service: 11.00am
(10.30am July and August)
Church website: www.stmacharsranfurly.org
Open Fridays 10.00am-12.00 noon. Bridge of
Weir Gala Week in June
CHURCH OF SCOTLAND ⊘ 🗋 ⬦ 💻 wc

ST MACHAR'S, RANFURLY

838 RENFREW OLD PARISH CHURCH

NS 509 676

26 High Street, Renfrew
The Church of Renfrew was bestowed
by King David on the Cathedral
Church of Glasgow in 1136. Within
the present lancet Gothic 1862
sanctuary are two late medieval
monuments, a hooded vault with
recumbent effigies and an altar tomb.
In Renfrew town centre. Regular bus
services from Glasgow and Paisley.
Sunday Services: 11.15am and 6.30pm
Doors Open Day, September
CHURCH OF SCOTLAND ♿ ⬦ wc **B**

RENFREW OLD PARISH CHURCH

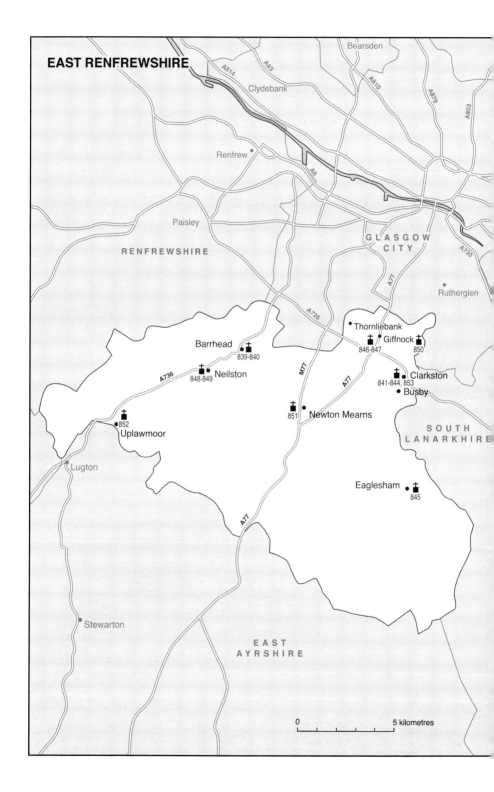

EAST RENFREWSHIRE

EAST RENFREWSHIRE

839 ARTHURLIE PARISH CHURCH, BARRHEAD

NS 501 588

Ralston Road/Main Street, Barrhead

Built 1967 to replace the 1796 'whitewashed kirk'. Designed by Honeyman, Jack and Robertson of Glasgow. High roof and long aisles. The open pews, constructed from the same light hardwood (ramin) as the cross, font, lectern and choirstalls, create an understated unity. Stained glass by Gordon Webster in the style 'Dalles de Verre'. The grounds, laid out by Bessie McWhirter, are open to all.

Services: Sunday 11.00am; Wednesday 10.45am

Church website: www.arthurliechurch.org.uk

Open by arrangement with Church Officer, telephone 0141 881 1792

CHURCH OF SCOTLAND 🦽 (side entrance) Ⓢ 🗎 wc

840 ST JOHN'S, BARRHEAD

NS 508 592

Aurs Road, Barrhead

Built in 1961, architect Thomas S Cordiner, after the old building was burnt down in 1941, before its centenary Mass. Note the prevalence of Greek iconography over Latin and the recurrence of the motif of St John. Tabernacle door designed by Hew Lorimer and presidential chair by John McLachlan. Rushworth and Dreaper organ. Services: Saturday Vigil 6.30pm; Sunday 10.00am, 12.00 noon and 6.30pm; Exposition of the Blessed Sacrament, in the oratory, Monday to Friday 10.30am to 10.00pm. All welcome for private prayer

Open by arrangement with Presbyery House, telephone 0141 876 1553

ROMAN CATHOLIC 🦽 (side door) Ⓢ wc

ST JOHN'S,
BARRHEAD

841 GREENBANK CHURCH, CLARKSTON

NS 574 568

Eaglesham Road, Clarkston

The Church designed by McKissack & Rowan was opened in 1884. The chancel, furnishings and stained glass windows were added in 1937. A mural by Alistair Gray in the transept was completed in 1979. The Centenary Chapel was opened in 1984.

Sunday Services: 9.30am and 11.00am

Church website: www.greenbankglasgow.org.uk

Open by arrangement, telephone Church Officer

0141 644 2839

CHURCH OF SCOTLAND 🦽 Ⓢ wc

GREENBANK CHURCH, CLARKSTON

842 ST AIDAN'S, CLARKSTON

NS 573 574
Mearns Road, Clarkston
Hall Church built 1924 and present church 1951, architects Noad & Wallace.
Building has a steel frame and brick interior. Red sandstone facing matches Hall.
Stained glass including a pair of windows by Susan Bradbury 1998.
Sunday Services: Holy Communion 8.00am, Sung Eucharist 10.00am,
Evensong/Evening Prayer 6.30pm
Church website: www.staidans.freeserve.co.uk

Open Wednesdays 9.00-11.30am
SCOTTISH EPISCOPAL [♿] [Ⓙ] [☕]

843 ST JOSEPH'S, CLARKSTON

NS 575 572
2 Eaglesham Road, Clarkston
First church built also as a school in
1880. Replaced by a modern building
on same site in 1971. Stained glass
windows by Shona McInnes and

ST JOSEPH'S, CLARKSTON

tapestries by Joanna Kinnersly-Taylor. Services: Saturday Vigil 6.00pm; Sunday
Masses 8.30 am, 10.00 am, 12.00 noon and 6.00pm; weekday Masses 10.00am and
7.00pm Monday-Friday; Saturday 10.00am.
Open all day
ROMAN CATHOLIC [♿] [wc] [Ⓙ] [☕]

844 STAMPERLAND CHURCH, CLARKSTON

NS 576 581
Stamperland Gardens, Clarkston
Congregation's first service held in an air raid shelter of a local garage in 1940.
Thereafter a local shop was occupied at 38 Stamperland Crescent before a hall
church was built in 1941 (now hall of church). Present modern building erected
1964, architect J Thompson King & Partners. Concrete bell-tower. Three stained
glass windows by Gordon Webster, previously in Woodside Parish Church. Pipe
organ 1897 by Lewis & Co of
Brixton and earlier in Regent
Place UP Church, Dennistoun,
Glasgow. Furnishings include
items from 1938 Glasgow Empire
Exhibition Church. Bas-relief of
mythical pelican on outside wall.
Sunday Services: 9.45am and
11.00am
Open by arrangement, telephone
Norman Bolton 0141 638 3502
CHURCH OF SCOTLAND [♿] [Ⓙ]

STAMPERLAND CHURCH, CLARKSTON

845 EAGLESHAM PARISH CHURCH

NS 572 518

Montgomery Street, Eaglesham

The present attractive church with clock steeple was designed
by Robert McLachlane and completed in 1790. It replaced
churches on this site since early times. Former United Free
Church is now the Church Halls and Carswell United
Presbyterian Church refurbished as 'The Carswell Halls' (both
located on Montgomery Street). 'Father' Willis organ and fine
embroidered pulpit falls by Kathleen Whyte and Fiona
Hamilton. Covenanter graves in churchyard. Sunday Services:
9.30am and 11.00am, except June to August 10.30am

Church website: www.eaglesham-parish-church.com

EAGLESHAM
PARISH CHURCH

Open Tuesday and Thursday 10.00-12.00 noon, 2.00-4.00pm and Doors Open Day, September,
or by arrangement, telephone the Beadle 01355 303411

CHURCH OF SCOTLAND & ⑦ 📖 wc B

846 GIFFNOCK SOUTH PARISH CHURCH

NS 559 582

Greenhill Avenue, Giffnock

A 'hall church' (now Eglinton Hall) was opened in
1914. The present church was begun in 1921 and
dedicated in 1929. It is by Stewart & Paterson in late
Gothic style with blonde sandstone. There is a fine

GIFFNOCK SOUTH PARISH CHURCH

collection of stained glass windows, including six by Gordon Webster. There are
three recent windows, one by Sadie McLellan and two by Brian Hutchison.
Sunday Service: 11.15am

Church website: www.glasgowkirks.org.uk

CHURCH OF SCOTLAND & ⑦ wc B

847 ORCHARDHILL PARISH CHURCH, GIFFNOCK

NS 563 587

Church Road, Giffnock

Church and hall built in Gothic Revival style, H E Clifford
1900. Of local stone with a red tiled roof, squat tower with
spiral wooden stair and roof turret. Extensions carried out in
1910 and 1935. Stained glass 1936-86 by Webster, McLellan,
Wilson and Clark. Wood panelling 1900-35. 2-manual pipe
organ, Hill, Norman & Beard. Embroidered pulpit falls 1993.
On east side of Fenwick Road, north of Eastwood Toll. Buses
from Glasgow Buchanan and trains from Glasgow Central.

Sunday Services: 10.00am, 11.15am and 6.30pm (part year only)

ORCHARDHILL PARISH
CHURCH, GIFFNOCK

Church website: www.orchardhill.org.uk

Open by arrangement, telephone Church Officer 0141 589 4353, or Secretary 0141 638 3604

CHURCH OF SCOTLAND & ⑦ B

848   NEILSTON PARISH CHURCH

NS 480 574

Main Street

There has been a Christian presence on the site for over 1,000 years. Originally a single-storey building, the church was enlarged 1746-98, including the balcony. Further alterations 1820. An important feature is a Gothic window above the vault of the Mure family of Caldwell. Stained glass by Stephen Adam. Nearby is a memorial to John Robertson, a native of Neilston, who built the engine for *The Comet*, the first steamship on the Clyde. Circular mort-house of 1817.

Sunday Service: 11.00am

Open by arrangement

CHURCH OF SCOTLAND 🦽 wc ② ☕ 📖 **B**

849   ST THOMAS'S, NEILSTON

NS 479 573

70 Main Street, Neilston

Built 1861 and dedicated to St Thomas the Apostle as a tribute to the work to make the parish succeed. The tower was added in 1891. Services: Monday-Saturday Mass 10.00am; Saturday Vigil 6.00pm; Sunday 9.00am, 10.00am

Open daily

ROMAN CATHOLIC 🦽 wc ☕ 📖

ST THOMAS'S, NEILSTON

850   NETHERLEE PARISH CHURCH

NS 557 590

Ormonde Avenue, Netherlee

Built in neo-Gothic style of red Dumfriesshire sandstone by Stewart & Paterson 1934. Oak panelling and furnishings beautifully carved. Lovely stained glass. City buses via Clarkston Road. Sunday Services: September to May, 11.00am and some at 6.30pm; June to August 9.30am and 11.00am

Open by arrangement, telephone Mr McVey 0141 637 6853

CHURCH OF SCOTLAND

🦽 ② 📖 ⚱ ☕ wc **B**

NETHERLEE PARISH CHURCH

851 MEARNS PARISH CHURCH, NEWTON MEARNS

NS 551 556

Junction of Eaglesham Road and Mearns Road

Religious settlement and site since AD 800, the present church dates from 1813 and was extensively renovated in 1932. Organ originally from Glasgow City Hall. Stained glass windows by Gordon Webster and James McPhie. South wall tapestry donated by the late Lord Goold. A phosphor-bronze weathercock weighing two and a half cwts atop the bell-tower was erected in the late 1940s. Gate posts in the form of sentry boxes date from the era of the 'Resurrectionists'. Sunday Services: 9.30 and 11.00am

Open by arrangement, telephone the Minister 0141 616 2410

CHURCH OF SCOTLAND [♿] [wc] [②] **B**

MEARNS PARISH CHURCH,
NEWTON MEARNS

852 CALDWELL PARISH CHURCH, UPLAWMOOR

NS 435 552

Neilston Road, Uplawmoor

Simple country church built 1889 William Ingram. Memorial glass sculpture depicting the Trinity by Ralph Cowan 1989. Garden of Remembrance dedicated 1997. Off B736 Barrhead–Irvine. On main street. Sunday Service: 11.00am; Summer timetable, July to August 10.00am; Wednesday brief act of worship 12.00 noon

Open daily 11.00am-3.00pm. Soup lunch in hall adjacent October to March, Friday 12.00 noon-1.30pm

CHURCH OF SCOTLAND [⌂] [wc]

CALDWELL PARISH
CHURCH, UPLAWMOOR

853 WILLIAMWOOD PARISH CHURCH

NS 567 576

Seres Road, Williamwood

Built in 1937 as a church extension charge, the church is a fine example of mid-1930s church architecture. Original and somewhat austere interior upgraded and enriched. Historical and other information available. By rail from Glasgow Central to Williamwood or Clarkston, 10 minutes walk from both stations. Bus services from Glasgow to Eaglesham, alight at Clarkston. Sunday Service: 11.00am

Open February to June and September to December, weekdays, 9.45am-12.00 noon.

Other information, telephone 0141 638 2091

CHURCH OF SCOTLAND [♿] [②] [🍴] [⌂] [☕]

WILLIAMWOOD PARISH CHURCH

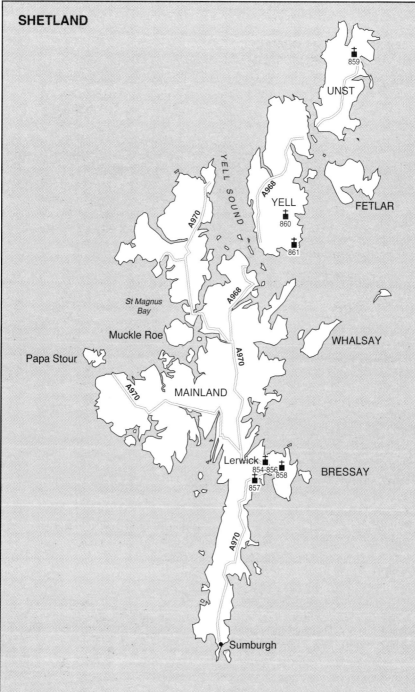

SHETLAND

UNST

859

YELL SOUND

A970

A968

YELL

860

861

FETLAR

St Magnus
Bay

A968

Muckle Roe

A970

WHALSAY

Papa Stour

A970

MAINLAND

Lerwick

854-856

858

857

BRESSAY

A970

A970

Sumburgh

0   10   20 Kilometres

SHETLAND

Local Representative: Dr Ramsay Napier, 4 Sletts Park, Lerwick, ZEI OLN
(*telephone* 01595 693716)

854 ST COLUMBA'S, LERWICK

HU 478 411
1 Greenfield Place
Designed by James Milne of Edinburgh and built 1828 with interior and apse of
1895 by John M Aitken, the church is recognised as a fine example of neo-classical
architecture in the north of Scotland. Splendid horse-shoe gallery. Organ by
Bryceson Bros of London, 1871, one of the earliest in the Church of Scotland.
Stained glass window depicting the figure of Jesus by Danish sculptor
Thorvaldsen. Sunday Service: 11.15am

Open by arrangement, telephone the Minister 01595 692125
CHURCH OF SCOTLAND 🦽 wc 🔇 📖 **B**

855 ST MAGNUS EPISCOPAL

HU 479 411
Greenfield Place, Lerwick
Designed by Alexander Ellis in Early English style and built 1862-64. Battlemented
tower added 1891. Alterations to chancel by Alexander Ross, 1899. Windows by
Sir Ninian Comper (moved here from the chapel of the former House of Charity
in 1973). Services: Monday-Friday 7.45am and 5.30pm; Sunday Morning Prayer
10.00am, Sung Eucharist 10.45am, Evening Prayer 6.30pm, Compline 8.00pm
(summer)

Open at all times
SCOTTISH EPISCOPAL 🦽 wc ☕ 📖 **B**

ST MAGNUS EPISCOPAL

856 ADAM CLARKE MEMORIAL METHODIST CHURCH, LERWICK

HU 475 412
Hillhead
Built 1872 and named after the Rev
Adam Clarke (1760-1832), President of
the Wesleyan Methodist Conference,
who greatly encouraged the
development of Methodism in Shetland.
The building suffered severe storm
damage in 1992 and reopened after
major refurbishment in 1994. Stained
glass window in memory of William
Goudie, a Shetlander designated
President of the Wesleyan Methodist
Conference in 1922, who died before
taking office. Sunday Services: 11.00am and 6.15pm
Open by arrangement, key available at adjacent Manse, telephone 01595 692874
METHODIST & wc ⊘

ADAM CLARKE MEMORIAL
METHODIST CHURCH, LERWICK

857 GULBERWICK CHURCH

HU 443 389
2 miles south of Lerwick
A handsome and simple church built in 1898 with Orkney stone facings. The
windows behind the pulpit are filled with cathedral squares. Picturesquely situated
in the village of Gulberwick with a graveyard overlooking the sea.
Sunday Service: 10.00am
Open by arrangement, telephone the Minister 01595 692125
CHURCH OF SCOTLAND 📖 **c**

858 BRESSAY CHURCH

HU 493 410
One mile from ferry
A typical harled kirk with belfry of the early 19th century, built 1812 to replace an
earlier kirk of 1722 which in turn replaced Bressay's three ancient chapels. The
church boasts two beautiful stained glass windows of St Peter and St Paul of
1895. At each of the windows are memorial tablets. The church overlooks the bay
and its seals. Sunday Service: 3.00pm
Open by arrangement, telephone the Minister 01595 692125
CHURCH OF SCOTLAND 📖 **B**

859 HAROLDSWICK METHODIST CHURCH, UNST

HP 646 134
Haroldswick, Unst
The most northerly church in Britain. The
present building 1993 was designed by a
Shetland architect, based on a simplified form
of a Norwegian wooden stave kirk. Most of
the work was done by local voluntary labour.

HAROLDSWICK METHODIST CHURCH, UNST

The interior beams and panelling are
Scandinavian pine and the lightness, warmth and proportion of the worship area
are striking. New bell turret for the 1867 bell has just been completed. Sunday
Service: 11.00am or 6.00pm (alternate Sundays)
Open all the time
METHODIST ♿ wc

860 EAST YELL METHODIST CHURCH, YELL

HP 517 855
Otterswick, East Yell
Built 1892 to serve the needs of the
local community, this lovely 'Chapel in
the Valley' is noted for its simple beauty,
warmth of its welcome and ecumenical
nature of its congregation. The chapel
has been described as a 'little gem'.
Much admired unique pulpit fall,
designed and crafted locally, depicting
the Lamb of God. Sunday Services:
10.45am or 2.45pm (alternate Sundays)
Open all the time
METHODIST ♿ wc

EAST YELL METHODIST
CHURCH, YELL

861 ST COLMAN'S EPISCOPAL

HU 520 798
Burravoe, Yell
A little rural gem in Arts & Crafts Gothic. Designed by R T N Spier and built
1900. Apsidal end and spirelet. Herring-bone patterned panels to doors, timber
choir stalls and pews. Folding Gothic timber chair by Morris & Co and painted
front to the timber altar depicting the Worship of Heaven. Services: Eucharist 3rd
Sunday every month 2.45pm plus 1st Sunday June to September
Summer Flower Festival Service: 1st Sunday in July, 2.45pm
Open at all times
SCOTTISH EPISCOPAL ♿ wc **B**

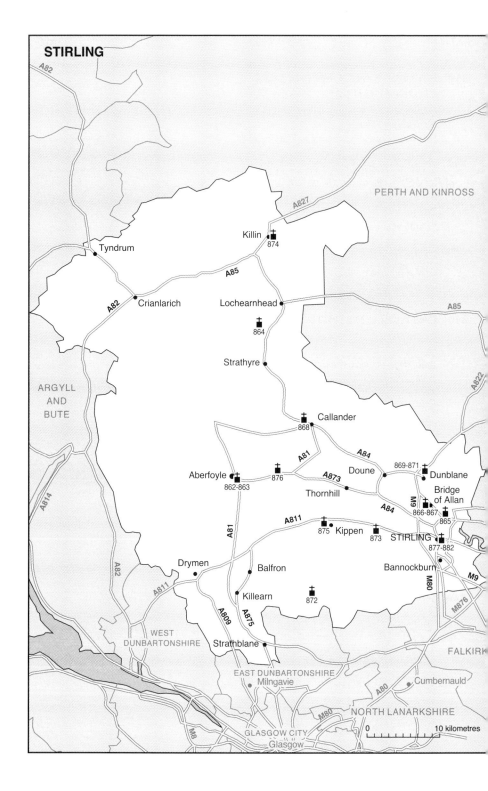

STIRLING

A82

PERTH AND KINROSS

A827

Killin
874

Tyndrum

A85

Crianlarich

A82

Lochearnhead

A85

864

ARGYLL
AND
BUTE

A822

Strathyre

Callander
868

A81

A84

Doune

869-871

Dunblane

A814

Aberfoyle
862-863

876

A873

Thornhill

Bridge
of Allan

M9

866-867

865

A84

A82

A811

875 Kippen

873

STIRLING

877-882

A811

Drymen

Balfron

Bannockburn

M9

A82

A809

Killearn

872

M80

M876

A875

Strathblane

FALKIRK

WEST
DUNBARTONSHIRE

EAST DUNBARTONSHIRE

A80

Cumbernauld

Milngavie

M80

NORTH LANARKSHIRE

M8

GLASGOW CITY
Glasgow

0   10 kilometres

STIRLING

Local Representative: Mr Louis Stott, 10 Trossachs Road, Aberfoyle, FK8 3SW (*telephone* 01877 382784)

862 ABERFOYLE PARISH CHURCH

NN 518 005
Loch Ard Road, Aberfoyle
John Honeyman designed this church which
sits at the foot of Craigmore and on the
banks of the River Forth. In early-Gothic
style 1870, it replaced the old kirk of
Aberfoil on the south bank of the river
reached by crossing the hump-backed
bridge. The new church was enlarged in

ABERFOYLE PARISH CHURCH

1884 to include transepts. The interior is elegant with the minimum of
ornamentation. Magnificent roof timbers. Stained glass, including a window by
Gordon Webster 1974. 2-manual pipe organ 1887 by Bryceson Brothers, London.
On the B829. Linked with Port of Menteith. Sunday Service: 11.15am
Open Saturday afternoon in August for church sale. Other times,
telephone Mr I Nicholson 01877 382337
CHURCH OF SCOTLAND ② 📖 wc **B**

863 ST MARY'S, ABERFOYLE

NN 524 010
Main Street, Aberfoyle
The church was deigned by James Miller, who also designed Gleneagles Hotel. It
was built 1892-93 by workers from the local slate quarry. The stone came from
Ailsa Craig by railway (free of charge) to test the weight capacity of the new
branch railway. Oak panelled reredos. Organ by Henry Willis.
Sunday Services: Sung Eucharist 9.30am; 1st Sunday; 11.00am other Sundays
Open by arrangement with Mrs M Johnson, telephone 01877 382611
SCOTTISH EPISCOPAL ② wc

864 BALQUHIDDER PARISH CHURCH

NN 536 209
Handsome parish church in dressed stone, built 1853 by David Bryce. Exhibition of
the history of the church. Bell donated by Rev Robert Kirk (1644-92), a notable
boulder font and the supposed gravestone of St Angus, possibly 9th-century. The
ruins of the old parish church are in the graveyard where there are many
intriguing carved stones, including that of Rob Roy MacGregor. A84 at
Kinghouse. Linked with Killin. Sunday Service: 12.00 noon
Open daily. Summer Music Sunday evenings during summer months
CHURCH OF SCOTLAND ♿ wc **B**

BALQUHIDDER PARISH CHURCH

865 LOGIE KIRK, BY BLAIRLOGIE, STIRLING

NS 829 968

The tower, square and pedimented and surmounted
by an octagonal belfry, was designed by William
Stirling of Dunblane 1805. The remainder of the
church, an elegant whinstone box, by McLuckie &
Walter of Stirling 1901. Stained glass windows
include one by C E Kempe and two modern windows
by John Blyth. Fourteen oak panels depicting scenes
from the Bible enclose the chancel and pulpit. The
ruined Old Kirk of Logie, with its good selection of
17th and 18th-century gravestones, is nearby. In idyllic
rural setting at foot of Dumyat and in the shadow of
the Wallace Monument. A91, four miles north-east of
Stirling. Sunday Service: 11.00am

Church website: www.logiekirk.co.uk

Open Sundays, August 2.00-5.00pm or by appointment, telephone 01786 475414

CHURCH OF SCOTLAND ♿ 🐕 🚻 📖 ⚲ ☕ wc B

LOGIE KIRK,
BY BLAIRLOGIE, STIRLING

866 HOLY TRINITY PARISH CHURCH, BRIDGE OF ALLAN

NS 791 974

Keir Street, Bridge of Allan

Built in 1860 and enlarged later, the church contains
chancel furnishings designed in 1904 by the eminent
Scottish architect, Charles Rennie Mackintosh. The
church has an attractive timber roof and excellent
stained glass windows by Kempe family, Ballantine
and Adam. Organ by Lewis 1884, with additions. On
corner with Fountain Road, opposite Somerfield car
park. Bus service from Stirling to Royal Hotel, one
block. Rail service to Bridge of Allan Station,
10 minutes walk. Sunday Service: 11.00am

Open June to September, Saturdays 10.00am-4.00pm

CHURCH OF SCOTLAND ♿ 🐕 🚻 📖 wc B

HOLY TRINITY PARISH CHURCH,
BRIDGE OF ALLAN

867 ST SAVIOUR'S CHURCH, BRIDGE OF ALLAN

NS 792 973
Keir Street, Bridge of Allan
Church adjacent to rectory 1857, architect
John Henderson, and later enlarged 1871-72
by Alexander Ross. Halls added to rectory
1893. Vestry added 1928. West window by
Robert Anning Bell, Stephen Adam Studios,
1922. Pipe organ, Forster & Andrews 1872.
By road, bus and rail services from Stirling.
On corner with Fountain Road. Sunday
Services: Said Eucharist 8.00am, Sung
Eucharist and Sermon 10.00am
Open generally 10.00am-5.00pm
SCOTTISH EPISCOPAL   ♿ **B**

ST SAVIOUR'S CHURCH, BRIDGE OF ALLAN

868 ST ANDREW'S, CALLANDER

NS 624 080
Leny Road
Sheltered by a magnificent cedar of Lebanon, this pretty little church was
consecrated in 1857. The architects were either J, JW & WH Hay or 'the
stonemason at Stronvar' who worked on the parish church at Balquhidder for
David Bryce in 1853. Enlarged by the addition of transepts in 1886. Organ by
Abbot and Smith of Leeds 1898. Sunday Service: Holy Communion 11.00am 1st,
2nd and 3rd Sunday, 9.30am 4th and 5th Sunday
Open by arrangement, telephone Ms Gunkel 01877 330798
SCOTTISH EPISCOPAL   ♿ wc **B**

869 DUNBLANE CATHEDRAL

NN 782 014
The Cross
One of Scotland's noblest medieval churches, the lower part of the tower is
Romanesque, but the larger part of the building is of the 13th century. Six late
15th-century choir stalls survive. The Cathedral was restored by Sir Robert Rowand
Anderson between 1889 and 1893. Screen, pulpit, lectern and font by Anderson.
Choir stalls and organ case by Sir Robert Lorimer. Important ensemble of stained
glass by Clayton & Bell, Gordon Webster, Douglas Strachan, C E Kempe. The six
magnificent choir windows are by Louis Davis. Sunday Services: 9.15am (summer),
10.30am (winter)
Open April to September 9.30am-6.30pm, October to March 9.30am-4.30pm.
Closed Tuesday afternoons, Friday and Sunday mornings
CHURCH OF SCOTLAND   ♿ ⓦ 📖 **A**

870   SCOTTISH CHURCHES HOUSE CHAPEL, DUNBLANE

NN 783 014
Kirk Street, opposite Cathedral
Uncovered in 1961 during restoration of buildings which became Scottish
Churches House. Medieval in origin, possibly a chapel of one of several
ecclesiastical residences which then surrounded the Cathedral. Fine barrel-vaulted
roof. Restored for use as the chapel of Scottish Churches House, an ecumenical
Conference House and Retreat Centre. Daily House Prayers: 9.00am
Church website: www.scottishchurcheshouse.org
Open at all times
ECUMENICAL   ② 🏠 wc **B**

871   ST BLANE'S CHURCH, DUNBLANE

NN 783 014
High Street/Sinclairs Street Lane, Dunblane
Open 1854 as Free Church which through
unions became East United Free Church and
East Church of Scotland. United with former
Leighton Church in 1952 to become St Blane's
Church. Stained glass includes windows from
Leighton Church, other windows by Roland
Mitton. Interesting tapestries in vestibule
including a reproduction of 'The Light of the
World' by Holman Hunt. Pipe organ 1860 by
Peter Conacher, perhaps the earliest example of
his work in Scotland. Sunday Services: 11.15am
(10.15am June to August), and 6.30pm
Open by arrangement, telephone the Minister 01786
822268, Dr Duncan 01786 822657, or
Mr Cattan 01786 822142
CHURCH OF SCOTLAND   wc ② 🏠 **B**

ST BLANE'S CHURCH, DUNBLANE

872   FINTRY KIRK

NS 627 862
Fintry Village
The present church, built in 1823, was constructed around the original kirk of
1642, and the congregation continued to worship in the old sanctuary while
building went on around them! On completion, the inner church was demolished.
The bell was transferred from old to new and is still in use today. Early 20th-
century stained glass, including a First World War memorial window. Session
House in the kirkyard added 1992. Linked with Balfron. Sunday Service: 10.00am
Open Easter Saturday, and Saturdays May to September, 2.00-4.00pm
CHURCH OF SCOTLAND   ② 🍴 ☕ wc **B**

FINTRY KIRK

873 GARGUNNOCK PARISH CHURCH

NS 707 943

Manse Brae, Gargunnock

Situated in very beautiful rural location. Village church 1650 on pre-Reformation foundation, renovated 1774 and 1891. Three individual outside stairs to three separate lairds' lofts. Two good 20th-century stained glass windows. War memorial by Lorimer. Mountain indicator. Graveyard. Five miles west of Stirling, off A811. Sunday Service: 11.30am

Open by arrangement, telephone 01786 860678

CHURCH OF SCOTLAND 🛉 📖 ℝ **B**

GARGUNNOCK PARISH CHURCH

874 KILLIN AND ARDEONAIG PARISH CHURCH, KILLIN

NN 571 330

Main Street, Killin

Distinctive white-harled octagonal classical church built in 1744 by the mason Thomas Clark to a design by John Douglas of Edinburgh. Inside it has been altered from a 'wide' church to a 'long' church. The Fillan Room, a small chapel for prayer in the tower, was created in 1990. In front of the church is a monument to Rev James Stewart (1701-89), minister of Killin, who first translated the New Testament into Scots Gaelic (published 1767). At the eastern end of the village. Serves Morenish Chapel (see Perth & Kinross); linked with Balquhidder. Information about Services in Morenish Chapel from Tourist Information by Falls of Dochart in village. Sunday Service: 10.00am

Open May to October during daylight hours

CHURCH OF SCOTLAND 🔊 🚾 **B**

KILLIN AND ARDEONAIG
PARISH CHURCH, KILLIN

KIPPEN PARISH CHURCH

875 KIPPEN PARISH CHURCH

NS 652 849

Fore Road, Kippen

Built 1827 by William Stirling, extensively redesigned 1924-26 by Reginald Fairlie
and Eric Bell. Exceptionally graceful, Latinate in style, and incorporating a
splendid and perfectly combined display of (mainly) 20th-century Christian art,
including works by Sir Alfred Gilbert, Alfred Hardiman, James Woodford and
Henry Wilson, as well as local craftsmen. Stained glass by Herbert Hendrie.
Sunday Service: 11.30am

Open 9.00am-4.30pm (dusk in winter) (presently under review)

CHURCH OF SCOTLAND 🦽 (ramp available for wheel chairs) WC ② 📖 **B**

876 PORT OF MENTEITH CHURCH

NS 583 011

On the shore of the Lake of Menteith, a church built in 1878 to designs by John
Honeyman on a site of earlier churches with medieval connections. Simple
rectangular plan, Gothic style, with square tower containing carillon of eight bells.
Victorian pipe organ, probably by Brook. Surrounded by a graveyard and a few
minutes walk from the ferry to Inchmahome where the ruined 13th-century
Augustinian Priory may be visited. On B8034 beside the Lake Hotel.
Linked with Aberfoyle. Sunday Service: 10.00am

Open by arrangement, telephone Mr G Ellis 01877 385201

CHURCH OF SCOTLAND ② 📖 WC **B**

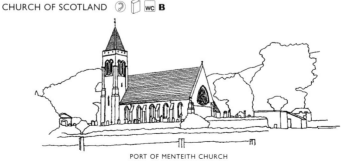

PORT OF MENTEITH CHURCH

877 ALLAN PARK SOUTH CHURCH, STIRLING

NS 755 933
Dumbarton Road, Stirling
Peddie & Kinnear 1886 with the interior
modernised for the centenary in 1986 by Esmé
Gordon. Radical change under consideration to
bring interior and grounds to the requirements
of the 21st century. Two large circular and three
smaller stained glass windows to commemorate
the fallen in the two World Wars, the ministry of
the Rev Alan Johnston and members of the
Kinross family. Sunday Service: 10.00am January
to June, 11.30am July to December
*Open by arrangement, telephone Church Secretary
01786 471998. Office hours Tuesday, Wednesday
and Friday 11.30am-2.30pm*
CHURCH OF SCOTLAND wc ⊘ **B**

ALLAN PARK SOUTH CHURCH, STIRLING

878 THE CHAPEL ROYAL, STIRLING CASTLE

NS 790 941
There has been a chapel in the castle since at least 1117. It became the Chapel
Royal of Scotland in the time of James IV in about 1500. The present building
was built in 1594 by James VI for the baptism of Prince Henry. It was redecorated
in 1629 in advance of the visit in 1633 of Charles I. After being sub-divided to
serve military uses, there was a first phase of restoration in the 1930s, and the latest
phase of work was completed in 1996. A large rectangular building with
Renaissance windows and a central entrance framed by a triumphal arch along its
south front. Notable features include decorative paintings of 1629 by Valentine
Jenkin, a modern wagon ceiling reflecting the profile of the original, and modern
furnishings including a communion table cover designed by Malcolm Lochead.
Services by arrangement
Open April to October 9.30am-6.00pm; November to March 9.30am-5.00pm
NON-DENOMINATIONAL ♿ ⊘ ◻ ⌷ ⌴ (Castle Restaurant) **A**

THE CHAPEL ROYAL, STIRLING CASTLE

879 CHURCH OF THE HOLY RUDE, STIRLING

NS 792 937

St John Street, Stirling

The original parish kirk of Stirling, used for the coronation in 1567 of James VI, at which John Knox preached. Largely built in 15th and 16th centuries. Medieval open-timbered oak roof in nave. Choir and apse added in 1555, the work of John Coutts, one of the greatest master masons of the later Middle Ages. Notable stained glass. Largest pipe organ in Scotland, built by Rushworth & Dreaper 1940 and rebuilt 1994. Oak choir stalls and canopies 1965. Historic graveyard. Near to Stirling Castle. On Historic Stirling (open top) bus route.

Sunday Service: 11.30am January to June, 10.00am July to December

Open May to September, 10.00am-5.00pm. Venue for many concerts

CHURCH OF SCOTLAND 👩‍🦽 🍴 📖 ② wc ℞ **A**

880 HOLY TRINITY CHURCH, STIRLING

NS 793 934

Albert Place, Dumbarton Road, Stirling

One of Sir R Rowand Anderson's most distinctive churches 1878, close to Stirling Castle, old town and shops. Very close to town centre, on Historic Stirling (open top) bus route. Sunday Services: Eucharists 8.30 and 10.30am, Evening Prayer 6.30pm

Open mornings daily

SCOTTISH EPISCOPAL 👩‍🦽 ② **B**

HOLY TRINITY CHURCH, STIRLING

881 ST NINIAN'S OLD, STIRLING

NS 797 917

Kirk Wynd, St Ninian's. Stirling

Only the tower and bell of 1734 survive following desecration of the nave by Cromwellian troops and an explosion of munitions stored in the 13th-century church by Jacobites. Present building is of 1751 with remodelling 1937 by A A McMichael. Major restoration programme will enhance exterior and interior.

Sunday Services: 10.30am and 6.30pm (second Sunday in March, June, September and December)

Open by arrangement with Mr Robert Simpson, telephone 01786 813335

CHURCH OF SCOTLAND 👩‍🦽 ② 📖 wc wc **A** (Steeple) **C** (Hall)

ST NINIAN'S OLD, STIRLING

882 VIEWFIELD PARISH CHURCH, STIRLING

NS 795 938

Irvine Place, Stirling

The present building, seating 600, was erected in 1860 to replace the 1752 meeting house. The congregations have been part of the Secession of 1733, going through United Presbyterian and United Free Churches until joining the Church of Scotland in 1929. Interior largely as constructed, though the window of the creation story behind the pulpit is a modern intervention by Christian Shaw. Sunday Service: 11.00am

Open by arrangement with keyholder Mr Monteith, telephone 01786 461350

CHURCH OF SCOTLAND ♿ (from Irvine Place) Ⓘ WC

VIEWFIELD PARISH CHURCH, STIRLING

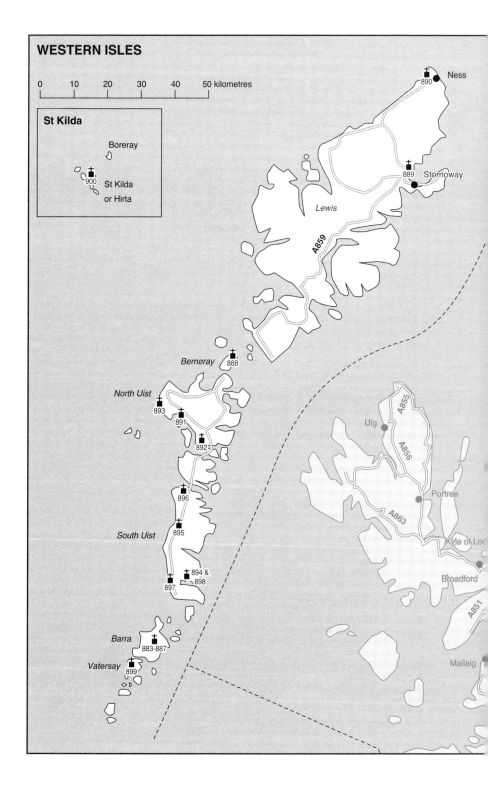

WESTERN ISLES

Local Representative: Atisha McGregor Auld, Ruisgarry, Isle of Berneray, by Lochmaddy, North Uist HS6 5BQ

OUR LADY STAR OF THE SEA, CASTLEBAY, BARRA

883 OUR LADY STAR OF THE SEA, CASTLEBAY, BARRA

NL 667 983

Castlebay, Barra

Opened Christmas 1886, architect Woulfe Brenan of Oban. Statue by Dupon of Bruges of Our Lady Star of the Sea. Stained glass of crucifixion in Sanctuary, and of Our Lady Star of the Sea installed as war memorial in early 1950s. Bell in tower; the clock chimes the hour during day and night. Sunday Service: 11.00am

Open at all times

ROMAN CATHOLIC ♿ (ramp access available) ◯ **B**

884 ST BRENDAN, CRAIGSTON, BARRA

NF 657 018

Craigston, Barra

Dating from 1805, the oldest church in the Isles of Barra. Restored 1858. Two etchings (scraperboard white on black) of St Brendan and St Barr, by Fr Calum MacNeill, retired priest of the diocese. Service: Saturday Vigil 7.00pm

Open at all times

ROMAN CATHOLIC ♿

885 ST VINCENT DE PAUL, EOLIGARRY, BARRA

NF 703 076

Built in 1964, the church has a tall roof with swept eaves. Small cemetary at Cille Bharra, burial place of MacNeil chieftans. Sunday: Mass 11.00am

Open at all times

ROMAN CATHOLIC

ST VINCENT DE PAUL, EOLIGARRY, BARRA

886 NORTH CHAPEL, CILLE BHARRA, EOLIGARRY, BARRA

NF 705 074

Twelfth-century church built on site of 7th-century foundation dedicated to
St Finbarr of Cork, Eire. Re-roofed with help from the Scottish Development
Department. Contains notable 12th-century runic stone (original now in the Royal
Museum, Edinburgh) and 16th-century grave-slabs with carvings of animals and
foliage. Mass on the feasts of the Celtic saints

Open at all times

ROMAN CATHOLIC

887 ST BARR'S, NORTHBAY, BARRA

NF 707 031

A simple lancet-windowed building
by G Woulfe Brenan 1906, with
porch and vestry added 1919. Small
bellcote on porch. Services daily:
Mass 7.30pm; Sunday 11.00am

Open at all times

ROMAN CATHOLIC

ST BARR'S, NORTHBAY, BARRA

888 BERNERAY CHURCH, ISLE OF BERNERAY

NL 552 801

Opposite war memorial

Built 1887, architect Thomas Binnie of Glasgow, for the United Free Church.
By uniting with the Established Church, now in ruins, it became the Church of
Scotland and still flourishes as such. HRH the Prince of Wales worshipped here
on a private visit in 1991. Berneray is now accessible by a causeway from North
Uist across the Sound of Harris. Sunday Services: 12.00 noon in English, 6.00pm
in Gaelic

Open by arrangement with Mr MacLean, telephone 01876 540249

CHURCH OF SCOTLAND [wc] ⊘ ⓘ

889 ST MOLUAG'S COMMUNITY CHURCH, TONG, LEWIS

NB 448 366

Opposite Tong School, on B895

In 1999 the building, which had formerly been a village shop and Post Office,
was converted into a church, opened and dedicated 2000. Sunday Service: Sung
Eucharist 11.00am (except first Sunday of month from May to September and
Easter Day – Service at Eoropaidh)

Open by arrangement, telephone 01851 820559

SCOTTISH EPISCOPAL [♿] [wc] [wc] ☕ (after Service)

890 ST MOLUAG, EOROPAIDH, NESS, LEWIS

NB 519 651

The building probably dates from the 12th century, but the site is believed to have been consecrated in the 6th century and is probably the place where Christianity was first preached to the people of Lewis. The church was restored in 1912 by Norman Forbes of Stornoway, under the guidance of the architect J S Richardson; the altars date from this restoration. The side chapel is connected to the main church only through a squint. The church has no heating, electricity or water; lighting is by candles and oil lamps. Two hundred yards from B8013 (signposted Eoropaidh from A857).

Services: 11.00am Easter Day, and on first Sunday of May to September

Open during daylight hours, Easter to last weekend in October.

Vehicular access impossible. In wet weather, path to church can be muddy

SCOTTISH EPISCOPAL **A**

891 CARINISH CHURCH, NORTH UIST

NF 820 604

Clachan an Luib, North Uist

The original Church of Scotland for North Uist and formerly a Free Church. The main feature is that the communion pews run down the length of the church so that those taking communion would sit side-on to the pulpit.

Sunday Service: 6.00pm, Gaelic once a month

Open by arrangement, telephone 01875 580219

CHURCH OF SCOTLAND wc **B**

892 CLACHAN CHURCH, NORTH UIST

NF 811 638

Built 1889 for the United Free Church, architect Thomas Bennie of Glasgow. Considerable difficulty was experienced procuring the site from Sir William Powlet Campbell Orde, Bart. After lengthy negotiations he reluctantly gave the present site at an annual rental of £3.9s. Sunday Service: 12.00 noon in English

Open by arrangement, telephone 01875 580219

CHURCH OF SCOTLAND wc ⟲

CLACHAN CHURCH, NORTH UIST

893   KILMUIR CHURCH, NORTH UIST

NF 708 706
West side of North Uist, close to Balranald RSPB Reserve
Originally North Uist Parish Church. Gothic T-plan
by Alexander Sharp 1892-94. In the south-west
inner angle is a two-stage tower, its battlemented
parapet enclosing a slated pyramidal spire. Inside, a
wealth of pitch-pine. One of the few remaining
Gaelic-essential charges; during the morning Gaelic
service one can hear, and participate in, the
precenting of Gaelic psalms. Sunday Services:
10.00am in Gaelic, 6.00pm in English.

KILMUIR CHURCH, NORTH UIST

Open by arrangement, telephone Mr Macbain 01876 510241
CHURCH OF SCOTLAND [wc] (⑨)

894   DALIBURGH/DALABROG, SOUTH UIST

NF 754 214
Built originally as South Uist Free Church in 1862-63, now Church of Scotland.
Manse completed 1880 and vestry/hall behind low wall added later. All harled.
Church rectangular in plan with three bays with round-headed openings and a
single window in either gable. Door and apex belfry to south gable. Pulpit with
panelled front. Communion table and war memorial based on design of that at
Howmore by Archibald Scott. Sunday Service: 11.00am
Open at all times
CHURCH OF SCOTLAND [wc] (⑨) **B**

895   HOWMORE CHURCH, SOUTH UIST

NF 758 364
Simple austere building by John McDearmid
1858, set in open land overlooking the Atlantic.
Acts as landmark for west-coast fishermen.
One of few churches in Scotland with central
Communion table. Nearby are remains of
13th-century church. Sunday Service: 12.30pm
Open at all times
CHURCH OF SCOTLAND [♿] [wc] **B**

HOWMORE CHURCH, SOUTH UIST

896   IOCHDAR CHURCH, EOCHAR, SOUTH UIST

Built 1889 as a Mission House by David MacIntosh, a small, compact church
with traditional pews and central pulpit. The church particularly lends itself to
quiet prayer and meditation. Sunday Service: 6.00pm first Sunday of the month
Open by arrangement, telephone Mrs Stephenson 01870 610401
CHURCH OF SCOTLAND

897 OUR LADY OF SORROWS, SOUTH UIST

NP 758 165
Garrynamonie
Built 1965, Architect Richard J McCarson, with a
monopitch roof. Above Blessed Sacrament altar is
a ceramic on the theme of the Sacred Heart by
David Harding of Edinburgh who was also
responsibile for original mural of Our Lady of
Sorrows at the entrance. This was replaced in 1994
by the present mural reflecting the sorrows of the contemporary world by Michael
Gilfeddar, commissioned by Canon Galbraith. Service: Saturday Vigil 6.30pm
Church website: www.pa44.dial.pipex.com
Website name: Catholic Church, Western Isles, Scotland
Open throughout each day
ROMAN CATHOLIC

OUR LADY OF SORROWS, SOUTH UIST

898 ST PETER'S, SOUTH UIST

NF 745 211
Daliburgh
Big harled church of 1868 with a birdcage bellcote on the south gable and a tall
concrete hoop bellcote on the 1960s porch. North sanctuary added 1907.
Services: Sunday Mass 11.30am
Church website: www.pa44.dial.pipex.com
Website name: Catholic Church, Western Isles, Scotland
Open throughout each day
ROMAN CATHOLIC   C

899 OUR LADY OF THE WAVES & ST JOHN, VATERSAY

NL 646 961
Uidh, Vatersay
Small functional church for celebration of Mass and other church services.
Reached by causeway from Barra. Sunday Service: 3.30pm
Open at all times
ROMAN CATHOLIC

900 CHRIST CHURCH, ST KILDA

NF 100 994
Village Bay, St Kilda
The stimulus for the kirk, designed by Robert Stevenson, came from the Rev
Dr John Macdonald who visited St Kilda several times in the early 19th century.
The church fell into disrepair after evacuation in 1930. Renovated over a period of
20 years since coming into the care of The National Trust for Scotland in 1957.
St Kilda is Scotland's first World Heritage Site. Services by arrangement
Open by arrangement, contact The National Trust for Scotland, telephone 01631 570 000
INTER-DENOMINATIONAL

CHURCHES WITH A
HISTORIC SCOTTISH CONNECTION

901 THE CHURCH OF SCOTLAND IN CARLISLE
NY 3956
Chapel Street, Carlisle
Built 1834, altered 1979 and extended 1994. A city centre church, the interior is
arranged over two floors with halls and kitchen on the ground floor and sanctuary
on the first floor. The extension provides three floors housing ecumenical One World
Centre, coffee lounge and Fair Trade shop. Two minutes from main 'Lanes' shopping
area and civic centre; five minutes from the cathedral, castle and parks; ten minutes
from Tullie House Museum. Two minutes from bus station in Lowther Street.
Sunday Service: 11.00am; also 6.30pm 1st Sunday (except January, July and August)
Open Monday to Friday 10.00am-2.00pm.
Coffee lounge and Fair Trade shop, open Monday to Friday 10.00am-2.00pm
CHURCH OF SCOTLAND 🦽 ⑦ ☕ wc **A**

902 CROWN COURT, COVENT GARDEN, LONDON
Adjacent to Fortune Theatre, Russell Street
Historic London church in the heart of Theatreland. The 'Kirk of the Crown of
Scotland' dates from 1909, replacing an earlier church of 1711. Longest established
Presbyterian Church in England. Royal arms of George I above communion table.
Baptismal font of Iona marble. Superb stained glass.
Sunday Services: 11.15 and 6.30pm; Thursdays 1.10-1.30pm
Church website: www.crowncourtchurch.org.uk
Open July and August, 11.30-2.30pm Tuesday, Wednesday and Thursday.
At other times, telephone the Church Secretary on 020 7836 5643
CHURCH OF SCOTLAND ⑦ 🍴 📖 wc

903 ST COLUMBA'S, LONDON
Pont Street, London
The present building, re-dedicated in 1955, replaced
the original building destroyed by incendiary bombs
in 1941. The architect was Sir Edward Maufe. Fine
rose window, 'The Creative Spirit of God' by Moira
Forsyth. The London Scottish Chapel contains the
Rolls of Honour of the London Scottish Regiment.
The arms of the Scottish Counties, painted in
heraldic colours, are carved at the base of the tall
windows all round the church. Services: Sundays
11.00am and 6.30pm; Wednesdays 1.00pm
Church website: www.stcolumbas.org.uk
Open 9.30am-5.00pm, Monday to Friday
CHURCH OF SCOTLAND ⑦ 📖 wc wc **Grade II**

ST COLUMBA'S, LONDON

THE STORY OF SCOTLAND'S CHURCHES SCHEME

Ann Davies, SCS Advisory Council Member

In its tenth anniversary year Scotland's Churches Scheme really has something to celebrate.

From original, small beginnnings in East Lothian, it now covers the whole of Scotland with more than 900 churches in membership and a country-wide network of twenty-four local representatives.

The acceptance by HRH the Princess Royal to become Patron in this celebratory year is an acknowledgement of the unique opportunity the Scheme offers the national and community life of Scotland and is a recognition of its development and expansion.

The Scheme encourages and assists churches of all denominations to open their doors and tell their own stories, to focus on their ecclesiastical heritage and to inspire a greater awareness among communities of all buildings designed for worship and active as living churches.

With the nation-wide recognition of the value of the project have come further initiatives in assisting congregations in visitor welcome, promotions and interpretation. A scheme to encourage more organ playing is backed by the Inches Carr Trust whose generosity enables member churches and organists to develop their musical gifts and promote greater use of the instruments in churches large and small.

Scotland's Churches Scheme has its roots in the 'Ministry of Welcome' created in 1984 by enthusiast, Christine Milligan, at St Mary's Church in Haddington. It reflected the growth in interest among tourists to Scotland.

In 1989 came the 'Come and See' award, designed to promote church tourism in the UK and sponsored by the Ecclesiastical Insurance Group. Christine Milligan's proposal – 'Come and See

Scotland's Churches' – was the only Scottish entry for the competition and took the award, with the Diocese of Lincoln.

A busy period of research followed in which, with the support of the Scottish Tourist Board and Napier University, Edinburgh, 2400 churches in Scotland were surveyed on the state of their visitor management. An advisory committee, representing principal denominations, assisted and a pilot study of three churches was undertaken: Killin Parish Church, St Mary's Episcopal Cathedral, Edinburgh and Coats Memorial Church in Paisley. This culminated in the publication by the Scottish Tourist Board of a guide to setting up a ministry of welcome – 'Unlocking the Door'.

The great step forward however was taken in 1993 when John Hume, then the Chief Inspector of Historic Buildings in Scotland, suggested a project along the lines of Scotland's Gardens Scheme with an annual handbook giving times of opening and a brief description of featured churches.

Armed with this idea, Christine Milligan approached Sir Jamie Stormonth Darling of the National Trust for Scotland for his advice. He saw at once the potential of this idea and, with his help, Shane Duff, John Laurie and Brian Dale as legal adviser were brought in. Stewart Brown was persuaded to chair a small Executive Committee and an Advisory Council was set up. Scotland's Churches Scheme was launched on 5th May 1994.

The enthusiasm of the initial Trustees has not waned and the impact made by the Scheme has surprised and delighted a wide range of supporters. The first guidebook was published in 1995 featuring 128 churches. The number in the 2004 edition is 903.

Annual Gatherings to launch the now familiar guidebook have been held in Edinburgh, Glasgow, Stirling, Aberdeen and Linlithgow and its scores of exquisite illustrations, drawn by John Hume, are making it a collector's item at home and overseas.

When Her Majesty Queen Elizabeth the Queen Mother agreed to become patron and Lady Marion Fraser was appointed the first president, a rapid period of development was signalled as trustees, executive and advisers sought to extend the ways in which they could support churches in membership.

At the end of 1997 Christine Milligan retired and was succeeded by Dr Brian Fraser. Attention now turned to developing the volunteer network of local representatives who were 'recruiting' entries for the guidebook as well as providing a vital link with the Scheme centrally.

Originally four representatives were appointed, but this has now grown to 23 covering every region of the country, from the most northerly church in Shetland to the most southerly in Galloway, from the south-east coast out to Tiree and Barra in the far west and even to St Kilda.

A regular Newsletter keeps members up to date and a series of 'How to' leaflets has been broadly welcomed for the practical advice and encouragement it offers. 'How to research your Church's History' has made members look at their buildings with new eyes.

'How to present your Church's Story' has produced many innovative ideas while 'How to welcome Visitors to your Church' has offered well tried suggestions and guidelines. 'How to Improve your Church's Security' is the latest addition.

Ten years on, the vision of the Scheme remains and is best summed up in one of its stated aims: to promote the common purpose of mission through the ministry of welcome for visitors, tourists and pilgrims.

ST MARY'S COLLEGIATE CHURCH, HADDINGTON

SCOTLAND'S CHURCHES SCHEME

ENCOURAGES CHURCHES TO:

- Open their doors with a welcoming presence
- Tell the story of the building, its purpose and the faith which inspired it
- Care for visitors in a sensitive and enriching way
- Work together with others to make the Church the focus of its community

SUPPORTS CHURCHES WITH:

- The publication of its comprehensive guidebook – *Churches to Visit in Scotland*
- Free advice on all aspects of visitor welcome, publicity, interpretation and exhibitions
- A network of local representatives in direct contact with headquarters
- Effective national publicity

SCOTLAND'S CHURCHES SCHEME GRATEFULLY ACKNOWLEDGES SUPPORT FROM:

THE CRUDEN FOUNDATION

THE DULVERTON TRUST

THE EAST-WEST TRUST

THE GARFIELD WESTON FOUNDATION

THE INCHES CARR TRUST

THE MANIFOLD TRUST

THE OPEN CHURCHES TRUST

THE P F CHARITABLE TRUST

THE RUSSELL TRUST

SCOTTISH & NEWCASTLE PLC

THE WEBSTER CHARITABLE TRUST

AND SEVERAL ANONYMOUS PRIVATE BENEFACTORS

DONATIONS

Please consider making a donation to Scotland's Churches Scheme, either in an individual or corporate capacity, so that this guide may become an indispensable part of the Scottish calendar, and the permanent financial future of the Scheme is secured.

Options, including Gift Aid which generates additional monies through the reclaim of tax already paid by donors, are:

[a]   Gift Aid
[b]   Gifts through the Charities Aid Foundation
[c]   Give As You Earn schemes operated by employers, and
[d]   Bequests in a Will, which are exempt from Inheritance Tax

Information and forms for [a] and [b] may be obtained from:

Scotland's Churches Scheme
Dunedin, Holehouse Road
Eaglesham
Glasgow G76 0JF

Telephone: 01355 302416
Fax: 01355 303181
E-mail: fraser@dunedin67.freeserve.co.uk
Website: churchesinscotland.co.uk

- ✂

Donation Form

I enclose £   as a donation to Scotland's Churches Scheme

Name

Address

Postcode

CHURCHES TO VISIT IN SCOTLAND

To:

The Director, Scotland's Churches Scheme,
Dunedin, Holehouse Road, Eaglesham, Glasgow
Telephone: 01355 302416
Fax: 01355 303181 *E-mail:* fraser@dunedin67.freeserve.co.uk
Website: churchesinscotland.co.uk

Please send me details and an application form for entry in the next Guidebook

Name
_____

Address
_____

_____

Postcode
_____

Name of Church
_____

Address of Church
_____

_____

Postcode

Further copies of the current Guidebook are available from the above address
at £8.99 paperback (£11.99 including p&p); or contact:
NMS ENTERPRISES LIMITED – PUBLISHING
National Museums of Scotland, Chambers Street, Edinburgh EH1 1JF
Telephone: 0131 247 4026
or
SCOTTISH CHRISTIAN PRESS
21 Young Street, Edinburgh EH2 4HU. *Telephone:* 0131 260 3110

SCOTLAND'S
GARDENS SCHEME

We had a great start to the garden season in 2003 with many visitors being able to enjoy the snowdrop openings which this year were the best for many years. Our annual handbook *Gardens of Scotland* went on sale by the second week of February and this year featured in the best sellers lists until May. However many people still find that it is sometimes difficult to find a copy in their local retailers, so remember to complete the form at the end of the book and we will then send you a copy at the start of the season.

This year we also launched our new website under www.gardensofscotland.org where you can see which gardens are open every week of the year throughout Scotland. We hope that you will find it easy to follow and that the map will guide you to the gardens without difficulty. We will also be adding more colour photographs to enable the visitor to have an idea as to what they can see when they visit the gardens.

Scotland's Gardens Scheme was founded in 1931 and follows much the same procedures as was started all those years ago. We do however find that the competition from other charities is growing each year, and as our sole source of income is by the opening of gardens under the Scheme we do badly need your support to enable us to help our principal beneficiaries and those charities which are personally chosen by our owners. We can promise you a lovely day out and generally an excellent tea as well!

Remember to look out for our large plant sales. Plants are carefully matured throughout the season and then put on sale at very reasonable prices. The sales staff are also on hand to offer free advice as to what might grow in that awkward spot in your garden and this service has become a major feature of the sales. Also look out for lectures on the Scheme and other subjects being held in your areas throughout the year. We wish Scotland's Churches Scheme yet another successful year, and would be very happy if we were able to attract the same number of new gardens to our Scheme as you manage to attract new churches to join yours. This is surely an indication of your ongoing success.

Scotland's Gardens Scheme
22 Rutland Square
Edinburgh EH1 2BB

Telephone: 0131 229 1870
Fax: 0131 229 0443

Email: office@sgsgardens.netco.uk
website: www.gardensofscotland.org

CHURCH
RECORDERS

NADFAS

Scottish churches do not immediately promise rich pickings. Most of the present day buildings are 19th century replacements of pre-Reformation parish churches or former Free Churches. Consequently we do not expect to find the thumb-print of our ancestors on their bare walls and anonymous furnishings.

The activities of Church Recorders, who are volunteer members of the National Association of Decorative & Fine Arts Societies (NADFAS) show how a closer scrutiny of church interiors can illuminate both past and present. Church Recorders make a comprehensive Record of the furnishings and some of the fabric with text, photographs, drawings and historical research; often much of intrinsic and historical interest is found.

Sadly, today there is much vandalism, theft, and loss of precious artefacts. The Records, which are paid for by NADFAS Societies, provide a permanent, detailed inventory invaluable for repairs and insurance.

The Record is of interest to parishioners, visitors, and serious scholars. Guides in churches can obtain information from it, but it must be stressed that the Record is confidential.

One copy is presented to the church, others are lodged with official bodies such as the Church Authority and the Royal Commission for Ancient and Historic Monuments of Scotland.

The sum of knowledge gained, and the value of the work, is inspiring NADFAS Societies in Scotland to record churches of all denominations.

Churches that have been, or are being recorded are indicated by the above logo.

Further information can be obtained from:

The Church Recorders Scottish Representative
NADFAS HOUSE
8 Guildford Street
LONDON WCI IDT

Telephone: 020 7430 0730

THE OPEN CHURCHES TRUST

What Scotland's Churches Scheme is doing in Scotland and this Trust in England and Wales are complementary. Your Scheme has huge support and a very impressive list of open churches.

The main work of the Trust at present is to put on roadshows for Diocesan areas, which tackles all the problems of opening a place of worship to the public. There is a huge growth of organisations which are tourist motivated and which lead to the opening of a large number of such places. The North West Multi-Faith Tourism Association operates from Manchester to Dumfries and incorporates synagogues, temples and mosques. With big operations in North Yorkshire, Rotherham, Mid Bedfordshire, Kent, Sussex and Wales, the Open Churches Trust is now working with a mass of friends, all with the same objectives.

I realise that a great many of your churches will be open but without stewards. Our roadshow demonstrates the real value of stewards.

We reckon that a stewarded church attracts double the number an unstewarded church attracts.

The continual growth of your Scheme is an inspiration to us all. By our new roadshow we hope to start catching you up on the number of churches open.

We must never forget that the prime purpose of an open church is to allow people to use it. Tens of thousands of people every day pop into an open church for ten minutes of peace, quiet, contemplation and prayer. This is a reflection of the stressful times we live in and the need for a haven. All open churches provide this.

Perhaps one of the most important new features of the Trust's work is the insistence that on the roadside beside an open church is a well-made sign saying: THIS CHURCH IS OPEN. This increases visitor numbers enormously.

THE OPEN CHURCHES TRUST
c/o The Really Useful Group Ltd
22 Tower Street, London WC2H 9TW

Telephone: 020 7240 0880
Fax: 020 7240 1204
E-mail: oct@reallyuseful.co.uk
Website: www.openchurchestrust.org.uk

THE SCOTTISH REDUNDANT CHURCHES TRUST

EAST CHURCH, CROMARTY, ROSS-SHIRE

AIMS:
- To take into ownership the best examples of redundant places of worship of all denominations in Scotland.
- To preserve and protect their fabric.
- To maintain them for the benefit of the local community and the nation.
- To provide public access to them.

Incorporated as a Charitable Company in 1996, the SRCT owns four redundant churches throughout Scotland: St Peter's Church, Orkney, Cromarty East Church, Ross-shire, Pettinain Church, Lanarkshire and Tibbermore Church, Perthshire. These outstanding examples of our rich ecclesiastical heritage are repaired and preserved as 'sleeping' churches, open to visitors and made use of by local people for occasional worship and community events.

Changes in social and cultural attitudes, the decline in the church-going population and the high cost of maintaining ageing buildings mean that an increasing number of historic churches throughout Scotland are in limited use or have become redundant. The SRCT is the only national body that aims to protect, preserve and care for churches of all denominations whilst maintaining public access to them.

We rely on fundraising, donations and legacies to continue our work and to support the repair projects in the churches we own. If you would like to contribute towards saving Scotland's ecclesiastical heritage, or would like more information about the work of the SRCT and the Friends Groups and events at our churches, please contact: Victoria Collison-Owen, Scottish Redundant Churches Trust, 4 Queen's Gardens, St Andrews, KY16 9TA. *Telephone:* 01334 472032. *Fax:* 01334 470767. *E-mail:* SRCTrust@aol.com.

The Scottish Redundant Churches Trust, a Charitable Company Limited
by Guarantee, SC162884. Scottish Charity SC024407

SCOTTISH CHRISTIAN PRESS

resources for youth ministry,
children's ministry and adult education...

Scottish
Christian PRESS

visit us at
www.scottishchristianpress.org.uk

Get a Grip series
£7.99
- 'the best Christian material for youth that I
have found'

Kids in Kirk series
£6.50
- 'how to' guides to children's ministry

All books available from
BookSource Glasgow
orders@booksource.net or phone
08702 402 182

See **more** on the
back inside cover of
Churches to Visit in Scotland!

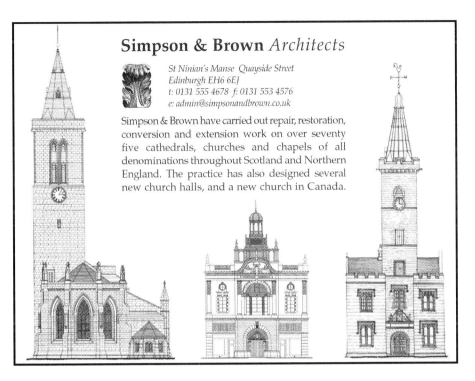

NEW MEETING & CONFERENCE ROOMS

Trades Hall, Glasgow

Two new conference rooms in a stripped Adam style have been created on the top floor of this historic building closely inspired by the original Adam design and encompassing a shallow curved niche on the long sides towards the centre of the building. Well lit and with computer points their capacity is up to 40 (depending on layout).

These rooms have adjacent disabled and other toilet accommodation and small kitchen. Also adjacent is a new room containing educational and interpretational material about the part played by the Incorporated Trades in the growth of Glasgow as a commercial and industrial centre and their role in the city today.

Basic hire for a half day meeting £125 each (£175 for the full day) rising to £350 on Saturdays (inclusive of VAT)

You can find out more about the Trades Hall on www.bbnet.demon.co.uk/thall or telephone the **booking office on 0141 248 5566 (tel/fax).**

Building: 85 Glassford Street, Glasgow G1 1UH.
Office/Bookings: 310 St. Vincent Street, Glasgow G2 5QR.

INDEX OF ARTISTS

Number refers to church entry, not page

INDEX OF CHURCHES

Number refers to church entry, not page